Another Europe

Given the recent focus on the challenges to representative democracy, and the search for new institutions and procedures that can help to channel increasing participation, this book offers empirical insights on alternative conceptions of democracy and the actors that promote them.

With a focus on the conceptions and practices of democracy within contemporary social movements in Europe, this volume contributes to the debate on the different dimensions of democracy, especially on representation and participation. The book explores the transnational dimension of democracy and addresses a relevant, and little analysed aspect of Europeanization: the Europeanization of social movements. From a methodological point of view, the research innovates by covering a group of individuals traditionally neglected in previous studies: social movement activists. The various chapters combine analysis of the individuals' attitudes and behaviour with that of the organizational characteristics, procedures and practices of democracy.

Providing a cross-national comparison on the global justice movement, the theoretical challenges of the new wave of protest and the rich empirical data this book will appeal to students and scholars of sociology, political sociology, social movement studies, and transnational as well as comparative politics.

Donatella della Porta is professor of sociology in the Department of Political and Social Sciences at the European University Institute, Italy.

Routledge/ECPR studies in European political science
Edited by Thomas Poguntke,
Ruhr University Bochum, Germany on behalf of the European Consortium for Political Research

The Routledge/ECPR Studies in European Political Science series is published in association with the European Consortium for Political Research – the leading organization concerned with the growth and development of political science in Europe. The series presents high-quality edited volumes on topics at the leading edge of current interest in political science and related fields, with contributions from European scholars and others who have presented work at ECPR workshops or research groups.

1 **Regionalist Parties in Western Europe**
   Edited by Lieven de Winter and Huri Türsan

2 **Comparing Party System Change**
   Edited by Jan-Erik Lane and Paul Pennings

3 **Political Theory and European Union**
   Edited by Albert Weale and Michael Nentwich

4 **Politics of Sexuality**
   Edited by Terrell Carver and Véronique Mottier

5 **Autonomous Policy Making by International Organizations**
   Edited by Bob Reinalda and Bertjan Verbeek

6 **Social Capital and European Democracy**
   Edited by Jan van Deth, Marco Maraffi, Ken Newton and Paul Whiteley

7 **Party Elites in Divided Societies**
   Edited by Kurt Richard Luther and Kris Deschouwer

8 **Citizenship and Welfare State Reform in Europe**
   Edited by Jet Bussemaker

9 **Democratic Governance and New Technology**
   Technologically mediated innovations in political practice in Western Europe
   Edited by Ivan Horrocks, Jens Hoff and Pieter Tops

10 **Democracy without Borders**
Transnationalisation and conditionality in new democracies
Edited by Jean Grugel

11 **Cultural Theory as Political Science**
Edited by Michael Thompson, Gunnar Grendstad and Per Selle

12 **The Transformation of Governance in the European Union**
Edited by Beate Kohler-Koch and Rainer Eising

13 **Parliamentary Party Groups in European Democracies**
Political parties behind closed doors
Edited by Knut Heidar and Ruud Koole

14 **Survival of the European Welfare State**
Edited by Stein Kuhnle

15 **Private Organisations in Global Politics**
Edited by Karsten Ronit and Volker Schneider

16 **Federalism and Political Performance**
Edited by Ute Wachendorfer-Schmidt

17 **Democratic Innovation**
Deliberation, representation and association
Edited by Michael Saward

18 **Public Opinion and the International Use of Force**
Edited by Philip Everts and Pierangelo Isernia

19 **Religion and Mass Electoral Behaviour in Europe**
Edited by David Broughton and Hans-Martien ten Napel

20 **Estimating the Policy Position of Political Actors**
Edited by Michael Laver

21 **Democracy and Political Change in the 'Third World'**
Edited by Jeff Haynes

22 **Politicians, Bureaucrats and Administrative Reform**
Edited by B. Guy Peters and Jon Pierre

23 **Social Capital and Participation in Everyday Life**
Edited by Paul Dekker and Eric M. Uslaner

24 **Development and Democracy**
What do we know and how?
Edited by Ole Elgström and Goran Hyden

25 **Do Political Campaigns Matter?**
Campaign effects in elections and referendums
Edited by David M. Farrell and Rüdiger Schmitt-Beck

26 **Political Journalism**
New challenges, new practices
Edited by Raymond Kuhn and Erik Neveu

27 **Economic Voting**
Edited by Han Dorussen and Michaell Taylor

28 **Organized Crime and the Challenge to Democracy**
Edited by Felia Allum and Renate Siebert

29 **Understanding the European Union's External Relations**
Edited by Michèle Knodt and Sebastiaan Princen

30 **Social Democratic Party Policies in Contemporary Europe**
Edited by Giuliano Bonoli and Martin Powell

31 **Decision Making Within International Organisations**
Edited by Bob Reinalda and Bertjan Verbeek

32 **Comparative Biomedical Policy**
Governing assisted reproductive technologies
Edited by Ivar Bleiklie, Malcolm L. Goggin and Christine Rothmayr

33 **Electronic Democracy**
Mobilisation, organisation and participation via new ICTs
Edited by Rachel K. Gibson, Andrea Römmele and Stephen J. Ward

34 **Liberal Democracy and Environmentalism**
The end of environmentalism?
Edited by Marcel Wissenburg and Yoram Levy

35 **Political Theory and the European Constitution**
Edited by Lynn Dobson and Andreas Follesdal

36 **Politics and the European Commission**
Actors, interdependence, legitimacy
Edited by Andy Smith

37 **Metropolitan Governance**
Capacity, democracy and the dynamics of place
Edited by Hubert Heinelt and Daniel Kübler

38 **Democracy and the Role of Associations**
Political, organizational and social contexts
Edited by Sigrid Roßteutscher

39 **The Territorial Politics of Welfare**
Edited by Nicola McEwen and Luis Moreno

40 **Health Governance in Europe**
Issues, challenges and theories
Edited by Monika Steffen

41 **Republicanism in Theory and Practice**
Edited by Iseult Honohan and Jeremy Jennings

42 **Mass Media and Political Communication in New Democracies**
Edited by Katrin Voltmer

43 **Delegation in Contemporary Democracies**
Edited by Dietmar Braun and Fabrizio Gilardi

44 **Governance and Democracy**
Comparing national, European and international experiences
Edited by Yannis Papadopoulos and Arthur Benz

45 **The European Union's Roles in International Politics**
Concepts and analysis
Edited by Ole Elgström and Michael Smith

46 **Policy-making Processes and the European Constitution**
A comparative study of member states and accession countries
Edited by Thomas König and Simon Hug

47 **Democratic Politics and Party Competition**
Edited by Judith Bara and Albert Weale

48 **Participatory Democracy and Political Participation**
Can participatory engineering bring citizens back in?
Edited by Thomas Zittel and Dieter Fuchs

49 **Civil Societies and Social Movements**
Potentials and problems
Edited by Derrick Purdue

50 **Resources, Governance and Civil Conflict**
Edited by Magnus Öberg and Kaare Strøm

51 **Transnational Private Governance and its Limits**
Edited by Jean-Christophe Graz and Andreas Nölke

52 **International Organizations and Implementation**
Enforcers, managers, authorities?
Edited by Jutta Joachim, Bob Reinalda and Bertjan Verbeek

53 **New Parties in Government**
Edited by Kris Deschouwer

54 **In Pursuit of Sustainable Development**
New governance practices at the sub-national level in Europe
Edited by Susan Baker and Katarina Eckerberg

55 **Governments, NGOs and Anti-Corruption**
The new integrity warriors
Edited by Luís de Sousa, Barry Hindess and Peter Larmour

56 **Intra-party Politics and Coalition Governments**
Edited by Daniela Giannetti and Kenneth Benoit

57 **Political Parties and Partisanship**
Social identity and individual attitudes
Edited by John Bartle and Paolo Belucci

58 **The Future of Political Community**
Edited by Gideon Baker and Jens Bartelson

59 **The Discursive Politics of Gender Equality**
Stretching, bending and policy making
Edited by Emanuela Lombardo, Petra Meier, Mieke Verloo

60 **Another Europe**
Conceptions and practices of democracy in the European social forums
Edited by Donatella della Porta

Also available from Routledge in association with the ECPR:

Sex Equality Policy in Western Europe, *Edited by Frances Gardiner*; **Democracy and Green Political Thought**, *Edited by Brian Doherty and Marius de Geus*; **The New Politics of Unemployment**, *Edited by Hugh Compston*; **Citizenship, Democracy and Justice in the New Europe**, *Edited by Percy B. Lehning and Albert Weale*; **Private Groups and Public Life**, *Edited by Jan W. van Deth*; **The Political Context of Collective Action**, *Edited by Ricca Edmondson*; **Theories of Secession**, *Edited by Percy Lehning*; **Regionalism Across the North/South Divide**, *Edited by Jean Grugel and Wil Hout*

Another Europe

Conceptions and practices of democracy in the European social forums

Edited by Donatella della Porta

LONDON AND NEW YORK

First published 2009
by Routledge
2 Park Square, Milton Park, Abingdon, Oxon OX14 4RN

Simultaneously published in the USA and Canada
by Routledge
711 Third Ave, New York, NY 10017

Routledge is an imprint of the Taylor & Francis Group, an informa business

First issued in paperback 2013

© 2009 Selection and editorial matter, Donatella della Porta; individual chapters, the contributors

Typeset in Times by Wearset Ltd, Boldon, Tyne and Wear

All rights reserved. No part of this book may be reprinted or reproduced or utilized in any form or by any electronic, mechanical, or other means, now known or hereafter invented, including photocopying and recording, or in any information storage or retrieval system, without permission in writing from the publishers.

British Library Cataloguing in Publication Data
A catalogue record for this book is available from the British Library

Library of Congress Cataloging in Publication Data
Another Europe: conceptions and practices of democracy in the European social forums/edited by Donatella della Porta.

p. cm. – (Routledge/ECPR studies in European political science; 60)
Includes bibliographical references and index.

1. Political participation–Europe. 2. Social movements–Europe.
I. Porta, Donatella della, 1956–

JN40.A56 2009
322.4094–dc22   2008050124

ISBN13: 978-0-415-47464-1 (hbk)
ISBN13: 978-0-415-84608-0 (pbk)
ISBN13: 978-0-203-87703-6 (ebk)

Contents

List of figures	xi
List of tables	xii
List of contributors	xiv
Acknowledgements	xvii
Series editor's preface	xviii

PART I   1

1 **Another Europe: an introduction**   3
 DONATELLA DELLA PORTA

2 **The ESF organizing process in a diachronic perspective**   26
 CHRISTOPH HAUG, NICOLAS HAERINGER, AND
 LORENZO MOSCA

3 **Communicating the European Social Forum**   46
 LORENZO MOSCA, DIETER RUCHT, AND SIMON TEUNE
 (WITH THE COLLABORATION OF SARA LÓPEZ MARTIN)

4 **Models of democracy: how activists see democracy in the movement**   65
 MASSIMILIANO ANDRETTA AND
 DONATELLA DELLA PORTA

5 **Democracy from below: activists and institutions**   86
 DONATELLA DELLA PORTA AND MARCO GIUGNI

PART II 109

6 **The social bases of the GJM mobilization and democratic norms** 111
MASSIMILIANO ANDRETTA AND ISABELLE SOMMIER

7 **The organizational dimension: how organizational formality, voice, and influence affect mobilization and participation** 128
CLARE SAUNDERS AND MASSIMILIANO ANDRETTA

8 **Novel characteristics of the GJM: a (latent) network analysis approach** 149
MASSIMILIANO ANDRETTA, IOSIF BOTETZAGIAS, MOSES BOUDOURIDES, OLGA KIOUFEGI, AND MUNDO YANG

9 **Parties, unions, and movements: the European Left and the ESF** 173
MASSIMILIANO ANDRETTA AND HERBERT REITER

10 **Protest and the forum: forms of participation in the global justice movement** 204
MARCO GIUGNI, ALESSANDRO NAI, AND HERBERT REITER

11 **Another Europe: some conclusions** 225
DONATELLA DELLA PORTA

Appendix 239
References 248
Index 266

Figures

1.1	The research model	12
3.1	A scheme of external communication flows informing about the ESF	48
7.1	Typology of organizations in the GJM	132
7.2	Level of perceived deliberativeness within one's most important group	141
7.3	Deliberation as normative models among members	144
7.4	Comparing satisfaction with groups' democracy and incongruence between perceived practices and norms	145
8.1	Crossing structural embeddedness and participation in GJM events abroad	160–1
8.2	Latent networks according to leaders and simple members' (structural) embeddedness	164–5
8.3	Crossing structural embeddedness and deliberative-participative values	168–9
10.1	Use of general forms of participation	213

Tables

1.1	Internal and general democratic values explicitly mentioned in the selected documents	7
2.1	Chronology of European meetings in the ESF organizing process	28
2.2	The thematic axes of the ESF events	36–7
3.1	Who or what incited you to partake in the ESF?	51
4.1	Typology of democratic conceptions	72
4.2	Participation in decision making in own group and in the GJM	73
4.3	Degree of satisfaction with decision making in selected institutions	74
4.4	Participation in GJM events by activists' normative models of democracy	75
4.5	Identification with GJM by activists' normative models of democracy	76
4.6	Linear regression analysis with 'satisfaction with GJM democracy'	82
5.1	Trust in institutions of ESF participants in Florence, Paris, and Athens	89
5.2	How much do you agree with the following statements?	92
5.3	Opinion of ESF participants in Florence and Athens about which institutions should be strengthened to achieve global social movement's goals	94
5.4	Previous political activities of ESF participants in Athens, Florence, and Paris	97
5.5	Strategies the global movement has to use in order to enhance democracy	98
5.6	Estimates of effects of selected independent variables on levels of trust for representative institutions	102
5.7	Estimates of selected independent variables on solutions to improve democracy	104
5.8	Estimates of effects of selected independent variables on strategies of political mobilization	105
6.1	Evolution of the current social situation of participants in the ESF	116

6.2	Evolution of the current social position of the 'professional activists' in two ESFs	119
6.3	Type of activists by sociographic variables	120
6.4	Level of experience in similar events and identification with the global movement according to gender and age group	122
6.5	Democratic ideals by sociographic profiles	124
7.1	Expectations of types of organizations' extent of activist participation in mobilization, action repertoires, and decision making	135
7.2	ESF participants' involvement in GJM protest at home and abroad by organizational type	137
7.3	Significant differences in ESF participants' action repertoires by organizational type	138
7.4	Perceptions of democracy working within the group	141
7.5	Normative ideals of democracy	143
8.1	Bivariate non parametric correlations (Kendall's tau-b) between network indicators in each country network	156
8.2	Level of embeddedness for each type in each country	157
9.1	Groups indicated as organizers of seminars or workshops at the Athens ESF	186
9.2	Participants EPA Vienna, 10–12 May 2002	187
9.3	Traditional and radical left activists by type of democratic regime	190
9.4	The involvement of leftist activists in the GJM	193
9.5	Typology of activists and perceived organizational democratic practices	195
9.6	Typology of activists and normative democratic models	196
9.7	Typology of activists and level of incongruence and satisfaction with democracy in the group	198
10.1	Past and present action repertoires of ESF participants in Florence, Paris, and Athens	212
10.2	Relationship between views about decision making processes and general forms of participation	216
10.3	Relationship between views about strategies to enhance democracy and general forms of participation	217
10.4	Relationship between views about strategies to tame globalization and general forms of participation	218
10.5	Effects of selected independent variables on general forms of participation	219

Contributors

Massimiliano Andretta is Assistant Professor at the University of Pisa where he teaches Political Science, Political Communication and Participation and Social Movements. He has published several articles and book chapters on the topic of social movements. Among his recent publication we mention *Globalization from Below: Transnational Activists and Protest Networks* (Minnesota University Press, 2006; with Donatella della Porta, Lorenzo Mosca, and Herbert Reiter), and an article that appeared in the *European Foreign Affairs Review* with the title 'Imagining Europe: Internal and External Non State Actors at the European Crossroads' (2007; with Nicole Doerr).

Iosif Botetzagias is Lecturer at the Department of the Environment, University of the Aegean, Greece, teaching Environmental Politics and Sociology. His research interests include green parties and environmental NGOs, new social movements and social networks analysis.

Moses Boudourides is an Associate Professor of Applied Mathematics at the University of Patras, Greece. His research is on social networks, social movements, collective choice, science and technology studies, dynamic systems and chaos/complexity theories.

Donatella della Porta is Professor of Sociology in the Department of Political and Social Sciences at the European University Institute. Among her recent publications on social movements are: *The Global Justice Movement* (Paradigm, 2007; with Massimiliano Andretta, Lorenzo Mosca, and Herbert Reiter), *Globalization from Below* (The University of Minnesota Press, 2006; with Abby Peterson and Herbert Reiter), *The Policing of Transnational Protest* (Ashgate, 2006; with Manuela Caiani), *Quale Europa? Europeizzazione, Identità e Conflitti* (Il Mulino, 2006; with Mario Diani), *Social Movements: An Introduction*, 2nd edition (Blackwell, 2006; with Sidney Tarrow), and *Transnational Protest and Global Activism*, (Rowman and Littlefield, 2005).

Marco Giugni is researcher at the Laboratoire de Recherches Sociales et Politiques Appliquées (resop) and teaches at the Department of Political Science at the University of Geneva. He has authored or co-authored several books and articles on social movements and contentious politics. His research interests include: social movements and collective action, immigration and ethnic relations, unemployment and social exclusion.

Nicolas Haeringer is researcher at the Centre de Recherche en Sociologie des Organisations, University of Paris Dauphine

Christoph Haug is doctoral researcher at the Social Science Research Center in Berlin and at Freie Universität Berlin. His research interests include: social Forums, decision making in social movements, civil society in Africa, and theories of the public sphere.

Olga Kioufegi is researcher at the University of Patras, Greece.

Sara Lopez Martin is currently finishing her PhD in the department of Political Science of the Complutense University of Madrid. Her research interests concern social movements and political uses of the Internet.

Lorenzo Mosca is currently research fellow at the Bocconi University (Milan). He has been involved in several European projects such as YOUNEX, DEMOS and EUROPUB. He has published extensively in international peer-reviewed journals and articles in books translated into English, Spanish, French, German and Italian.

Alessandro Nai is Assistant in the Department of Political Science at the University of Geneva. His interests and competences are particularly in political behaviour of citizens in a direct democracy, and, more specifically, in cognitive strategies put up by individuals in decision making.

Herbert Reiter is a historian and researcher at the European University Institute in Florence. Among his recent publications are *Globalization from Below* (Minneapolis, The University of Minnesota Press, 2006; with Donatella della Porta, Massimiliano Andretta, and Lorenzo Mosca), and *The Policing of Transnational Protest* (Ashgate, 2006; with Donatella della Porta and Abby Petersen (eds)).

Dieter Rucht is Professor of Sociology and co-director of the research group 'Civil Society, Citizenship and Political Mobilization in Europe' at the Social Science Research Center, Berlin. His research interests include political participation, social movements, and political protest.

Clare Saunders is Lecturer (RCUK Fellow) in Politics and International Relations at the University of Southampton. Prior to this, she was a Research Associate at the University of Kent, working with Christopher Rootes on the Demos project.

Isabelle Sommier is Professor at the Sorbonne, Paris. Among her books are *Le Renouveau des Mouvements Contestataires à l'heure de la Mondialisation* (Paris: Flammarion, collection Champs, 2003; with Olivier Fillieule and Eric Agrikoliansky (eds)), *Généalogie des Mouvements Altermondialistes en Europe: Une Perspective Comparée* (Paris: Karthala, 2008), and *Radiographie* *du Mouvement Altermondialiste* (Paris: La Dispute, 2005; with Eric Agrikoliansky (eds)).

Simon Teune works at the Social Science Research Center, Berlin. His research interests are: social movements, protest, and culture. He is preparing a PhD dissertation dealing with the communication strategies of global justice groups during the anti-G8 protests in Germany 2007.

Mundo Yang studied Political Science at the Free University of Berlin and is currently a Research Fellow with the research group 'Civil Society, Citizenship, and Political Mobilization in Europe' at the Social Science Research Center, Berlin. His main research interests are: the public sphere, mass media and protest politics.

Acknowledgements

This book reports the results of part of the comparative research project Democracy in Europe and the Mobilization of the Society (Demos 2004). The Demos project is financed by the European Commission, Sixth Framework Programme Priority 7, Citizens and Governance in a Knowledge Based Society, and (for the Swiss case) the Federal Office for Education and Science, Switzerland. It is coordinated by Donatella della Porta (European University Institute), partners are: University of Kent at Canterbury, UK, Christopher C. Rootes; Wissenschaftszentrum Berlin fuer Sozialforschung, Germany, Dieter Rucht; Università di Urbino, Italy, Mario Pianta; Centre de Recherches Politiques de la Sorbonne (CRPS), Universitè Panthéon-Sorbonne, France, Isabelle Sommier; Instituto de Estudios Sociales de Andalucía, Centro Superior de Investigaciones Cientificas (IESA-CSIC), Spain, Manuel Jiménez; and Laboratoire de Recherches Sociales et Politiques Appliquées (resop), Université de Genève, Switzerland, Marco Giugni. Collaborators to the research included, at different times, Massimiliano Andretta, Marko Bandler, Angel Calle, Hélène Combes, Nicolas Haeringer, Nina Eggert, Raffaele Marchetti, Lorenzo Mosca, Alessandro Nai, Herbert Reiter, Clare Saunders, Simon Teune, Mundo Yang, and Duccio Zola. We are especially grateful to the thousands of activists who trusted, encouraged and helped our understanding of the European Social Forum. As often, our gratitude goes to Sarah Tarrow, for her careful editing of the manuscript.

Series editor's preface

As the financial crisis is shaking the foundations of the global economy and pushing states to the edge of bankruptcy, much of the criticism and protest of the variegated alter-globalist movement(s) suddenly sounds a lot more realistic and plausible. Anyone who has still doubted the seriousness of the crisis might finally have become convinced of the opposite when listening to statements by the chairmen of multinational banks advocating regulation and a stronger role of the state. As a matter of fact, global leaders are taking refuge in policy measures which are bordering on state socialism. To be sure, suggesting the partial nationalization of banks, as it happened in the heartland of neo-liberalism, would have been regarded as a complete and utter sign of political extremism merely 12 months ago.

However, the aspirations of these movements reach beyond policy change. Reminiscent of previous waves of mobilization of extra-parliamentary protest action, there is much talk about unity of form and substance. In other words, many believe that policies can only be changed if the way politics is done is also radically transformed. Global politics in its present form is not just criticized for its undesirable outcomes in terms of social justice, the failure to move sufficiently fast on measures to slow down climate change or to guarantee human rights, to mention but a few of the central goals. It is also the representative, delegatory and essentially elitist nature of global (and domestic) politics which is seen with considerable disaffection and criticism.

Openness to participation, deliberation and respect of diversity are regarded not only as instrumental for achieving better policies; they are also seen as ends in themselves. From this perspective, these movements present a formidable challenge to established politics around the globe. But do they live what they preach? How much internal democracy is to be found in the movements which, after all, cannot function without some degree of internal functional differentiation and elite building? And what do movement activists themselves think about these democratic ideals? How widely are they shared in a movement which is essentially a movement of movements, a broad coalition of very diverse actors, some of which are highly formalized, even elitist while other are more grassroots oriented and loosely structured?

These are some of the questions which are addressed in the current volume that concentrates on data collected during the Athens European Social Forum

(EFS) of May 2006 but draws comparisons to earlier meetings elsewhere. Using participant observation, document analysis and a mass survey of movement activists, a team coordinated by Donatella della Porta sheds important light on the internal dynamics of the EFS. This includes processes of internal organization and coordination, external alliances and linkages with parties of the Left and, above all, the nature of democratic practices inside the movement. To be sure, the latter is methodologically challenging as sample representativeness is a major problem when polling a population (i.e. a movement) that has neither clearly defined boundaries nor a high degree of organizational stability.

As was to be expected, the results show that there is considerable diversity. Document analyses reveal, for example, that different modes of internal democracy can be found, and delegation and the majority principle are quite widespread despite a sometimes more idealistic rhetoric. Also, normative aspirations are not always realized in practice yet there is a high degree of satisfaction with the functioning of democracy within the movement. When it comes to contacts with parties of the traditional Left, relationships were difficult, particularly when these parties were in government even though the ESF often received important organizational support from these parties.

Above all, the book shows that the ESF is a unique political 'actor' in that it represents an open space for discussion, deliberation and participation, marked by a considerable degree of respect for diversity and high scepticism towards vertical power. At the same time, multiple memberships are widespread and many who get involved in the ESF are also active in far more traditional forms of collective action. It remains to be seen how strong possible 'contamination effects' will be in the long run. However, who would have predicted a year ago that the Gordon Brown would partially nationalize banks....

Thomas Poguntke, Series Editor
Florence, November 2008

Part I

1 Another Europe

An introduction

Donatella della Porta

> We, women and men from social movements across Europe, came to Athens after years of common experiences, fighting against war, neoliberalism, all forms of imperialism, colonialism, racism, discrimination and exploitation, against all the risks of an ecological catastrophe.
>
> (Assembly of the Movements 2006)

With these words, the activists participating in the Assembly of the Movements of the European Social Forum (ESF) in Athens presented themselves, remembering 'years of common experiences'. The ESF in Athens is the fourth social forum held on a European scale, with the aim of providing a space for the encounter of thousands of social movement organizations and tens of thousands of activists. In their document, the activists claim to have been part of a successful fight against neoliberalism: 'This year' – they state – 'has been significant in that a number of social struggles and campaigns have been successful in stopping neoliberal projects such as the proposed European Constitution Treaty, the EU Ports Directive, and the CPE in France' (ibid.).

The targets of this struggle are identified in a number of international governmental organizations (IGOs), including the EU:

> Movements of opposition to neoliberalism are growing and are clashing against the power of trans-national corporations, the G8 and organizations such as the WTO, the IMF and the World Bank, as well the neoliberal policies of the States and the European Union.
>
> (Ibid.)

In fact, at the first ESF in Florence (in 2002), the activists already rooted their movement in a history of struggles targeting IGOs. As the Call of the European Social Movements stated:

> We have come together from the social and citizens movements from all the regions of Europe, East and West, North and South. We have come together through a long process: the demonstrations of Amsterdam, Seattle, Prague,

> Nice, Gothenburg, Genoa, Brussels, Barcelona, the big mobilisations against neoliberalism as well as the general strikes for the defence of social rights and all the mobilisations against war, show the will to build another Europe.
>
> (ESF 2002)

In a similar way, stressing the internal diversity as an enriching characteristic of their movement, the Declaration of the Assembly of the Movements at the third ESF, held in London in 2004, claimed:

> We come from all the campaigns and social movements, 'no vox' organisations, trade unions, human rights organisations, international solidarity organisations, anti-war and peace and feminist movements. We come from every region in Europe to gather in London for the third European Social Forum. We are many, and our strength is our diversity.

'Coming together', 'diversity', 'another Europe': these are all expressions repeated over and over in the documents of the European Social Forum. In this introductory chapter, I will discuss, first, why and how the issue of democracy is relevant in research on contemporary social movements. Second, I will explain why the European Social Forum is a significant (and 'critical') case study. I will then present the research methods, focusing in particular on the survey of activists at the fourth European Social Forum.

Democracy and/in contemporary social movements: where is the challenge?

The basic assumption of our research is that the consideration of democracy plays an important role in social movement organizations and, conversely, social movements are important actors in contemporary democracies. Although their activities are not limited to the political system, social movement organizations often interact with it: by protesting, they present claims to various levels of governance; they encounter 'street level bureaucrats' such as police officers; they lobby various branches of the public administration; and they are increasingly contracted to provide public services addressed to specific constituencies (women, migrants, and others).

Beyond addressing demands to decision makers, however, social movements also express a fundamental critique of conventional politics, thus shifting their endeavours from politics itself to meta-politics (Offe 1985). Since the 1970s, the 'new social movements' have also been said to present important innovations vis-à-vis dominant conceptions in the workers' movement: among them are decentralized and participatory organizational structures; defence of interpersonal solidarity against state and corporate bureaucracies; and the reclamation of autonomous spaces, rather than material advantages (ibid.). In doing so, social movement organizations develop proposals – ranging from limited reforms to ambitious utopias – for alternative democratic practices.

The dimension of internal democracy is all the more important for collective actors that have few material incentives to distribute and must therefore gain and keep the commitment of their members on the basis of shared beliefs. This is especially challenging for a base of activists that appear as very demanding, critical, and auto-critical when issues of internal democracy are at stake. Social movement organizations are in fact self-reflexive actors that tend to debate the issue of democracy as it applies to their internal lives (Melucci 1989). Recent research has confirmed the high degree of critical discussion on the implementation of internal democracy present in social movements (della Porta 2005c). Past experiences are reflected upon, showing important learning processes. Although no satisfactory solution has yet emerged to address the main organizational dilemmas – between, among others, participation versus efficacy, equality versus specialization, and so on – experiments develop, innovating on the old, and unsatisfactory, models.

On both the external and the internal dimensions of democracy, social movements have been said to affirm the legitimacy (if not the primacy) of alternatives to representative democracy, criticizing both liberal democracy and the 'organized democracy' of political parties. Their ideas resonate with

> An ancient element of democratic theory that calls for an organization of collective decision making referred to in varying ways as classical, populist, communitarian, strong, grass-roots, or direct democracy against a democratic practice in contemporary democracies labelled as realist, liberal, elite, republican, or representative democracy.
>
> (Kitschelt 1993: 15)

To these (more traditional) participatory values, some emerging ones have been linked, such as attention to communication, practices of consensus building, emphasis on the inclusion of diverse groups and, especially, respect for such diversity (della Porta 2005b; della Porta and Reiter 2006a). Contemporary social movement organizations experiment with consensual methods of decision making, and values such as plurality, diversity, and inclusivity are mentioned in their fundamental documents (della Porta 2009). Investigating recent movements, Francesca Polletta stressed that activists:

> Expected each other to provide legitimate reasons for preferring one option to another. They strove to recognize the merits of each other's reasons for favouring a particular option ... the goal was not unanimity, so much as discourse. But it was a particular kind of discourse, governed by norms of openness and mutual respect.
>
> (Polletta 2002: 7)

These aspects resonate with the emerging debate in political theory and the social sciences in general on so-called discursive or deliberative democracy, especially with the approaches locating democratic deliberation in voluntary groups (Cohen

1989), social movements (Dryzek 2000), protest arenas (Young 2003: 119) or, more in general, enclaves free from institutional power (Mansbridge 1996).

In our research, we address in particular the conceptions and practices of democracy that have developed in the global justice movement (GJM), mobilizing transnationally and demanding social justice and participatory and/or deliberative democracy. We have defined the GJM as the loose network of organizations (with varying degrees of formality, and even including political parties) and other actors, engaged in collective action of various kinds, based on the shared goal of advancing the cause of justice (economic, social, political, and environmental) among and between peoples around the globe (della Porta 2007a). This means that we focus on an empirical form of transnational activism, without claiming to cover all the existing manifestations of that abstract concept. We operationalized our definition by looking at collective identities, non-conventional action repertoires, and organizational networks (see della Porta 2007a). While we focus here on surveys of movement activists, the comparative research project Democracy in Europe and the Mobilisation of the Society (Demos) (covering France, Germany, Great Britain, Italy, Spain and Switzerland, and the transnational level), upon which this volume draws, includes an analysis of documents and websites of organizations of the GJM (della Porta and Mosca 2005; della Porta and Reiter 2006a), semi-structured interviews with nongovernmental organizations (della Porta and Mosca 2006), and participant observation of movement groups and their experiences with participatory and/or deliberative decision making.

We assume that the issue of democracy is particularly relevant for the GJM given its external and internal challenges. First of all, the GJM reacts to deep transformations in representative systems that include power shifts from the national to the international level as well as from the state to the market (della Porta 2005c). Additionally, internal democracy is particularly relevant for a multifaceted, heterogeneous movement (which has significantly defined itself as a 'movement of movements') that incorporates many social, generational, and ideological groups as well as movement organizations from various countries. As the first studies on this subject are pointing out, this movement has a more pluralistic identity, a more loosely connected organizational structure, and a more multiform action repertoire than those characteristic of previous movements (Andretta et al. 2002, 2003; della Porta and Mosca 2003; della Porta 2007a). Moreover, the global justice activists develop 'tolerant' identities as opposed to the 'totalitarian', or at least organizational, identities of the past (della Porta 2005b).

Other parts of the Demos project confirmed that the issue of democracy continues to be a very relevant one for social movements. To give just one example, our analysis of the documents of 244 social movement organizations showed that most mention democratic values in their main documents (see della Porta and Reiter 2006a). Looking at the values concerning internal democracy (Table 1.1), participation is still a main point of reference in social movement organizations' (SMOs) visions of democracy, mentioned by one-third of the organizations as an internal value. It is a founding principle not only for the 'purest' forms of SMOs,

Table 1.1 Internal and general democratic values explicitly mentioned in the selected documents[1]

Internal democratic values	%	General democratic values	%
Autonomy of the territorial levels***	38.5	Participation	51.2
Autonomy of member organizations**	33.1	Difference/plurality/ heterogeneity	47.1
Participatory democracy	27.9	Equality	34.0
Inclusiveness	20.9	Dialogue/communication	31.6
Consensual method	17.2	Inclusiveness	25.8
Non-hierarchical decision-making	16.0	Transparency	23.8
Criticism of delegation and/or representation	11.1	Individual liberty/autonomy	21.7
Deliberative democracy	7.0	Autonomy (group; cultural)	18.9
Limitation of delegation	6.6	Representation	6.1
Rotation principle	6.6		
Mandate delegation	6.1		

Source: della Porta and Reiter 2006.

Notes
1 N = 244, with the exception of ** not applicable for 114 (46.7%) groups, because they do not mention organizations as members; and *** not applicable for 62 (25.4%) groups, because they do not mention territorial levels of organization.

but also for trade unions and left-wing political parties. However, additional values emerge specifying (and differentiating) the conceptions of participatory democracy. Appeals to the limits of delegation, the rotation principle, mandated delegation, criticism of delegation, or deliberative democracy as internal organizational values are present, although not widespread (between 6 and 11 per cent). References to consensual and non-hierarchical decision making are more significant (17 and 16 per cent, respectively), and even more frequent references are made to inclusiveness and the autonomy of local chapters or member organizations (between 21 and 29 per cent). Looking at general democratic values, it is remarkable that the documents in as much as half of the sample refer to plurality, diversity, and heterogeneity as important democratic values, at a level very near to that of (more traditional) participation. Equality is mentioned in the analysed documents in about one-third of our sample and values such as transparency, inclusiveness, and individual freedom in about one-fourth. Significantly, representative values are mentioned by only 6 per cent of our organizations.

Research on democracy and movements

Although recognizing the importance of social movements in and for democracy, social movement research has traditionally focused more on the external than on the internal dimension, and more on the effects of representative democracy on social movement characteristics than vice versa. Especially since the

1980s, with the increasing interest in social movements by political scientists, European scholars have used the concept of political opportunities, developed by American scholars, in cross-national research projects. Alexis de Tocqueville's famous contrast between a 'weak' American government and a 'strong' French one is usually an implicit or explicit starting point for analyses linking institutional factors – or 'regimes' in Tilly's definition (1978) – with social movement development (Kriesi 2004: 71). The idea that states' strength or weakness influences social movement strategies remains central to the literature on collective action in general, and on revolutions in particular.

Especially in the 1990s, large comparative research projects explored the effects on social movements of some main dimensions of comparison among European countries such as centralization versus decentralization of power (Rucht 1994: 303–12; Kriesi et al. 1995); the characteristics of national political cultures (Kitschelt 1986; Kriesi et al. 1995); the influence of a country's democratic history (Flam 1994; della Porta and Reiter 1998); the prevailing model of industrial relations (Joppke 1993; Tarrow 1989; della Porta 1996); and the alliance with parties of the Left (della Porta et al. forthcoming). In contrast, only a few attempts were made to address the effects of social movements on representative democracies, and these attempts mainly focused on macro-dimensions (see Giugni et al. 1998, 1999; Giugni 2004).

With few remarkable exceptions (in particular, Lichterman 1996; Polletta 2002), the conceptions of democracy in social movements were not often investigated, and when they were it was mainly with a focus on the debate on their organizational forms, often returning to the traditional cleavage between those who praised organizations as effective instruments of mobilization (Gamson 1990; McCarthy and Zald 1987) and those who feared an iron law of bureaucratization (Piven and Cloward 1977). Although some researchers have singled out various forms and trends of organizational structures and developments (for instance, Kriesi 1996; Rucht 1996; della Porta 2003b) and stressed the typical network forms of movements (Gerlach and Hine 1970; Diani 1995; see della Porta and Diani 2006a for a review), an instrumental vision tended to prevail. As Clemens and Minkoff (2003: 156) have recently noted, with the development of a resource mobilization perspective, 'Attention to organisation appeared antithetical to the analysis of culture and interaction. As organisations were understood instrumentally, the cultural content of organising and the meanings signalled by organisational forms were marginalised as topic for inquiry'. Moreover, empirical research pointed out the limits of direct forms of democracy, in particular the 'tyranny of the structureless', the closed nature of small groups to newcomers, and the risks of a 'hidden' leadership (among others, Freeman 1974; Breines 1989).

The main (although not the only) questions asked in the last decades have therefore focused on macro-causes for the development of social movements, and the instrumental role of social movement organizations in mobilizing environmental resources. These are relevant questions that will also remain central for contemporary movements. However, the emerging conflicts have also raised the need to refocus our attention from social movements as dependent variables, to social movements as (to a certain extent) 'independent' and conscious actors, producing changes not only on the outside, but also on the inside. Internal communication and democratic practices are relevant angles for the analysis of movements that are both innovative and pluralistic. In our analysis of the GJM, in fact, we want to shift attention towards what we can define as the emergent properties of protest.

In his conceptualization of an 'eventful temporality', Sewell (1996) suggests considering the capacity of some events to interrupt or challenge existing structures. In fact, research on the GJM started to pay attention to a sort of cross-fertilization in action ('contamination', to use the Italian neologism), recognizing some of the emerging characteristics of protest. Action campaigns and the networking structure of the global movement produce a situation of intense interaction among various individuals and organizations. This creates a process of 'contamination in action' through mechanisms of multiplication of individual belonging and organizational networking, which in turn facilitates frame-bridging, the transformation of identities and the creation of informal links (della Porta and Mosca 2006). As we will see in this volume, transnational protests such as the ESFs are especially 'eventful'.

Research on individual activists

With its focus on conceptions and practices of democracy within social movements, our research aims at an innovative contribution to a long-lasting and important debate. Summarizing, we look at social movements as spaces for the elaboration of conceptions of democracy and initial experimentation with them, focusing attention especially, but not only, on the micro-dimension of individual conceptions and experiences.

Research on activists has addressed both their social background and their political attitudes and behaviour. Social science research on political participation has traditionally stressed a class divide: participation emerges as limited and selective, increasing with social status (Lagroye 1993: 312). Higher levels of participation were identified, *ceteris paribus*, among the better educated, the middle classes, men, the medium age cohort, married people, city residents, the ethnic majority group, and citizens' involved in voluntary associations (Milbrath and Goel 1977). Usually, higher social status implies more material resources (but also more free time) to invest in political participation, but also a higher probability of being successful (via personal relationships with powerful individuals) and especially a higher sense of personal achievement. Psychological disadvantages overlap with social disadvantages, reducing the perception of one's own 'droit de parole' (Bourdieu 1979: 180).

Research on social movements has looked at the social characteristics of activists, reaching some similar conclusions. First, it has often been observed that the new social movements recruit from a specific social base, mainly comprising components of the middle class (Kriesi 1993). Second, in order to account for the overrepresentation of young and student activists, the concept of biographical availability was used to identify the circumstances that increase free time and limit family responsibilities, reducing constraints to participation in movement actions (see McAdam 1988). The increase in unconventional forms of participation over the last few decades had only a limited equalising effect regarding gender, age, and education (Topf 1995: 78).

Questions about support for protest have re-emerged in the social science discussion of contemporary global social movements, prompted by the heterogeneity of activists in protest campaigns centring on debt relief, international trade rules and barriers, global taxation, fair trade, peace, as well as European institutions. From the normative point of view, for a 'movement of movements' the inclusivity towards the social groups the movement aims at representing is a relevant, and often discussed, issue (Doerr 2006a, 2006b; Haug 2006). Research on the GJM has contributed some useful information on the social backgrounds of its activists, who emerged as well-educated and predominantly middle-class; male and middle-aged groups were not overrepresented. The research has also identified a re-emergence of the labour conflict.

A second important set of questions refers to the political background of participants, their values and previous experiences. Especially with the growth of political participation and the enlargement of research on unconventional forms of action, the debate about the degree and sources of selectivity has re-emerged, although with a new focus on the role of collective identities in overcoming individual lack of resources. Alessandro Pizzorno (1966) had already long ago noted that politics tends to refer to systems of solidarity that are at the basis of the very definition of interest. In fact, interests can be identified only with reference to a specific value system; values drive individuals to identify with wider groups in society, providing a sense of belonging and the willingness to mobilize.

In this perspective, participation is an action in solidarity with others that aims at protecting or transforming the dominant values and interest systems (ibid.). The process of participation therefore requires the construction of solidarity communities within which individuals perceive themselves and are recognized as equals. Identification as awareness of being part of a collective facilitates political participation. It is not the 'social centrality' (to which Milbrath refers), but the centrality with respect to a class (or a group) that defines an individual's propensity to political participation. This explains why some groups, composed of individuals that are endowed with low status, are able to mobilize more effectively than other groups under certain conditions. Additionally, research on participation in protest events has stressed the role of social networks in mobilizing activists (Klandermans 1997). Participation is therefore explained not only by individual resources, but also by collective and relational ones.

If the construction of a collective identity is a precondition for action, it is also a consequence of it. In fact, participation itself changes individual identity, increasing the sense of belonging to some groups and weakening other potential identifications. In collective action, identity is produced and reproduced (della Porta and Diani 2006). Barricades for revolutionaries, strikes for workers, occupations for students are actions oriented to influence public authorities, but also have an internal effect insofar as they strengthen 'class consciousness' – or, in more modern terms, collective identification. Participation therefore, in a sort of virtuous circle, increases a sense of belonging, encouraging more participation. During action, participants tend to identify not only the 'self' (the 'us' they identify with), but also the 'other' (the opponents, considered as responsible for an unjust situation). It is indeed 'in action' that the process of 'cognitive liberation' – that is, the attribution of a social, and addressable cause to an individual problem (McAdam 1988) – develops.

Also in this direction, research on the activists of the GJM has already contributed important knowledge on the role of multiple memberships, previous experiences of mobilization as well as individual networks in the paths towards and within political activism. In fact, many activists (especially older ones) had participated in previous waves of protest and in the civil society groups that emerged from them: students often had experiences in student groups, women in feminist collectives, workers in trade unions. The social bases of the 'global' protest seem, indeed, to reflect the range of political cleavages already mobilized, without the clear emergence of a 'new cleavage' – for example, between the 'winners' and the 'losers' of globalization. The dominant identification with the 'Left' of the political spectrum testifies in fact to the re-emergence of conflicts on social inequalities, which had been considered as largely pacified (della Porta 2006).

On both the social and the political backgrounds of the activists of the GJM, our research aims at contributing new, systematic, and comparative data. We also want, however, to go beyond these sets of questions focusing on the role of these various dimensions of participation in influencing conceptions and practices of democracy. A main assumption of our research is indeed that the general principles of democracy such as power (kratos) by/from/for the people (demos) can be combined in different forms and with different balances: representative versus participatory, majority versus deliberative and so on. As for the social basis of our protest, we will discuss the extent to which new generations, women, middle classes, or precarious workers are carriers of specific visions of democracy. In terms of political careers, we will observe to what extent various paths of political socialization, multiple belongings, degrees of identification and commitment to the movements as well as the judgements upon representative institutions are linked to the democratic conceptions of activists.

The general analytic model we developed in our research is reported in Figure 1.1 (numbers in parentheses refer to questions included in the questionnaire; see appendix).

Democracy in the European social forum: a critical case study

This volume will focus on the European social forums, using as far as possible a cross-time perspective that takes into account the evolution and transformations

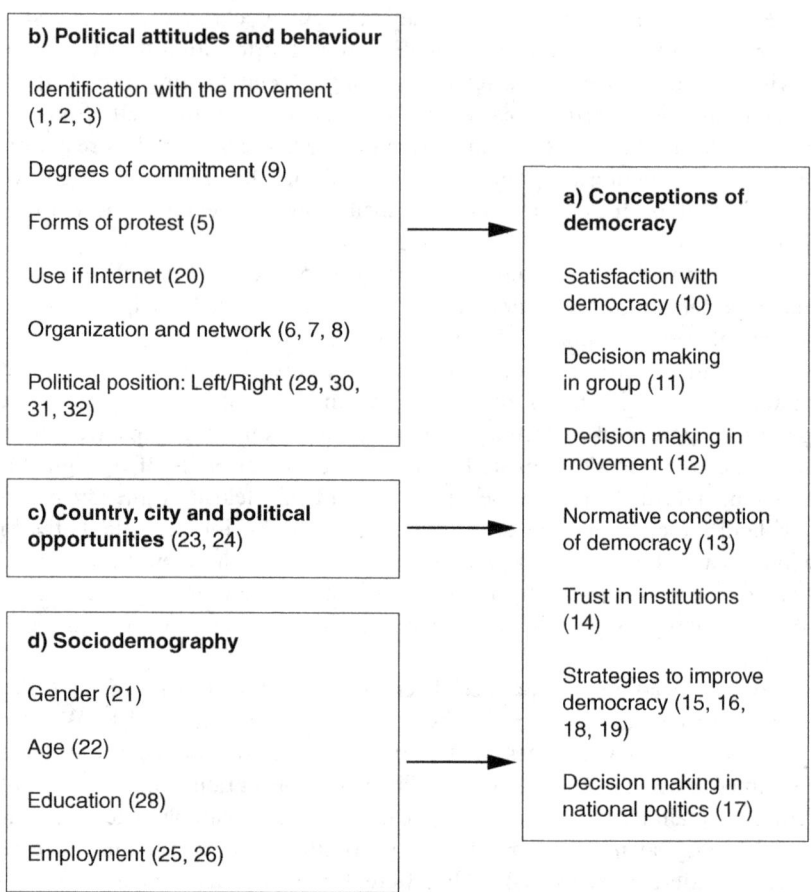

Figure 1.1 The research model.

among the four forums. The social forums are an innovative experiment promoted by the global justice movement. Counter-summits against the official summits of IGOs (especially the G8, World Bank and IMF, WTO, and EU) represent the more conflictual forms of protest at the transnational level. In contrast to a counter-summit, which is mainly oriented towards public protest, the Social Forum is set up as a space for debate among activists. Although the first large-scale social forum, the World Social Forum (WSF), was indirectly oriented to 'counter' another summit – as it was held on the same date as an alternative to the World Economic Forum (WEF) in Davos (Switzerland) – it also presented itself as an independent space for encounters among civil society organizations and citizens.

Since the very beginning, the WSF showed a large mobilization capacity. The first meeting, held in Porto Alegre in January 2001, was attended by about 20,000 participants from over 100 countries, among them thousands of delegates of NGOs and social movement organizations. Its main aim was the discussion of 'Another possible globalisation' (Schoenleitner 2003). Since then, the number of organizers and participants as well as the organizational efforts of the subsequent WSFs (in Porto Alegre in 2002 and 2003, then in Mumbai in 2004 and again in Porto Alegre in 2005) increased exponentially. The WSF also gained large media attention. According to the organizers, the WSF in 2002 attracted 3,000 journalists (from 467 newspapers and 304 radio or TV stations), a figure that doubled to more than 6,800 in 2005 (Rucht 2005: 294–5). As Dieter Rucht (2005: 291) observed,

> During its relatively short existence, the WSF has become an institution in its own right and can be seen as a kind of huge showcase for a large number of issues, groups, and claims.... Within the short period of their existence, WSFs have become a trademark that has begun to overshadow its competitor, the World Economic Forum, in respect to public attention. It is also a structure that, according to its slogan 'Another world is possible', raises many hopes, energizes many participants, links large numbers of issues and groups, and – last but not least – contributes to the creation of an overarching identity and community as expressed in the vision of a meeting place for the global civil society.

Since 2001, social forums have also developed at the macro-regional, national, and local levels. Pan Amazonian social forums were held in Brazil and Venezuela in 2004; African social forums in Mali and Ethiopia; Asian social forums in India (Sommier 2005: 21). Among them, the European Social Forum (ESF) played an important role in the elaboration of activists' attitudes towards the European Union, as well as the formation of a European identity. The first ESF took place in Florence on 6–9 November 2002. Notwithstanding the tensions before the meeting,[1] the ESF in Florence was a success: not only was there not a single act of violence, but participation went beyond the most optimistic expectations. Some 60,000 participants – more than three times the expected number – attended the 30 plenary conferences, 160 seminars, and 180 workshops organized at the Fortezza da Basso; even more participated in the 75 cultural events in various parts of the city. About one million participated in the march that closed the forum. More than 20,000 delegates of 426 associations arrived from 105 countries – among others, 24 buses from Barcelona; a special train from France and another from Austria; and a special ship from Greece. Up to 400 interpreters worked without pay to ensure simultaneous translations.

The second ESF, held in Paris in 2003, involved up to 60,000 individual participants and 1,800 groups (including 70 unions), in 270 seminars, 260 working groups and 55 plenary sessions (with about 1,500 participants in each); 3,000 activists worked as volunteers, 1,000 as interpreters. According to the organizers,

150,000 people participated in the final march. The third ESF, in London in 2004, involved about 25,000 participants and 2,500 speakers in 150 seminars, 220 working groups and 30 plenary sessions, as well as up to 100,000 participants at the final march. The fourth, in Athens in 2006, included 278 seminars and workshops and 104 cultural activities listed in the official programme; there were 35,000 registered participants, and up to 80,000 participated in the final march.[2]

The choice of the ESF as a case study is related to its peculiar nature as an experiment in alternative practices of democracy. In this sense, we are not selecting an average protest event, but a critical moment when participants are aware that democracy is a central stake in the internal life of the movement as well as in the society at large. Not by chance, the ESF is represented in the press as 'an exchange on concrete experiences' (*La Stampa*, 10 November 2003), 'an agora' (*Liberazione*, 14 November 2003), a 'kermesse' (*Europa*, 3 November 2003), a 'tour-de-force of debates, seminars and demonstrations by the new global' (*L'Espresso*, 13 November 2003), 'a sort of university, where you learn, discuss and exchange ideas' (*La Repubblica*, 17 October 2004), 'a supranational public space, a real popular university, but especially the place where to build European nets' (*Liberazione*, 12 October 2004). Vittorio Agnoletto, spokesperson of the Genoa Social Forum (which organized the anti-G8 protest in 2001), writes of the ESF as a 'non-place':

> It is not an academic conference, even though there are professors. It is not a party international, even though there are party militants and party leaders among the delegates. It is not a federation of NGOs and unions, although they have been the main material organizers of the meetings. The utopian dimension of the forum is in the active and pragmatic testimony that another globalisation is possible.
>
> (*Il Manifesto*, 12 November 2003)

The common basic feature of a social forum is the conception of an inclusive public space. The charter of the WSF defines it as an 'open meeting place'. Participation is open to all civil society groups, with the exception of those advocating racist ideas and those using terrorist means, as well as political parties as such. Its functioning, with hundreds of workshops and dozens of conferences (with invited experts), testifies to the importance given (at least in principle) to knowledge. In fact, the WSF has been defined by one of its organizers as 'a market place for (sometime competing) causes and an "ideas fair" for exchanging information, ideas and experiences horizontally' (Schoenleitner 2003: 140), which promotes exchanges in order 'to think more broadly and to construct together a more ample perspective' (ibid.: 141). The same participants in their comments published online recall the image of 'academic seminars'.[3] Writing on the ESF in Paris, sociologists Agrikoliansky and Cardon (2005: 47) stressed its pluralistic nature:

> Even if it re-articulates traditional formats of mobilisations, the form of the 'forum' has properties that are innovative enough to consider it as a new entry in the repertoire of collective action.... An event like the ESF in Paris

does not indeed resemble anything already clearly identified. It is not really a conference, even if we find a program, debates and paper-givers. It is not a congress, even if there are tribunes, militants and *mots d'ordre*. It is not just a demonstration, even if there are marches, occupations and demonstrations in the street. It is neither a political festival, even if we find stands, leaflets and recreational activities. The social forums concentrate in a unit of time and space such a large diversity of forms of commitment that exhaustive participation in all of them is impossible.

What unifies these different activities is the attempt at providing a meeting space for the huge number of loosely coupled groups that form the archipelagos of the GJM. Its aims include enlarging the number of individuals and groups involved, but also laying the groundwork for a broader mutual understanding. Far from aiming at eliminating differences, the open debates should help to increase awareness of each other's concerns and beliefs. The purpose of networking (through debating) was already openly stated at the first ESF in Florence, where the Declaration of the European social movements announced:

> We have come together to strengthen and enlarge our alliances because the construction of another Europe and another world is now urgent. We seek to create a world of equality, social rights and respect for diversity, a world in which education, fair jobs, healthcare and housing are rights for all, with the right to consume safe food products produced by farmers and peasants, a world without poverty, without sexism and oppression of women, without racism, and without homophobia. A world that puts people before profits. A world without war. We have come together to discuss alternatives but we must continue to enlarge our networks and to plan the campaigns and struggles that together can make this different future possible. Great movements and struggles have begun across Europe: the European social movements are representing a new and concrete possibility to build up another Europe for another world.

The openness towards 'the others' is considered in some activists' comments as a most relevant attitude in order to 'build nets from the local, to the national to the supranational'.[4] In this sense, social forums belong to emerging forms of action that stress, by their very nature, plurality and inclusion.[5]

The advocated inclusivity and horizontality is certainly not fully implemented in the concrete experiences of the forum. Degrees of structuration, inclusion, and representation are always at the centre of discussion. Democracy in the forum is a constant topic, with tensions between different models (horizontal versus vertical, but also as oriented to action or discussion) testified by the different structures present within the forums. Again in Agrikoliansky and Cardon's words,

> In order to avoid the destructuration typical of these types of reticular spaces, the 'central' organizational structures try to give coherence and a

meaning to the alter-globalist movement. This effort at coordination is implemented on different terrains and especially in the architecture of the places of debates and exchanges, that constitute the very body of the ESF.

(2005: 48)

Similar to scientific conferences or party congresses, the plenary conferences offered a central focus, but also choreographically confirmed the division between a stage for the few and the stalls for the crowds. Differently structured, with people mostly seated in circles and intervening in a more informal way and as individuals more than as representatives of an organization, the seminars and the workshops (ateliers) should instead allow for the development of European networks from below on specific issues, as the frequent exchange of addresses at the end of each session testifies for (ibid.: 70).

Although it functions as an arena for the encounter of many and heterogeneous groups and activists, the ESF is a dynamic process. The focus of the initiatives in part changed, in part expanded from one ESF event to the next. At the second ESF, in Paris, there was increasing attention to defining a position towards the European Union, with the call for a 'Europe of the citizens and the peoples' and against the form and the outcomes of the European Convention and EU policies on agriculture, migration, and social issues. Increased focus was given to gender issues, unemployment and precarious work, housing, and the rights of the most excluded (Sommier 2005: 25). The choice of London for the third ESF was justified, among other reasons, by the peculiarity of the British movements 'struggling at the heart of neo-liberal power' vis-à-vis the continental groups. The third ESF saw a growing focus on the issue of the war in Iraq and the position towards migrants and Muslim citizens in Europe and in the world – an issue that had already emerged in Paris with the debate around the participation of Tariq Ramadan, accused of anti-Semitism for an open letter published on the ESF website, in which he criticized certain French intellectuals. In Athens, the large presence of Turkish activists and Eastern Europeans reflected an emerging attention towards the people and movements on the 'periphery' of the EU. The organizational formula and practices of the ESF subsequently changed as a result of this process (see Chapter 4 in this volume).

These transformations also interacted with some apparent changes in the participants at the various events. Surveys of the first, second, and fourth ESFs[6] indicate first of all a large presence of participants with previous experience in events promoted by the GJM – with a clear growth of this category between Paris (slightly more than half) and Athens (almost four-fifths; although the growth is not so significant in comparison with the Florentine event). Looking at the frequency of participation in this type of event, in Athens there was a dramatic growth in veterans of GJM events, with about 40 per cent having participated often (ten times or more). These data reflect the longer history of the GJM by 2006, but also the increasing number of strongly committed activists at the ESF in general, and in our sample in particular. It is also coherent with the trend in degrees of identification in the GJM, where we notice an important increase in the percentage of those who declare a strong identification with it (from 24 per cent in Florence to 39 per cent in Athens, although the peak here is in Paris) and a parallel decline in those who are not at all or only slightly identified with the GJM (from 23 per cent in Florence to 16 per cent in Paris and then 13 per cent in Athens).

The research: methods and caveats

The research on the ESF presented in this volume is based upon three main empirical methods: a qualitative discourse analysis of the documents (organizational documents, activists' reports online, newspapers articles and so on); participant observation at meetings of the ESF and at the European Preparatory Assembly, where decisions about the location and the programme of the ESF were taken; and surveys of activists at the ESF. Regarding the analysis of the documents, we should stress the richness of the materials, but also its selective nature. Our analysis does not therefore endeavour, at this level, to cover all the available documents. In order to reach an understanding of the multilevel nature of the organizational process of the ESF, as well as of the interactions with its complex environment (especially of potential allies and mass media), we focused on the documents published in the languages covered by our team (English, French, German, Italian, and Spanish), and that were available online. These documents helped us to locate the micro, individual dimension of beliefs and motivation within an organizational environment. Although only loosely structured, the participant observation at the meetings and in the areas where the forums took place allowed us a better understanding of the meanings the participants gave to those spaces and the ways in which they lived in them.

More systematic has been the collection of data at the individual level, mainly based upon a survey of the participants at the fourth European Social Forum in Athens, compared when possible with the data collected at similar endeavours at the first ESF in Florence (della Porta *et al.* 2006a) and the second ESF in Paris (Agrikoliansky and Sommier 2005). Social movement scholars have considered the individual dimension through interviews oriented to assess paths into participation in protest events (Klandermans and Oegema 1987), patterns of activists' radicalization (della Porta 1995), and the long-term effects of socialization in social movements (McAdam 1988). Research on these issues has employed mainly semi-structured or in-depth interviews and life histories; surveys have been rarer. Although sometimes used for discussing the characteristics of 'protest-oriented' citizens (Barnes and Kaase 1979; Dalton 1996; Norris 2002), surveys on the entire population have usually been considered as minimally useful for analysis of social movements, since their members are generally too few to allow for statistically significant analyses. Logistical and epistemological concerns specific to research with questionnaires to activists have to be added to those related to surveys in general.

In the few cases in which structured questionnaires have been used, social movement activists have typically been surveyed during demonstrations. A recent assessment of the social science literature in the field mentions only three surveys of protest events before the late 1990s: a comparison of four rallies that were held in 1970 and 1973 in the US (Seidler et al. 1976; Meyer et al. 1977; Meyer and Seidler 1978); a survey of demonstrators at a national anti-nuclear rally held in Washington, DC in 1979 (Ladd et al. 1983); and another at a march in Sheffield to protest the visit of Prime Minister Margaret Thatcher (Waddington et al. 1988). In the 1990s, such surveys began to spread, with three such projects conducted in 1994 at protest marches in France (see Favre et al. 1997; Fillieule 1997) and four in 1998 at marches in Belgium (van Aelst and Walgrave 2001).

Beginning in 2000, however, surveys at protest events have increasingly been used in the wave of the global cycle of protest that became visible in Seattle in 1999. Among others, the Gruppo di Ricerca sull'Azione Collettiva in Europa (GRACE) at the University of Florence surveyed participants at the anti-G8 protest in Genoa and the Perugia–Assisi Peace March in 2001, and at the first European Social Forum in Florence in 2002 (Andretta et al. 2002, 2003, 2006a); the Groupe de Recherches sur l'Activisme Altermondialiste (GRAAL, University of Paris Sorbonne) and the Centre de Recherche sur l'Action Politique (CRAPUL, University of Lausanne, Switzerland) covered the anti-G8 protest in the French-Swiss region of Evian–Lausanne–Geneva and the second European Social Forum in Paris, both in 2003 (Fillieule et al. 2004; Fillieule and Blanchard 2006; Agrikoliansky and Sommier 2005). A survey was conducted in eight countries during the 15 February Global Day of Action in 2003 against the war in Iraq (Walgrave and Rucht forthcoming). Additionally, Bedoyan and van Aelst (2003) surveyed a protest march in Brussels on 14 December 2001, Roth and Rucht studied protests against unemployment in four German cities, and Eggert and Giugni (2007) surveyed the events in Zurich and Davos in 2004. Beyond providing data on the sociographic and political backgrounds of the activists as well as their individual attitudes and behaviours, the above-mentioned research also helped to raise some main methodological caveats in this specific use of survey data.

We shall start here by acknowledging the general limitations of surveys as heuristic devices. In terms of representativeness, the surveys must address problems related to sampling error (not all members of the population have the same chance of being included in the sample); drop-out errors (related to the specific characteristics of those who refuse to be interviewed); errors in understanding (respondents answer without understanding the questions); missing value errors (a certain percentage does not respond to specific questions). For well-known reasons, surveys focus on individuals: indeed, they are not the best way to analyse either concrete organizational praxis or organizational values (Dryzek 2004). Additionally, they have to be used with care (and possibly triangulated with other, more qualitative techniques), when we want to study values or motivations in-depth. In fact, the very instrument of the survey discourages the active participation of interviewee and interviewer, reducing creativity and flexibility in the search for homogeneity and standardization. Besides the difficulty of assessing the influence of interviewees' attempts to provide 'socially desirable answers or rationalization', surveys tend to produce superficial or standardized responses: 'feelings and emotions, people's uncertainties, doubts, and fears, all the inconsistencies and the complexities of social interactions and belief systems are matters that are not easily tapped with survey questionnaires' (Klandermans and Smith 2002: 27). In the analysis reported in this volume, we tried to take into account these limits by triangulating the information collected through the survey with that coming from other methods (among them in depth interviews and participant observation; see below).

Another question, with implications for the representativity of the sample, concerns the status of the specific surveyed demonstrations vis-à-vis the social movement to be investigated. While in fact social movements are complex networks of networks, characterized by a changing degree of density, social movement events rarely involve all components equally. Additionally, given the high material and psychological cost of travelling, national and, especially, local activists are largely overrepresented: at the first ESF, for instance, the largest component of participants was from Tuscany, and Italians were of course more numerous than non-Italians. Samples that may respect the composition of a certain event fairly well, therefore, do not reflect the characteristics of national and (even less) transnational movements. The counter-summits targeting the EU are in fact greatly influenced by the characteristics of the national movements that organize and host them: a demonstration targeting the EU in pro-EU Belgium will have different social and political bases from a similar one in Euro-sceptic Sweden (see, for example, Bédoyan and van Aelst 2003 on the EU counter-summit in Brussels at the end of 2001, and Peterson 2006 on the EU counter-summit in Gothenburg in 2002).

Additionally, especially among locals, protest events attract newcomers as well as people who are only marginally involved in a movement. Surveys at protest events address situations in which

> Participation is generally not submitted to any condition. People do not need to be a member of an organisation, they usually do not have to register (apart from the case of Social Fora where you have to pay fees), etc. That means that the reference population, the crowd itself, can be composed of core militants, sympathizers, bystanders, sight-seers, lost people, tourists and sometimes opponents! A crowd can't be considered as equal to a social movement constituency. Its heterogeneity is far more important and different in nature.
>
> (Fillieule and Blanchard 2006)

The sample therefore represents the specific characteristics of these sub-samples of the movement population. The variety in terms of degree of commitment, identification, and previous experience actually enriches the possibility of analysis, but one should be cautious in generalizing results to the smaller circles of the most committed activists. In our research, we shall address these concerns by comparing the Athens ESF with other protest events that have been previously surveyed. Additionally, we shall compare sub-samples of the population with different degrees of commitment to the GJM.

An additional problem refers to the representativity of the sample, and it is linked to the sampling procedure. Pierre Favre, Olivier Fillieule, and Nonna Mayer (Favre *et al.* 1997) were among the first scholars to devise a method to randomly sample demonstrators. As Fillieule and Blanchard (2006) recently summarized, 'since it is not possible to use a sampling strategy based on quotas, one has to use a probabilistic method, that is to say, to guarantee that all possible participants would have equal opportunity of being interviewed'. To devise a technique that would support this aim, the researcher has to consider the symbolic allocation of spaces in a demonstration, as well as demonstrators' habits. As Fillieule pointed out,

> People do assemble at a meeting point, march under a banner, depending on multiple belongings, following a march order that is predetermined by the organisers. Others are more erratic, travelling from one group to another, from the very heart of the demonstration to its margins. These numerous spatial and temporal distributions have a clear consequence: one must use two different methods, depending on which stage of a demonstration is concerned, the assembling phase or the march itself.
>
> (1997: methodological appendix)

Taking into account this 'use' of the marches by the participants, a two-step sampling procedure has been proposed. A first step involves the distribution of questionnaires at the gathering space, usually 'divided in advance into sectors clearly identified by some spatial distinguishing marks' where activists of different groups converge. In each sector, the interviewers select 'the Xth person in a group' (Blanchard and Fillieule 2006). In a second phase, questionnaires are administered during the protest march itself, with the interviewers usually divided into two teams moving one from the start and one from the end of the march. In order to offer all participants equal chances to be interviewed, further surveys at demonstrations have also usually sampled the Nth person in every Nth row of a march (e.g. van Aelst and Walgrave 2001). However, this sampling method proved difficult to implement at very large demonstrations. At the Global Days of Action against the war on Iraq, activists interviewed during a cross-national research project were mainly selected at the beginning and the end of the marches (in some cases involving between half a million and two million participants), being careful to select randomly in various sectors of the squares or parks where demonstrators converged (see Rucht and Walgrave forthcoming).

Still different criteria have been used to select interview partners at social forums, which are static events. The sample for a survey conducted during the days of the anti-G8 protest in Genoa in 2001 included people selected randomly over the various initiatives ('theme-based piazzas', debates, campsites and so on), so as to construct a sample that included the various 'souls' of the movement (Andretta *et al.* 2002). The sample for the survey of the first European

Social Forum in Florence in 2002 was similarly constructed (della Porta *et al.* 2006a), as was the one at the counter-summit against the G8 meeting in Evian, which involved a cross-border demonstration between France and Switzerland (Fillieule *et al.* 2004). This was also the strategy we used at the Athens ESF, trying to exploit the nature of the event as a long-lasting meeting, during which it was possible to find time to complete and return the questionnaire. In fact, our team was mainly located at the main entrance of the forum and gave the questionnaire to those entering. Most members of the Demos team, plus some additional collaborators (a total of 19 researchers), participated in the distribution and collection of the questionnaires that took place as planned at the fourth European Social Forum in Athens on 3–6 May 2006.

In all these cases, since purely random sampling is impossible given the lack of knowledge on the universe of participants, the representativity of the sampled interviewees is a critical issue, to be monitored in relation to the known dimensions of the universe. For the GSF survey, the composition of the surveyed sample by organizational area was compared with the estimates of the number of participants from the different networks provided by the organizers on the eve of the protests.[7] For the first ESF survey, the distribution of the sample according to nationality was compared with that of those enrolled at the forum (della Porta *et al.* 2006a). For our survey, we have tried to gain similar information on the country distribution as collected at registration.

Especially for transnational protest events, basic decisions affecting the representativity of the sample refer to the language used in the questionnaires. Since activists may be expected to be more willing and able to respond to a questionnaire in their mother tongue, the decision whether, in how many, and in which languages to translate the questionnaire affects the final sample. For instance, although using more or less the same techniques for sampling, the choice of distributing questionnaires only in Italian at an anti-G8 survey was reflected in a sample almost entirely composed of Italians, while the translation of a questionnaire into English, French, Spanish, and German distributed at the first ESF produced a multinational sample (della Porta *et al.* 2006a). In our survey in Athens, we translated our questionnaire into all the languages of the countries involved in the Demos project and, additionally, into Greek.

A fourth element affecting the representativity of our sample is, as for other surveys, the return rates. Due to logistical difficulties, interviews can rarely be carried out face-to-face. Respondents are thus asked either to return the questionnaire at a collecting point, or to mail them back. The return rate of questionnaires at the 15 February Global Day of Action varied, for instance, between 37 per cent of the questionnaires distributed at the Spanish march and 54 per cent of those distributed in the Netherlands (Walgrave and Verlhulst 2004). Other questionnaires have yielded similar results (van Aelst and Walgrave 2001). About 1,200 questionnaires (more than 30 per cent) were returned to our Demos desk at the entrance of the ESF premises. Given the logistical challenges of our survey, this return rate – similar to those obtained in previous research – can be considered as satisfactory (van Aelst and Walgrave 2001). Of course, the peculiarities of the respondents in terms of age, gender, and education can bias the results. Two possible ways to address this issue have been suggested: First, a comparison between results of interviews run face-to-face and returned questionnaires in postal surveys (della Porta forthcoming); and second, the recording of some information from those who refuse to take the questionnaire.

In addition, specific to surveys at demonstrations are the highly emotionally charged environments where they are distributed (and, possibly, collected). As Blanchard and Fillieule (2006) noted,

> People attending a protest event or a political rally are by nature in an expressive situation. They do actually express their feelings and their opinions, if only by being there, by chanting and shouting slogans, by raising their fists, by wearing masks or costumes, by holding banners or placards. Two consequences follow. One is that people's willingness to participate is generally optimal, apart for those groups and individuals who reject as a whole poll techniques and sociological surveys as being part of the 'dominant order'. The other is that in case of face-to-face interviews, people will certainly pay little attention to the questions since they are engaged at the same time in a collective action, surrounded by colleagues, friends, relatives and the whole crowd.

Additionally, the completion of questionnaires can become a collective action, and the pressure to adhere to the group values is strong. These problems of validity can be considered in designing the questionnaire (avoiding long and complex questions, keeping the completion time low, focusing on actual behaviours) as well as, of course, in the interpretation of the data.

We tried to consider these caveats in the preparation of our research, distribution of questionnaires and interpretation of results. Above all, we devoted time and energy to designing a questionnaire that was short enough to discourage dropouts, and with clear questions (valid indicators). In particular, taking into account previous experiences with surveys, we used some already tested questions focusing on socio-demographic characteristics, trust in institutions, and previous experiences of participation of the activists – that is, variables that we would expect to affect decision making processes and the development of deliberative processes. We had instead to develop questions on the much less studied dimensions of democracy inside and outside movements. Our interest in the micro-dimension of the conceptions and practices of democracy is reflected in some questions focusing on respondents' normative conceptions and actual perceptions of democratic practices, at three levels of the group, the movement, and the political institutions in general.[8]

This volume

With its focus on conceptions and practices of democracy within contemporary social movements in Europe, our volume aims at contributing to the crucial debate on the various dimensions of democracy, between representation and participation. Given the recent focus on debates in political science and political sociology on the challenges to representative democracy, and the search for new institutions and procedures that can help to channel increased participation, the research we present offers empirical insights on alternative conceptions of democracy and the actors that support them. Additionally, with the attention paid to the transnational dimension of democracy and the emerging conception of 'another Europe', the volume addresses a relevant and little analysed aspect of Europeanization: the Europeanization of social movements. From a methodological point of view, the research innovates by covering (through a large-N survey of activists) an until recently neglected population of individuals: social movement activists. Additionally, the various chapters combine the analysis of the individuals' attitudes and behaviour with that of organizational characteristics, procedures, and practices of democracy.

The volume is divided into two main parts, the first focusing on the meso, organizational level, and the second on the micro, individual one.

The first section, to which this introductory chapter belongs, describes the organizational and communicative aspects of the European Social Forum. Chapter 2 covers the ESF organizational process in a diachronic perspective. Cristopher Haug, Lorenzo Mosca, and Nicolas Haeringer discuss the organizational dimension of social movements, through an analysis of the main tensions and decision making procedures at transnational meetings of the European Preparatory Assembly. The organizational process emerges as a contested space, with tensions related to the interaction of different organizational cultures but also capacity for self-reflection. In Chapter 3, 'Communicating the European social forum', Lorenzo Mosca *et al.* analyse the communication within/by the forums, and their relationship to conceptions of democracy. Communication is also a contested terrain, with opposition between professional and participatory conceptions of media work. Complex networks of communicators address different publics, with great capacity to interact with sympathizers, but resonance in the mainstream press.

Chapters 4 and 5 bridge the first and second parts by providing information on both the forum and the activists who participate in it. In Chapter 4, 'Models of democracy: how activists see democracy in the movement', Massimiliano Andretta and Donatella della Porta focus upon conceptions of democracy, presenting the various dimensions of our main dependent variable (in particular, a typology is built crossing two dimensions: (*a*) majoritarian versus consensual; (*b*) delegated versus direct). While activists tend to value participation, the implementation of general democratic principles in the social forum process is often debated and contested, sometimes in consensual, sometimes in agonistic ways. In Chapter 5, 'Democracy from below: activists and institutions', Donatella della Porta and Marco Giugni look at the proposals to reform existing institutions, through the analysis of activists' attitudes towards democracy as they emerge from the survey results as well as from internal debates/documents. Focusing on attitudes towards multilevel governance – in particular the European institutions – and the emerging conception of politics, the chapter confirms high mistrust in representative institutions but also widespread belief in the need to build alternative institutions of multilevel governance together with attempts to build concrete alternatives in everyday life.

The second part is devoted to individual conceptions of democracy and the explanations for them. In Chapter 6, 'The social bases of the GJM mobilization and democratic norms', Massimiliano Andretta and Isabelle Sommier focus on the degree of social inclusion in the ESF, covering the gender, age, educational, and employment background of the activists and the ways in which these dimensions influence activists' conceptions of democracy. The debate on the inclusivity (and exclusion) in the ESF is also addressed. In Chapter 7, 'The organizational dimension: how organizational formality, voice, and influence affect mobilization and participation', Clare Saunders and Massimiliano Andretta address the organizational backgrounds of the activists and the forum, explaining democratic visions on the basis of participation in formally structured versus grassroots types of organizations. In Chapter 8, on 'Novel characteristics of the GJM: a (latent) network analysis approach', Massimiliano Andretta, Iosif Botetzagias, Moses Boudourides, Olga Kioufegi, and Mundo Yang focus on networking in the movement, applying network analysis to the survey data. The multiple and multilevel memberships of the activists allow us to identify the role played by organizations active on various issues in the ESF networks mobilized in different countries. Organizational belonging is also relevant for the analysis carried out in Chapter 9, on the forum and the Left, this time for its ideological aspect. Massimiliano Andretta and Herbert Reiter consider here the political alignments of the activists and their effects on visions of democracy. Survey data and internal documents on the issue of institutional alliances are used as illustrations of the way in which the institutional Left interacts with the forum at the local, national, and supranational levels. The forum process emerges here also as a space where varying left-wing actors and conceptions of the Left meet each other, with some cooperation and much competition. Interactions within and without the ESF are, finally, addressed in Chapter 10, on 'Protest and the forum', where Marco Giugni, Alessandro Nai, and Herbert Reiter, look at repertoires of protest as part and parcel of the activists' conception of democracy. Looking also at the ESF as a form of protest and at the protests that take place within and around the forum, as well as at those by the ESF, the chapter highlights the internal tensions around strategic choices, but also the convergence around a multi-form repertoire combining more institutional and more disruptive forms of protest.

In the concluding chapter, Donatella della Porta synthesizes some main results of the research, locating them within the broader social science debate on democracy, as well as discussing the potential for generalizing the findings on the ESF to wider trends in contemporary social movements. In particular, research on the World social forums is reported in order to distinguish what is typically European and what is not in the transnational process observed in the volume.

Notes

1 With centre-right politicians but also many opinion leaders expressing a strong fear of violence in a city considered particularly fragile because of its artistic value (to the point of suggesting limitations to the right of demonstration in the 'città d'arte').
2 Data on participation are from the entry 'European social forum' in Wikipedia. Online, available at: http://en.wikipedia.org/wiki/European _social_forum accessed 24 December 2006.
3 See, for example, www.lokabass.com/scriba/eventi.php?id_eve=12, accessed 20 December 2006.
4 See, for example, www.lokabass.com/scriba/eventi.php?id_eve=62, accessed 20 December 2006.
5 Similar forms of protest that favour networking and successively 'contamination' (or cross-fertilization) are the 'solidarity assemblies', a series of assemblies where multiple and heterogeneous organisations active on similar issues are called to participate with their particular experiences; or the 'fairs of concrete alternatives', whose aim is to link various groups presenting alternatives to the market economy ranging from fair trade to environmental protection (della Porta and Mosca 2006).
6 See below for a methodological presentation of the surveys.
7 Since the figures were used for logistical purposes (such as finding lodging for the incoming activists), they were expected to be quite reliable.
8 Since ours was the first attempt to develop a questionnaire on conceptions and practices of democracy, we devoted a long and intense time to questionnaire testing and redrafting. We pre-tested different versions of the questionnaire and analysed the results, paying special attention to missing values and variations in responses. First, the German team in collaboration with the EUI team developed a draft questionnaire containing questions on activism, group affiliation and concepts of democracy. Different versions of the questionnaires were tested in the UK and Germany in 2005, and twice in Italy in 2006. In Britain, a pre-test was run at the anti-G8 protest at Gleneagles in July 2005, where the British team undertook short face-to-face interviews with 493 participants in the Make Poverty History march, and distributed 2,000 longer self-completion questionnaires to marchers (with a response rate of 28 per cent). In Germany, a revised questionnaire was used to survey participants at the first national Social Forum in Erfurt, 21–24 July 2005, where 785 questionnaires were handed out in the registration area and 310 returned (response rate of approx. 40 per cent). A still different version of the questionnaire was tested by the EUI team during the march against the Bolkestein directive, which, in parallel with marches in other European cities, was held in Rome on 15 October 2005. During this event we distributed 723 questionnaires, 475 (65.6 per cent) of which were fully completed and returned. These tests indicated that the questionnaire had to be shortened and that some variables/values needed to be rephrased, cut, or substituted. After a consortium meeting, a working committee started a long deliberation process that was concluded with a 'fair consensus' on the final draft, which was once again tested in Italy in April 2006 with satisfying results: about 30 participants in a seminar organized by Italian NGOs (a conference by Serge Latouche in Florence) filled out the questionnaire in a complete way.

2 The ESF organizing process in a diachronic perspective[1]

Christoph Haug, Nicolas Haeringer, and Lorenzo Mosca

Introduction

As stated in the WSF's Charter of Principles[2] (document 5 – full document list at end of this chapter – henceforth: Charter), social forums are meant to be open spaces of discussion. However, this space is not given, but actively created. It is a challenge to coordinate the loose network of individuals, groups, and organizations that assemble under the banner global justice movement (GJM) in such a way that the desired open space of discussion emerges. Within the framework of a volume addressing the issue of democracy in the ESF process, this chapter focuses on the political challenges of this process, considering in particular the political controversies and conflicts as moments in which principles and common values are revealed, tested, and transformed. In this perspective, our analysis is relevant for anybody who wants to reflect on contemporary forms of transnational democracy.

Organizing such a huge and complex process raises three types of challenges. The first is about coordination: although it is a transnational process, the ESF is based on nationally and locally rooted actors. Coordinating them involves a complex interaction between the transnational level and the various national ones. The second challenge concerns the ESF's relative autonomy from other spheres, including the political one: it aims at being a space for civil society organizations, set apart from state and party politics (Charter, articles 5 and 8). However, organizing the event implies negotiating with local and national authorities, as well as relying (at least partially) on political parties and their mobilizing capacities. The third challenge is deeply rooted in the ESF's project itself: as an open space, it constantly aims at inclusion and mobilization for common action. While the first two challenges are mainly related to practical and ideological issues as well as diverging interests within the movement, this third challenge is part of what Polletta has called 'democratic dilemmas' (2002: 12): 'the problem ... that maximizing one set of participatory democracy's benefits may come at the expense of maximizing another' (ibid.: 13). Each section of this chapter addresses one of these challenges. Adopting a diachronic perspective, our main aim is to single out changes or even trends in the six-year development of the ESF organizing process.[3]

Our account of this process is based on personal interviews with various organizers, participant observation in the European Preparatory Assemblies

(EPAs), analysis of documents (reports, meeting minutes, articles, websites and mailing lists), and a review of the relevant literature.

Levels of co-ordination: rooted transnationalism

The ESF has – at least formally – adopted a horizontal form of organization, based on anti-hierarchical principles of inclusion rather than a classic system of representation. The European Preparatory Assembly (EPA), which is at the core of this organizational process, constitutes an ad hoc transnational space for coordination. Considering, however, that social movement organizations are still mainly structured at the national or even the local level (della Porta *et al.* 2006, 2007b; Agrikoliansky *et al.* 2005), it comes as no surprise that the role of national environments is neither fully abolished nor ignored at the EPA meetings. In this section, we will describe and analyse this form of rooted transnationalism of the ESF organizing process. Our focus is on the transnational level; we will not discuss the dynamics within national coordinating bodies, as this would imply a case study approach rather than a diachronic perspective.

The European Preparatory Assembly: an open body at the core of the process

The EPA is driven by the same principles that guide the ESF itself, except – of course – that the EPA does take decisions, although only those directly related to the organizational process of the forum. It is an open space where delegation of political power is prohibited and decisions made by consensus (Aguiton and Cardon 2005: 7). EPAs are held roughly every two to three months in varying countries in order to involve diverse geographical areas in the preparatory process.[4] Despite the transnational character of these meetings, the absence of a European budget forces local EPA organizers to cover the costs of the meeting, except for travel expenses, which are covered by the participants themselves or by a solidarity fund. This makes it difficult for movements in the 'poorer' countries of the former Soviet bloc to organize an EPA because they also lack support from more established institutions. As one Eastern interviewee told us: 'The Westerners cannot imagine that the whole Social Fora in the East are branded as terrorists and as anti-democratic!' (interview 1).

An EPA consists of several plenary sessions held on Saturdays and Sundays, as well as several working group sessions. Three working groups (WGs) established at the first EPA have continued ever since: the WG on organization (dealing with issues of communication, finance, logistics, interpretation, and travel), the enlargement WG, and the programme WG (setting the framework of the forum programme). The latter is by far the most attended and most active, as it deals with issues shaping the character of the forum – for example, defining the thematic axes and merging seminar proposals. Because of this workload and political importance, it holds an additional meeting outside the EPAs at least once before every Forum (see Table 2.1).

Table 2.1 Chronology of European meetings in the ESF organizing process

Meeting*	Date	Months since previous EPA	Place	Number of participants[1]
EPA[2] 1.1	9–10 March 2002		Brussels	
EPA 1.2	10–12 May 2002	2	Vienna	242 (M)
Coord.[3] EPG[4]	10 June 2002	–	Rome	30 (M)
EPA 1.3	13–14 July 2002	2	Thessaloniki	>200 (M)
Coord. EPG	7–8 September 2002	–	Brussels	~50 (P)
EPA 1.4	4–6 October 2002	3	Barcelona	~150 (P)
First ESF	**6–10 November 2002**	**1**	**Florence**	**60,000**
EPA 2.1	7–8 December 2002	1	Saint-Denis	272 (M)
EPA 2.2	8–9 February 2003	2	Brussels	213 (M)
EPG	28 February 2003	–	Geneva	
EPG	25 April 2003	–	Berlin	
EPA 2.3	26–27 April 2003	2½	Berlin	~300 (P)
EPA 2.4	19–20 July 2003	3	Genoa	~300 (P)
EPG	27–28 September 2003	–	Bobigny	
EPA 2.5	29–30 September 2003	2	Bobigny	~150 (P)
Second ESF	**12–15 November 2003**	**1½**	**Paris et al.**	**51,000**
EPA 3.1	13–14 December 2003	1	London	~200 (P)
EPA 3.2	6–7 March 2004	3	London	255 (M)
EPA 3.3	16–18 April 2004	1½	Istanbul	~250 (P)
Coord.	29–30 May 2004	–	Paris	~50 (P)
EPA 3.4	19–21 June 2004	2	Berlin	~200 (P)
EPA 3.5	4–5 September 2004	2½	Brussels	223 (M)
EPG	13 September 2004	–	Paris	
Third ESF	**15–17 October 2004**	**1½**	**London**	**20,000**
EPA 4.1	18–19 December 2004	2	Paris	~200 (P)
Coord.	15–16 January 2005	–	Brussels	33 (P)
EPA 4.2	26–27 February 2005	2	Athens	305 (M)
EPA 4.3	21–22 May 2005	3	Prague	176 (R)
EPA 4.4	24–25 September 2005	4	Istanbul	467 (M)
EPA 4.5	8–9 January 2006	4	Vienna	215 (R)
EPA 4.6	4–5 March 2006	2	Frankfurt	130 (C)
EPG	1–2 April 2006	–	Athens	65 (C)
Fourth ESF	**4–7 May 2006**	**2**	**Athens**	**35,000**
EPA 5.1	4–5 November 2006	6	Frankfurt	~130 (C)
Coord.	11 January 2007	–	Brussels	~20 (P)
Coord.	19 February 2007	–	Paris	~25 (P)
EPA 5.2	31 March–1 April 2007	5	Lisbon	178 (R)
EPA 5.3	15–16 September 2007	5½	Stockholm	164 (R)
EPA 5.4	1–2 December 2007	2½	Istanbul	197 (R)
EPG	2–3 February 2008	–	Paris	31 (R)
EPA 5.5	23–24 February 2008	2½	Berlin	176 (R)
EPG	26–27 April 2008	–	Malmö	~46 (R)
EPA 5.6	7–8 June 2008	3½	Kiev	~150 (P)
EPG	12–13 July 2008	–	Brussels	~32 (P)
Fifth ESF	**17–21 September 2008**	**3**	**Malmö**	**13,000**
Sixth ESF	2010 (scheduled)		Istanbul	

Sources: Minutes, reports, registration lists and authors' participation.

Notes

* Working groups on enlargement and organization have been meeting outside the EPAs. Their meetings are not listed here.
1 These figures need to be seen as estimates taken from the official registration lists (R), minutes (M), count (C) by one of the authors or reports from other participants (P). The numbers for the actual forums are those declared by each ESF organizing committee and may be based on different methods of estimation.
2 EPA – European Preparatory Assembly.
3 Coord. – meeting of a smaller ad hoc coordinating working group (not a full EPA).
4 EPG – European Program Group meeting outside an EPA.

Besides these standing WGs, ad hoc groups are set up to prepare discussions on issues like the decision making method or to accomplish coordinating tasks between the EPAs. Although some EPA participants have pushed for the creation of a continuous steering committee, such suggestions have never found enough support to form a 'consensus'.

The importance of the so-called 'thematic networks' is steadily growing. Meeting on Fridays before the actual EPA, they facilitate coordination among movements of different countries or different political currents working on the same thematic field.[5] In a way, this networking phase can be described as a 'Mini-ESF'.[6] Many interviewees have described the network meetings as the most important and most inspiring aspect of the preparatory process. Even though the EPAs derive their importance from their status as the highest decision making body of the organizing process, many participants perceive the EPA weekends much more as an opportunity for transnational coordination and exchange than as a decision making space.

Dynamics of transnationalization

If we ask about the relevance of the transnational level in the course of the process, we can distinguish symbolic relevance (in the sense of the presence of a shared ideal) and material relevance (in the sense of effective influence of transnational decisions on the design of the forum).

As the ESF process was initiated directly at the WSF 2002 by highly transnationalized activists, the transnational dimension was highly valued from the beginning, despite the fact that the national organizing committees in the host countries did most of the practical work. The national organizers of the first ESF (Florence) had high expectations regarding transnationality: They actively encouraged decisions to be taken at EPAs rather than within their own national committees, and they actively defended transnational decisions against groups in their own countries. However, it was not always easy to reach such decisions in the first place (interview 6). Perhaps the relative weakness of the transnational level (in terms of actual decisions) was due to the significant competition between the Italian and the French 'delegations': disappointed not to be the first ESF host, the latter used the transnational level to raise vetoes on a series of decisions concerning finances and the participation of political parties in the organizing committee (interview 10). To avoid such conflicts in the future, it was then agreed that decisions regarding the composition of domestic organizing committees should not be taken by the EPA. If we consider the transnational realm as transcending national boundaries (as opposed to the international realm, where national entities interact based on their 'national autonomy'), then the beginning of the process was not transnational but international, although the transnational aspect had high symbolic value.

In the preparatory process of the second ESF (Paris), the relation between symbolic and material transnationalization was reversed: French organizers first searched for a consensus within the very large and diverse French initiative committee and then defended their national decision at the EPAs (interview 9). The ideal of a transnational process was clearly subordinated to inclusiveness at the national level. At the same time, the EPAs gained 'material' weight as participation grew due to the success of the first ESF. The will of a growing number of organizations and movements engaged on the transnational meetings could not be entirely ignored.

It was in the preparations for the third ESF (London) that this material relevance started to become also symbolically relevant: EPA participants were commonly referred to as 'the Europeans' as opposed to 'the British'. The British organizing committee was reluctant to accept, let alone implement, the will of the EPA, and a power struggle between the EPA and national organizers loomed for the first time. As one activist notes: 'If any of the decisions taken here [at the EPA] are implemented, it will be because the key people in the host country want to see them implemented, not because it was what the EPA decided' (Maeckelbergh 2004). British organizers made clear that the ultimate decision making power lies with the national groups responsible for the finances. However, in some decisions (such as the number of plenary sessions), they had to yield to the will of 'the Europeans' (Becker 2004b). Compared to the international competition between the French and the Italians two years earlier, the process had now become more transnationalized, though mostly at a symbolic level.

In the preparations for the fourth ESF (Athens), the transnational level also gained material relevance as various conflicts within the Greek organizing committee (GOC) were brought to the EPAs and solved there. The dissenting faction within the GOC (which was widely criticized for pursuing its own interests rather than promoting the organizing process) had to yield to the decisions of the EPA, which supported the stance of the majority of the GOC.

After the fourth ESF, it was proposed that a pan-European organizing committee with funding from all European countries be in charge of organizing the fifth edition. This plan proved unfeasible; but the fifth ESF was nevertheless the first one set up by a transnational organizing committee composed of organizations from Sweden, Norway, Denmark, and Finland.

Nationality as a 'container' in transnational decision making

The relevance of national delegations has persisted throughout the process, and they are frequently referred to in EPA discussions (EPA minutes almost exclusively state the positions of 'national delegations' or agreements among them). These 'delegations' constitute a 'container' for coordination and regulation, with the 'shield' of nationality around them: the various actors can explain their positions and explore disagreements without having to negotiate their core political identity (e.g. Trotskyite, communist or unionist, etc.). In the process of transnational decision making, a first vision of what a consensus could look like is built under the banner of 'being Italian' or 'being French', and so on. The ongoing decay of 'nationality' as a political category enables the activists to use it as an ambivalent container reflecting the persisting relevance of national contexts, at the same time giving space for irony and reflexive distance towards its contents. In addition, it facilitates transnational consensus building by effectively 'delegating' part of the political struggles into the national arena. Put differently, transnational consensus becomes possible because dissent can be shunted into subordinate national spheres.

By using 'nationality containers', an atmosphere of friendship is created (because nobody would feel hostility against a particular nation) and entrenched political struggles are made discursively irrelevant, opening up opportunities to discuss new issues. This facilitates mutual listening and learning, not only internationally but also within countries: once cooperation between two organizations from one country has been established, they are likely to be sustained nationally.

The invisible backbone: transnational personal networks

The ESF process was initiated by highly transnationalized activists who met at the WSF. In other words, the ESF process did not simply *grow out of* national contexts but was also *induced into* the national context of each host country.

This process repeated itself in every host country: a transnational elite brings the ESF to its home country and mobilizes national civil society to join the process. The idea is to bring new actors on board and keep them, thus enlarging and perpetuating transnational networks. However, this process faltered in 2004 due to a non-Europe-oriented national organizing process in the UK, where no new 'transnational activists' stayed in the organizing process, leaving existing transnational networks (mostly dominated by Italians and French) to maintain the transnational co-ordination.

While this certainly strengthened the transnational level in the ESF process and enhanced trust and emotional bonds through collective experiences, it also made it more difficult for new activists to join these existing personal networks and to obtain information about ongoing decision making processes. Resisting this natural process of social closure of a group that has worked together for several years seems to be the main challenge of the ESF process today. As Polletta noted, 'the same social relations that have sometimes made it easy to practice [participatory democracy] have also made it difficult to sustain' (2002: 21).[7]

Though problematic from the perspective of inclusivity, this transnational network of activists functions as the backbone and memory of the ESF organizing process.[8] It ensures organizational continuity and constitutes a 'counter-balance to strong powers' (interview 4) such as big unions and certain transnational networks whose organizational logic and political strategy is very different from that of the ESF process, such as the International Socialist Tendency (IST) led by Britain's Socialist Workers Party (SWP).[9]

The backbone of the ESF organizing process is an informal personal network of activists who have long participated in the process and thus share common experiences related to it. Its core is the central knot of several pre-existing transnational networks: The Attac network has played a vital role as a network of transnationalized activists with relatively good connections to their constituency in various European countries, especially in bringing the ESF to Scandinavia. The Fourth International,[10] the European Left (EL), and the Internationalist Socialist Tendency (IST) remain less visible in public, though not without influence. This background of party related networks is the cause for the conflicts regarding party participation, which we will analyse in the next section.

Concluding this part, we can observe that, in a long-term perspective, the trust and mutual understanding that is built in these personal networks seems to be the essential backbone of the organizing process.

Dependency and autonomy

The ESF is built as a space for civil society organizations and movement activists, independent from the political sphere. However, until now, the need for public funds has made it difficult to bypass (left) political parties in the mobilization process. Moreover, the relation to the WSF makes the situation even more complex, positioning the ESF organizing process in a field between dependency and autonomy.

The relation of the ESF to the WSF

In contrast to the WSF, the ESF was set up in a transnational space that was already constituted as a political space (the European Union), that is, a locus of power. In this European context, the ESF was thought to contribute to the building of a joint European social movement. For this reason, Italian activists began supporting consideration of not only the open space oriented charter of Porto Alegre, but also the more action oriented call from the Assembly of Social Movements (issued at the end of WSF in 2002) as the ESF's founding document. The idea was to root the ESF into the loose European networks of the social movements, giving them some common focus for action against the neoliberal policies of the EU rather than just an empty open space (Aguiton and Cardon 2005: 19ff.).

However, this move was perceived by members of the WSF International Council (IC) as an attempt to bypass the principles of open space codified in the Porto Alegre Charter (article 6). The IC threatened not to accredit the ESF as part of the WSF process; from then on, relations between the EPA and the IC alternated between soft conflicts and cold cooperation. Repairing those tensions depended mostly on those few activists who participated in both bodies.

Though these initial tensions have been resolved, European organizers have been careful to protect their autonomy and avoid incorporation as a regional edition of the WSF – that is, as a forum where global issues are debated from a European perspective, rather than one where European issues are discussed with a global perspective. For example, they refused to present the fourth ESF in Athens as part of the polycentric edition of WSF 2006 (which was organized in Venezuela, Mali, and Pakistan under the umbrella of the IC).[11]

The ESF and political parties

The Porto Alegre Charter clearly forbids political parties to participate in the forum, stating that 'neither party representation nor military organisations shall participate in the forum' (article 8). Nonetheless, European parties have consistently demonstrated the interest and the will to interact with both the forum event and its organizing process. EPA 1.2 (see Table 2.1) drew up several guidelines making the ESF process quite accessible to political parties, allowing their representatives to participate in national delegations at the EPAs. In addition, party leaders, cadres, and members were able to register as party delegates at the ESF, thus indirectly acknowledging parties as legitimate organizations within the ESF. The WG on organization later decided 'that political parties (while they cannot organize or speak at the conferences and seminars) can organize workshops [i.e. small scale activities without simultaneous translation; the authors] as parties, provided they are not simply promoting themselves' (document 10). At the EPAs, however, party politics continue to be proscribed, and those participants active in a political party register as members of non-party organizations.

This ambiguous situation has been under continuous criticism; but in practice, it has been largely up to the national organizers to find a pragmatic solution. Regarding the fourth ESF in Greece – a country where political activism is strongly rooted in political parties – the Greek organizers stated: 'we think that the present situation of the relations between the political parties and the forum is sufficient and functioning. We can't see a way of changing it.'[12] This is confirmed by the experience of the Nordic Organising Committee, where a definite ban on parties in the organizing process did not prevent active party members from assuming key positions.

The EPA's 'choice not to choose' (that is, to retain an ambiguous relationship to parties) seems to be a viable compromise between the principle of minimizing competitive politics and the aim of including a maximum number of activists. It accommodates the role of left parties for many social movements in Europe but at the same time provides a mechanism to 'keep them under control' (interview 3), preventing their competitive logic of maximization of votes (Rucht 1993: 266) from taking over the cooperative organizing process.

Finance and public institutions

Even though the ESF is a 'non-governmental' space (Charter, article 8) wary of being co-opted by government officials, the EPA never managed to establish guidelines on how to relate to public institutions during the organizing process. While some EPA participants who organized the first ESF stated that one of the first EPAs put a ban on private funding, it is clear that such a ban cannot be enforced, nor is it practically achievable (interviews 5, 9, 10, 11). To date, every edition of the ESF has relied on support from public institutions to varying degrees.

For the first ESF, the Tuscany region and city of Florence provided the rooms and translation equipment, worth approximately €400,000 in the ~€1 million budget (document 7). The second ESF went further in the relationship with public institutions. In order to raise money from four different municipalities, it was hosted in four different cities: Bobigny, Ivry, Paris, and Saint-Denis. In the end, public subsidies covered 85 per cent of the total costs of €3.2 million. Together with other revenues of about €1 million, this led to an unexpected surplus, which was used to fund the ESF memory project (document 13).

The acceptance of such a large amount of public funds was openly criticized during EPAs. But while in both France and in Italy funding remained unconditional (that is, it was not actively used to influence the contents of the forum), the Greater London Authority headed by Mayor Ken Livingstone used their £480,000 'donation' (approximately €720,000, about one-third of the total budget; see Lee 2004: 3) to exert considerable influence over the organizing process of the third ESF. Although the 'bureaucratic grip' (Becker 2004a, see also document 8) of Livingstone and his allies caused considerable conflicts, the EPA decided not to risk a clash that would lead to cancellation of the ESF, choosing to think in terms of an 'English exception'. In the end, EPA participants preferred a 'bad' Forum to no Forum at all.

It was the declared aim of the Greek organizers of the fourth ESF to show that one can host a 'cheap' Forum without relying on public funding. With a total cost of €1.1 million (document 6), they succeeded in drastically cutting expenses;[13] but the revenues from cultural events were not as high as expected due to bad weather, lower merchandise sales, and less space hired by organizations for stalls. With a shortfall of €300,000, the finance committee speculated 'that the trade unions and the local authorities will respond to our call for financial support' (document 6) in order to settle the deficit.

Although entry fees contribute significantly to the relative autonomy of the forum, they have been a subject of debate ever since the first edition. As an Italian activist remembers:

> There was a tough discussion concerning the fact that we should grant access even to those who cannot afford the entrance fee to the Forum. This was to maintain the principle of the Forum as an open space ... the matter of granting access to everybody was solved in the Italian style with the idea of a free one-day visitor pass.
>
> (Interview 2)

The cost of the entry pass peaked in London (ranging from £10 to £30 compared to €3 to €5, depending on income, in Paris (Lee 2004: 3), even though the EPA pushed for lower rates.

Between inclusion and mobilization: the ESF's democratic dilemmas

Aguiton and Cardon (2005) have identified tension between two general goals inherent in all Social Forum processes: enlargement and building collective action. The core political innovation of the 'Forum form' (Lee 2004: 5) is to 'try the impossible' and pursue both goals at the same time: neither rushing ahead as an avant-garde, leaving most people behind, nor getting lost in endless discussions. In this section, we will illustrate the different aspects of this general tension (and attempted solutions) as they become manifest in the ESF organizing process.

Geographical, social and political enlargement of the ESF process

Not only is the postulated openness of the ESF event restricted by financial constraints, but participation in the EPA meetings is highly dependent on material (time, money) and immaterial resources (language and rhetoric skills, personal networks, reputation, and so on) (Doerr 2007; Haug 2007a, 2007b). In order to encourage participation from poorer countries, participants from Western countries are asked to contribute to a solidarity fund,[14] used to subsidize travel expenses for participants from Central and Eastern Europe (including Turkey).

While the 'enlargement to the East' is a frequently addressed issue, the social enlargement of the process (that is, the inclusion of marginalized social groups) is virtually unaddressed at the transnational level, leaving this issue to be solved within countries. So far, the issue remains largely unsolved, probably because the broad inclusion of socially disadvantaged people would not only require extensive funds but would also entail renegotiating a number of agreements that were easily reached amongst middle-class activists but would be more difficult in a socially more heterogeneous crowd.

The political enlargement (that is, the inclusion of new political sectors) is mostly addressed from a perspective of including the more moderate parts of the movements, especially the trade unions. The 'inclusion' of the radical parts is pursued by the autonomous spaces, which have mushroomed at the fringes of the official Forums and incorporated groups that were absent or reluctant to join the official ESF (Nuñes 2004). Despite their sometimes anti-ESF-rhetoric, the autonomous spaces follow a 'one-foot-in one-foot-out' strategy (Juris 2005a: 262–5) towards the main ESF, using the ESF event (but not so much the organizing process) as an occasion to build networks, both within the autonomous spaces and between these and the main ESF (documents 11 and 12).

The political differences between the autonomous spaces and the main ESF lie not so much with the thematic priorities (for the thematic diversity of the ESF, see Table 2.2) but in the different organizational cultures which, while existing all through the process, were prominently framed as 'horizontals versus verticals' during the preparation of the third ESF in London. From a 'horizontal' perspective, the organizing process of the ESF was exclusive, top-down, and power-laden, preventing any alternative forms of coordination to evolve, thus thwarting the possibility of an emerging other world. In the context of the above mentioned tension between inclusion and mobilization, the organizers of the autonomous spaces leaned to the inclusion side, assigning high symbolic value to a process devoted to equality and inclusion of minorities, making even seating

Table 2.2 The thematic axes of the ESF events

	Thematic axes	No. of plenaries	No. of seminars
2002	1 Globalization and liberalism	6	66
	2 War and peace	5	31
	3 Rights – Citizenship – Democracy	6	47
	Dialogues	5	–
	Alternatives	3	–
	Windows on the world	6	–
	Total	31	144
2003	1 Against war, for a Europe of peace and justice, of solidarity, open upon the world	6	
	2 Against neo-liberalism, against patriarchy, for a social and democratic Europe of rights	6	
	3 Against the logic of profit; for an ecologically sustainable society of social justice and for food sovereignty	6	
	4 Against merchandising processes; for a Europe of democratic information, culture and education	6	
	5 Against racism, xenophobia and exclusion for the equality of rights, dialogue between cultures; for a Europe open to migrants, refugees and asylum seekers	6	
	Dialogues and confrontations	2	
	Strategies	6	
	Opening onto the world	10	
	Focus	7	
	Total	55	262[a]
2004	1 Democracy and fundamental rights	5	34
	2 War and peace	6	25
	3 Against racism, discrimination and the far right: for equality and diversity	5	22
	4 Corporate globalization and global justice	5	24
	5 Social Justice and solidarity: against privatization (deregulation), for workers, social and women's rights	6	41
	6 Environmental crisis, against neo-liberalism and for sustainable societies	5	16
	Total	32	155[b]
2006[c]	1 War and peace	–	23
	2 Europe's role in liberal globalization	–	15
	3 Immigrants in Europe	–	14
	4 Discrimination, racism, the far right	–	10
	5 Recognized social rights such as public spaces, public services and social protection	–	23
	6 Lack of security, poverty, exclusion	–	7
	7 The workplace: productivity, growth, unemployment/full employment	–	14
	8 Environment, sustainable development, energy, water, climate	–	13

	9 What democracy and which fundamental rights does Europe need?	–	9
	10 Economic policies in Europe	–	7
	11 Right to education and culture, role of the media	–	16
	12 The feminist alternative	–	11
	13 Agriculture, food sovereignty, European small scale farmers	–	8
	14 Where is the EU headed?	–	5
	15 Movement strategy	–	21
	16 Repressive law and order policies in Europe	–	8
	17 Urban policy	–	5
	Total	0	209
2008[d]	1 Working for social inclusion and social rights – welfare, public services and common goods for all	–	29
	2 Working for a sustainable world, food sovereignty, environmental and climate justice	–	19
	3 Building a democratic and rights based Europe, against 'securitarian' policies. For participation, openness, equality, freedom and minority rights	–	14
	4 Working for equality and rights, acknowledging diversities, against all forms of discrimination. For feminist alternatives against patriarchy	–	12
	5 Building a Europe for a world of justice, peace and solidarity – against war, militarism and occupations	–	26
	6 Building labour strategies for decent work and dignity for all – against precarity and exploitation	–	24
	7 Economic alternatives based on peoples' needs and rights, for economic and social justice	–	18
	8 Democratizing knowledge, culture, education, information and mass media	–	22
	9 Working for a Europe of inclusiveness and equality for refugees and migrants – fighting against all forms of racism and discrimination	–	12
	10 Social movements, the state and future of the global justice movement (cross thematic)	–	28
	Total	0	198

Source: printed programmes.

Notes
a At the second ESF seminars were not assigned to the 'main lines'.
b Three seminars do not belong to an axis.
c Thematic areas were not included in the printed programme due to lack of space (email from Yannis Almpanis, Greek organizing Committee, 20 November 2007). The numbers listed here are those decided by the final EPG meeting.
d Thematic axes as decided at EPA 5.5. The tenth axis was added by EPA 5.6.
e Six seminars were assigned to two axes.

arrangements (circular or confrontational) a political issue. For more traditional organizations such as trade unions and party-socialized officials, such an 'obsession with procedural issues' is often hard to understand, let alone put into practice. Apart from the organizers of the autonomous spaces, Attac and organizations from Scandinavian countries (Bohn 2004; Marsdal et al. 2004) have especially criticized the lack of formal procedures and transparency in the ESF organizing process (see also Haug 2007b). This grassroots perspective is symbolically represented in the logo of the fifth ESF in Scandinavia. Whether the Nordic organizing committee succeeds in implementing it remains to be researched. Our analysis ends with the fourth ESF in May 2006.

Programme and 'visibility'

According to the WSF charter, nobody is authorized to speak on behalf of the forum (article 6). This leaves the organizers of the ESF little room for sending political messages to the general public,[15] preventing them from favouring too much the action side of the process. However, many organizers found that for 'selling' the forum to the media, promoting it and mobilizing people, the mere repetition of the abstract opposition to 'neoliberalism and to domination of the world by capital and any form of imperialism' stated in article 1 of the charter was not enough. The national organizers of each Forum have been particularly keen to get extensive media coverage to empower them in their national struggles when the forum event is over and moves to another country.

As a way out of this dilemma, the programme of the forum has been structured along 'thematic axes' (see Table 2.2). By subsuming the seminars taking place within the open space of the forum under such headings, certain themes (or even political messages) were emphasized over others, giving them some visibility in the general public.

Because of their (supposed) high symbolic relevance, the exact wording of these programmatic axes has always been strictly controlled by the EPAs,[16] which devote much time to this discussion. In the preparations for the second ESF (see Agrikoliansky and Cardon 2005), for instance, it was thoroughly discussed whether the axes should have neutral titles (e.g. 'war'), protest-like titles (e.g. 'against the war'), or titles that mention alternatives or positive visions (e.g. 'for peace and justice'). The relevance of Europe and EU institutions was also contested. Even when the general topic of an axis has been agreed upon, the exact wording still remains a subject of intense debate (e.g. should the environment axis mention 'ecology', 'sustainable development', or 'climate change'?). The ESF's words are precious, and any allusion or elusion can mark openness or exclusion to a whole set of actors. Wordings easily prioritize one group's struggles over another's; every term has different connotations depending on its discursive context. Only this political characteristic of language together with diverging political preferences among the organizers helps in understanding how the sometimes clumsy and somewhat arbitrary titles (Table 2.2) end up in the final programme.

These debates vividly illustrate the fundamental importance of the construction of meaning in and by social movements (Gamson 1992). However, the tensions within the ESF organizing process are not limited to the 'mere' production of meanings. The preparations for the first three editions of the ESF saw a fierce struggle for the distribution of speakers in the jointly organized *plenaries* or *conferences*. While *seminars* and *workshops* (which constitute the vast majority of activities within the forum) are 'self-organized'[17] and designed as spaces for dialogue, the plenaries whose speakers are agreed upon at the EPAs are big assemblies with celebrities and intellectuals addressing a huge audience with little or no time for interaction. The first ESF saw 30 such 'conferences', and the second had 55 'plenaries'. Since negotiations about speakers' names or national quotas were very time-consuming, most EPA participants wanted to abandon plenaries in the third ESF (interviews 3, 5, 6). However, British organizers resisted, proposing 13 plenary sessions. Since such a small number would have made the struggle for speakers even harder, EPA 3.3 pushed the number up to 30. The names of the speakers and facilitators were then agreed upon at the final meeting of the European Program Group (document 2).

In the preparations for the fourth ESF, the organizers made considerable changes in the format of the programme. Big plenaries were officially abandoned (though large rooms for over 1,000 people were made available to hold 'big seminars'), and the programme was built in a two step web-based consultation process (Cardon and Haeringer 2008): in the first stage of the so called '*consulta*', activists throughout Europe were asked 'which kind of themes do you want to be discussed in the next ESF?' and 'which are, according to you, the priorities for the other Europe we want?' (document 3). The suggestions were then combined to form a list of 14 (EPA 4.3) and later 17 (EPA 4.4) themes that was agreed upon without much hassle.[18]

Since plenaries no longer had to be negotiated, the main controversy regarded the second stage of the *consulta*, the merging procedure for seminars: a total of about 800 had been proposed by organizations from across Europe, and these had to be merged into a final 210 due to limited capacity of rooms and simultaneous translation provided by the Babels network of volunteer interpreters. (Alternatively, seminar organizers could decline translation services and have their seminar listed as a workshop.) Although a set of criteria was decided upon after a series of controversial meetings during EPA 4.6 (document 4), the actual merging process ignored these criteria and relied on the debate amongst 65 activists from across Europe, who came together in the final two-day meeting of the European Program Group.

Looking at the overall developments since 2002, we can say that the building of the ESF programme has changed in two ways. First, the proportion of the programme organized centrally has continuously decreased due to the abolition of plenaries and the introduction of a two stage consultation process. In order to ensure broader inclusion and avoid power struggles, local ESF organizers gave up one of their few real sources of political power in the process.[19] Second, within the centrally organized part, the importance of the transnational level has grown. As we argued above, the importance of the deliberations on the European level has increased, although the national organizing committee remains influential as most of the actual work is done there. Both of these developments can be interpreted as a shift towards the inclusion side of the mentioned dilemma in the organizing process, leaving the action side to the thematic networks and alliances, which were formed during the ESF events and some of which meet regularly before the EPAs. With regard to the ideal proclaimed by the charter of Porto Alegre, this is – generally speaking – a progress toward actually putting that ideal into practice.

Complex representation

Building on Walzer's (1983) concept of 'complex equality', Polletta described the relations 'in which some within the group are permitted more authority than others in areas in which they have special expertise' (2002: 13). This partly applies to the situation at the EPAs, but we prefer to speak of *complex representation* since our interviews clearly show that many participants – even some within the leadership – perceive the situation as unequal.[20] To the participant observer, it soon becomes clear that certain people are carefully listened and replied to, while the chattering sound from the audience sometimes increases when 'less important' individuals or known 'screwballs' take the floor. This selective listening is not only related to content or style of speech. More important is the status of the speaker: representatives of unions and national delegations, speakers from Attac (especially those representing the two big Attac chapters, Germany and France), as well as pioneers of the ESF process known for their commitment to the common cause and representatives from the current ESF organizing committee are considered 'important'.

But measuring the 'weight' of each speaker simply in terms of the size of the constituency he/she represents would miss the point. The EPAs are not based on a static system of representative power. This is why we label this system of representation as *complex*. As described by Polletta (2002: 13), the authority of speakers is granted not per se but in relation to their field of expertise. For the ESF organizing process, it is not of primary importance that someone represents a large number of people, but that this 'representative' has comprehensive knowledge of his/her constituency. In order to build a successful Forum, it is important to know and understand people's motivations, their political cultures, their way of thinking. In other words, the logic is not 'you have to listen to me because I represent 1 million members', but rather 'I can tell you something about how this issue is seen within my organization (or my region, my country, my community). If you want these people to participate in the ESF, you might want to consider what I have to say.'

For participants acustomed to formal systems of representation, where delegates are courted simply because of their status as formal representatives, the system of complex representation in the EPA can look like disrespect towards their status as an important representative. For others who reject the principle of delegating power to representatives, complex representation seems questionable when people do have more to say 'just because' they represent big organizations. The system of complex representation at the EPAs is different from both organizational cultures, and understanding it requires complex knowledge of EPA participants, what they represent, and how they represent it. With regard to the tension between mobilization and inclusion mentioned at the beginning of this section, this form of 'negotiation' incorporates both sides: participants who do not formally represent anything can successfully make an argument and are thus included, while at the same time endless discussions can be avoided by weighing arguments with regard to the speaker who makes them, thus making joint action possible.

However, this solution remains fragile and entails at least three problems. First, there is no common currency for 'importance'. The criteria for the weight of each speaker (regarding a specific issue) are neither consensual amongst participants, nor explicit. This leads not only to misunderstandings and hidden conflicts, but also to a situation where – ironically – marginalized speakers cannot legitimately struggle for recognition because equal recognition is already formally granted to everyone (since everyone may speak). A right to be listened to does not exist. As a result, harsh critique can be voiced against the marginalized when they openly accuse individuals (e.g. the session chair) of exclusion, manipulation, or unfair behaviour, because such an affront violates the rules of friendly conduct. A culture of consensus and friendship, which is necessary to create an inclusive atmosphere and mutual trust needed for the system of complex representation to work, ironically leads to marginalizing those who do not comply with the shared standards established amongst friends.

The second problem is a process of closure due to relevance of personal networks of trust and shared experience. The EPA leadership is not inaccessible, as they welcome any help and 'expertise' to contribute to the process. But they welcome especially *new* expertise, and because of the immense experience accumulated within the leadership group, *new* expertise is difficult to find. People who can *contribute to the process* are highly valued; but what is considered as a valuable contribution is defined by those who are already there.[21]

Third, complex representation is vulnerable to groups that want to use the ESF process to maximize their own political profit. For example, the Greek SWP affiliate SEK has long opposed the ESF coming to Greece, fearing that their relative weakness within the Greek Left (interviews 7, 8; Becker 2002) would become evident; in the actual preparations for the fourth ESF, members of the SEK have done hardly any of the practical work and took on tasks mostly to control certain processes (interviews 7, 8). Despite such behaviour, the SWP is taken seriously because of its considerable mobilization potential. The relative strength of the SWP and its affiliates on the transnational level lies in their hierarchical organization, international contacts, active members, and strategic occupation of mobilizing themes currently en vogue (and ignored by other organizations), as well as, perhaps most importantly, their practice of acquiring leadership positions in campaigns and alliances reaching far beyond their own constituency. Thus, SWP members acquire a certain amount of knowledge relevant in the system of complex representation, but they use it in a strategic way. In other words: not cooperating with the SWP is likely to cause more trouble than including it. The impetus of including *all* parts of the (left) movement against neoliberalism is at the core of the organizing process and motivates organizers to include even those who follow different logics within their own organizations.

Concluding remarks

Looking at the history of the ESF organizing process reveals a number of interesting research issues that we can only briefly address here, while summarizing some main results.

First, the obvious gap between the movements of Western and Eastern Europe needs to be addressed not only by the movements but also by movement research. Creating better understanding of the different cultures and political–economic contexts of movements in the East and in the West may even be a prerequisite for bridging the gap within the ESF process.[22]

Second, the dynamics of the autonomous spaces that reside at the fringes of the forum but at the same time represent a vital part of the 'forum form' (Aguiton and Cardon 2005: 5) might be a key to understanding the internal dynamics of the global justice movement as a movement of movements.

Third, the relation between the forum as an open space of discussion and the Assembly of Social Movements directed towards collective action could develop into a crucial test of the cohesive power of the charter of Porto Alegre as a catalyst for the development of new organizational forms.

Fourth, little research has yet been done on the impact of the new organizational culture of the social forums on political parties and vice versa. While 'contamination in action' (della Porta and Mosca 2007) is clearly taking place *within* the movements, such a process can be expected to be much more difficult *between* parties and the movements, since they explicitly adhere to different logics of *external* action. As an interest issue for further investigation: Does the division of labour between parties and movements persist, or is there a convergence of both within the ESF?

Fifth, the interaction of different organizing cultures in a very heterogeneous movement has not yet been studied on a micro-level. In the context of theories of deliberative democracy, it seems highly relevant to explore how consensus decisions are made under such conditions.[23]

Finally, the dynamics of transnationalization described above indicate that studying transnational meetings can reveal mechanisms and processes facilitating and restricting real transnationalization (as opposed to internationalization).[24]

Selected interviews

1 Mirek Prokeš, UNITED for Intercultural Action/Defence for Children International/Initiative for Social Fora, Czech Republic, interviewed 30 March 2007 in Lisbon.
2 Gregorio Malavolti, Italy, Arci/DS, spokesperson of the Florence local social forum and organizing secretary, Italian organizing committee, interviewed 21 December 2006 in Florence.

3 Piero Bernocchi, COBAS, Italy, interviewed 16 September 2007 in Stockholm.
4 Panayotis Yulis, Network for Political and Social Rights (Epohi)/Greek Social Forum, Greece, interviewed 7 January 2006 in Vienna.
5 Anders Svensson, Solidarity without borders/Socialist Party, Sweden, interviewed 14 September 2007 in Stockholm.
6 Frank Slegers, Belgian Social Forum, interviewed 15 September 2007 in Stockholm.
7 Anonymous member of the Greek organizing committee, interviewed 2 April 2006 in Athens.
8 Conversation with three anonymous members of the Greek organizing committee, 5 November 2006 in Frankfurt.
9 Erhard Crome, Rosa-Luxemburg-Foundation, Germany, interviewed 14 September 2007 in Stockholm.
10 Bruno Paladini, COBAS/MAT, Italian organizing committee, interviewed 11 January 2007 in Florence.
11 Stefano Kovac, ICS/Arci, Italian organizing committee, interviewed 24 January 2007 in Florence.

Documents

1 Proposals from Methodology Group, 23 August 2007. Online, available at: www.fse-esf.org/spip.php?article236 accessed 20 November 2007.
2 Minutes of the European Program Group meeting in Paris, 13 September 2004. Online, available at: www.fse-esf.org/spip.php?article61 accessed 20 November 2007.
3 Minutes of the European Preparatory Assembly, 25–27 February 2005 in Athens. Online, available at: www.fse-esf.org/spip.php?article13 accessed 20 November 2007.
4 'Merger process version 4 ENG-FR.doc', Frankfurt, 7 March 2006.
5 World Social Forum Charter of Principles. Online, available at: www.forumsocialmundial.org.br/main.php?id_menu=4&cd_language=2 accessed 20 November 2007.
6 'Financial committee of the 4th E.S.F.: temporary review', distributed at EPA 5.1, November 2006 in Frankfurt.
7 Minutes of the European Preparatory Assembly, 4–6 October 2002 in Barcelona. Online, available at: www.fse-esf.org/spip.php?article44 accessed 20 November 2007.
8 Reflections and analysis: the WOMBLES, the ESF and beyond. Online, available at: www.wombles.org.uk/article20060454.php accessed 18 November 2007.
9 ILC Asia Bulletin no. 3. Online, available at: www.owcinfo.org/ILC/Asia_WC/AWC_bulletin_03.html accessed 18 November 2007.
10 'Report of the [Italian] Organization Committee in Thessaloniki 13th July [2002]'. Online, available at: http://web.archive.org/web/20021219052133/www.fse-esf.org/article.php3?id_article=76.

11 'Towards an Autonomous Space at the European Social Forum in Florence November 2002'. Online, available at: www.nadir.org/nadir/initiativ/agp/pgaeurope/leiden/autonomous_space.htm accessed 18 November 2007.
12 'A Call for Democracy in the ESF Process'. Online, available at: https://publish.indymedia.org.uk/uk/servlet/OpenMir?do=getpdf&id=286049&forI E=.pdf accessed 18 November 2007.
13 'Budget of the ESF–FSE 2003', undated Excel file, confirmed as final budget by Marc Mangenot, member of the finance commission of the French Organising Committee, email of 29 March 2008.

Notes

1 This chapter was written jointly, but each author contributed the following empirical sections: Christoph Haug wrote sections 'The European Preparatory Assembly: an open body at the core of the process', 'Nationality as a "container" in transnational decision making', 'The invisible backbone: transnational personal networks', and 'Complex representation'; Nicolas Haeringer wrote sections 'The relation of the ESF to the WSF', 'Geographical, social and political enlargement of the ESF process', and 'Program and visibility'; and Lorenzo Mosca wrote sections 'Introduction', 'Dynamics of transnationalization', 'The ESF and political parties', and 'Finance and public institutions'.
2 The Porto Alegre Charter has been widely adopted as the social forums' founding document.
3 At the time of this writing, highly interesting developments are taking place as the ESF moves to Sweden, a country so far not very involved in the ESF process. Our systematic analysis, however, ends with the fourth ESF in Athens. See document for more recent discussions within the process.
4 Between 150 and 350 persons from more than 20 countries involving roughly between 60 and 120 different organizations usually participate in the EPAs.
5 Thematic networks active at EPAs include: Labour and Globalization, Babels (interpreters), Charter of Principles for Another Europe, Education, Migrants and Migration, Public Services, Anti-War, Women and Feminists, Local Social Forums, Anti-G8, Memory of the ESF process, Stop EPAs (European Partnership Agreements), Against Repression, Environment and Climate Change, Trade Unions, Precarity, Tax Justice. Whether or not any of these meet depends on the initiative of someone organizing them (i.e. requesting a slot in the programme).
6 Some network meetings are held like seminars, with prepared input and thematic discussions and planning of collective action.
7 In her study of meetings of American social movements, Polletta (2002: 4, 16–21) found three interactional frameworks for participatory democracy: 'religious fellowship, tutelage and friendship' (ibid.: 20). The EPAs are too big and too heterogeneous for everybody to agree on the same model. Nevertheless, *friendship* is clearly the framework that the informal EPA-leadership adheres to. It is characterized by 'the *informal* quality of decisionmaking and its *intimacy*.... Decisions were made by informal consensus, and tasks were allocated or volunteered for on the basis of participants' preferences and skills' (ibid.: 19).
8 After the Paris ESF, a memory project was set up. However, this only partly deals with the *organizing* process (as distinct from the content of the forum) and obviously cannot replace the living memory of experienced activists.
9 For a more detailed account on the practices of the SWP, see the partisan but nevertheless enlightening journalistic reports published in the *Weekly Worker* (online, available at: www.cpgb.org.uk/esf) as well as the numerous reflections by activists involved in the preparations for the London ESF (e.g. Böhm *et al.* 2005).

10 Other networks also claim heritage to the Fourth International, which split in 1953 (Wikipedia 2008). Here, we refer to the 'Reunified Fourth International' associated with Ligue Communiste Révolutionnaire (LCR) in France, internationale sozialistische linke (isl) in Germany, Socialistiska Partiet (SP) in Sweden, and others.
11 These issues were discussed during a meeting between European members of the IC and its international secretariat on 19 June 2005 in Barcelona.
12 Email sent on the ESF mailing list, 11 January 2005.
13 The costs for simultaneous translation had been reduced considerably by buying interpretation equipment based on ALIS technology (see Chapter 3 in this book) instead of renting commercial equipment.
14 Usually €10 for individuals and €50 per organization.
15 Levêque (2005: 81–2) shows that even official press conferences did not treat political issues but limited themselves to quantitative and logistical information (how many participants, etc.).
16 When participants at EPA 5.4 sensed a tendency of the Nordic organizers to decide the thematic axes on the national level, an additional meeting of the European Program Group was immediately scheduled to ensure European (leaders') participation.
17 'Self-organized activities' is a term also used by the WSF to indicate that Forum organizers merely provide the room and translation (as well as listing it in the official programme), while the content of the seminar or workshop is decided by those organizations who registered it.
18 The same procedure was used in the preparations for the fifth ESF. This time, the finalizing of the themes at EPA 5.5 was more controversial, as the Nordic organizers aimed to reduce the number of themes and move from a negative rhetoric of 'against' to a positive one of 'building alternatives'.
19 This decision was inspired by a similar one made by WSF's International Council.
20 Polletta (2002: 13) states that 'complex equality may be perceived by *outsiders* as inequality' [our emphasis]. Since our interviewees are not outsiders, it seems inadequate to use the term 'complex equality'.
21 Most 'EPA leaders' show some openness to the Nordic political culture currently introduced into the process; but structural changes, such as reducing plenary time and working more in small groups at the EPAs, do meet some resistance.
22 In terms of bridging the gap between social movement researchers of Eastern and Western Europe, the *European Protest Movements* research network initiated by Martin Klimke, Joachim Scharloth, and Kathrin Fahlenbach (online, available at: www.protest-research.eu) represents a step in the right direction.
23 Christoph Haug's ongoing PhD project on 'Discursive decision making in meetings of the global justice movements' addresses this question. See also della Porta and Rucht (forthcoming).
24 Haug (2008) shows how this question can be linked with similar questions in the field of research on the European public sphere.

3 Communicating the European Social Forum[1]

Lorenzo Mosca, Dieter Rucht, and Simon Teune (with the collaboration of Sara López Martin)

Introduction

Since the first World Social Forum (WSF) in January 2001, social forums have developed as spaces for sustained and intensified communication across thematic and ideological divisions within the global justice movements (GJMs) (della Porta 2005b; Rucht forthcoming). After the first WSF meeting and its follow-ups received wide media coverage and proved attractive and successful in the eyes of the participants, the social forum process was soon extended to the continental, national, and local levels.

In contrast with the elitist World Economic Forum (WEF) that usually gathers in the Swiss mountain resort Davos, the social forums are conceived as an inclusive attempt to establish a transnational public sphere from below (Ylä-Anttila 2005; Doerr 2007; see also Chapter 1 in this volume). Accordingly, the organizers face the task of communicating the forum in an open, transparent, and inclusive way. By 'communicating the forum', we mean a manifold and only partially planned process that includes (a) informing and attracting potential participants, and (b) explaining the goal of the forum to the local citizenry and the wider public. Communicating the forum also has an internal dimension, namely coordinating the various groups that are involved in its organization. In the following, however, we will largely neglect this latter aspect and concentrate, instead, on the two dimensions of external communication in the context of the European Social Forum (ESF).

First, forum organizers aim at attracting as many participants as possible. The more widespread and detailed the communication concerning the nature, location, and content of the event, the more likely it is to mobilize movement constituencies. Involving participants from all over Europe implies a significant effort in communication that, to be successful, requires the lowering of barriers to participation related to language, resources such as money needed to travel, and time to attend the forum. Second, and probably more important, the ESF is conceived as a mass event that sends a message not only to the wider public in the respective host city or country, but possibly to European citizens at large. For this purpose, the organizers must think about how to reach their external target groups and audiences.

In the first section of this chapter, we will focus on the external communication of the forum by providing a general overview of the available channels. Second, we will investigate how movement constituencies are reached and mobilized. Third, we will describe how the ESF is presented to external audiences, ranging from the inhabitants of the hosting city to the European or even worldwide mass publics which, at best, learn about the ESF via media reports. Finally, we summarize the main findings of our research.

An overview on communication channels in the ESF process

Before describing in detail the attempts to communicate the ESF, we will provide an overview of the interactions that take place based on a simple concept of communication (cf. Shannon and Weaver 1949). The process always includes an *addresser* who wants to convey a message. Considering the target and the effect s/he is aiming at, the addresser chooses a *channel* that s/he thinks is appropriate to get the message across. Any act of communication has an *addressee* who is supposed to receive the message. Obviously, the decoding of the message, and thus the success of the communication, is dependent on many factors such as context, relationship between addresser and addressee, characteristics of the channel, and what Thompson (1995: 171) calls the 'hermeneutic process of appropriation', as meanings are redefined by the addressees.

Looking at the ESF, we are primarily interested in information about the event that is spread by three kinds of addressers: (*a*) the ESF organizers (e.g. the European Preparatory Assembly (EPA)[2] and the local organizing committee); (*b*) global justice movement organizations (GJMOs) and activists who may be supportive or critical of the official event;[3] and (*c*) the ESF participants (see Figure 3.1). These types of addressers aim at informing others about the ESF as such, its concept, programme, and agenda. Critical activists and participants may raise problematic aspects of the ESF, for example related to its organization and development. All of these groups also want to convey their experiences during the event.

As indicated above, these addressers want to reach various target groups. The first group includes potential participants and interested citizens (movement constituencies in Figure 3.1) who share basic claims expressed at the ESF. These people need mainly information referring to 'logistics' (what is going to happen where and when, how to get to the venue, where to sleep, and so on). Especially when they do not attend, activists are interested in a description and evaluation of the ESF and the events connected to it. The channels used by the addressers to reach movement constituencies are primarily posters, leaflets, and alternative media (ESF- and other websites, email lists, radio, video, newsletters, and brochures). Potential participants in the ESF are also informed via unmediated forms of communication, namely in preparatory events and assemblies of their respective group or organization. Personal networks also play an important role in communicating the forum to potential participants.

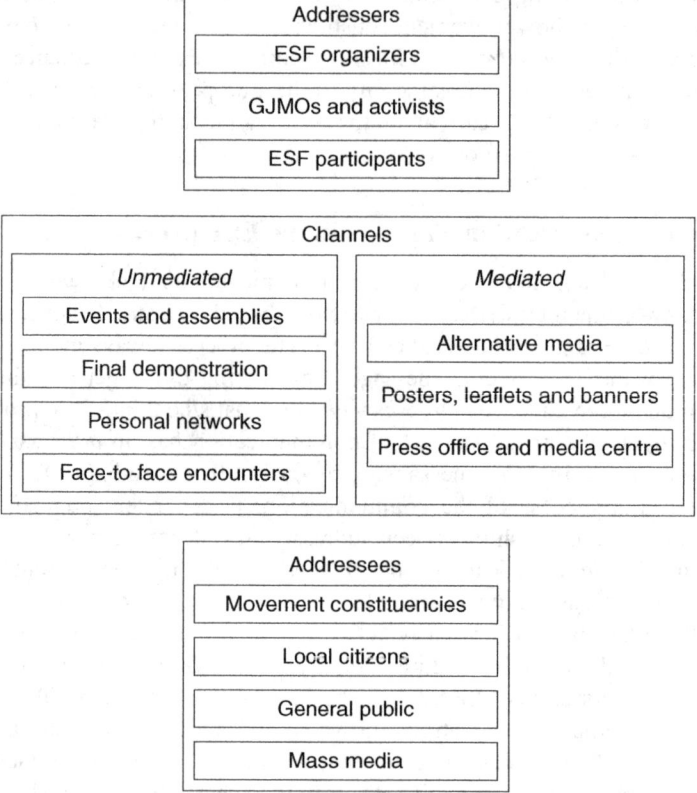

Figure 3.1 A scheme of external communication flows information about the ESF.

The second group that is addressed consists of local citizens. Communication with these individuals aims at raising their interest in the ESF and fostering the critique of neoliberalism for which the event stands. This target group must be prepared for the event because locals are confronted with the ESF most directly, both during demonstrations and at the ESF venue. At the same time, last-minute participants might be recruited from the population of the host city or its surrounding area. Local citizens are informed early via local media, posters, banners, and face to face contacts. Cultural events such as concerts or art exhibitions offer local citizens an opportunity to get in touch with the ESF and to learn about the claims of the global justice movements, without necessarily getting involved.

A third and more diffuse addressee is the 'general public'. Beyond the local citizens, it includes all those who are not involved in the ESF or do not support it. Ordinary European citizens, but also political and economic elites are targeted to let them know about the activists' dissident perspectives on European and global politics. ESF press offices and media centres address the general public directly or indirectly (via mass media).[4]

The fourth addressee is the commercial and public mass media. As there are few physical encounters with the vast majority of European citizens the forum aims to sensitize, most communication with them occurs via mass media. Therefore, ESF organizers have always tried to secure truthful and positive media coverage. Although knowledge about the ESFs has been widespread and the mass media paid considerable attention to the early forums, this success did not result from a consistent pre-existing strategy on the part of forum organizers (see Plöger 2007: 115 for the WSF). Rather, a number of other factors come into play.

First, the channels used to spread information about the ESF are dependent on structural factors such as the receptiveness of the target group and availability of the channel to the addresser. However, the way these channels are used may become a contested issue in the preparation of a social forum. Which strategy is eventually deployed is contingent on the dominant view in the organizing committee.

Second, the context plays a decisive role for decisions on communication. The first ESF in Florence had to address a partly hostile environment – notwithstanding the support by the centre-left regional and city administration – as the national media, the national government (centre-right), and some opinion-makers associated the forum with the riots during the protests against the G8 summit in Genoa in July 2001 (Andretta *et al.* 2002). The environment was much friendlier for the ESF in Paris, which was supported by public authorities and received positive media resonance in the host country. The London forum was marked by internal conflicts between 'horizontals' and 'verticals' related, among other issues, to the key role played by local public institutions in the organizing process. The organizers of the fourth ESF in Athens opted for a more inclusive path, with efforts to attract participants from Central and Eastern Europe. However, like the forum in London, the Athens ESF suffered from a decrease in public attention. Apart from the composition of the organizing committees, contextual characteristics of each forum have contributed to different layouts in the communication of the ESF.

Third, the way in which communication flows is also influenced by internal factors. For example, the initiative of individuals does play an important role in small groups that are based on (mostly) voluntary engagement. The ESF might present itself to the public with an elaborate website because one of the organizers is knowledgeable about new technologies and devotes much time to website management. Yet the organizers of another ESF may not have such expertise and accept a website that is not attractive to journalists and uninvolved citizens.

Informing and mobilizing participants

Reaching out for participants: the ESF organizers

Although communication is considered to be central to mobilization processes like those of the ESF, its role tends to be underestimated in the analysis of social movements (Kavada 2005). To mobilize participants for the ESF, it is vital to spread basic information as widely as possible. People should learn what the ESF is, when and where it takes place, and the logistical details for participation. While information from the EPAs is mainly restricted to basic facts such as the programme of the ESF, the host city, and the exact date, details of the organization are usually established and communicated by the local organizing committee. The local ESF organizers release the call for participation and design the mobilizing media such as posters, flyers, and the website.

As one of the main aims of a social forum is to connect pre-existing groups, most ESF participants are core activists of the GJMs (cf. Chapter 7 in this volume). This is especially so because the costs for participation in the ESF are quite high for those activists who do not represent a group or an organization or live in the host city. Due to the time and money required to travel to another country, it is rare for participants without any previous commitment to travel long distances for a glimpse of the ESF. The range of potential participants also has an effect on the flows of communication. At least for participants from outside the host country, their inclusion in existing networks very likely facilitates the dissemination of information. Most of the core activists exchange information about the ESF in the networks in which they are engaged. If not, they are likely to know how to access the necessary information (e.g. through the ESF website – www.fse-esf.org). By and large, ESF organizers trust these channels of communication, choosing to invest little energy in mobilization efforts beyond the activist core and sympathizers of the GJMs.

Throughout the preparatory process, information about the ESF is spread mainly through participants in the EPAs. As members of organizations and networks, EPA participants disseminate knowledge about the EPA discussions in their home country in emails, assemblies, and personal communication. This implies that GJM activists from a country with low participation in the EPA (for example, Portugal) are less likely to be informed about the ESF than those in countries with a high involvement in the social forum process (for example, Italy or France). Beyond these unmediated forms of communication, reports from the EPAs are also available via a specific mailing list and on the ESF website.

However, the Internet does not replace direct interactions. In an analysis of the mobilization for the ESF in Paris, Kavada (2005) found that while the Internet facilitates access to information, it does not substitute for face-to-face contacts, which continue to be crucial in motivating people to attend the ESF. These findings are supported by the results of a survey conducted by the Centre de Recherches Politiques de la Sorbonne during the Paris ESF. When participants were asked what pushed them to attend the ESF, personal contacts and organizations scored higher than mediated forms of communication as a trigger to participation (see Table 3.1). Yet, Internet, mass media, posters, and leaflets do play a role in stimulating participation. This is particularly true for those participants with little prior involvement in movement networks. Attendees who were neither members of an organization involved in the forum nor experienced with more than one GJM street demonstration more often cited alternative and mass media as motivators to visit the ESF.

Table 3.1 Who or what incited you to partake in the ESF?

Sources of motivation to attend the ESF	Involvement		
	Low	High	Total
Own organization	6.9	25.3	19.6
Friends	15.9	17.5	17.0
Media	14.1	9.2	10.7
Internet	13.6	9.2	10.6
Other organization	9.7	10.7	10.4
Colleagues	6.4	7.7	7.3
Family members	8.2	5.7	6.5
Posters/leaflets	8.7	5.2	6.3
Acquaintances	7.9	4.8	5.8
Total	31.2	68.8	100.0
(N)	(390)	(861)	(1,251)

Source: CRPS survey at the ESF in Paris.

This finding clearly shows that if forum organizers aim at attracting newcomers in addition to long-standing activists, more energy should be invested in forms of mediated communication. If, however, the main target is committed activists, the breadth of participation depends on the organizations and personal networks that are involved in the preparation of a forum rather than on mediated forms of communication.

Covering the forum by and for activists

In the days before, during, and after an ESF, the event is covered from an activist perspective. Following the tradition of independent coverage of major GJM events that started with the protests against the World Trade Organization in Seattle in 1999, structures facilitating this sort of coverage can be found at each ESF. The idea that emerged in Seattle was to confront the negative coverage of the mainstream media with up-to-date reports produced 'from below'. During the ESFs, the organizers tend to renounce an official voice for the forum, which is conceptualized as an open space for discussion and networking rather than a political actor. Instead, information is produced and widely disseminated by the Media Centres (MC)[5] created for every ESF event. As shown below, the organization of MCs has often raised conflicts among organizers whose management and integration into the local organizing committee differed significantly. These conflicts are merely based on different concepts of democracy.

In order to provide alternative coverage of the Florence ESF, the MC followed the model developed for the Genoa protest against the G8 summit (July 2001), where Indymedia-Italy played an essential role (Di Corinto 2001; Cristante 2003). However, the MC became a site of conflict between two groups in charge of managing it: one affiliated with Indymedia and grassroots radio responsible for the technical requirements (e.g. computer connectivity, etc.), and the other more closely associated with the hard core ESF organizers, committed to spreading organizational and logistical information about the forum, for instance through the website. The conflict evolved around the degree of openness of the MC. Grassroots media activists of the first group promoted unrestricted access for all participants (Interview 1), while the second group sought to limit access to accredited personnel only. Eventually, the latter group decided to distinguish between movement and mainstream media, reserving two different areas in the MC. As resources were limited, ordinary activists were not allowed to access the MC. The grassroots media activists strongly opposed this decision and tried explicitly to boycott it (Interview 2). During the forum, many laptops were stolen from the MC, seriously hampering the centre's functioning. According to one interviewee, people participating in the autonomous spaces in Florence also thought that technological resources located in the MC should be available to all activists:

> We were quite annoyed as the ESF organisers did not provide us with a good [physical] space, and we had negotiated a lot with them in order to obtain various resources. But in the end, what they promised us was never accomplished. Then we had to take the law into our hands ... we went across the forum and thus re-appropriated some materials of the media centre.
> (Interview 3)

The experience of stolen laptops in Florence persuaded the ESF organizers to restrict access to the MC in the subsequent ESFs. In the Paris ESF, prospective users needed accreditation and had to show a card in order to enter the MC. As a response, an alternative Independent Media Centre (IMC) with limited equipment was created in the autonomous space of Métallos Médialab (PGA 2007).

In London (2004), the management of the MC was even more problematic since all 'alternative' media were excluded from accessing the MC. In the words of one media activist: 'Press passes for the ESF were to be available to "proper" journalists with National Press Cards' (Jones 2004). This led to the creation of an alternative IMC with over 70 computers in the Camden Centre. However, the seizure by FBI agents of two Indymedia computer servers on 7 October 2004 (without providing any justification) made independent coverage of the ESF even more difficult. Because of this intervention, about 20 national and regional sites of the international network (among them the British, Italian, Portuguese, and parts of the German site) were no longer available.

A different MC policy was adopted in Athens (2006), where the MC was open to everybody while some computers were reserved to 'official' and 'alternative' journalists. Wireless access was also provided in the building hosting the ESF, allowing Internet connections to every laptop located in the area. However, this did not discourage autonomous spaces close to Indymedia from setting up an 'alternative' MC.

In addition to the alternative coverage targeting those who could not attend the event, the first ESF in Florence hosted a project aimed at informing the ESF participants on site. During the preparation of the forum, some activists raised the idea of a bilingual, self-financed, and self-produced newspaper (with eight pages per issue) to cover the event. Ultimately named *Social Press*, the newspaper was realized by a working group on communication from the local Milan social forum, with collaboration from the Florence social forum and the ESF press office (Interview 4). During the forum four issues were produced and distributed. Its producers estimated that they had to sell at least 1,000 copies to cover its expenses; in the end, between 18,000 and 19,000 copies were sold. According to its self-understanding,

> The newspaper wants to give a voice to networks, cities and people belonging to the movement of movements ... it will devote space to the events and the programme of the forum privileging, however, the great issues of debate and the individual experiences forming it. Each number will also provide one page focusing on the city of Florence. Every day it will cover in-depth one particular topic: labour and migrations, technologies, war, food and health.
> (*Vita*, Italian weekly non profit magazine, 5 November 2002)

During the Florence forum, some efforts were made to keep track of the discussions taking place throughout the event. More than 100 voluntary students were involved in the project 'Operation Scriba manent' promoted by the University of Florence and the COSPE, a local NGO, with the aim of collecting information on workshops and seminars through a uniform grid. They wrote more than 100 reports covering 50 workshops and more than 80 seminars (Martelli and Panzani 2002). The information was later stored and organized on a web server and has been, until recently, accessible through a search engine.

However, until 2003 projects to store information about the ESF remained uncoordinated. After the forum in Paris, there were attempts to collect information about the ESF in a more systematic way in order to build a comprehensive 'memory'. When it became clear that funds remained at the end of the forum, it was decided to use the extra budget to support a series of groups already working on the memory project. Funds were given to the action research network Euromovements and to Nomad, an international network for 'developing alternative technologies aimed at empowering people'.

While Euromovements created tools to systematize and store knowledge produced within the ESF process, Nomad developed a technological system to enable simultaneous translation in multi-linguistic settings like the ESF. Nomad operated in close association with Babels, a political network of volunteer interpreters and translators created on the occasion of the first ESF to secure the right of all people to express themselves in the language of their choice.

At the beginning of the ESF process, a large proportion of the overall ESF budget was devoted to translation.[6] Costs for interpretation were reduced significantly in later forums, where all translations were managed by Babels volunteers. During the preparatory process for the 2006 ESF in Athens, a group of

Greek activists along with others from Nomad built on the experience of past forums to develop an Alternative Interpretation System (ALIS), which broadcasted translations via FM radio waves (Gosselin 2005). ALIS was based on open source software, providing low cost recording (and streaming) of ESF talks. This also made the discussions accessible to those who could not attend the meetings.

In Athens, the idea of creating a memory of the event was published in the programme and discussed in a specific seminar. Here, the Memory Project was physically located in a room reserved to the archiving and creative documentation of the event. Some of the seminars are very well documented in audio, text, and photos. However, while many data collected on each ESF are available on the Internet, they cannot be found on a common site. Moreover, the written documents are mostly monolingual in Italian, French, or English.

Presentation of the forum to external audiences

The ESF is not only organized as a temporary meeting place for activists from all over the continent; it is also designed as a protest event conveying the message that 'another Europe is possible' to those who do not attend. In an evaluation of the third ESF in London, Attac France contends that the forums have become the 'most visible public expression of the alterglobalisation movement' (Attac France 2004). Because social movements usually aim at persuading citizens about the need for societal and political changes, they have to convey to the population at large their view of reality, for example, to identify problems and their causes, as well as possible solutions (Klandermans 1984; Snow and Benford 1988).

ESF activists try to get their message across in several ways. Local citizens may be addressed by posters or banners, protest activities, or cultural events. For a more intense contact, locals can be encouraged to get in touch with the participants, visit the forum's venue, and get a glimpse of the activities there. Communicating the forum to non-involved people who are physically distant from the venue is more difficult. To reach them, mass media are indispensable. Even though the relation between established mass media (TV, radio, and the press) and social movements is tense and media often ignore or distort information on protest events (Rucht 2004), all ESFs have tried to convey their message via mass media. This is particularly difficult at the European level due to the lack of pan-European media. In order to overcome these limits, forum organizers tend to focus on the national context whose media system, journalists, and language they are familiar with.

Usually, the local organizers are responsible for media relations and the major demonstration during the ESF. But they are, of course, not the only group that has an interest in external communication. Every single organization, group, or network that comes to an ESF may have its own ideas and preferences regarding the forum as an opportunity to appear in public. As a consequence, the participants favour a number of differing and sometimes conflicting communication strategies.

Communicating the European social forum 55

The basic means to communicate the ESF to the public developed over time and tended to reappear in every subsequent ESF. Of course, the various targets and respective channels of communication do not have the same importance in every ESF, since every national (or local) organizing committee defines its preferences anew.

Presentation of the forum to the local public

Attempts to familiarize local citizens with the ESF have taken very different shapes in each of the four forums. The most basic strategy has been to publicize the event in the city through posters and banners. Beyond the mere eye-catching effect, this presentation also seeks to invite uninvolved citizens to come to the site and to prepare the ground for more substantial communication. At the venue, the market-like atmosphere of many stands and booths stuffed with information about very different actors and issues may be another reason for locals to come. Organizers also try to gain mainstream media coverage by writing press releases, holding press conferences, and naming press officers who are permanently accessible for journalists.

In addition, the ESF organizers have tried to stage low threshold events that allow locals to mingle with movement activists. One strategy, which proved successful in Athens, consists in organizing cultural events such as concerts and art exhibitions. Every night, concerts were organized in which nationally known artists performed on three stages across the spacious venue. Many young locals attended the concerts, some of whom took the opportunity to stroll through the central hall picking up information from the stalls. In Porto Alegre (Brazil), WSF participants tried to call attention to their claims in a series of events labelled 'street dialogue'. Public street theatre and music shows were organized to attract citizens who were otherwise not involved in the forum. Similar events were occasionally reported from the ESFs. Especially in Florence, where the ESF was confronted with a negative public image prior to the event, activists engaged in a dialogue with the citizens of the host city and tried to overcome prejudices about the forum via face-to-face communication.

Focusing on this aim, a working group of Florence's local social forum launched the campaign 'Firenze Città Aperta' (Florence Open City) in September 2002, initially criticizing and then bypassing the national organizing committee. The latter was perceived to be highly involved in political discussions, but scarcely engaged in preparing the city for this international event. As one promoter recalls, 'I think that the national organisational committee wanted to gain international credibility from this event. For that reason the attention devoted to the local level and the city was inadequate' (Interview 5).

Some activists belonging to the local social forum were particularly worried about the relationship with the local citizenry. Many had participated in the anti-G8 protests in Genoa in 2001, where, after a negative press campaign, many locals seemed to fear the protesters (Andretta *et al.* 2002). Also for the first ESF, mainstream media described the forum's participants as radical 'no globals' coming to Florence to devastate the city and its cultural assets (della Porta et al. 2006). The door-to-door campaign aimed, through direct conversations with citizens and shopkeepers, to convince them that there was no reason to fear the ESF. Accordingly, the activists presented themselves as responsible citizens interested in discussing issues that were of fundamental importance for the future of humankind.

Despite these efforts, some more radical groups criticized the forum as being closed, exclusive, and isolated within the citadel (the ancient fortress that hosted most of the ESF activities). Some groups therefore tried to geographically extend the forum to the city, recalling the experience of the Genoa protest where the various organizational networks assembled in 'thematic squares' to communicate their ideas to the local citizens. This strategy was also meant to communicate with people who were not interested in the forum but who might accidentally pass by one of these squares.

The protest march

The march concluding each forum is considered to be an important opportunity to communicate the forum to the population of the hosting city and beyond (on the role of protest in the ESF, cf. Chapter 10 in this volume). Due to the mass of participants, these marches are not only visible to the bystanders but are also reported in local, national, and foreign media. Usually, the participants in the forum are joined by other political groups from the host country, thereby presenting a broad spectrum of claims and issues related to the general idea that 'another Europe is possible'.

In Florence, a significant effort was made to involve local citizens in the final demonstration. During the march, volunteers positioned themselves along the route to create a bridge between demonstrators and passersby. In the two weeks preceding the event, the volunteers had contacted residents along the route to explain the idea of the social forum and the final demonstration, and to develop an atmosphere of mutual trust (Interview 6). Ultimately, these people welcomed the 500,000 demonstrators, and the final march attracted positive and significant media coverage.

In Paris, the final demonstration per se did not attract great media coverage, probably because it was smaller than in Florence and no violent incidents were expected. However, the forum in general did get extensive coverage, Moreover, this coverage tended to be positive, especially in left-wing media.[7]

In London, by contrast, the public image of the movement was undermined by the conflicts surrounding the whole organizing process. Such conflicts had already emerged in the preparatory stage and during the forum itself at the occasion of a plenary session in which Ken Livingstone, the left-wing Mayor of London, was expected to speak (Papadimitriou et al. 2007: 11). Subsequently, grassroots activists took to the street for a demonstration against the official ESF dominated by trade unions and the local authorities. Conflicts between 'verticals' and 'horizontals' were also visible during and after the final demonstration, when some horizontal activists were kept from speaking on the official stage and even arrested by the police (ibid.). Thus, activists had difficulties in displaying a positive image of the movement during the demonstration.

In their evaluation of the forum in Athens, the organizers emphasized the high number of local citizens who had visited. They also pointed to the number of some 70,000 protesters in the final march, interpreting this as a success in politicizing people in Greece.[8] However, the march was also discredited by some of the media because of the violent clashes between some radical demonstrators and the police. In addition, fistfights among rival groups within the demonstration provoked strong criticism from the organizers and some external groups. Not surprisingly, the local organizers, who had a heated internal debate about this incident, were not eager to discuss it in a larger setting such as the concluding Assembly of the Social Movements, let alone mention it vis-à-vis mass media.

Probably with the exception of Florence where a partial link between ESF participants and the local citizenry was created due to the awareness campaign, few 'ordinary' citizens tended to join these marches. To these citizens, the march is more a colourful spectacle than a political framework in which they wish to belong. However, one must also acknowledge that the marches are not only an outward-directed activity but also serve to strengthen the collective identity of forum participants, who enjoy the relaxed atmosphere and 'power in numbers' (DeNardo 1995).

Presentation of the forum to the general public

Even though the organizers notoriously claim informing and directly interacting with the local public as a priority, their evaluations of past ESFs suggest that mass media resonance is perceived as one of the most important criteria for a successful forum. Of course, the organizers are aware of the problematic and ambivalent role of mass media. As the prime source of information for uninvolved citizens, mass media is considered an important target to spread the message. At the same time, the forum organizers have good reason to be sceptical about this channel of information. It is well known that a range of factors tends to produce a distorted picture of the forums, among them the mechanisms of news production, the selection of aspects that are considered worth reporting, and the political and social distance of many journalists and editors from non-institutional politics.

Anticipating these difficulties, the organizers of the first ESF in Florence developed a complex structure of communication to deal with journalists: a press office set up just one month before the forum[9] and a group of six spokespersons (among them three women) representing the local social forum. In contrast, the national organizing committee was not represented by any spokesperson. This was a deliberate choice to differentiate the event from the Genoa anti-G8-protests in which a single person, Vittorio Agnoletto, was appointed as spokesman of the Genoa Social Forum, the main platform coordinating the anti-G8 protests.

However, the absence of official spokespersons created a misunderstanding for many newspapers, which tended to identify representatives of the local forum with the ESF as a whole. Forum organizers clearly wanted to mark the distinctiveness of the ESF through a 'strategy of a plurality of voices' (Interview 7), thus dissociating themselves from more traditional left organizations such as political parties. This kind of strategy was problematic, as it ignored the fact that most journalists did not want to talk with unknown people and were instead searching for 'scoops', 'celebrities', and publicly recognized 'leaders' of the movement (such as those who organized the Genoa Social Forum).

The outcome of the last press conference preceding the official opening of the forum is quite telling. While the organizers had agreed to have some well-known 'leaders' outside the press room, journalists started to interview them immediately after the press conference. In the end, those recognized leaders gained much more media coverage than the press conference itself (Interview 2). The spokespersons of the local social forum also reported having accompanied some journalists to explain the forum during the event. According to them, journalists hoped to find confrontation and tried to confirm prefabricated clichés (Interviews 5 and 8).

During the preparations for the ESF in Paris in 2003, the organizers again considered interaction with mass media to be a key problem. In an analysis of the relationship between the ESF and the media, Sandrine Lévêque (2005) portrays the tension between adapting to the needs of mass media and criticizing them. The ESF in Paris certainly made a leap forward in the professionalization of public relations (PR) work. A press centre was established at the venue to supply journalists with the needed infrastructure. As mentioned above, it was accessible only to accredited journalists, while alternative media activists had their own media centre nearby. In order to give a voice to the polyphonic event, two part-time spokespersons were hired. They distributed one press release in French, English, Spanish, and Italian every day of the forum to a list of 2,000 journalists. Email and telephone contacts for both spokespersons were offered on the website. The archiving of the media coverage was professionally conducted by an external company that filed reports from September to November 2003. The interest by the media was already impressive even before the start of the event, with 300–400 journalists attending a press conference prior to the ESF.

In light of this professional media relations work, it is no surprise that press resonance was considered as an important indicator for the success of the event as a whole. This aspect occupied half of the evaluation report that was produced by the paid staff after the event (Lévêque 2005: 77). These steps towards professionalization were taken to reach the main aims in public relations: visibility[10] and a coherent and positive image of the forum. Yet, the aim to present the event as 'univoque' (ibid.) or – as one of the spokesperson said in an interview – 'as if the forum was a person' (Interview 9) resulted in a separation between political and organizational aspects. The spokespersons decided to present the ESF as a concept or structure, abstaining from clear political messages. Not surprisingly, members of the organizing committee considered the PR work as a flop. The vague political statements by the press officers and their focus on logistics were of little interest to the journalists (Lévêque 2005: 81). As in Florence, many journalists ignored or circumvented the press officers, using pre-existing contacts to interview political 'celebrities'.

Even though the organizers emphasized professional media contacts, the criticism of mass media by activist groups played an important role in the discussions of the ESF. Lévêque identifies three strands of criticism (2005: 83). The first was represented by experts in discussions and workshops dealing with 'processes of marketization of information'. The second strand of criticism emanated from three forums organized by leftist and/or alternative media: 'Archipel des revues', 'Métallos Médialab' and 'Projet K', harbouring Marxist media. The third strand was represented by journalists' trade unions that discussed the problems of news production in the framework of the ESF. The prominence of critical media at the ESF in Paris fits well into a national trajectory of the *mouvement altermondialiste*. In France, *Le monde diplomatique*, a monthly left journal that played an important role in the foundation of Attac and as a site for a critical debate of globalization, was a natural ally for the ESF organizers.

Although the event in 2004 had a PR layout similar to the event in Paris, the adaptation to the needs of commercial journalism was even more visible in London. Here, the most important difference compared to the structure in Paris was the monopolization of media relations by one person. As a service for journalists, the London website was the first ESF site to include a section to access press releases and information about accrediting. According to the website, 600 journalists seized the opportunity to report on the ESF.[11] The criticism raised against the PR work in London resembles in part the general objections against the organization of the forum. Critics interpreted the fact that only one person was in charge of media contacts as an expression of the hierarchical style of the organization as a whole.[12] Criticism was also expressed about the fact that the Greater London Authority (GLA) sponsored and controlled the ESF website, with access limited to a small group. The GLA imposed a logic of 'good management', externalizing the website administration to a private software company that was paid £40,000 for its work. In a first phase, grassroots activists raised their voices, as they wanted to be involved in the development of the ESF official website. In the words of one activist belonging to the 'horizontals':

> I remember that we called the company and asked to have access to the database but they replied that we were not among their clients as they have signed a contract with the ESF office in London. Even the European organisers wrote many letters to the London office claiming that that information belonged to everybody but they did not give up.
>
> (Interview 16)

As Jones (2004) has stated:

> [While] the e-commerce functionality [of the website] was deemed crucial to the ESF ... the requirements for the other website functionalities were

never opened up for public discussion. All public interactivity was rejected and too few people were trusted to participate and administer the site.

As a result, the horizontals created a collaborative website based on Wiki that could be directly edited by registered users. According to Kavada (2007), the site managed by the verticals functioned essentially as a 'shop window', while the horizontals' site operated as a 'collaborative lab' reflecting different communication logics: a broadcasting, top-down logic in the former, and a collaborative, bottom-up logic for the latter.[13]

Although a handful of seminars dealt with the biases of commercial news production and the opportunities of self-organized community media, the self-critical debate that characterized the ESF in Paris was not prominent in London. While the Paris ESF found a rough balance to fulfil the needs of both mass media and alternative media, the latter were largely neglected in the official event in London.

In the Athens ESF in 2006 – as a reaction to the criticism of the London ESF and an expression of the collectivist spirit of the organizers – a group of five activists carried out the media work, one of them identifiable as an ESF press officer. The concept of the press team was similar to that developed by the organizers of the Florence ESF. The self-understanding of the Greek press team was to facilitate contacts between journalists and activists rather than providing a professional service to mass media. However, the team's press releases were available in Greek and English only. A press centre was established at the venue, but the website had no special features for journalists. In an interview, some organizers reported that access to the national media was – among other factors – made possible through those journalists who were on friendly terms with the activists.[14]

Conclusion

The comparison of ways to communicate the four ESF meetings has shown some continuity but also some specificities based on the different contexts and preferences of the hosting organizers. Let us first summarize the observations on communication targeting the immediate movement adherents.

In general and first, the organizers of the ESFs deal with a structured field of activist organizations and networks with their own means of communication. For the most part, it suffices to reach only several of these groups and networks which, in turn, distribute information to both their own constituencies and to other groups via email lists, newsletters, gatherings, and so on. These groups and organizations are attentive to a forthcoming ESF and will therefore take note of calls for participation, suggestions for the programme, and so on. It seems that these second-step flows of information occur largely on the basis of the same language or nationality.

In between the individual ESF gatherings, the three to four annual meetings of the EPAs play an important role, both in providing input for (and sometimes soft pressure on) the local organizers, and in distributing information on the ESF to the countries and organizations the participants in the EPAs (mostly informally) represent. In addition, the local organizers actively inform and mobilize groups and networks in their respective political contexts, not least because they also have to raise money to make a big meeting such as an ESF possible. In all ESF meetings, support from local authorities was granted, though to very different degrees, with least support in Athens and Florence. In addition, direct communication during and after the ESFs occurs in meetings of the EPAs and various committees and groups, including those who are concerned with the evaluation of the ESFs. Finally, a communication structure of media specialists is gradually evolving with the goal of creating a document-based 'memory' of the ESFs that can be accessed via the Internet. They also seek to organize an evaluation process based on questionnaires and reports after the event.

Second, the organizers and participants of the ESFs address people and audiences that cannot be considered as part of the movement constituency. Here again, mediated and direct forms of communication are used. Besides the wider public opinion, the reaction of the local citizenry is of crucial importance. Influenced by various sources, among which mass media are probably most decisive, the locals may take a positive or a negative attitude towards the ESF. The first ESF in Florence (in 2002) took place after a hostile media campaign, as especially the national government and conservative media evoked the fear of violence. This prompted forum activists to invent forms of communication that were appropriate to such a situation. A number of creative campaigns directly addressed local citizens, seeking to spread the image of a peaceful event.

The public attitude was much more relaxed and supportive for the second ESF in Paris (in 2003). In this situation, forum organizers could use and strengthen more professional media relations to attract broad attention, although this was criticized during workshops as too much of an adaptation to the logic of mass media. The forms of communication that could be observed at the third forum in London (in 2004) reflected an organizational process that grassroots activists criticized as being 'vertical' and 'bureaucratic'. The monopolizing communication strategy, however, could not compensate for the fading interest of mass media in the event, as a preliminary media analysis not presented here has shown (see Rucht and Teune 2007).

Though in Athens the negative trend of London continued with a decline in public attention, a qualitative change in the communication and mobilization strategy was evident. First, the fourth ESF was organized in a more open and transparent way. Second, the Greek organizers succeeded in mobilizing large groups of participants from Central and Eastern Europe who had not taken part in the preceding social forums in Western European countries. Third, the debates evolving around the question of how to communicate the forum to the public had consequences. Adaptation to the expectations and needs of professional journalists was perceived as negative once it became the single most important aim of communication. In the aftermath of the London ESF, activists abandoned this strategy, re-emphasizing the importance of alternative media and resisting journalists' demands for a single spokesperson.

The analysis of the external communication of the ESF process has also taught us a lesson about democracy in movements. During the preparatory process, measures have been developed to allow for transparency of and easy access to information. These goals are mainly pursued via the ESF website and email lists. However, the strong reliance on the Internet tends to exclude activists without access, that is, mainly poor and poorly educated people. Furthermore, the prevailing means of communication privilege those activists who are part of a dense network in a country with a high interest in social forums in general. Accordingly, these activists tend to be more included in the preparatory process and to have better access to relevant information than other activists.

Concluding our analysis, we wish to stress two points. First, the ESFs are much more than just a series of short-term gatherings. Though these physical encounters are the most visible highlights, the ESF constitutes an ongoing process in which an open, transparent, democratic, and interactive structure of internal and external communication is sought – and partially achieved. Over time, a highly informal and flexible infrastructure is emerging to fulfil this task. In this process, the need for efficacy (via professionalization, division of labour, and so on) conflicts with the aim of a participatory and 'horizontal' form of communication. The balance between these poles is constantly adjusted anew according the differential weight of the players in various steps of the ESF process.

Second, our analysis has shown the difficulties in communicating the ESF to an audience not related to the global justice movements and their allies. In this respect, mass media beyond the control of ESF organizers remain crucial. With regard to established mass media, the movement activists have to find the right balance between adapting, at least to some extent, to these media's needs and mechanisms while at the same time insisting on procedures and messages that do not compromise the movements' cause.

Interviews

1 Jason Nardi. WSF, working group on communication. Italy.
2 Cristiano Lucchi. ESF press officer. Italy.
3 Member of the ESF Memory Project.
4 Marco de Filippi. Founder of *Social Press*, working group on communication. Italy.
5 Tommaso Fattori. Spokesperson of the Florence local social forum and national organising committee. Italy.
6 Massimo Torelli. Initiator of the awareness campaign 'Firenze Città Aperta'. Italy.
7 Bruno Paladini. Member of the national organising committee. Italy.
8 Sara Nocentini. Spokesperson of the Florence local social forum and national organising committee. Italy.
9 Member of Arcilesbica, spokesperson of the Florence local social forum. Italy.

10 Former director of OneWorld Italy, administrative staff, working group on communication. Italy.
11 Founder of Social Press, working group on communication. Italy.
12 Spokesperson of the Paris ESF. France.
13 Interview with four members of the Greek organizing committee. Greece.
14 Member of Espacio Alternativo. Spain.
15 Member of Ecologistas en Acción. Spain.
16 Member of the Asamblea contra la Mercantilización de la Información (ACME). Spain.
17 Member of Kokkino (RED). Greece.
18 Member of Socialist Worker Party (SWP). United Kingdom.
19 Member of the international network People's Global Action. Spain.

Notes

1 We wish to thank Ariane Jossin and Christoph Haug for sharing their knowledge about the ESF process with us. The article was collaborative, but each author contributed specifically to an empirical section; Lorenzo Mosca wrote the section 'Presentation of the forum to external audiences' but also contributed to the other sections.
2 The EPA is an informal transnational infrastructure that shapes the organizing process of the ESF at the continental level (see Chapter 2 in this volume). Hence, groups beyond the host country are involved in the ESF process and want to give advice and/ or have a say in the basic content and shape of the specific ESF meeting.
3 All of the ESFs have – to varying degrees – triggered criticism by radical activists who urged a self-organization of the forum 'from below' in a framework that was called 'autonomous spaces', promoting a radical stance in contrast to allegedly moderate claims within the official forum. Dependent on the openness of the preparatory process and the resonance of the groups that dominated the forum's organization, the autonomous spaces were defined as complementary or oppositional to the 'official' ESF.
4 However, local organizers also have face-to-face meetings with public authorities to negotiate the areas where a forum is held, the route of the final demonstration, and so on.
5 Not to be confused with Independent Media Centers (IMC) sometimes co-existing with the 'official' media center of the ESF.
6 In Florence, €300,000 were spent for equipment and €100,000 for professional interpreters. While professional interpreters were contracted for the plenary conferences (interpreted in English, French, German, Italian, and Spanish), volunteers worked in the seminars (interpreting in three languages).
7 The forum was also an issue for conservative media. Even though some articles had a critical or derogatory tone, the coverage was quite exhaustive, maybe partly as a reaction to the hype produced by leftist media. Therefore, the Paris ESF received a broader coverage than the three other ESFs in 12 European newspapers (see Rucht and Teune 2007).
8 In particular, that so many people could be mobilized independently from the Greek Communist Party was seen as a leap forward in the autonomy of the Greek social movements (see Almpanis 2006).
9 The nucleus of the press office formed part of the national organizing committee (approximately 40 people) and consisted of three press officers who were supported by a group of 20 to 30 volunteers (nearly all of them journalists) (Interview 2).
10 One element of the public relations concept was to display a unifying symbol for the event as a whole. The ESF logo, applied to T-Shirts and paraphernalia, was very

salient in Paris, even being used by the mass media in their reports about the forum. The logo also symbolized the identity of the social forum process on an international scale. For example, the European network of local social forums and the social forum in Germany used it as a template for their own logos.
11 Online, available at: www.ukesf.net/en accessed 25 January 2007.
12 Also, the nomination process for the press officer was deemed not transparent. A summary of the criticisms are online, available at: www.euromovements.info/upload/esf_media.doc accessed 25 January 2007.
13 The experience of the London ESF resulted in an emphasis on the European dimension of the organizational process (see also Chapter 2 this volume). After the London forum, it was agreed that the website concerning the ESF process would be developed under the control of the EPA, while the site concerning the ESF event (allowing for registration and providing logistic information) would be managed by the national organizing committee (EPA 2005).
14 In addition, the organizers tried to benefit from a domestic law that assures airtime in public media regarding 'social messages'. To their regret, this opportunity was not effectively used because of organizational and practical flaws (Interview 10).

4 Models of democracy
How activists see democracy in the movement

Massimiliano Andretta and Donatella della Porta[1]

Democracy as a multidimensional concept

The ESF has been an arena for debate and networking, but also a space where various conceptions of democracy have emerged and been developed. In addition to calls for a fluid, open, and inclusive organizational structure,[2] the internal debate between supporters of 'vertical' and 'horizontal' conceptions of democracy was already emerging at the first ESF in Florence. The representatives of local social forums called for a 'rootedness in the territory', the creation of open assemblies, and a fluid structure, stressing the importance of the non-organized. By the second ESF, a main criticism addressed the role of the more 'institutional' organizations, accused of imposing a hierarchical and non-transparent structure on what is supposed to be an open and consensual process (Sommier 2005: 29ff.). The local social forums were particularly critical of a 'top down' approach. These critiques were instrumental in the creation of autonomous spaces.

During the Parisian ESF, but not within it, a self-managed village –organized by No vox and the Réseau Intergalactique and visited by about 6,000 activists (ibid.: 38) – as well as the formation of a libertarian and anarchist social forum testify to the search for alternative, horizontal forms of action. Some activists feared a sort of 'institutionalization' of the ESF that, in Paris, was accompanied by the forum of the European trade unions and the forum of the local authorities (with more than 200 participants), with high visibility of institutional actors (including the unions, even their European federation), especially in the press. Although many articles stressed the plurality of the movement, disproportionate voice was given to the mayors who hosted the forum, as well as to the representatives of political parties, unions, and local governments that were present. From within the movement, the organization of the second forum was criticized not only for the fragmentation of the events in five distant places, but also for the municipality's decisions to rent buildings from private firms for the forum and to hire private policemen who prohibited entrance once the seats were all taken. There was also criticism of the organizers' tendency to ally along national lines.[3]

The internal debate in the GJM between 'horizontal' and 'vertical' conceptions of democracy took more dramatic forms at the third ESF in London, where the local London Social Forum, together with other informal groupings, accused the main organizers (among them the Socialist Workers Party, Globalise Resistance, Socialist Action, and some unions) of imposing 'top down' organizational decisions. The tensions developed into an open contestation of the final events and led to some arrests among the autonomous activists. They represented, in fact, a turning point in the evolution of the ESF process. Even before the London ESF, one of the prominent speakers of the GJM, Susan George, in praising the decision of the WSF to abolish plenaries, had written:

> I was disappointed, on the other hand, that the 2004 European Social Forum in London still clings to the supposed necessity of plenaries even though there will be fewer than in previous years. Sorting out who gets to speak on what platform on what subject and with whom; how many speakers are allotted to each country and to each organisation; mixing them carefully according to gender, hue, hemispheric origin and I suppose religious profession, sexual orientation, height, weight and God knows what else; requiring each year long and multiple meetings all over Europe – all this has proven, as far as I can tell, a colossal waste of everyone's time and money. Let's get serious, people ... in future Social Forums I would hope we could stop the silly jockeying for speech slots, refrain from endless repetition and ceremonial condemnation, determine what issues we really need to talk about, get organised beforehand to do so, then hit the ground running.
>
> (George 2004)

In London, the tensions between 'horizontals' and 'verticals' escalated when the former openly contested the final plenary session, accusing the organizers of being dominated by 'an oligarchy of parties and unions' and denouncing the aggressive attitudes of the marshal body and the police at the final march (*La Repubblica*, Bologna, 19 October 2004). A press release of the radical Italian union Cobas criticized the attitudes of the British organizing committee (in particular the Socialist Worker Party, Socialist Action and some unions), who were accused of monopolizing the speech after the final march and repressing internal contestation. Another radical union, Sin Cobas, criticized the 'traditional closure of British politics, that also involves the radical Left' as responsible for the exclusion of the 'multitudes of less-well structured groups' from the decision making process. The 'problem of democracy and efficacy' was widely discussed: some activists lamented the fact that only a few people got to decide: 'those who speak in the assemblies are always male, white and 50 years old' (*Liberazione* 19 October 2004).

In an open online forum to discuss the event, the London ESF was in fact judged a success, but 'with many internal problems, with difficulties, delays'. There were 'many young people, a lot of desire to participate – not always fulfilled – a great desire not to throw away the most interesting political novelty of the first few years of this century' (Salvatore Cannavò of the Italian daily *Liberazione*[4]); but also 'a lack of curiosity of the organisers to look beyond Blair and one's own ideological borders, beyond the opposition to the war', and by the 'feeling that the great majority of the alter-globalist peoples are fed up with the call for "bringing politics back in the first place", of the war between organisations, of the tricks used to have the last word' (Anna Pizzo, of the Italian weekly *Carta*). A specific criticism addressed the centralization of the preparatory process, in the hands of 'a dictatorship – the idea that those who have a say are the ones who can afford the Easyjetters' fare to international meetings', as well as the fact that local social forums had an inadequate part in the official programme. Unlike the Paris ESF, the costs of setting up networking 'spaces' for them were not covered by the London ticket price or venue-finding arrangements. Local social forums 'had to make their own arrangements in the "alternative" spaces apart from one seminar at Alexandra Palace' (according to a collective assessment published by the London Social Forum).

The document 'A Different ESF is Possible', issued by activists participating in the UK Local Social Forum Network, declared that 'The British process to build for the ESF has been, from the proposal to have it in London onwards, organised without an open, democratic, inclusive process.' The involvement of the Greater London Authority (GLA) in the process was considered by some activists as especially challenging for the democratic quality of the forum process, as:

> They are led by a small group of people from Socialist Action, one of the somewhat conservative factions of the Fourth International. They work according to an explicit managerial philosophy and an interpretation of democracy which is in many ways quite the opposite of the participatory democracy of Porto Alegre. This small group – no more than around 12 – of political managers has disproportionate power because, although Livingstone is formally a member of the Labour Party, he is not under any live democratic party pressure like the mayors of Florence, Paris and Porto Alegre ... for the political managers of the GLA the way to implement the will of the democratically elected mayor is through tough professional management and a minimization of the layers of mediation between the mayor's senior management and the delivery of the service.
> (Online, available at: judmila.org/~pueblo/cgi/semamap/grepin1. cgi?item=%22power%22–572k accessed 22 April 2008)

Praising the 'Florentine miracle' of harmonious collaboration among different groups, the Italian alternative union Cobas also stigmatized the 'authoritarian, hegemonic, and exclusive practices' of several British groups (from SWP to the unions), which had created strong tensions with the 'horizontal' groups.

Even more fundamental was the criticism of the lack of transparency of the decision making process as a whole. In the words of a young unionist from Attac Denmark, Lars Bohn,

> In democratic terms, I will have to say we failed. And that is serious. We claim to want to create another world, and even that this is possible. But if we can't even create a trustworthy democratic alternative within our own

ranks, how can we expect people from the outside to trust us to create the conditions for a more democratic world?

(Bohn 2004)

This activist, who had participated in the European Preparatory Assembly, criticized not only the lack of information on the agenda and of minutes on the decisions taken, but also what he calls a breach of trust by the British organizers about the decision to hold the final march under the slogan 'No to Bush, no to war' while 'it was a clear decision of the ESF preparatory assembly that the main slogans of the demo should be some that covered the whole ESF: war, privatisation, racism'. He sadly concluded,

> Maybe that's how democracy works in England. But seen from at least a Scandinavian point of view this is a major break of trust. If this had happened here, the group behind it would surely be excluded from further participation in any kind of common cooperation. Not by an authoritarian body, but just because nobody would have enough trust to cooperate with them anymore.

In a similar vein, Attac Austria, Bulgaria, Finland, France, Germany, Hungary, Italy, Norway, Poland, Romania, Spain, Sweden, Switzerland, Wallonia–Brussels, Denmark, and Flanders, rethinking the working method within the process, stressed that

> The guiding principle has to be striving for a process building from below, in the sense that it has to start from the considerations of different movements and organisations, including the many who are currently not following the process, but nevertheless consider it most important.
>
> (Sandimgetriebe no date)

The European Preparatory Assembly is said to have struggled for 'openness and inclusivity, while transparency and accountability for decision making has been neglected'.

The challenge of building up a common model of democracy for diverse groups and people is generally recognized in the movement, and the criticism of the organization of the ESF produced some structural changes. In particular, the plenary sessions were reduced in London, and then abolished in Athens, in order to leave more space for 'bottom up' networking, with specific assemblies (of women, of precarious workers, of migrants, of young people, and so on) oriented to build common initiatives. Additionally, 'parallel' spaces for the critical groups have been semi-institutionalized (although with different agreements) in the organization of the forum. The Athens ESF was considered by most activists to be an improvement upon the previous ESF – as an Italian activist stressed in a mailing list, 'less ideological and more concrete', with more capacity to build transnational networks on specific issues. Here as well, however, it was recognized that the quality of the debate in the (well attended) final Assembly of the Social Movements was not very deliberative, with 'all those who intervene who think they have something fundamental to say, even though they almost never succeeded, or were interested, in following up the line of reasoning and of the previous intervention' (ibid.). In fact, the launching of common initiatives derived largely from the informal meetings in the previous days.

Along with criticism of the ESF decision making process and proposals for improving it, various conceptions of democracy do emerge within the ESFs. Defending the organization of the London ESF, one of the organizers from the SWP, Alex Callinicos, states that 'One difficulty in this process has certainly been that participants have very different conceptions of democracy and often showed little tolerance of definitions different from their own'. While in Italy and France the activists of these various areas of the GJM had already come together in common struggles, building links of reciprocal trust, in the UK the organization of the ESF was their first collaboration.[5]

Conceptions of democracy are certainly discussed within the forums. In these debates, tensions often emerge between a more traditional political approach and one stressing the autonomy of the civil society. During the seminar 'In search for a lost democracy' at the second ESF, politics is defined as 'a common good, as air, water, or peace', which 'does not have to be delegated only to professional politicians'. In parallel, democracy is considered as 'a concrete practice, not a theory', stressing the need for building counter-expertise through the common work of experts and citizens. At the debate on 'Politics: common good?', there was stigmatization of the 'ideology of expertise', but also of the conception of the party as a vanguard. Although the existing (present and past) left-wing governments were criticized for their support of the privatization of public services and the reduction of social rights, the role of the parties was discussed, with some participants stressing the link between the old labour movement and contemporary alter-globalists. The seminar on 'How to win the majorities to the ideas of the alterglobalist movement?' also discussed the relationship between movements and parties in a moment of 'crisis of political representation'. In the debate on 'Which perspectives for the altermondialist movement', participants praised the mobilization capacity of the GJM in activating protest and convincing the public, but also stigmatized its failure to influence institutional decisions.

If influencing power seems most important to some activists, others insist on the necessity of avoiding power. At the seminar titled 'Resisting means to create the utopia, here and now', the role of some spiritual and utopian bases (humanization of work, limits to consumption, sharing of knowledge) for the development of individual imagination and freedom was emphasized. In several meetings, the testimonies of religious people engaged in social movements addressed the articulation between political commitment and spiritual beliefs, proposing inter-religious dialogue, refusal of the use of religion as an instrument of power and domination, and spiritual resistance to liberal globalization.

The debates on power also addressed inequalities within the ESF itself – for instance, the debate 'All citizens for a Europe that rejects misery', which criticized the lack of space left to very poor people in the movement; or 'Participatory democracy and exclusion', which discussed the preconditions for real participation of people 'in conditions of exclusion'. The presentation of the seminar entitled 'The alterglobalist movement reflects on its words, symbols and the problem of language' read as follows:

> The alter-globalist movement developed gradually as a full actor. This undeniable force depends on its capacity to aggregate the most different cultures and streams, stating diversity as its intrinsic richness. Yes, but ... coexistence and cooperation in the largest diversity (of cultures and practices, codes and references, or even values) easily implies the return to logics of power, and can develop into the practical inability to manage diversity ... The movement has to face a dialectic between the will to preserve and promote diversity and the desire (and need) to build alternatives to the dominant system, and therefore to adopt a profile to a certain extent 'unitary'.

A reflection on communication is suggested as a way to produce 'a fertile diversity', developing from a debate on the very way in which the movement is named in the different countries: from *altermondialiste* or counter-globalist in France, to a 'movement of movements', 'against liberal globalization' or for another possible world in Italy; or anti- or alter-globalization in Spain. Different conceptions of democracy are also linked to different protest strategies, including judicial cases, conferences, exemplary action, lobbying, observatories, local street festivals, free universities and encyclopaedias, laboratories, theatres, movies, and alternative experiments (such as social enterprises, fair trade).

Reflecting on these various conceptions (and dimensions) of democracy within the ESF (and the global justice movement in general), one of the main purposes of our research is the analysis of models of democracy as they are elaborated 'from below', implemented both in the internal organization of social movements and in their interaction with institutional politics. A first assumption is that, although representative models of democracy remain dominant, they are challenged from the point of view of legitimacy as well as efficiency: declining confidence in conventional forms of political participation is accompanied by the perception of poor performance by representative democratic governments. Other models of democracy (re)emerge as possible correctives for the malfunctioning of representative democracy; in fact, experiments in participatory and deliberative forms of democracy are underway within political institutions as well as by political and social actors. In this context, various conceptions of democracy coexist, stressing different indicators of democratic quality (see Chapter 1 this volume).

A second assumption is that general principles of democracy can be combined in different forms and with different balances. In fact, in our work, we did not aim at measuring degrees of (quality of) democracy (or conceptions thereof), but instead at constructing a typology of the various models of democracy that are present, in a more or less 'pure' form, in GJM organizations and processes.

Models of democracy 71

In this sense, we want to analyse in detail the plurality of visions and practices of democracy expressed by GJM organizations and activists.

In particular, debates tend to develop within the movements on two main dimensions. First, participatory conceptions that stress inclusiveness of equals (high participation) are contrasted with those based upon the delegation of power to representatives (low participation). In this sense, we studied the continued presence of direct forms of democracy that put a strong emphasis on the assembly; and, in contrast, the extent to which the processes of institutionalization of social movement organizations (often stressed in social movement research in the last two decades) have spread a principle of delegation of power.

A second dimension refers to *consensus/deliberation* and looks at the emphasis on decision making methods that assign a special role to public discussion, the common good, rational arguments, and transformation of preferences. These aspects are particularly embedded and valorized by the *method of consensus* that poses an even stronger emphasis on the decision making process per se than on the outcome of such a process. In the various parts of the Demos research, we have used a typology of democratic forms of internal decision making (see della Porta and Reiter 2006a; della Porta and Mosca 2006) that crosses the two dimensions of participation (referring to the degree of delegation of power, inclusiveness, and equality) and deliberation (referring to the decision making model and to the quality of communication). It is important to keep in mind, however, that the variables used to construct the typology were different in the different parts of our research, reflecting the differences in the research instruments and the types of sources used.

Analysing the main documents of GJM organizations, with the aim of identifying the visions of democracy, inside and outside the movement, we narrowed it down to four basic conceptions (or models) of internal democracy (della Porta and Reiter 2006a). In the *associational model*, the assembly is composed of delegates and – even in those cases in which the assembly consists of all members and is defined as the main decision making organ – everyday politics is managed by an executive committee; moreover decisions are taken by majority vote. When, according to the selected documents, delegates make decisions on a consensual basis, we speak of *deliberative representation*. When decisions are made by an assembly that includes all members, and no executive committee exists, we have an *assembleary* model, when decisions are taken by a majority, and *deliberative participation*, if consensus and communicative processes based on reason together with participation are mentioned as important values.

As we can see in Table 4.1, over half of the 212 organizations in our sample, covering the GJM in six European countries (Italy, France, Spain, Germany, Switzerland, and Great Britain) as well as at the transnational level, support an associational conception of internal decision making.[6] This means that – at least formally – a model based upon delegation and the majority principle is quite widespread, and indeed expected, given the presence in the GJM of parties, unions, and NGOs. It is, however, only part of the picture: we classified 14.6 per cent of the organizations as assembleary, since in the documents we

Table 4.1 Typology of democratic conceptions

Participation		High	Low
		Associational model (%)	Assemblary model (%)
Consensus	Low	Visions 59.0 Practices 35.6 Norms 19.1	Visions 4.6 Practices 2.5 Norms 35.9
	High	Deliberative representation Visions 15.6 Practices 32.7 Norms 8.2	Deliberative participation Visions 10.8 Practices 29.2 Norms 36.7

Sources: On visions (N = 212), della Porta and Reiter 2006; on practices (N = 184), della Porta and Mosca 2006; on norms (N = 1,055), Demos survey at the fourth ESF in Athens.

analysed, they stressed the role of the assembly in a decision making process that remains tied to aggregative methods such as voting or bargaining. In an additional one-fourth of the organizations, the deliberative element comes to the fore, with 15.6 percent of organizations applying consensus within an associational type (deliberative representation) and 10.8 per cent applying it within an assembleary model (deliberative participation).

Consensus is even more prominent if we move, as we did in another part of our research, from the written documents to the accounts of movement practices by representatives of the GJM organizations (della Porta and Mosca 2006). Acknowledging that constitutions and written documents are not always followed in everyday activities, and that praxes are often different from norms, we in fact complemented the information obtained on organizational ideology with interviews on organizational functioning, as perceived and reported by their speakers.[7] In this part we operationalized the dimension of *participation/delegation* by distinguishing groups characterized by a central role of the assembly in their decision making processes from all other types of organizations (executive-centred, leader-centred, mixed models, and so on). On the dimension *deliberation/majority voting*, we separated groups employing consensus from organizations employing different decisional methods (simple majority, qualified majority, mixed methods, and so on). Here as well, our research testifies to the presence of various types of organizational decision making in the GJM, confirming that social movements are characterized by 'considerable variation in organisational strength within and between movements' (Klandermans 1989: 4).

Of the 202 out of the overall 212 cases that we could classify (in 4 per cent of the cases it was not possible to collect enough information on the main decision making body or on the method of decision making), almost one-third fall into the deliberative-representative category, where the principle of consensus is mixed with the principle of delegation. Another 36 per cent adopt an associational model that is based on majoritarian voting and delegation, while about 30 per cent of the groups bridge a consensual decision making method with the principle of participation (refusal of delegation to an executive committee); only 2.5 per cent of the selected organizations mix the principle of delegation with the majoritarian principle (assembleary model).

The fact that interviewees tend to stress consensus more than the organizational documents do can be explained in various ways: respondents might be more up to date and accurate in describing the actual decision making in their groups, or they may want to give a more positive image of decision making in their organizations. Whatever the explanation, norms of consensus appear as very much supported by the movement organizations.

This result also emerges from an analysis of the normative models of democracy proposed by the activists we interviewed in Athens (see again Table 4.1), although there the emphasis is towards participation. In this sample, the rate of support for associational models of democracy further declines to one-fifth of our population (N = 1,055), and the percentage of deliberative-representative reaches only 8.2 per cent. From a normative point of view, indeed, the ESF participants are attracted by either assembleary or deliberative-participative models (about one-third each). Participation and deliberation are considered, therefore, as main values for 'another democracy'.

In order to locate these results within a broader picture of the activists' appreciation of how democracy works in different contexts, we first have to consider whether the activists perceive these models as being implemented in their own groups and in the GJM in general. When shifting from norms to practices, the activists describe a reality that is not as participatory and deliberative as in their ideal conceptions. Participation in decision making is, in fact, considered to be limited to a small number of activists, at least by 40 per cent of the respondents when assessing meetings of their own groups and 60 per cent when assessing the meetings of the GJM in general (see Table 4.2). As for decision making procedures, on the other hand, activists see the meetings of the GJM as more

Table 4.2 Participation in decision making in own group and in the GJM

	In the meeting of the group (%)	In the meetings of the GJM (%)
a Who decides…		
Few participants	13.1	21.4
Enough participants	27.9	38.1
Almost all participants	30.3	26.1
All participants	28.6	14.3
Total no.	857	970
b How do you decide…		
Voting	30.1	17.3
Sometimes voting	20.5	31.3
Sometimes consensus	24.5	32.2
Consensus	24.9	19.4
Total no. 854	1,205	

consensual than those of their own groups, while recognizing in both a tendency towards either decisively privileging consensus (in about one-fourth for their own group and about one-fifth for the GJM in general) or mixing voting and consensus (in slightly less than half of responses for group meetings and about two-thirds of responses on the GJM).

Notwithstanding this incongruence between norms and practices, the activists express a high degree of satisfaction with the way in which democracy works in the movement, especially if compared with the very critical judgement on the democratic practices in representative institutions (see Table 4.3). Satisfaction with how democracy works in the groups is indeed very high, with a tiny minority of either very unsatisfied or moderately unsatisfied – although (confirming the self-reflexive nature of activism) about half of the sample express moderate satisfaction and as much as one-third are totally satisfied. Overall, activists also expressed satisfaction with decision making within the GJM, although in this case moderate satisfaction prevails (in about two-thirds of respondents), and about one-fourth is moderately unsatisfied. Degrees of satisfaction are very low, however, when we move to attitudes towards public institutions: here, dissatisfaction is virtually unanimous (with about two-thirds very unsatisfied and one-fourth moderately unsatisfied) and refers equally to the national, EU, and UN institutions (see Chapter 5 in this volume).

We can expect models of democracy to interact with the degree of previous participation in movement events: the more a person believes in participation and consensus building, the more likely s/he should be to make his/her voice heard. We asked our respondents how much they had taken part in previous events organized by the GJM. The sample had high variance on this: only about one-fifth was first-timers, and another 11 per cent had participated only once, while about one-third had participated between two and five times and as many as 40 per cent more than five times. First-timers are less likely to emphasize consensus, while those with more previous experiences of participation stress both consensus and participation (see Table 4.4). Although statistically significant, the correlation coefficient is not very high, indicating that consensus and deliberation are indeed values that spread beyond the most active participants.

Table 4.3 Degree of satisfaction with decision making in selected institutions

Degree of satisfaction	Satisfied with decision making process in (%)				
	Your group	GJM	National political system	EU	UN
Very unsatisfied	2.6	5.2	65.0	65.0	66.2
Moderately unsatisfied	12.7	24.6	24.9	25.4	26.5
Moderately satisfied	54.1	64.0	8.3	8.7	6.1
Very satisfied	30.6	6.2	1.7	0.9	1.2
Total	937	1,031	1,107	1,105	1,096

Table 4.4 Participation in GJM events by activists' normative models of democracy

Normative models of democracy	Participation in other GJM events before Athens (%)			TOTAL (No.)	% Who participated in at least one event before Athens	Mean[1]
	Never before	2–5 times	More than 5			
Associational	25.2	36.6	38.1	202	74.8	5.16
Deliberative representative	15.1	43.0	41.9	86	84.9	5.98
Assembleary	21.3	45.6	33.1	375	78.7	4.78
Deliberative participative	14.6	37.8	47.7	384	85.4	6.20
Total	19.1	40.8	40.1	1,047	80.9	5.47
Measures of association	Cramer's V = 0.11***				Cramer's V = 0.11***	ETA = 0.14***

Note
1 The mean of the participation in GJM events before Athens was calculated by assigning to each original category of the question the mean of its range. Thus, while the categories 'never before' and 'only 1 time' have been recoded as respectively '0' and '1', the third category 'between 2 and 5 times' was recoded as '3.5', the fourth category 'between 6 and 10 times' as '8', and the last category 'more than 10 times' as '12'.

We might also imagine that cosmopolitanism, as indicated by experiences in protest and demonstrations in other countries, could increase trust in consensus building and participation, as these values have emerged as particularly widespread in transnational events (see, for example, Doerr and Haug 2006). Our sample, where participants are equally divided between those who did and did not participate in protest events abroad, confirms in fact that 'cosmopolitan' activists are more attracted by deliberative models of democracy: among those who support a deliberative-participative normative model of democracy, 58 per cent have participated in other protest events of the global justice movement outside their own country (as compared to 49 per cent of those who support a deliberative-representative model, 47 per cent of those who support an associational one, and 44 of those who support an assembleary one). Here as well, the correlation coefficient indicates a statistically significant but not particularly strong relation between the two variables (Cramer's V = 0.12***). If cosmopolitans are more supportive of consensus and participation, the other activists also tend to join them on very similar values.

Together with experiences of participation in protest events, at home and abroad, subjective degrees of identification with the global justice movement might also be expected to influence attitudes towards democracy. In particular, those who identify more with the movement can be expected to express more support for those values that emerged as particularly relevant for the GJM organizations – inclusiveness, participation, and consensus (della Porta and

Table 4.5 Identification with GJM by activists' normative models of democracy

Normative models of democracy	Identification with GJM			Total (100%)	% Enough or much identified	Mean (value 0–3)
	No or little	Enough	Much			
Associational	21.0	43.0	36.0	200	79.0	2.13
Deliberative representative	12.8	57.0	30.2	86	87.2	2.16
Assembleary	13.7	48.8	37.5	371	86.3	2.23
Deliberative participative	9.1	49.1	41.8	383	90.9	2.32
Total	13.4	48.5	38.2	1,040	86.6	2.24
Measures of association	Cramer's V = 0.10***				Cramer's V = 0.12***	ETA = 0.11**

Reiter 2006a). Our data from the ESF in Athens indicate, first of all, a very high degree of identification with the GJM among our respondents. Less than 1 per cent declared that they did not identify with the GJM, and a very low 12.4 per cent identified only a little. The remaining part identified either quite a lot (47.4 per cent) or very much (39.4 per cent). Crossing degrees of identification with normative conceptions of democracy, our analysis indicates a statistically significant correlation: with the growth of identification, support for consensual and participatory decision making increases (see Table 4.5). Here too, the correlation is not particularly strong, indicating quite widespread support for the more participatory and consensual values.

Satisfaction with GJM democracy: what for and how it is achieved

Satisfaction with democracy within social movements is a crucial question, since SMOs have relatively few resources to convince members to participate in costly actions such as protest. To be sure, symbolic incentives, such as group solidarity, identification with a larger collective, and mutual recognition, together with material resources, make non-conventional collective participation possible (della Porta and Diani 2006). However, it is difficult to imagine that activists would bear the costs of participation if they were totally dissatisfied with the way in which decisions on actions and aims to pursue are taken. Moreover, if a movement openly declares that it will fight for political power to be democratized, it must try to implement some coherent internal decisional practices. It seems reasonable that activists would refrain from getting politically involved in a movement which, largely, does not (attempt to) practice what it preaches. As Coy has suggested:

> Decision making is the oil that greases the wheel of social movement organising. Done poorly, it can bring a social movement organization to a rather

abrupt halt, disrupt movement coalitions, or eventually contribute to the abeyance or even a demise of entire movements. On the other hand, when decision making is done well, it serves to advance the movement toward achievement of its organising and programmatic goals. And when social movement decision making is done especially well, it may even stand as both a symbol and a concrete manifestation of the kind of social and political relations the movement is trying to organise in the wider world beyond the movement itself.

(Coy 2003: vii)

The GJM network of networks, made of a flexible and heterogeneous net of organizations and individuals, is a critical case for studying the implications of how internal decision making works. Not only does it openly challenge the functioning of external (representative) democracy by criticising its exclusionary logic and its poor performance, but above all its very existence depends on the management of internal controversies on what to do and how, and on the direct participation of activists from different parts of the world. Should internal democracy be perceived as 'very badly done', the net would collapse and activists would drop out. As mentioned above, the data from our survey show a very high degree of satisfaction with democracy working at the GJM level, that is, in decision making settings such as the preparatory assemblies for the organization of the ESFs, the actions organized at the transnational levels such as the 'Stop Bolkestein' or the anti-war campaigns, and other types of networks.

If empirical evidence supports the claim that satisfaction with internal democracy matters for the organization of the GJM, it is worth investigating the factors that facilitate it. According to our data, satisfaction with internal democracy significantly correlates with the degree of identification in the GJM: while as much as 79 per cent of dissatisfied (not at all or little satisfied) activists declare that they identify (enough or much) with the movement, the percentage increases to 93 per cent for the (moderately or much) satisfied (Kendall's tau-b coefficient = 0.243, significant at 0.001 level). Identification is in turn correlated with participation in GJM events: the means of participation figure is 2.3 for those with little or no identification with the GJM and about 6.0 for the highly identified activists (ETA = 0.265, significant at 0.001 level). Put in another way, only 54 per cent of the non-identified, but as many as 84 per cent of the identified activists declared having participated in GJM events at least once before the ESF in Athens; and 27.3 per cent of the former, as compared to 54 per cent of the latter, have done so at the transnational level (outside their own country).

Thus, satisfaction with internal democracy seems to be an important 'resource' for identification with the GJM and, then, for participation. Why activists are satisfied with democracy in the GJM is thus the question we will try to answer in the remainder of this section.

Obviously, only those who participate directly in GJM decision making settings can directly experience how democracy works there. The others may express their satisfaction by trusting the people involved, who tell them their story of the decisional processes, or simply by judging the results of their decisions. After all, activists may simply think that if the movement is able to bring together so many organizations and activists from different countries and political backgrounds, there must be an open and democratic decision making process that allows this to happen. In a different perspective, however, activists who do not directly participate in the decision making settings of the movement may express dissatisfaction with democracy because they feel excluded. According to our data, however, there are no relevant differences with regard to satisfaction between actual participants in the GJM decision making settings and activists involved in GJM events but not directly involved in decision making: 68 per cent of activists not directly involved in GJM decision making settings and 69 per cent of those involved are moderately or much satisfied!

Another factor that can influence the degree of satisfaction is the normative idea of democracy the activists hold: the higher the standard of democracy one ideally supports, the more difficult it could be for him/her to be satisfied with real and concrete decision making. For instance, if it is true, as Mansbridge (2003: 229) contends, that a deliberative normative model of democracy meets the ideals of many social movement activists, it is also true that such a model is difficult to implement in concrete decisional processes. This may lead to some dissatisfaction.

We can test this hypothesis by correlating satisfaction with GJM democracy with activists' level of agreement with four statements on 'how political decisions should be taken'. The first statement sets two groups in opposition: those who think that primarily the *quality of argument* should make a difference, regardless of who voices the argument; and those who think that *resourceful* and active groups/individuals should have more weight. The second statement distinguishes between those who think that it is always important that the opponents accept each other as *equal* and those who believe that, in political conflicts, there are situations in which *mutual acceptance is not important*. The third statement separates those whose normative idea of democracy is compatible with *delegation of power* from those who think that the *participation of all* interested persons should always be a priority; and finally, the last statement sets those who believe that decisions should be taken by *voting* in opposition to those who are convinced that they should be taken by *consensus*. Each of these statements was presented in a polarized form; activists could position themselves on a scale ranging from 0 (argument, equal discussants, delegation, and voting) to 3 (resources, no mutual acceptance, full participation, and consensus).

If we correlate those statements with the satisfaction scale (from 0 to 3), no statistically significant differences can be found except with the last item (voting versus consensus) (Kendall's tau-b = -0.08, significant at 0.01 level). A normative idea of democracy based on consensus is (very weakly) correlated with dissatisfaction with democracy in the GJM. Nonetheless, the correlation is low and limited to the indicator of consensus versus majoritarian conceptions. If we correlate an additive index of deliberativeness of the normative view of democracy with satisfaction, this hypothesis is statistically and substantially rejected (Kendall's tau-b = −0.04, not significant).[8]

Finally, we can ask whether the activists' perceptions of how democracy works at the GJM level influence their levels of satisfaction. This is what most scholars supporting deliberative democracy would expect: according to them, in fact, satisfaction should be higher, and decisions more legitimated, when the decisional process is perceived as more participative and deliberative. Among others, Bernard Manin (1987: 345) describes deliberation as 'the process by which everyone's will is formed' in such a way that the outcome is legitimate; Joshua Cohen (1989: 21) claims that 'free deliberation among equals is the basis of legitimacy'; Seyla Benhabib (1996: 69) sees deliberation as 'a necessary condition for attaining legitimacy'; and Amy Gutmann (1996: 344) suggests that 'the legitimate exercise of political authority requires ... decision making by deliberation among free and equal citizens'. If this is true, we should find that activists who perceive the GJM democratic settings as deliberative are more satisfied with internal democracy than the others.

However, some scholars have questioned the legitimizing effect of deliberation, arguing that it can carry 'conservative or antidemocratic connotations usually overlooked by well-intentioned theorists' (Sanders 1997: 348). Deliberation also has some 'cons': it may support the status quo when consensus hides covert conflicts; it takes a lot of time, favouring those who can spend more of it; and it creates incentives to use veto power as a bargaining chip (Mansbridge 2003). It also implies the need for skills – such as the ability to make rational or reasonable arguments – which are unequally distributed (Sanders 1997); and it can lead to a transformation of preferences towards those who are more able to promote 'good' arguments, rather than with the common good (Stokes 1998). Many of these statements will be controlled in other chapters, where the type of organization to which activists belong and their sociographic attributes (gender, education, age, and so on) will be at the centre of the analysis. In this section, we will see if the perception of deliberative settings leads to more or less satisfaction towards democracy within the GJM.

If we apply the typology for the normative democratic models shown in Table 4.1 to the perceptions of how democracy works in the GJM, we can observe that about 31 per cent of activists perceive it as 'associational', 28 per cent as 'deliberative-representative', about 18 per cent as 'assembleary' and about 24 per cent as 'deliberative-participative'. The cross-tabulation of this typology with satisfaction shows that activists who perceive democracy at the GJM level as 'assembleary' and 'deliberative-participative' are more satisfied than those who perceive it as 'associational' or 'deliberative-representative'. Of the four items measuring the perceived model of GJM democracy, only the one measuring voting versus consensus is not correlated with satisfaction: the Kendall's tau-b coefficients for the correlations with the arguments versus individual or group resources, equal/non equal treatment, and degree of perceived participation in decision making items are respectively 0.254, 0.235, and 0.202 (all significant at 0.001 level). The correlation between satisfaction and the index of perceived deliberation in GJM decision making[9] is also statistically significant and high (0.218, at 0.001 level). Actually, satisfaction with GJM democracy increases from 67 per cent among those perceiving an associational model, and 60 per cent of those perceiving a deliberative-representative model, to 79 per cent among the activists perceiving either an assembleary or a deliberative-participative model (the Cramer's V of the cross-tabulation is 0.17, significant at 0.001 level).

The most likely explanation for why the perception of deliberation brings about legitimacy, or at least satisfaction, is that 'consensus decision making processes interact with the emotional life of movement participants, particularly when dealing with internal movement conflicts' (Coy 2003: viii), and this is particularly important in a heterogeneous transnational movement such as the GJM.

The last factor to look at in this section is the level of congruence between activists' normative ideals of democracy and their perceptions of how democracy actually works within the GJM. The hypothesis in this case is that the less the congruence between normative ideals and actual perceptions of democracy, the less satisfied activists will be. In order to operationalize the degree of congruence, we can calculate the differences between the activists' scores on normative ideals and those on the GJM's perception of democracy. This is rather simple to do, since activists were asked to show their level of agreement with the same kind of statements for both normative and actual models. As mentioned, each item varies from 0 to 3; thus, the differences for each pair of items (between the perception of delegation/participation in GJM decision making, and how an activist values delegation/participation as democratic ideals) can vary from –3 to +3 (that is, if an activist perceives that only a few people participate at the GJM decision making, the relative value is 0, but s/he would prefer full participation as democratic ideal, whose value would be 3, the difference is –3), with 0 representing the value for a perfect congruence between normative ideals and the perception of actual decision making (in our example, if an activist perceives the participation of whoever wants to in GJM decision making – value 3 – and values full participation as a democratic ideal – value 3 – the difference is 0). Consequently, the further the value is from 0, the less the congruence between perceived practices and ideal models of decision making.

To calculate an index that measures the level of 'incongruence' regardless of its direction, we transformed the negative values into positive ones: for each item we get an index that varies from 0 (full congruence) to 3 (full incongruence). We also calculated a synthetic additive index, which adds the four indexes and divides the sum by 4.[10] According to the latter, activists showing full congruence (0) and full incongruence (3) both amount to only about 5 per cent; 50 per cent show a relatively high degree of congruence (1) and about 40 per cent a relatively high degree of incongruence (2). The correlations between all indexes of incongruence with (dis)satisfaction with democracy within the GJM show that the more incongruent the (normative and perceived) models, the less the activists are satisfied.[11] If we recode the synthetic additive index of congruency in two categories, 77 per cent of the (more or less) 'congruent' activists are satisfied, as compared to only 61 per cent of the (more or less) 'incongruent' ones. Thus, according to our findings, satisfaction with democracy within the GJM is a function of two main factors: how democracy is perceived at that level, and the congruence between this perception and the normative ideals of democracy that activists hold.

Interestingly, the two findings point in two different directions: while the first one confirms that, as 'deliberative' scholars have been arguing, deliberation has a legitimizing effect for decision making – the second one would limit this only to individuals who hold a deliberative-normative model of democracy. For those who support a different normative model (associational, assembleary, and so on), what counts is the distance between their ideals and their perception of the actual democratic practices: the greater this distance, the lower their satisfaction, whatever the model.

Indeed, the level of incongruence is a function of the models of democracy perceived at the GJM level: more than 58 per cent of activists who perceive the GJM as 'associational' or 'deliberative-representative' find those models far from their democratic ideals, while this percentage goes down to 24 and 27 per cent when activists perceive an 'assembleary' or a 'deliberative-participative' setting (the Cramer's V of the cross-tabulation is 0.326, significant at 0.001 level).

Finally, we can have a more accurate view of the relevant factors which explain (dis)satisfaction with internal democracy, if we use a regression analysis with satisfaction as the dependent variable and the indicators of perceived democratic models and incongruence as independent variables. Such an analysis will allow us not only to see which factor better explains satisfaction, but also which dimension matters the most.

As can be seen in Table 4.6, if we only test the impact of the dimensions of incongruence, the most important explanatory variables refer to the 'argument/ resources' and the 'equals/non acceptance' dimensions: the more the activists' ideals are dissonant with their perceptions of democratic settings in the GJM on those dimensions, the less they are satisfied with democracy at that level. On the 'argument/resource' item, 76.4 per cent of 'more or less' congruent activists are (moderately or much) satisfied, as compared to 55.6 per cent of the 'more or less' incongruent ones; on the 'equals/non acceptance' dimension, the finding is similar (74.4 per cent versus 58 per cent). On the contrary, the incongruence on the other two dimensions (delegation/participation and vote/consensus) is not relevant to satisfaction.

However, if we now introduce the dimensions of the perceived GJM democratic settings in the regression, the picture changes. In Model 2, in fact, no dimension related to incongruence has an impact on the dependent variable, while two dimensions of the perceived GJM democracy significantly explain part of the variation. Those are the 'equals/non equals' and the 'delegation/ participation' dimensions. To report this another way, 58 per cent of the activists who believe that participants are not treated as equals in the GJM democratic settings and 62 per cent of those who perceive a mechanism of delegation declare themselves to be satisfied with democracy in the movement, while the

Table 4.6 Linear regression analysis with 'satisfaction with GJM democracy' (0–3) as dependent variable

Independent variables	Model 1		Model 2	
	Standardized b	Sig.	Standardized b	Sig.
Degree of incongruence in...				
Item 1 (arguments/resources)	–0.183	0.000	–0.070	n.s.
Item 2 (equals/non acceptance)	–0.109	0.004	–0.037	n.s.
Item 3 (delegation/participation)	–0.056	n.s.	–0.043	n.s.
Item 4 (voting/consensus)	–0.021	n.s.	0.018	n.s.
Perceived dimensions of democracy in GJM				
Item 1 (arguments/resources)	–	–	–0.099	n.s.
Item 2 (equals/non acceptance)	–	–	–0.106 (equals)	0.037
Item 3 (delegation/participation)	–	–	0.113 (participation)	0.007
Item 4 (voting/consensus)	–	–	–0.007	n.s.
R square	0.071		0.103 Sig. F change,	0.000

percentage of satisfied activists increases to 77 per cent and 79 per cent respectively for those who perceive equal treatment of participants and the openness of decision making settings to whoever wants to participate. Once full participation and equality are perceived, satisfaction increases whatever the method of decision making (vote or consensus), and whatever the level of incongruence between their democratic ideals and the way in which GJM democracy is perceived. To conclude, although both incongruence and perception of how democracy works within the GJM contribute to explaining satisfaction, the latter offers a more powerful explanation.

All the findings reported in this section allow us to build a model to explain participation in GJM events and activities that emphasizes the role of internal decision making or, put in another way, an explanation of how collective action is built through norms. Participation is in fact a function of identification (Kendall's tau-b is 0.329, significant at 0.001 level), which in turns depends (also) on the degree of activists' satisfaction with how democracy works in the GJM (Kendall's tau-b is 0.241, significant at 0.001 level), the latter being higher when an open (meaning participatory) and equal decision making process is perceived to be at work (Kendall's tau-b coefficients are respectively 0.202 and 0.235, both significant at 0.001 level).[12]

Conclusions

In this chapter, we addressed the democratic normative dimension of political activism in the GJM. We highlighted the fact that although the GJM has promoted a normative idea of democracy that values both full participation and consensus, the ESF process has often been criticized for its actual democratic practices. An internal conflict between 'vertical' and 'horizontal' activists has created dissatisfaction with the way in which decisions are taken when a European Social Forum is being organized. Referring to the data on the organizational level, we showed that in fact, the organizations that participate in the GJM activities are characterized by varying views of democracy. The organizational statutes, expressing (like the constitution of a state) their fundamental values, confirm tensions between delegation and participation, majority vote and consensus. In comparison with organizational documents, the interviewed representatives of the organizations put more emphasis on consensual decision making, and the activists surveyed at the ESF stressed participation as a normative value. The activists themselves reported that in their group, and similarly in the GJM, the normatively supported principles of full participation of all members and consensual decision making are not always met. Nonetheless, activists participating at the ESF in Athens seemed to be very satisfied with democracy working at the group level and in the GJM meetings. We also found that participation in the GJM strengthened participative and deliberative visions of democracy.

The fact that many activists stress full participation of all those interested and consensus when they are asked to judge what makes decision making fully democratic reveals an incongruence between their values and practices that has been worth analysing. Incongruence between activists' democratic values and their perception of how decisions are taken during the GJM's meetings seems, in fact, to explain part of the variation in satisfaction with democracy in the movement. Moreover, we found that activists' satisfaction in the GJM meetings is higher when they perceive that those who defend different and conflicting opinions treat each other as equals, and especially when the full participation of all those who are interested is promoted.

This is an interesting result for the theory of democracy, since deliberative theorists have long debated the legitimating effect of deliberation. Besides being congruent with normative ideals of democracy, participative and consensual decision making settings are also effective, in the sense that decisions are legitimized by the very procedure through which they have been taken. Moreover, it seems that the procedure of inclusion fosters those 'civic skills' that citizens need to get involved in politics: in the GJM the inclusion in decision making generates a satisfaction with democracy that is highly correlated with identification with the movement and participation in collective actions. Far from being only theoretically relevant, those findings confirm that democracy is not only a matter of ideals, but also a matter of how to get those ideals practised here and now.

Notes

1 Donatella della Porta is the principal author of 'Democracy as a multidimensional concept'; Massimiliano Andretta is the principal author of 'Satisfaction with GJM democracy: what for and how it is achieved' and 'Conclusions'.
2 See, for example, www.lokabass.com. Online, available at www.lokabass.com/scriba/eventi.php?id_eve=12 accessed 12 December 2006; see also Chapter 1 in this volume.
3 See, for instance, the criticism by Bernard Cassen in *Le Monde diplomatique* of the Italian pressure to hold the first ESF in Florence.
4 This and the following quotes are taken from documents published online in 'ESF: Debating the Challenges for its Future', newsletter collecting articles and reflections on the third ESF. Online, available at: www.euromovements.info/newsletter/index.htm accessed 24 December 2006.
5 According to Callinicos,

> At different stages this process embraced a very wide range of forces – stretching from the Trade Union Congress and mainstream NGOs to autonomist groups with a history of intermittent violence such as the Wombles. Holding this coalition together would have been difficult in any circumstances. Of course, the Italian and French comrades also have developed very broad coalitions, but it was probably an advantage that these had been constructed well in advance of actually organizing the ESF, so that people had an experience of working together. In Britain, by contrast, the *altermondialiste* networks that had participated in the earlier Forums were relatively weak. A coalition had to be created from scratch to organise the London ESF. This involved bringing together very diverse organisations with no history of working together and huge differences in political culture. Working together would have been hard in any circumstances.
>
> (ESF no date)

6 In each country and at the transnational level, we selected about 30 organizations that had been involved in the main initiatives of the GJM (among them the European social forums), insuring variance especially on the main issues addressed. Lists of organizations that had signed calls for action of social forums (at the national, European, and global levels) and other important movement events were used to single out the groups belonging to the 'core' of the GJM's networks. A common sampling strategy was agreed upon in order to collect comparable data, covering SMOs representing different streams within the movement (environmentalist, pacifist, women's rights, unions, gay, migrant and human rights activists, squatters, and so on), organizations that stemmed from the GJM (local social forums, Attac), as well as websites of media close to the GJM (periodical magazines, radio stations, newspapers, and networks of independent communication). See della Porta (2009).
7 Though we aimed at covering the same organizations for the two types of analysis (documents and interviews with representatives), this was not always possible. We did interview the representatives of about 90 per cent per cent of the organizations whose documents were analysed in the previous part of the research.
8 For the operationalization of the index, we first dichotomized the four items by assigning the value 1 when 'arguments', 'equality', 'participation' and 'consensus' are considered important, and the value 0 when the opposite ('resource', 'non acceptance', 'delegation', 'vote') is true. Eventually we summed the four dichotomies in our index, which then varies from '0' (no deliberativeness) to '4' (full deliberativeness).
9 We operationalized the index of perceived deliberation in GJM in same way as the index of activists' normative deliberativeness (see note 8).
10 This means that the synthetic index will also vary from 0 to 3.
11 The Kendall's tau-b of the correlations (N = 792–839) are as follows: -0.227^{***} for item 1; -0.177^{***} for item 2; -0.079^{**} for item 3; -0.104^{**} for item 4, and -0.196^{***}

for the synthetic additive indexes of deliberation (at the normative and at the descriptive level).
12 The R square resulting from a regression analysis with participation in GJM events (collective action) as dependent variable and the identification, satisfaction, and the two items, full participation and equality, of the perception of GJM internal democracy as independent, is 0.164, significant at 0.001 level.

5 Democracy from below
Activists and institutions

Donatella della Porta and Marco Giugni

> Although the EU is one of the richest areas of the world, tens of millions of people are living in poverty, either because of mass unemployment or the casualization of labour. The policies of the EU based on the unending extension of competition within and outside Europe constitute an attack on employment, workers and welfare rights, public services, education, the health system and so on. The EU is planning the reduction of workers' wages and employment benefits as well as the generalisation of casualization. We reject this neo-liberal Europe and any efforts to re-launch the rejected Constitutional Treaty; we are fighting for another Europe, a feminist, ecological, open Europe, a Europe of peace, social justice, sustainable life, food sovereignty and solidarity, respecting minorities' rights and the self-determination of all peoples.
> (Declaration of the Assembly of the Movements of the fourth European Social Forum 2006)

This is how the Declaration of the Assembly of the Movements of the fourth European Social Forum in Athens addresses the European Union on 7 May 2006. It rejects neither the need for a European level of governance, nor the existence of a European identity (that goes beyond the borders of the EU), but criticizes EU policies and asks for 'another Europe': a feminist, ecological, open, supportive, and just Europe. Similarly, the previous Assembly of the Movements, held at the third ESF in 2004, stated:

> We are fighting for another Europe. Our mobilisations bring hope of a Europe where job insecurity and unemployment are not part of the agenda. We are fighting for viable agriculture controlled by the farmers themselves, a farming industry that preserves jobs, and defends the quality of the environment and food products as public assets. We want to open Europe up to the world, with the right to asylum, free movement of people and citizenship for everyone in the country they live in. We demand real social equality between men and women, and equal pay. Our Europe will respect and promote cultural and linguistic diversity and respect the right of peoples to self-determination and allow all the different peoples of Europe to decide

upon their futures democratically. We are struggling for another Europe, which is respectful of workers' rights and guarantees a decent salary and a high level of social protection. We are struggling against any laws that establish insecurity through new ways of subcontracting work.

In these statements, as in many others, the ESF confirms its attention to interactions (although challenging ones) with the institutions of global, multilevel governance. Although addressed within a global discourse, Europe and European institutions are at the centre of attention. It is on these positions that this chapter focuses.

Research on social movements has often stressed the relationship between 'conventional' and 'unconventional' politics – or challengers and polity members, to use Tilly's (1978) expression. A major contribution of the 'political process' approach to social movements has indeed been its stress on the continuities in various forms of political participation in general, and between the characteristics of democratic regimes and the forms of protest in particular. Not only does democracy rise from 'disorder' (Tarrow 1989), but institutions shape social movements, their strength and their strategies. In fact, studies on social movements have often highlighted the role of political opportunities in facilitating participation, with the underlying assumption that it increases as access to public decision making becomes at least in part more open, the administrative units more decentralized, and the legislative, executive, and judiciary powers more distinct. Furthermore, the availability of allies, divisions within the government, or institutional reforms that ease bottom-up access are said to facilitate collective mobilization (Tarrow 1994; della Porta and Diani 2006).

The attention to the 'external dimension' of democracy is also linked to the strategic need to address some challenges to democracy, as it has traditionally been implemented in representative, liberal democracies. The movement for a globalization from below grew at a time of dramatic changes in the political process that have in fact affected the opportunities for protest. First, the growth of international governmental institutions challenges the principles and institutions of representative democracy that have been built up within the nation state (Held and McGrew 2000). Second, neoliberal economic policies, by increasing the power of multinational corporations, have reduced the capacity of traditional state institutions to control and steer the market (Pizzorno 2001; Crouch 2004).

Beyond suggesting policy changes, in a more reformist or radical fashion, the ESF is addressing these challenges through a critique of representative forms of democracy. In this endeavour, the movement is redrawing the boundaries of politics, broadening them in a more participatory direction (della Porta *et al.* 2006a). The self-definition as 'a movement for a globalization from below' stresses the fundamental criticism of 'top-down' representative democracy. The ESF criticizes supranational institutions not only for the specific policies they adopt, but also for their deficits in terms of democratic accountability. On the other hand, national representative democracies are stigmatized for being powerless – or at best inadequate to guide globalization – and for the growing insufficiency of mechanisms of electoral accountability faced with the greater power of the executive vis-à-vis parliament as well as the personalization of politics through the manipulative use of the mass media (della Porta and Tarrow 2005).

In this chapter, we will address the 'external' dimension of the conceptions of democracy by focusing on three main aspects: (*a*) trust in various types of institutions; linked to this, (*b*) the solutions envisioned for 'another democracy', with particular attention to the territorial level of governance; and, finally, (*c*) the preferences for a strategy of political mobilization, with interactions with the various public institutions, or the focus on more autonomy and the construction of 'free space'. We address these issues in two steps. In the first and the second parts, we discuss attitudes towards institutions located at various levels of governance as well as more general views of democracy and politics by participants in the ESF, based on descriptive analyses of our data. Here in particular, we stress changes over time by comparing the data on the fourth ESF in Athens with evidence from previous ESFs. In looking at differences over time, however, we shall keep in mind the different composition of the first three ESF events, particularly with regard to their location and, therefore, the large presence of activists from the host country. In the third part, focusing exclusively on the data from the ESF in Athens, we adopt a more explanatory approach in order to see what factors are associated with differences in participants' trust in different types of institutions, in the solutions they envisage to strengthen governance and democracy, and in their strategies of political mobilization.

Multilevel governance and trust in institutions: localist, nationalist or cosmopolitan?[1]

Previous surveys have indicated that activists internalize their organizations' criticism of representative democracy. Among the participants who protested against the G8 in Genoa, trust in representative institutions tended to be low, although with significant differences regarding the single institutions (see also della Porta *et al.* 2006a). In general, some international organizations (especially the EU and the United Nations) were seen by activists as more worthy of respect than their national governments, but less so than local bodies. Research on the first ESF confirmed that diffidence towards the institutions of representative democracy is spread cross-nationally, although particularly pronounced where national governments are either right-wing (Italy and Spain at the time), or perceived as hostile to the GJM's demands (as in the UK). Not even national parliaments, supposedly the main instrument of representative democracy, were trusted, while there was markedly greater trust in local bodies (especially in Italy and France), and, albeit somewhat lower, in the United Nations. The EU scored a trust level among activists that was barely higher than that for national governments.

Similar data on the second and the fourth ESF confirm the general mistrust in representative democratic institutions, especially in national governments, followed by the EU and then the UN (which were more trusted by the activists in Florence and in Paris), with more trust in local institutions (although much less than in the first and second ESFs), despite some qualification (della Porta 2007a). Among other actors and institutions, we might notice a much lower level of trust in the church and mass media, as well as in the unions in general, and a similarly low trust in the judiciary and (even lower) in political parties (Table 5.1). Rather, activists continue to trust social movements (and, a bit less, NGOs) as actors of a democracy from below. In sum, in seeking 'another Europe', one central feature is mistrust of parties and representative institutions. The common location of activists on the left of the political spectrum is blended with a high interest in politics, defined as politics 'from below', but mistrust in the actors of institutional politics. Mistrust is higher among the surveyed activists in 2006 than in 2002 and 2003.

A look at the minutes of the debates and other documents about the forums helps to locate the criticism of representative institutions in a broader frame. In this part, we shall look in particular at the positions towards Europe, a central focus of the ESF. A general complaint is that the EU uses its competences on market competition and free trade to impose neoliberal economic policies, while the restrictive budgetary policies set by the Maastricht parameters are stigmatized as jeopardizing welfare policies. The privatization of public services and increasing flexibility of labour are criticized as worsening citizens' wellbeing

Table 5.1 Trust in institutions of ESF participants in Florence, Paris, and Athens (valid cases only)

Type of institution[1]	Florence 2002		Paris 2003		Athens 2006	
	%	N	%	N	%	N
Local institutions	46.1	2,365	43.1	2,034	26.6	1,122
National government	6.1	2,451	11.6	1,997	11.5	1,126
National parliament	14.9	2,428	–	–	20.5	1,130
European Union	26.9	2,444	17.3	2,002	14.5	1,141
United Nations	29.6	2,444	31.7	1,985	18.1	1,136
Political parties	20.4	2,423	23.0	2,007	21.2	1,120
Unions	16.1[2]	–	57.5	2,025	49.0	1,122
Social movements	–	–	90.0	2,067	85.7	1,139
NGOs	–	–	77.3	2,002	66.8	1,132
Social movements and NGOs	89.4	2,464	–	–	–	–
Church	17.2	2,441	15.5	1,987	9.1	1,135
Mass media	12.4	2,449	9.3	2,010	3.9	1,142
Judiciary	36.7	2,429	–	–	33.8	1,136
Police	7.3	2,454	–	–	10.7	1,132

Notes
1 The degree of trust was translated into a dichotomous variable in the following way: 'not at all' and 'little' = 'no'; 'a fair amount' and 'a lot' = 'yes'.
2 The data refers to respondents to the non-Italian version: N = 417. In the Italian version, respondents were asked about their trust in specific unions, with the following results: trust in Cisl/Uil: N = 229; 8.9%; trust in Cgil: N = 1,104, 42.8%; trust in grassroots trade unions: N = 990, 38.4%.

and job security. Under the slogan 'another Europe is possible', various proposals were tabled at the first ESF, including 'taxation of capital' and, again, the Tobin Tax. At the second ESF, the European Social Consult stated,

> We have learnt to recognise the strength of coordinated action and the vulnerability of the 'untouchable' organisations of capitalism. We need to deepen our contact and communication with society, decentralizing our struggle and working in local and regional context in a coordinated way with common objectives ... the European Union is being shaped under the neoliberal politics. The European constitution comes to reinforce it and next year it will be our main goal to fight it.
> (http://workspace.fse-esf.org 2007)

In particular, the constitutional treaty is feared as the 'constitutionalization of neoliberalism'. A participant at the seminar 'For a democratic Europe, a Europe of rights and citizenship' claimed that

> The first part of the text is similar to a constitution. But the third one, which focuses on the implementation of concrete policies, goes beyond the normal frame of a constitution. It constitutionalises competition rights. Making rigid the policies to be followed, it takes away from the citizens all possibilities to change the rules. It is an unacceptable practice because it is anti-democratic. Anyway, all changes are made impossible by the need to obtain a unanimous vote by 25 states.

In the third part, 'everything is subordinated to competition, including public services, the relations with the DOM-TOM, and the flow of capital (something that, by the way, makes any Tobin Tax impossible)'.

The activists criticize the lack of democratic accountability:

> At the local level we have very little influence on the decision making process, but our influence becomes null when it comes to questions such as the European constitution or the directives of the WTO or the IMF. We are even criminalised when we attempt it.
> (http://workspace.fse-esf.org 2007)

The WIDE-European NGO Network, together with the Rosa Luxemburg foundation, link democracy to the provision of basic services and goods such as education, health, and water, subordinated to democratic decisions involving the local community, stating that public services are the bases of fundamental rights and stressing the need to democratize the provision of public services.

Beyond concrete policy choices, criticisms are also addressed to the secretive, top-down ways in which these policies are decided. The Assembly of Social Movements at the third ESF asked, among others, for more participation 'from below' in the construction of 'another Europe':

At a time when the draft of the European Constitutional treaty is about to be ratified, we must state that the peoples of Europe need to be consulted directly. The draft does not meet our aspirations. This constitutional treaty consecrates neo-liberalism as the official doctrine of the EU; it makes competition the basis for European community law, and indeed for all human activity; it completely ignores the objectives of an ecologically sustainable society. This constitutional treaty does not grant equal rights, the free movement of people and citizenship for everyone in the country they live in, whatever their nationality; it gives NATO a role in European foreign policy and defence, and pushes for the militarization of the EU. Finally it puts the market first by marginalising the social sphere, and hence accelerating the destruction of public services.

Criticisms of the conceptions of democracy at EU level also address security policies, with a call for a Europe of freedoms and justice against a Europe *'sécuritaire et policière'*. At the first ESF, the EU stance on foreign policy was considered as subordinate to the US, environmental issues as dominated by the environmentally-unfriendly demands of corporations, and migration policy as oriented towards building a xenophobic 'Fortress Europe'. At the Paris ESF, the construction of a European judicial space was considered as a way to control police power. In particular, EU legislation on terrorism was criticized as criminalizing such broad categories as the young, refugees, and Muslims. EU immigration policies were defined as obsessed with issues of security and demographic needs (with a semantic shift from 'Muslim' to 'youth', and from 'youth' to 'potential terrorist'). The official lists of 'terrorist organizations' by various national and international institutions are considered as arbitrary, as they include even groups that had previously been funded by the EU. Repressive measures are also criticized as ineffective, and the need for political solutions is stressed. While terrorism is stigmatized, there is a call to 'take a clear stand for international law, including the right of people to fight occupation', but also to 'defend national sovereignty'.

As for the EU foreign policy, criticisms address the subordination of humanitarian politics and developmental aid to commercial and security aims, and the misrecognition of the important role of the local population. Solidarity groups denounce the role of European states and corporations in Haiti, Latin America, and Africa, expressing disapproval of aggressive EU trade policies and asymmetric negotiations of commercial treaties. In terms of defence policies, proposals tabled during the ESFs range from 'a Europe without NATO, EU- and US army bases' to multilateralism, from the refusal of a nuclear Europe to more resources for the UN and the request for a mention in the constitution of the refusal of war as an instrument of conflict resolution.

Activists present at the various ESFs share these criticisms of EU politics and policies. At the first ESF, interviewees from different countries stated in fact that the European Union strengthens neoliberal globalization, expressing scepticism about the capacity of the EU to mitigate the negative effects of globalization and to safeguard a different social model of welfare (Table 5.2). The data from the survey at the 2005 demonstration in Rome protesting the EU Bolkestein directive confirm this image (with even stronger disagreement on the capacity of the EU to mitigate the negative consequences of economic globalization) (della Porta and Andretta 2006). In both cases, activists were convinced that the EU favours neoliberal globalization and that it is unable to mitigate the negative effects of globalization and safeguard a different social model of welfare. At the first ESF, Italians expressed greater trust in the EU and British activists were more sceptical (followed by the French and Spanish activists). The differences, however, were small overall. Comparing the distributions on these items of the Italians at the ESF in 2002 with those of the anti-Bolkestein marchers in Rome, we can see that opinions remained stable and consistently pessimistic.

Table 5.2 How much do you agree with the following statements? (weighted sample first ESF)

a) The European Union attempts to safeguard a social model that is different from the neo-liberal one

	Italy	France	Germany	Spain	UK	Total ESF	Rome 2005
A little	43.7	35.8	43.6	38.5	26.1	36.8	37.7
Some	8.9	8.2	7.7	6.4	4.2	7.0	11.7
Very much	0.7	5.2	1.3	3.7	1.4	2.5	4.0
Total	100%	100%	100%	100%	100%	100%	100%
N	135	134	78	109	142	598	410

b) The European Union mitigates the most negative effects of neo-liberal globalization

	Italy	France	Germany	Spain	UK	Total ESF	Rome 2005
A little	51.1	27.9	48.6	40.4	21.7	36.6	40.5
Some	15.1	13.2	14.9	10.1	5.6	11.5	11.7
Very much	2.2	8.8	6.8	5.5	13.3	7.5	1.5
Total	100%	100%	100%	100%	100%	100%	100%
N	139	136	74	109	143	601	410

c) The European Union strengthens neo-liberal globalisation

	Italy	France	Germany	Spain	UK	Total ESF	Rome 2005
A little	18.7	6.0	4.9	6.3	5.4	8.6	11.8
Some	43.2	32.8	35.4	38.7	15.0	32.3	31.7
Very much	34.5	58.2	57.3	53.2	73.5	55.5	48.2
Total	100%	100%	100%	100%	100%	100%	100%
N	139	134	82	111	147	613	410

Multilevel governance: which solutions?

Although critical of existing institutions, the GJM does seem aware of the need for supranational (macroregional and/or global) institutions of governance. At one of the plenary assemblies of the second ESF, Italian activist Franco Russo stated: 'There is a real desire for Europe ... but not for any Europe. The European citizens ask for a Europe of rights: social, environmental and peaceful. But does this Constitution respond to our desire for Europe?'. The representative of the French union *federation G10 Solidaires*, Pierre Khalfa, declared that the constitutional treaty 'is a document to be rejected ... [but] the discussion of the project is the occasion for a Europe-wide mobilisation' (*Liberazione* 14 November 2003).

The image of 'another Europe' (rather than 'no Europe') is often stressed in the debates. During the second ESF, the Assembly of the Unemployed and Precarious Workers in Struggle stated that 'For the European union, Europe is only a large free-exchange area. We want a Europe based on democracy, citizenship, equality, peace, a job and revenue in order to live. Another Europe for another World'. In this vision, the building of 'another Europe imposes putting the democratic transformation of institutions at the centre of elaboration and mobilisation. We can, we should have great political ambition for Europe ... *Cessons de subir l'Europe: prenons la en mains*' (http://workspace.fse-esf.org 2006). Unions and other groups active in public service proclaimed 'the European level as the pertinent level of resistance', among others against national decisions. The 'No to the Constitutional draft' is combined with demands for a 'legitimate European constitution' produced through public consultation, 'a European constitution constructed from below'. And many agree that 'the Europe we have to build is a Europe of rights, and participatory democracy is its engine'. In this vision, 'the European Social Forum constitutes the peoples as constitutional power, the only legitimate power'. In a report on the seminar 'Our vision for the future of Europe', we read:

> Lacking a clear and far reaching vision the EU-governments are stumbling from conference to conference. In this manner the EU will not survive the challenges of the coming decades! Too many basic problems have been avoided due to a lack of a profound strategic position. In our vision we outlined an alternative model for the future of Europe. It contains a clear long term position on Europe making a clear choice for the improvement of the quality of life for all and for responsible and peaceful development.
> (http://workspace.fse-esf.org no date)

When moving from the assessment of existing institutions to imagined ones, the activists of the first ESF expressed strong interest in the building of new institutions of world governance: 70 per cent of the respondents were quite or very much in favour of this, including strengthening the United Nations, an option supported by about half our sample (Table 5.3). Furthermore, about one-third of activists agree that in order to achieve the goals of the movement, a stronger EU

Table 5.3 Opinion of ESF participants in Florence and Athens about which institutions should be strengthened to achieve global social movement's goals (valid cases)[1]

Type of institution[2]	Florence 2002		Athens 2006	
	%	N	%	N
Strengthen national governments	22.0	2,362	25.6	1,066
Strengthen European Union[3]	43.2	2,383	34.9	1,073
Strengthen United Nations	56.6	2,405	48.4	1,056
Building institutions of world governance[4]	64.6	2,400	92.5	1,127

Notes
1 Question from the Florence questionnaire: 'In your opinion, to achieve the goals of the movement it would be necessary to strengthen....'; question from the Athens questionnaire: 'In your opinion, what should be done to tame neo-liberal globalization? Strengthen...'.
2 The level of disagreement/agreement was translated into a dichotomous variable in the following way: 'strongly disagree' and 'disagree' = 'no'; 'agree' and 'strongly agree' = 'yes'.
3 The Florence questionnaire asked about the strengthening of EU or other international super-national institutions.
4 The Athens questionnaire asked about the building of new institutions that involve the civil society on the international level; the Florence questionnaire asked about the building of new institutions of world governance.

and/or other regional institutions are necessary (with higher support for the EU among Italian activists and very low support among British activists). Respondents in Athens confirmed a widely shared scepticism that strengthening the national governments would help in achieving the goals of the movement (only about one-fifth of the activists responded positively). Confirming the trends already observed on the battery of questions on trust in institutions, between the first and the fourth ESFs the belief in the need for building (alternative) institutions of world governance became unanimous (93 per cent of the respondents), with a lower percentage in Athens in support of strengthening the EU (from 43 to 35 per cent) and/or the UN (from 57 to 48 per cent).

The activists of the first European Social Forum expressed quite a high level of affective identification with Europe: only 18 per cent felt not at all attached, 34 per cent felt little attached, 37 per cent enough, and 11 per cent very much. This means about half of the activists feel enough or a strong attachment to Europe (also in this case with less support from British and Spanish activists and more from French, Germans, and Italians). The activists of the ESFs therefore do not seem to be eurosceptics, wanting to return to an almighty nation state, but rather 'critical Europeanists' (or 'critical globalists'), convinced that transnational institutions of governance are necessary, but that they should be built from below.

These individual positions are also in line with the debates in the ESFs. At the first ESF in Florence, specific proposals for changes in EU policies came from networks of social movement organisations and from NGOs often already active on specific issues. The European Assembly of the Unemployed and Precarious Workers in Struggle stressed the importance of developing claims at the EU level (for example, a minimal salary of 50 per cent of the average); a network of the unions of cadres proposed a *Charte de responsabilité de cadres a l'echelle europèenne*; groups involved in the promotion of Esperanto as well as associations from ethnic minorities developed proposals for linguistic and cultural rights; and the European social consult asked to 'strengthen and widen the European social fabric in a network that should be participatory, horizontal and decentralised, as much in the taking of the decisions as it is in putting them into practice' (http://workspace.fse-esf.org 2007). Proposals for economic reform were developed by the European Union for Research on Economic Democracy. Humanitarian NGOs debated measures against religious and ethnic discrimination, including the potential effects of EU directives and national legislation. Cuts in indirect taxation and assistance for weaker social groups as well as a strengthening of public services were also called for.

Concrete proposals to improve the quality of democracy were also developed at the second ESF. They ranged from the establishment of an annual day of action devoted to media democracy to the building of alternative media (workshop on Reclaim the Channels of Information: media campaigns and media protest); from the reduction of import taxes on medicines to the increase in use of non-conventional medicines (seminar on Health in Europe: equity and access); from the introduction of the right to asylum in the European constitution to the regularization of all undocumented migrants (workshop on Right to Migrate, Right to Asylum); from a European social charter that recognizes the right to decent housing to the occupation of empty buildings (workshop on Housing Rights in Europe: towards a trans-European network of struggles and alternatives); from the dialogue with local authorities to participation of the people in international experiences of cooperation (workshop on Decentralized Cooperation: a dialogue between territories as a response to global challenges); from quality control on hard drugs to the liberalization of soft ones (workshop on Perfect Enemies: the penal governance of poverty and differences). Specific debates focused upon issues such as EU policies on commercial agreements; youth rights in Europe; Christianity, Islam and Judaism in Europe; nationalist extremism in Europe; financiarization and workfare; the contribution of the Church to the construction of a new Europe; European policy on employment; Europe seen by African eyes; ecological crises in Europe; the place of Islam in Europe; and Islamophobia.

Europe remained similarly central at the fourth Forum, where seminars (the large majority with 'Europe' in their titles) discussed such diverse issues as the fight against poverty and institutional racism in Europe, the charter of common principles of another Europe and the restriction of liberties, health systems and NATO, camps for migrants and the Abdullah Ocalan case, education and relations with Southern Mediterranean countries, corporate politics and labour rights, relations with Latin America and with the UN, the populist Right and new oppositional actors, left-wing journalism and housing problems, the Bolkestein directive and precarious workers, the Lisbon and Bologna strategy and constitution building, local governance and the WTO, taxation and

Islamophobia, violence against women and student mobility, linguistic equality and basic income, the rights of the Roma and US military bases, agricultural policy and psychiatric hospitals, human trafficking and sanctions against Israel, monotheistic religions and a position towards Cuba.

In Florence, the Call of the European Social Movements already framed all of these themes under the label of a struggle against neoliberalism:

> We have gathered in Florence to express our opposition to a European order based on corporate power and neoliberalism. This market model leads to constant attacks on the conditions and rights of workers, social inequalities, and the oppression of ethnic minorities, and the social exclusion of the unemployed and migrants. It leads to environmental degradation, privatisation and job insecurity. It drives powerful countries to try and dominate the economies of weaker countries, often denying them real self determination. Once more it is leading to war.

The discourse on the defence of the common goods (such as water) is framed as oriented to overcome the culture of merchandising, but also as a conception of national sovereignty that refuses solidarity with the external world. At the same time, there is the attempt to enlarge the notion of Europe beyond the European Union and the fear of an exclusive European identity as representing the 'civilized' culture against the non-European civilizations. Critical of 'the arbitrary decision of the EU to cut funds to the National Palestinian Authority', the Declaration of the Assembly of the Movements of the fourth European Social Forum warned of the dangers of a polarization of global citizens along a 'clash of civilizations', which would justify further discrimination against the people of the South. It stated that: 'Conservative forces in the north and the south are encouraging a "clash of civilizations" aimed at dividing oppressed people, which is in turn producing unacceptable violence, barbarism and additional attacks on the rights and dignity of migrants and minorities'.

Politics, antipolitics, alterpolitics: how to change the world?

Beyond discussing the territorial dimension of power, the data on the trust/mistrust in different political and social actors also help to address another relevant issue. Social movements have traditionally been classified as political versus culturally oriented, or seeking power versus personal change. The GJM is pragmatic in the development of proposals for policy changes but at the same time also expresses little interest in 'taking power', insisting instead upon a search for the construction of alternative, free spaces.

Movement politics is in fact conceived as alternative to institutional politics and based on interaction between society and politics. The presence in the movement of activists with previous experiences in voluntary associations of various types is reflected in a conception of politics as direct commitment. As an Italian activist declared during a focus group:

I never went in for politics, but before I always did voluntary stuff... I think there's now this merger between voluntary work and politics in the strictest sense ... and this is maybe the novelty that gives the impetus, the fuel that makes the forces of two worlds that were perhaps a bit separate before come together.

(Della Porta 2005b: 193)

In general, we have to consider that our activists are well endowed with experience of political participation in various (conventional and less conventional) forms. Activities such as signing petitions, participating in assemblies, or marching in the street are performed by almost the totality of our sample. Activism or previous activism in political parties is higher in Athens than it was in Florence, a result that resonates with a growing interest in the ESF by activists of the more institutionalized organizations (Table 5.4). However, experiences with direct forms of action such as occupations and blockades are lower among the participants in Athens than they were in Florence, a trend that can be linked to the higher participation in these activities in Italy (della Porta et al. 2006a) as well as the

Table 5.4 Previous political activities of ESF participants in Athens, Florence, and Paris (valid cases)

Type of activity	Florence 2002		Paris 2003		Athens 2006	
	%	N	%	N	%	N
Persuaded someone to vote for a political party	51.8	2,494	–	–	54.1	1,193
Active for a political party	33.5	2,496	–	–	41.2	1,193
Signed a petition/public letter/referendum[1]	88.8	2,509	96.3	2,102	84.2	1,194
Distribution of leaflets	73.4	2,498	74.0	1,970	70.9	1,194
Assembly/discussion group[2]	91.3	2,512	83.3	2,010	–	–
Symbolic action	–	–	64.9	1,885	–	–
Non-violent direct action	–	–	–	–	54.7	1,193
Cultural action	–	–	–	–	58.2	1,194
Demonstration march	–	–	95.5	2,080	92.6	1,194
Strike	86.0	2,507	71.2	1,950	56.7	1,194
Boycott of products	65.8	2,494	74.7	2,003	68.8	1,194
Blockade/sit-in	67.9	2,480	47.7	1,865	31.2	1,193
Occupation of a public building	68.0	2,509	39.2	1,904	33.5	1,193
Occupation of abandoned homes/land	25.9	2,488	–	–	12.1	1,193
Violent attack on property	8.4	2,494	6.0	1,830	6.3	1,193

Notes
1 Florence questionnaire asks about signature of petition/public letter/referendum; Paris questionnaire asks about signature of petition; Athens questionnaire asks about signature of petition/public letter.
2 Paris questionnaire asks about participation in a reflection or discussion group; Florence questionnaire asks about participation in an assembly or congress.

progressive detachment from the forum of the more radical and 'horizontal' groups, which in fact attended parallel events in Athens. However, more than half of the participants in the fourth ESF declared having participated in non-violent direct actions, and about three-quarters of them in boycotts and leafleting.

In order to better understand the conceptions of politics in the GJM, we also asked participants of the Athens ESF to rank strategies oriented to enhance democracy according to their perceived importance (Table 5.5). The results attest to the activists' search for alternative conceptions of politics and democracy. The most traditional form of political participation, contacting political leaders, has the lowest level of support. This reflects the previously mentioned mistrust of parties and the belief that representative institutions are increasingly detached from citizens. The critique of parties – especially those potentially closest to the movement – concerns their conception of politics as an activity for professionals, even more than opposition to specific policy choices. The movement was said by one activist to stress 'a completely different model of self-representation, etc. that doesn't fit, doesn't gel with a party's way of selection from above' (della Porta 2005b: 196). The demand for politics coincides with a demand for participation against parties that have become bureaucracies founded upon delegation, stressing the (wrong) idea of politics as undertaken by professionals, interested at most in electorally exploiting the movement, while still denying its political nature.

Although significantly better supported, the participatory option of reliance upon protest as a main means of putting pressure upon decision makers is also considered as a priority (first or second option) by less than one-third of our interviewees. The movement's objective is in fact to 'make the world aware': in the words of one focus group participant, it 'does not have the objective of taking power, but of changing society in its relationships, in feelings, in relations with people, of building a different world; and a different world is built from below' (della Porta 2005b: 196).

In fact, respondents consider spreading information to the public to be more relevant than contacting politicians – which has indeed emerged in previous

Table 5.5 Strategies the global movement has to use in order to enhance democracy (%)

	Practise democracy in group life	*Take to the streets*	*Spread information to public*	*Promote alternative models*	*Contact political leaders*
Most important	27.6	15.8	26.7	35.7	7.4
Second most important	18.1	15.3	31.5	27.1	10.6
Third most important	21.5	22.1	24.9	18.4	9.3
Fourth most Important	22.7	30.2	13.9	13.5	13.9
Fifth most important	10.2	16.6	3.0	5.2	58.9
Total	100%	100%	100%	100%	100%
N	1,072	1,064	1,073	1,080	1,060

parts of our research as a privileged strategy also for the GJMOs (see Demos reports: della Porta and Mosca 2006; della Porta and Reiter 2006a). If the New Left in the 1970s was fascinated by a possible revolutionary seizure of power, activists in the GJM tend instead to present their action as oriented towards slow and gradual change. In this sense, one activist intervening in a focus group compared the movement to a river:

> The broader the river, the slower it flows ... sometimes it even seems as if it flows underground, just because it's so broad ... the movement is like water permeating and flowing everywhere, so that when it knocks the wall down it already owns the field.
>
> (Della Porta 2005b: 196)

Even more, the activists stress the importance of building alternative spheres of political engagement and discussion. They most often rank in the top position the practising of democracy in group life and, even more, the promotion of alternative political and social models. In the activists' perception, politics involves the search, through debates, for an emerging conception of the common good. In fact, the construction of 'convergence spaces' should 'facilitate the forging of an associational politics that constitutes a diverse, contested coalition of place-specific social movements' (Routledge 2003: 345). The 'forum' quality of some arenas such as the ESF is particularly relevant, as a place where 'critically collective discussion about members' interests and collective identities' develops (Lichterman 1999: 104). The importance of forming open spaces and concrete alternatives is, in fact, stressed in organizational documents. The coordination of the European Social Forum presents itself as having the task of constructing 'a wider public space in which the nets, associations, movements, social forums and different social actors can debate with each other and intertwine their content, practices and campaigns. A space that belongs to all' (quoted in Fruci 2003: 187). The Italian local social forums define themselves as open, public arenas for permanent discussion: a forum is, in this interpretation, 'a tribune for the local civil society' (ibid.: 174).

A critical stance toward institutional politics is confirmed by the attitudes towards and experiences of participation in experiments of participatory democracy, promoted especially at the local level. Particularly locally, so-called deliberative arenas have developed over the last decade, based on the principle of participation of 'normal citizens' in public arenas for debates, empowered by information and rules for high quality communication (Fung and Wright 2001). In Europe, deliberative arenas have been promoted in the forms of citizens' juries in Great Britain and Spain; *Plannunszelle* in Germany; Consensus Conferences in Denmark, *Conferences de citoyens* in France, as well as Agenda 21 and various experiments in strategic urban planning. The focus of these experiments – which imply the creation of new institutions and the devolution of decision making power, although with some coordination with representative institutions – is the search for a solution to specific problems by involving ordinary, affected people.

Actors associated with social movements have intervened in the development of some of these processes, sometimes as critical participants, sometimes as external opponents. In particular, participatory budgeting has been credited with creating a positive context for the development of associations, fostering greater activism, greater interconnectedness of associations, and a city-wide orientation (Baiocchi 2002). Various groups involved in the GJM have in particular sponsored the participative budgeting that allows citizens to decide upon part of their city's expenditure. Notwithstanding this basis for legitimacy, only one-third of our activists (30.7 per cent) strongly believe that these experiments will improve the quality of decision making, while 42.5 per cent are moderately optimistic and 14.3 per cent disagree (of those, 2.6 per cent strongly). Additionally, only 30 per cent have ever participated in such a process.

Explaining democratic views: trust, solutions, and strategies

So far we have addressed the 'external' dimension of democratic conceptions in a rather descriptive way, comparing in particular the findings from the survey we conducted at the 2006 ESF with those stemming from previous studies. In this part we give a more explanatory turn to our analysis. To do so we have conducted a series of multivariate regression analyses, taking as dependent variables, respectively, the level of trust ESF participants have with regard to various representative institutions (local governments, national governments, the EU, and the UN); solutions for improving democracy (strengthening national governments, strengthening the EU, strengthening the UN, and building new institutions at the EU level and at the international level); and strategies of political mobilization (contacting political leaders, practising democracy, considering that participation in decision making processes improves democracy, and participation in such processes).

We are interested in particular in assessing whether and to what extent commitment to the GJM and previous participation in political activities influence the democratic views of movement participants. Social scientists are in fact split on the question of whether the GJM can be considered as a social movement, although internally diverse ('a movement of movements' in the definition of the Italian activists), or as a coalition of different actors that occasionally come together around single campaigns (see della Porta and Diani 2006: chapter 1 on the differences between social movements and coalitions). In Europe, the internal cleavages in the GJM have indeed emerged with more or less disruptive consequences in different countries (della Porta 2007a). Beyond Europe, various positions towards public institutions have characterized the debate within the World Social Forum, with a 'reformist wing' open to negotiations with public institutions and a more 'radical wing' developing a more confrontational attitude (Smith *et al.* 2007). Different positions have emerged not only on the degree of cooperation with public institutions at various levels, but also on the very focus upon the traditional concern of 'seizing political power' versus an emerging emphasis upon the building of alternative, free space.

Within a 'coalitional' approach, we should expect these positions to align along pre-existing memberships in different types of organizations. Activists coming from different paths would maintain their own political affiliations and follow specific agendas. However, if the GJM is a 'movement of movements', cross-fertilization should occur among the different areas towards common positions. In parallel, degrees of commitment to the movement (both behavioural, as participation in GJM initiatives, and symbolic, as identification with the movement) could explain the support for different strategies of interaction with institutions. In the literature on political participation, in fact, core activists have been defined as 'vestals of ideological purity' and contrasted with the leaders and a broader base of reference more open to compromise (Pizzorno 1978). Moreover, research on political participation has linked, in various ways, gender, age, and social status with political attitudes, expecting for example that more radical strategies will receive more support from young, male, and student activists (see della Porta forthcoming).

In order to discuss potential explanations, we have included among the independent variables a selection of indicators concerning the respondents' level of commitment to the movement and their political attitudes and levels of participation in the movement (or the organizations adhering to it). Previous participation in protest activities carried out by the movement, a strong identification with the movement, and position within the movement (in particular, being a movement leader) may be expected to favour the development of a critical stance vis-à-vis the existing representative institutions as well as democracy as practised by and within those institutions. Similarly, general political attitudes and behaviours such as one's self-placement on the left/right scale, voting, working in a party or other political and civic organizations, and using radical means of participation (e.g. civil disobedience and violence against property) are likely to have an impact on the ways in which one conceives the relationship between citizens and political institutions. The assumption here is that the more radical the political views and the more unconventional the forms of participation, the less will be the satisfaction for institutional politics. In addition, we have included a number of socio-demographic characteristics that are traditionally used in political sociology and resource-based approaches to political participation (Dalton 2002; Lazarsfeld *et al.* 1944; Verba and Nie 1972). Here, we consider them mainly as control variables.

To begin with, according to our data, institutional trust does not seem to depend on the level of commitment to the GJM (Table 5.6). Apart from one exception, none of the indicators of commitment to the movement are associated with the level of trust ESF participants give to various institutions. Thus, neither having participated in protests carried by the movement, nor identifying with the movement, nor holding a leadership position within the movement can help to raise the amount of trust that people have in local governments, national governments, the EU, or the UN. The only significant coefficient refers to the impact of identification with the movement on trust for the UN; but the effect is very weak. Thus, participation in the GJM does not seem to be associated with mistrust in political institutions.

Table 5.6 Estimates of effects of selected independent variables on levels of trust for representative institutions (standardized regression coefficients)

	Trust local gov'ts	Trust nat'l gov'ts	Trust EU	Trust UN
Commitment to the movement				
Participation in protests of the movement	−0.03	−0.03	−0.08	0.03
Identification with the movement	−0.03	−0.02	−0.06	−0.04
Leader in the group	0.05	0.07	0.04	0.08*
Political attitudes and participation				
Self-placement on the left/right scale	0.18***	0.20***	0.29***	0.24***
Voted in last election	0.16***	0.15***	0.12***	0.12**
Worked in a political party	0.01	0.04	−0.02	0.01
Practised civil disobedience	−0.13***	−0.15***	−0.06	−0.12**
Used violence against property	−0.09*	−0.10**	−0.09*	−0.08*
Socio-demographic characteristics				
Woman	−0.07	0.01	0.01	0.03
Age	0.06	−0.10*	−0.03	0.10*
Education	0.07	0.05	0.10*	0.08*
Student	0.04	0.03	0.11*	0.11*
R^2	0.12	0.13	0.17	0.13

Notes
*$p \leq 0.05$, **$p \leq 0.01$, ***$p \leq 0.001$

By contrast, most of the variables concerning political attitudes and participation have a statistically significant effect. Here we have included an indicator of political orientation (self-placement on the left/right scale), an indicator of electoral participation (has voted in last election), an indicator of conventional participation (has worked in a political party), and two indicators of unconventional participation with different degrees of radicalism (has practised civil disobedience and has used violence against property). The only indicator that is not significant concerns conventional political action: having worked in a political party does not impact on ESF participants' trust on the four institutional levels. The other four variables are all consistently significant across the four institutions concerned (local governments, national governments, the EU, and the UN). First, trust is related to self-placement on the left/right scale. People who place themselves on the leftmost side of the political spectrum are more sceptical towards representative institutions (quite understandably, there are virtually no right-wingers among the respondents). This variable displays the strongest effect overall. Second, trust is also positively associated with having voted in the last election, suggesting a link between conventional political participation and attitudes towards multilevel governance. Third, the practice of civil disobedience – a form of action often used by the GJM (more than 40 per cent of respondents have used it in the past) – is negatively associated with the level of trust (except in the case of the EU). Fourth, a similar relationship can be observed for the use of violent forms of action, although the effects are slightly weaker than in the case of civil disobedience.

Thus, movement participants who make use of unconventional forms of political mobilization – in particular, disruptive and even violent forms – tend to distrust representative institutions at all levels This seems to confirm that the use of more unconventional forms of political participation resonates instead with a mistrust in institutions. It should be noted, however, that analysing the relationship between trust and political participation is quite problematic. Here we assume that the latter influences the former, but the causality in fact might well go the other way around. In other words, trust in institutions might encourage political participation rather than being a consequence of it, for example by producing social capital, as many studies have shown (e.g. Fennema and Tillie 1999; Putnam 1993, 2000). It could be the case that, when someone has little trust in existing institutions of representative democracy, he or she tends to adopt alternative (unconventional) forms of political mobilization rather than using the institutional channels for participation. This is confirmed by the positive association between trust and voting: those who have more trust are more likely to vote.

The socio-demographic characteristics of respondents are generally not strong predictors of trust in representative institutions, at least not in a systematic fashion. Age is negatively associated with trust in national governments, but positively with trust in the UN. Apparently, younger participants believe more in national institutions, while older ones trust international institutions more, a finding that is difficult to interpret. Finally, being a student increases the likelihood that one trusts the EU and the UN (but not the local or national governments).

The findings for the solutions envisaged by ESF participants to improve democracy at various levels of governance are consistent with those concerning trust (Table 5.7). The strongest effects are again those for political attitudes and participation, specifically the impact of self-placement on the left/right axis and having voted in the last election. Both aspects positively affect the solutions for improving democracy. The previous use of violence against property is also associated, but negatively, with the solutions envisaged. In contrast, the use of civil disobedience displays only one statistically significant coefficient (strengthening national governments); having worked in a political party is never significant.

Here, however, we should distinguish between two types of solutions: strengthening existing institutions (national or supranational), and building new institutions to involve the civil society (at the EU level and at the international level). With regard to the first type of solution, participants who place themselves only moderately on the left, who have voted in the last election, and who have never used violence against property give more importance to strengthening existing institutions, whether national governments, the EU, or the UN (there is also a negatively significant coefficient for the indicator concerning the practice of civil disobedience, but only on strengthening national governments). Thus, conventional political participation (i.e. voting) seems to instil in people not only trust towards representative institutions, but also the view that the latter

Table 5.7 Estimates of selected independent variables on solutions to improve democracy (standardized regression coefficients)

	Strengthen national governments	Strengthen EU	Strengthen UN	New institutions to involve civil society (EU level)	New institutions to involve civil society (int. level)
Commitment to the movement					
Participation in protests of the movement	−0.03	−0.12**	0.02	−0.08	−0.05
Identification with the movement	−0.02	−0.05	0.03	0.16***	0.17***
Leader in the group	0.03	0.10**	0.09*	0.06	0.01
Political attitudes and participation					
Self-placement on the left/right scale	0.19***	0.24***	0.22***	0.08	0.05
Voted in last election	0.09*	0.14***	0.17***	0.10**	0.06
Worked in a political party	0.01	0.00	0.00	−0.05	−0.03
Practiced civil disobedience	−0.13**	−0.07	−0.06	0.04	0.02
Used violence against property	−0.12**	−0.10**	−0.14***	−0.12**	−0.04
Socio-demographic characteristics					
Woman	0.06	0.00	−0.01	−0.04	−0.02
Age	−0.00	0.04	0.11*	0.12**	0.05
Education	−0.02	0.10**	0.09*	0.02	0.03
Student	−0.03	−0.03	0.07	−0.01	−0.02
R^2	0.10	0.16	0.15	0.10	0.05

Notes
*$p \leq 0.05$, **$p \leq 0.01$, ***$p \leq 0.001$

can be improved in some way; while unconventional political participation points in the opposite direction.

These results also hold, in part, for the second type of solution. However, the view that democracy needs the building of new institutions at the supranational level depends above all on identification with the movement. Participants who identify strongly with the movement are more open to solutions aimed at creating new institutions that involve the civil society rather than strengthening existing ones. If this applies to all categories of participants in general, movement leaders seem to be more open to strengthening supranational institutions, both the EU and the UN. Concerning identification with the movement, we should note that this variable is positively correlated with most of the indicators of trust, solutions, and strategies in bivariate analyses, but that these effects disappear when controlled in multivariate analyses, except for the two indicators we have just mentioned.

Finally, among the socio-demographic variables, only age and education have some statistically significant effect, but not consistently across the five indicators of solutions to improve democracy. Age has a positive effect on views on strengthening the UN and building new institutions to involve the civil society. Education is positively associated with strengthening the EU and the UN.

The findings for the strategies of political mobilization used to improve democracy are weaker than those concerning trust and solutions, both in terms of variance explained and the number of statistically significant coefficients (Table 5.8). We can therefore be quite brief and comment on each dependent variable separately. Contacting political leaders only depends on self-placement on the left/right scale. The coefficient is negative, suggesting that more leftist-oriented participants are more willing to use this strategy. Practising democracy in group life is only influenced by having worked in a political party. The belief that the involvement of citizens in decision making processes improves democracy is affected by four factors: movement leaders, participants who are less strongly left-oriented, those who have voted in the last election, and those who have not used violent forms of participation tend to evaluate more positively the involvement of citizens in decision making as a strategy to improve democracy.

Table 5.8 Estimates of effects of selected independent variables on strategies of political mobilization (standardized regression coefficients)

	Contact political leaders	Practice democracy	Citizens in decision making improve democracy
Commitment to the movement			
Participation in protests of the movement	0.02	0.03	−0.02
Identification with the movement	0.05	0.00	0.05
Leader in the group	−0.07	0.02	0.09*
Political attitudes and participation			
Self-placement on the left/right scale	−0.25***	−0.04	0.11*
Voted in last election	−0.03	0.04	0.10*
Worked in a political party	0.02	0.10**	0.01
Practised civil disobedience	0.02	−0.06	−0.04
Used violence against property	0.06	−0.05	−0.14**
Socio-demographic characteristics			
Woman	−0.06	−0.03	−0.02
Age	0.01	−0.05	0.07
Education	0.04	0.02	0.05
Student	−0.02	0.02	0.06
R^2	0.10	0.03	0.07

Notes
*$p \leq 0.05$, **$p \leq 0.01$, ***$p \leq 0.001$

The results for the latter aspect are somewhat stronger than for the previous two, although not easy to interpret. It seems that two types of cleavages emerge among activists: one is around the 'degree of radicalism' measured on the traditional left/right axis (where 'more radical' means 'more to the left'); but the other is a division between how much the movement should invest in addressing existing political institutions, and how much it should instead focus on the construction of alternative arenas. This debate is not totally new, being reflected in the research on new social movements in the differentiation between 'instrumental' versus 'cultural' (Rucht 1994), or 'political' versus 'countercultural' strategies (Kriesi *et al.* 1995). In the GJM, however, the construction of alternative space is presented openly as a political strategy (della Porta 2005b).

What can we conclude from this analysis of the relationship between certain characteristics of GJM participants and their views concerning representative institutions – and, more generally, concerning democracy and how to improve it in the context of multilevel governance? First, in general, democratic views are influenced by the political orientation of participants. Indeed, the left/right scale has quite consistently the strongest effect among those we have included in our analyses (especially for trust and solutions). The more left-oriented an activist, the less he or she tends to trust representative institutions and to envisage that democracy can be improved by strengthening existing institutions. Second, democratic views are also resonant with the participants' political behaviour, both conventional and unconventional, but in the opposite direction. On the one hand, increased electoral participation is associated with participants' level of trust in representative institutions. On the other end, the use of disruptive and even violent forms of action diminishes their trust in existing political institutions and their belief that democracy can be improved by strengthening existing institutions. Third, commitment to the movement does not appear to be a strong predictor of conceptions of democracy, at least as far as trust and strategies are concerned. However, participants who strongly identify with the movement tend to think that improving democracy is best accomplished by building new institutions to involve the civil society. Finally, socio-demographic variables such as gender, age, education, or employment status are only weakly associated with democratic views. Age and education play some role, but the findings are not very consistent across the indicators of trust, solutions, and strategies.

Movement (activists) and institutions: some conclusions

The relationship between social movements and institutional politics has been a central focus in political and social science debates (see della Porta and Diani 2006: chapter 8 for a review). On one hand, since the development of the political process approach in the 1970s, social movements have been considered as part of political systems, influencing and being influenced by the political institutions. On the other end, social movements have also been considered as challenging the institutional conception of politics, or even as agents of 'antipolitics'.

In this chapter we examined the trust GJM participants have in different types of institutions, the solutions they envisage to strengthen governance and democracy, and their strategies of political mobilization. We have done so in two ways: a more descriptive analysis that compared democratic views of participants in the Athens ESF with evidence from previous ESFs; and a more explanatory analysis aimed above all at assessing the impact of commitment to the GJM and previous participation in political activities upon the democratic views of movement participants in terms of trust, solutions, and strategies.

We have stressed that participants at the 2006 ESF display strong criticism and mistrust of representative institutions at various territorial levels, which are seen as entailing a democratic deficit and incapable of acting effectively against the social injustices brought about by neoliberal globalisation. As compared to what previous surveys of ESF participants revealed, they are also quite sceptical about strengthening those institutions as a solution to such a democratic deficit and lack of effectiveness, while they stress the need to build new institutions of world governance. The activists share, however, strong cosmopolitan orientations, with a homogeneous belief in the need to build alternative institutions of global governance. Refusing a 'return to the nation-state', the activists of the social forum instead present a challenge for European institutions. To these, they ask for alternative policies and participatory politics, demanding a 'Europe of rights' which is a 'social Europe' but also a 'Europe from below'. Finally, we have seen that their general views of democracy and politics are reflected in the search for alternative strategies of political mobilization.

The multivariate analyses carried out in the second part of this chapter have addressed the relationship between commitment to and participation in the movement, on one hand, and democratic views, on the other. The variables we included in our models only explain a small part of the variance in the dependent variable, whether trust, solutions or strategies (a bit more for trust); most of the variables do not have a significant effect. In particular, identification and participation in the GJM, as well as socio-demographic variables, do not appear to influence the level of trust or mistrust in political institutions.

Among the variables that do play a role, the most important by far are self-placement on the left/right scale and having voted in the last election. Both variables are consistently associated with most if not all the indicators of trust, solutions, and strategies we have used in our analyses. Thus, the democratic views of participants in the GJM in terms of their political stance towards the existing institutions (local or national governments, the EU, the UN), or towards new institutions as well as democracy in general, seem to depend more on traditional attitudinal aspects (such as position on the political spectrum) and conventional behavioural aspects (such as participating in elections) than on movement-related aspects such as participation in protests of the movement, identification with the movement, or position within the movement. This holds especially for trust in existing institutions and for solutions that strengthen such institutions, but less so for solutions that build new institutions to involve the civil society and for strategies of political mobilization. This is perhaps an indication that the most left-leaning activists and those who participate in conventional politics (elections) still believe that long-lasting institutions such as local or national governments, as well as supranational institutions such the EU or the UN, can be made more democratic in a more effective way and that, in contrast, the building of new institutions is a more difficult path to improving democracy. The research therefore indicated tensions between different visions of 'external democracy' and the main strategies needed in order to implement them, but no structured generational or ideological cleavages within the ESF in particular, and the GJM more broadly.

Note

1 Some ideas presented in this and the following paragraph have been developed from della Porta and Caiani, 2009.

Part II

6 The social bases of the GJM mobilization and democratic norms[1]

Massimiliano Andretta and Isabelle Sommier

The social bases of participation and democracy: an introduction

Since Seattle 1999, the GJM has succeeded in mobilizing many and diverse people in national and transnational events. In fact, diversity is much emphasized in the rhetoric of the movement. As stated in a document produced by the first World Social Forums (WSF): 'we are ... social forces from around the world (that) have gathered here at the World Social Forum in Porto Alegre. Unions and NGOs, movements and organizations, intellectuals and artists' (World Social Movements 2001: par. 1), and 'women and men, farmers, workers, unemployed, professionals, students, blacks and indigenous peoples, coming from the South and from the North' (ibid.: par. 3). The heterogeneity of the movement was also underlined by the document produced by the second WSF, stating not only that 'we are diverse – women and men, adults and youth, indigenous peoples, rural and urban, workers and unemployed, homeless, the elderly, students, migrants, professionals, peoples of every creed, colour and sexual orientation', but also that 'the expression of this diversity is our strength and the basis of our unity' (World Social Movements 2002, par. 2).

Indeed, some activists claim that the goal of social inclusion has been achieved in the GJM mobilization. According to one of them, the movement

> Put together different generations ... and this is the great novelty and the great richness because it puts together men and women, who are from 20 to 60 years old, who discuss together against the old leftist parties' logic that separated the men from the women, the young from the old.
>
> (Della Porta 2003a: 130)

In this chapter, we want to examine whether the GJM rhetoric on inclusion and heterogeneity, usually referred to at the organizational and movement levels (Andretta and Mosca 2003; della Porta *et al.* 2006a), is confirmed by the social heterogeneity of the movement's activists. This will be investigated in various ways. First, we want to see whether ESF participants are sociographically diverse or whether a particular social profile systematically prevails. At the same time, we will look at the social profiles of long term activists to see if the higher barriers to continuous commitment are overcome by social inclusion. Finally, we will look at the social bases of the GJM ideal of democracy: are the GJM's democratic norms based on inclusion (of anybody interested) and heterogeneity (of different opinions) internalized by all participants (inclusion), regardless of social profile (heterogeneity)?

Answering the question of which kind of people do participate in GJM protests and events is important to understanding whether the GJM claims on inclusion and heterogeneity are supported by our findings. From a theoretical point of view, the question is whether consolidated findings on the sociographic impact on both conventional and non-conventional political participation also apply to the GJM. Most studies on political participation have actually confirmed the 'old' Milbrath's hypothesis of social and cultural 'centrality', finding that the most politically active individuals have medium to high social status (in terms of income and education) and are prevalently male and (in the case of the US) white (Milbrath and Goel 1977; for a useful review, see van Aelst and Walgrave 2001). It is interesting to note that hypotheses initially elaborated for conventional political participation (such as voting) in old Western democracies have been also confirmed for unconventional forms of participation such as lawful demonstrations (Verba *et al.* 1995; Norris 2002), as well as in new European democracies (for both conventional and unconventional forms) (Bernhagen and Marsh 2007). Moreover, similar results emerged from studies using different methods from the traditional population survey, such as protest events analysis and surveys of demonstrations (van Aelst and Walgrave 2001; Bédoyan *et al.* 2004). However, according to the mentioned studies, the variables of gender and age play different roles in explaining conventional versus unconventional political participation: unconventional participants seem to be relatively younger and more gender balanced than conventional participants are.

The theory of social centrality explains political participation based on various mechanisms: 'central' people in fact are more likely to possess those resources that can easily be converted into political engagement – the time-and-money-based dimensions, in the terms of Verba *et al.* (1995); they have more knowledge that can be used in politics – what Bourdieu (1986) calls cultural capital; and they are connected with many others through various kinds of social relationships – what Bourdieu (1986) and Coleman (1988) would call social capital. In the words of Verba *et al.* (1995: 15), we can consider three reasons why people do *not* take part in politics: 'because they can't; because they don't want to; or because nobody asked them'. They can't because they lack the necessary material resources; they don't want to because they lack the cultural capital to understand politics and its importance; and nobody asks them to participate because their interpersonal relationships are too narrow and/or do not include participants.

Some authors have pointed out that the key variable is the 'organization' – that is, participation in collective action is predicted by membership in any kind of voluntary association (Verba and Nie 1972; Pollock 1982; Leighley 1996). This does not, however, bring about different results in terms of exclusion, since several studies found that, for instance, the less educated are less likely to belong to an organization or association (Verba *et al.* 1995; Dekker *et al.* 1997; Hooghe

1999); and the lack of formal membership in one organization also points to the scarcity of 'social capital'.

Moreover, even if the GJM has achieved broad social inclusion, thus contradicting most studies on similar phenomena, it will remain to be seen whether such inclusion is still guaranteed at a higher level of participation in the movement: to what extent are the social characteristics of the most active people, who are members of organizations, participate for a long period of time, have a leadership position in one group, and participate in the movement decision making, representative of the larger part of participants? Even if the mentioned studies on political (also non-conventional) participation do not investigate the level of activism, it seems logical to predict that the social selection of those who decide to become a full time participant, the so called 'sustained activists' (Downton and Wehr 1998), will be even higher.

Finally, we can also think another way to conceptualize the impact of one specific sociographic variable on participation and sustained participation – namely, age. People belonging to different age cohorts, in fact, have been socialized in different political contexts, with specific patterns of protest mobilization that could lead to different patterns of personal involvement in the movement. Following this logic, we can classify people more than 54 years old at the time of the fourth ESF (2006), who witnessed the 1968 waves of protest in most of the European countries; those between 45 and 53, who experienced the subsequent period of new social movement mobilization in the mid-1970s; people between 30 and 44, whose political socialization started in the so called phase of institutionalization of the new social movements (see della Porta and Diani 2006); and, finally, the younger participants (up to 29 years old), who we can mostly expect to have mobilized for the first time within the GJM.

We can also expect these sociographic dimensions to have an impact on the central focus of this volume: the participants' views of democracy. If, as we have said, the GJM promotes a new kind of democratic ideal that we call 'deliberative' (see the introduction to this volume), to what extent does activists' social profile determine their propensity to see this model as legitimate?

There are many good reasons to believe that individual sociographic features would affect the ideal models of democracy held by activists. The deliberative theorists do not deny the importance of certain (social) conditions for deliberation, hence for deliberative attitudes – level of education being the most often mentioned. Certainly, authors who criticize the deliberative theory point to the social inequality that such practices bring about: they take a lot of time, favouring those who can spend more of it (generally young people and students) (Mansbridge 2003); and they require skills – such as the ability to make rational or reasonable arguments – which are unequally distributed (Sanders 1997). If this is true, we should find a larger propensity to emphasize deliberation as an ideal model for democratic decision making among the more educated and younger people. At the same time, according to Inglehart (1977), the post-materialist value of direct participation should be emphasized more by people who overcame their economic needs and are better educated.

Thus, we should find more emphasis on direct participation among middle class and educated activists, even though some recent findings suggest that the traditionally excluded categories, such as women, unemployed, and many activists from the East and the South, who participated in the ESF process, highly value a participatory democracy ideal and sometimes lament the lack of direct involvement in GJM decision making (Andretta and Doerr 2007; Doerr 2007).

We may also add that activists' ideals of democracy can depend on the period in which they were socialized to political activities. The wave of protests of the late 1960s, in fact, has been interpreted as a call for a democracy of the ancients, based on direct involvement in political decisions, as opposed to the democracy of the moderns based on delegation of power and representation (Kitschelt 1993). At the same time, no previous movement has put as much emphasis on consensual and deliberative practices as the GJM. In this sense, a sociographic variable (age) can be classified to test whether particular cohorts, socialized in different waves of mobilization, hold peculiar ideals of democracy.

In the following, then, after a short description of the sociographic profiles of participants in three different ESFs, we will see if those sociographic variables also explain their level of involvement (sustained activism) – namely, whether participants belong to an organization, and their position in it (simple members or leaders), as well as the degree of engagement in GJM events or activities at both the national and the transnational level. Further on, we will see to which extent activists holding deliberative attitudes are sociographically different from those who remain anchored to traditional models of democracy. In the last section, we will draw conclusions by theoretically interpreting our findings.

Who are those people in the forum?

In order to analyse the degree of social inclusivity, we considered the distribution by gender, age, education, and employment of participants at the 2006 European Social Forum in Athens. To look at the evolution over time, we will compare the sociographic profile of participants in the Athens ESF with those obtained in similar surveys conducted during the first and second ESFs (in Florence in 2002 and in Paris in 2003).[2]

The gender ratio of ESF participants is relatively balanced, particularly during the second forum (48.9 per cent men, 51.1 per cent women), with the exception of the fourth ESF where we see an overrepresentation of men: 54.9 per cent, versus 45.1 per cent women. However, this difference in the overall sample is related to the overrepresentation of men in some specific countries, with more balanced gender participation for activists from France (47.4 per cent of women) and Spain (47 per cent) and an even larger presence of women in other national subsamples (see Germany, where women constitute 54.5 per cent), versus others with a male overrepresentation (especially, among Italians and Belgians, with 62.4 per cent and 59 per cent men, respectively).

As far as average age is concerned, it is not surprising that the average age is predominantly younger in the three ESFs than in the overall European population. Those under 25 represent respectively 47.5 per cent in the first ESF, versus 24.5 per cent of the 2003 sample and 29.3 per cent of the 2006 sample. Those under 40 represent respectively 82.9 per cent, 71 per cent, and 63 per cent, whereas those over 25 years old are 13.7 per cent, if we consider the overall European population.[3] The larger presence of young people in the 2002 ESF could be explained by the novelty of the first edition of the movement, when the GJM was in what Francesco Alberoni (1981) called the *statu nascenti* phase of a social movement and may have been perceived as more attractive by the younger generation. The early phase of a cycle could in fact be more appealing to the young (all the more so given the strikingly festive character of the first ESF), while the later consolidation of the GJM brought about some routinization and professionalization, which modified the profile of the participants. We will return to this below.

The level of education is high and increases at each succeeding edition of the forum. We found that 32.5 per cent of participants had a college or university degree at the first ESF, 69.4 per cent at the second, and 80.3 per cent at the fourth. The ratio of technical or professional qualification was stable during the two first forums, at around 15 per cent; but dropped considerably at the Athens ESF (4.6 per cent of the sample).[4] The high proportion of persons without diplomas (19 per cent) or with only a high school degree (34 per cent) at the first ESF can be easily explained by the particularity of the sample that was composed more than half by students. In parallel, the clearly higher educational level of the participants in the ESF 2003 sample (half had a graduate degree) must be related to their older profile and to their higher social position: among those with an occupation, 42 per cent were executive managers or held a high level intellectual occupation and 44.1 per cent held a middle level occupation. The comparison between the general population and the ESF samples points to a huge difference in the educational level. Except for the first ESF, most of the activists had a college education, while the European average is much lower (18 per cent according to the ESS 2002–3). In contrast, intermediate profiles (such as technical/professional educational) are much more frequent in the overall population (41.1 per cent). From this point of view, the ESF activists, with their high level of cultural capital, do not mirror the general level of education found in the European population. This is also evident in regards to their social situation at the time of the inquiries, compared to the entire population of the European Union from 1999 to 2004.

Even if the indicators used by the three surveys to analyse the social position of participants are too different to be compared accurately, some results are clear. First, the GJM activists are prevalently students. Despite differences among the different editions – with 54.8 per cent at the first, 23.7 at the second, and 38.3 per cent at the fourth ESF – they are consistently overrepresented in relation to their weight in the European population (only 6.6 per cent). While not of the same proportion, this over-representation is also found for educators, who were represented more than twice as frequently in Athens than in the general European population (7.6 and 3.8 per cent, respectively). In reverse, the working class is remarkably less present among GJM participants. For example, in Paris and Athens, manual workers were only 2.2 per cent (but 22.3 per cent in overall European statistics). The same is true for retired people (6.5 per cent of the sample but 21.5 per cent of the general European population), as would be expected given the age distribution in the ESF population.

The predominance of employees in the public sector remained stable between 2002 and 2006 (about 48 per cent of those surveyed). However, we can note a clear decline of the private sector, from 48 per cent in 2002 to 29 per cent four years later, reaching the lowest rate in Paris (22.6 per cent), as would be expected given the importance of the public sector in the French population and among activists (see Uadier and Bacache 2007). This decline is balanced by the associative sector, which increased spectacularly between Florence (1.2 per cent) and Athens (23.5 per cent) – a sign of the professionalization of the GJM, or at least of the ESFs, as we will see below.

Professionalization and sustained activism in the GJM

The availability of social movement professionals may play a decisive role in explaining sustained activism, which we define as a high commitment level and continued participation – although sustained activism can also develop among organizations that foster grassroots participation. However, the very sociographic factors that explain political participation in general may also have an impact on both professionalized and sustained activism, thus increasing exclusion.

Who does what, how much and for how long

If non-conventional political participation is socially selective, and GJM mobilization does not provide a clear exception, sustained activism should be even more so. In other words, the social barriers that exclude some people from participation could be even higher for intense engagement or activism. In their 'theory of sustained activism', developed on the peace movement, Downton and Wehr (1998), argue that once life patterns and processes of socialization – which they link to situational availability and attitudinal availability – make activism available for

Table 6.1 Evolution of the current social situation of participants in the ESF (column percentage)

	ESF 2002	*ESF 2003*	*ESF 2006*
Student	54.8	23.7	38.3
Homemaker	0.5	0.9	0.6
Unemployed, looking for a job	5.1	10.0	5.7
Retired/early retired	2.0	12.2	6.5
Working population	37.5	53.2	49.5
Total valid cases	2,429 (100.0)	2,120 (100.0)	1,144 (100.0)

individuals, sustained activism is more a function of social and collective factors than of individual characteristics. The authors refer in particular to

> The belief in the urgency and effectiveness of peace action, which gives it meaning; the development of an activist identity rooted in the ethic of helping others and feeling personally responsible to act for change; bonding to a peace group's ideology, organization, leadership, and community; continually clarifying the movement's vision and its long-term view of change.
>
> (Ibid.: 547)

Many of these factors are related to the organizational factor. Membership in one organization may be even more important to predicting sustained activism than general activism, because the organization provides the incentives necessary to overcome some basic barriers to collective action (Olson 1963) and offers the context in which members foster their identification with the movement. In fact, this is clearly confirmed by our data. To measure sustained activism in the GJM, we rely upon three dependent variables: participation in GJM events before Athens (general participation),[5] participation in previous GJM events in a different country from one's own (transnational participation); and participation in GJM decision making (decisional participation). The participants interviewed in Athens had varying levels of experience in the GJM: about 80 per cent had previously participated in at least one movement event before the 2006 ESF, half of whom (40 per cent of the total) declared having participated in six or more, and 50 per cent in events abroad. Furthermore, 63 per cent declared that this previous participation also implied some involvement in decision making processes.

Those indicators of sustained activism are strongly correlated with membership in one organization as well as identification with the GJM. Against about 43 per cent of members of one organization, only 15 per cent of 'loners' (participants with no membership) had participated in more than six events before Athens; members of organizations had participated on average a bit less than six times before Athens, while participants without organizations only a bit more than twice (Eta: 0.14***). Among organizational members, 53 per cent of leaders and paid staff had participated in more than six events, as compared to 39 per cent of simple members (ordinary or voluntary members) (Cramer's V = 0.14***). In addition, 54 per cent of members and 23 per cent of non members declared having participated in at least one event outside their country of residence before Athens (Cramer's V = 0.20***): among them, 66 per cent of leaders and 51 per cent of simple members (Cramer's V = 0.15***). Finally, 68 per cent of members of organizations declared also having participated in a GJM decision making setting, against 27 per cent of non members (Cramer's V = 0.27***); among members, the percentage rose to 78 per cent among leaders and paid staff, compared to 65 per cent of simple members (Cramer's V = 0.14***).

Identification with the GJM is also highly correlated with sustained participation. The non parametric Kendall's tau-b of the correlation between identification[6] and level of general participation before Athens is 0.33***: 54 per cent of those who declared being highly (quite a lot or very much) identified with the GJM had participated in at least one transnational event, versus only 27 per cent of those who declared a low level of (no or little) identification (Cramer's V = 0.18***); and 68 per cent of the former, but 35 per cent of the latter had participated in GJM decision making (Cramer's V = 0.23***). Although organized participants tend to express more identification than non members (90 per cent against 65 per cent, Cramer's V = 0.24***), identification seems to have an independent impact on sustained participation: the Kendall's tau-b of the correlation is 0.26*** among non members and 0.29*** among members.

Thus, the model of sustained activism elaborated by Downton and Wehr for the peace movement works quite well for the GJM too. Once activism is available for individuals, it is sustained by factors related to interactions with leadership, identity, and the organization. Leaders and paid staff members, whom we call 'professional activists', seem to play a decisive role in this process. However, it remains to be seen to which extent sociographic variables also play a significant role in the explanation of 'sustained activism'. In other words, is sustained activism even more selective than occasional participation? This is what we will test in the following, by looking first at the process of professionalization of the ESF, and second at those participants who appear to be more active (sustained activists) than others.

The social bases of professional activists

Professional activists are those who are part of the leadership or are paid staff members. They are the people who devote their time to mobilizing resources for movement activities. We have already mentioned an increase in the associative sector, interpreting it as a sign of professionalization. Another sign of the professionalization of the ESF is that 'professional activists' are more present in Athens than in Paris (unfortunately, we do not have comparable data for the first ESF) – 38 per cent of the fourth ESF sample versus 21 per cent of the second. 'Simple' activists without responsibilities or mandates represented, respectively, 62 and 79 per cent of the sample.

Are professional activists different from ordinary ones? According to the results of some logistic regressions, these two types of activists are not so different from a sociographic point of view. But three variables play a significant role in explaining the distribution among the three groups (professional activists, ordinary activists, and loners): employment sector (public, private, associative) (Cramer's V = 0.35***); employment status (0.20***); and age (0.14***). It is not surprising that professional activists, when employed, work predominantly in the public sector (44.6 per cent of them in 2006) and in the associative sector (35 per cent). These two categories are stable from 2003 to 2006 and represent four-fifths of both samples. The importance of the associative sector can be explained by two factors: On the one hand, contention is becoming more professionalized; and on the other, the economic crisis expands the space and the need for humanitarian or social commitment, which is increasingly provided by numerous associations with social and healthcare dimensions.

The fact that 'professional militants' are more easily found in this sector than 'ordinary militants' also speaks in favour of the theory of the professionalization of activism, with the boundary between activism and professional activities becoming increasingly porous with the development of what, paraphrasing Weber, we can define as a group that lives of and for political protest.

However, there is a peculiarity in the sociographic profile of professional activists in Athens compared to their Parisian counterparts. In fact, the most notable evolution concerning the social position of the professional activists is the clear decline of the working population (56 per cent in 2006 versus 73.5 per cent in 2003), while the proportion of students almost tripled: they represent more than one-quarter of professional activists in the Athens sample versus one-tenth of the Paris sample (see Table 6.2). In contrast, the proportion of retired people and unemployed remains stable (10 per cent and 7 per cent, respectively). Such an evolution is related to the different age structure of the two samples (see above).

The average age of the professional activists in the two ESFs is relatively stable. In 2006, those under 25 represent about 19 per cent of professional activists, as compared to 12 per cent in 2003. In the second ESF, 12 per cent were 60 years and older (versus 6 per cent in 2006); but no one under 18 was professional. In both cases, and not surprisingly, professional activists are older than ordinary activists. If the gender of professional activists was very balanced in 2003, the number of males in positions of responsibility witnessed a clear jump four years later, bringing the ESF back to the usual unequal division of political labour between genders (60 per cent men versus 40 per cent women). However, this aggregate picture hides the variation among countries: although more than 50 per cent of professionals are women in Greece (the only country where professional activists are predominantly female), 71 per cent in Italy, 62 per cent in Germany, about 58 per cent in Belgium, France, and Spain, and 55 per cent in Great Britain, are males.

Let us now look at the profile of loners, participants who declared not belonging to any organization (they were about 12 per cent in Athens). The loners are predominantly Greek (46.5 per cent). The ESF is an event that draws activists, but also people who are just curious or who have no organizational affiliation (Sommier 2008). Very few non-Greeks are 'loners': French, German, and Italian 'loners' represent one-tenth of their sample. Among the other nationalities, the

Table 6.2 Evolution of the current social position of the 'professional activists' in two ESFs (column percentage)

	ESF 2003	ESF 2006
Student	9.5	27.0
Homemaker	0.0	0.6
Unemployed, looking for a job	7.0	7.4
Retired/early retired	10.0	9.8
Working population	73.5	55.9
Total valid cases	409 (100.0)	326 (100.0)

ratio of 'loners' is even lower – especially among Spaniards (7.7 per cent), Belgians (2.1 per cent), and British (0.7 per cent). Geographical distance appears to be dissuasive for unaffiliated participants who are not part of an organizational infrastructure that facilitates travel. Loners are also younger: 68.8 per cent are under 25 years old, versus 49.3 per cent of the whole sample (see Table 6.3). The percentage of women regularly decreases along with the commitment: the ratio is higher in the 'loner sample', lower in the whole sample (45.1 per cent), and even lower in the 'professional sample', where they represent only 39.7 per cent.

Table 6.3 Type of activists by sociographic variables (Athens, column %)

	Type of activists			
	Loners	Ordinary	Professional	Total
Gender				
Men	52.5	52.8	60.3	55.3
Women	47.5	47.2	39.7	44.7
Total (N)	141	466	320	927
Cramer's V n.s.				
Level of Education				
Compulsory	4.4	8.9	8.6	8.1
Post-comp.	54.4	36.3	32.8	37.8
University +	41.2	54.9	58.6	54.1
Total N	136	463	314	913
Cramer's V 0.11***				
Age group				
Up to 29	68.8	45.4	34.9	45.4
30–44	16.3	21.4	27.4	22.7
45–53	7.8	14.3	19.8	15.2
54+	7.1	18.8	17.9	16.7
Total (N)	141	467	318	926
Cramer's V 0.16***				
Employment status				
Blue and white collars	10.3	22.5	39.5	26.5
Upper class (professionals, managers, employers)	10.3	13.4	17.4	14.3
Teachers	5.2	9.7	10.5	9.2
Unemployed	3.4	7.5	3.5	5.5
Retired	3.4	9.1	5.0	6.8
Students	67.2	37.8	24.0	37.6
Total (N)	116	373	258	747
Cramer's V 0.24***				
Working sector				
Private sector	50.0	33.5	16.6	27.5
Public sector	45.0	55.9	39.8	48.0
Associative sector	5.0	10.6	43.6	24.4
Total (N)	40	236	211	487
Cramer's V 0.29***				

Half of the loners do not have an occupation. Those who declared themselves employed are both in the private and the public sectors (50 and 45 per cent, respectively), and only 5 per cent in the associative sector. If we compare them with the global and professional activist samples, we can see how involvement in the GJM is associated with sector: the closer one is to the associative sector, the more likely one is to be a professional activist. Although to a lesser extent, this is also the case for the public sector (see Table 6.3).

The social bases of GJM sustained activism

If sociographic factors matter in order to explain organizational membership and position within one group (ordinary members, activists, leaders, and so on), we might expect that they matter even more as far as sustained activism is concerned.

According to our data, gender has only a small impact on the general level of participation in GJM events before Athens: average participation in the GJM was 5.7 for men (about 43 per cent participated in six or more events) and 5 for women (36 per cent in six or more events) (ETA: 0.07*). No impact can be statistically found for participation abroad and in GJM decision making. Instead, age is far more important to predicting sustained activism in unconventional participation. In line with the findings of traditional conventional participation studies, older people tend to participate more: young participants (under 29 years old) have on average participated in 4.5 events, while older participants always in more than six, the 45–53 years old category being the most active (6.6 times). The impact is even more visible for transnational participation and participation in GJM decision making (see Table 6.4).

The impact of level of education is less clear, the most active being the least educated (none or compulsory education) and the most educated (graduate and post-graduate) (see Table 6.4). However, employment status is relevant: contrary to the common statement that students are more active than others, our data show that they tended to participate as much as the upper class (professionals, managers, and employers) and the unemployed, but much less than blue and white collar workers (manual and non manual workers), retired, and teachers (see Table 6.4). However, if we control for the impact of employment status on sustained activism by age, we see that among the youngest participants (up to 29 years old), the differences between students and other participants are not statistically significant (both students and others had participated in about 4.5 events before Athens, while 40 per cent of the former versus 35 per cent of the latter had participated in at least one event abroad). Those with a temporary job tended to participate less, especially in transnational events and in GJM decision making. Finally, as with professional activists, the employment sector is also important: most active are people occupied in the public sector or in the associative sector (staff, leaders, employed of associations, NGOs, unions, or parties) (see Table 6.4).

Thus, sociographic variables do have an impact on sustained activism in the GJM as well, although some of the findings do not necessarily confirm hypotheses elaborated in the studies on non-conventional participation: for instance, the

Table 6.4 Level of experience in similar events and identification with the global movement according to gender and age group

	Participation in previous GM events				
	In GJM events (average)	In 6 or more events (%)	In events abroad (% of yes)	In GJM decision making (% of yes)	Identification with the GJM (average)
Level of education					
Compulsory	5.7	45.5	49.4	70.4	2.2
Post-comp.	5.0	35.6	41.0	58.8	2.2
University +	5.7	41.9	56.8	65.6	2.3
Total	5.4	39.8	50.3	63.3	2.3
(N)	(1,163)	(1,163)	(1,146)	(934)	(1,129)
ETA/ Cramer's V	0.07*	0.07*	0.15***	0.08*	n.s.
Age groups					
Up to 29	4.5	31.6	36.6	53.8	2.1
30–44	6.0	44.1	56.1	68.3	2.3
45–53	6.6	50.9	63.0	74.1	2.5
54+	6.3	47.7	71.3	75.2	2.5
Total	5.4	39.7	50.1	63.1	2.3
(N)	(1,166)	(1,166)	(1,164)	(952)	(1,148)
ETA/ Cramer's V	0.19***	0.16***	0.27***	0.19***	0.26***
Employment status					
Blue and white collars	6.7	51.3	65.5	72.9	2.3
Upper class (professionals, managers, employers)	4.9	35.2	45.4	64.0	2.2
Teachers	5.6	40.9	61.1	70.0	2.3
Unemployed	4.8	32.1	48.1	66.0	2.4
Retired	6.4	48.3	70.0	71.7	2.6
Students	4.6	33.0	36.2	56.2	2.1
Total	5.4	39.6	50.1	64.2	2.2
(N)	(938)	(938)	(937)	(772)	(922)
ETA/ Cramer's V	0.19***	0.16***	0.26***	0.15***	0.23***
Working sector					
Private sector	4.5	30.5	39.2	58.3	2.3
Public sector	6.4	48.8	64.4	68.2	2.4
Associative sector	6.5	50.4	63.8	77.4	2.2
Total	5.9	43.8	57.0	67.4	2.3
(N)	(596)	(596)	(593)		(585)
ETA/ Cramer's V	0.18***	0.17***	0.23***	0.15***	0.11*

impact of age seems to be more related with the political socialization of the various generations (the most active are in fact those who experienced the waves of protest of the late 1960s and 1970s). Young and students are the least active, and although the most educated participate very much, the least educated do not participate less. Not only does the middle class participate less, but retired, unemployed, and blue and white collar workers show a very high degree of activism.

The social bases of activists' democratic views

Inclusion is not only a matter of participation in protest events, but concerns the very meaning of democracy. The GJM is said to be the bearer of a new model of democracy that we call deliberative democracy, which foresees the participation of all interested people in decision making, the use of rational argument to support opinions on available options of action, a tolerant attitude toward different opinions, and consensus as a procedure of decision closure. However, as already mentioned in the introduction to this chapter, there are reasons to believe that such a democratic ideal is supported by people with a particular social profile. To summarize the sociographic variables that can influence the democratic views participants hold, we refer to gender, age (according to political generation), education, and employment status.

We will test the impact of these variables separately on activists' degree of agreement with four statements on 'how political decisions should be taken', which, we recall (see Chapter 4), opposes the *quality of arguments* to *resources and power*; *tolerance* to *disrespect* of different opinions; *delegation of power* to *participation of all* interested persons; and finally, *voting* to *consensus*.[7]

If about 91 per cent of the full sample believes that the quality of arguments should always prevail over resources when a political decision is to be taken, surprisingly, younger people are a little less likely to accept this, while the oldest '68 activists' (54+) are the most 'argumentative'. Blue and white collar workers are a bit more inclined to believe that more resourceful and skilful individuals or organizations should have more weight. The latter applies especially to those who work in the private sector. However, only age appears to have a (small) statistically significant impact on the first item (see Table 6.5). Concerning the second item, no sociographic variable is found to be statistically significant, the percentage of those agreeing on mutual acceptance being about 88 per cent in each considered category.

When we consider the delegation/participation opposition, instead, age and employment status show a significant correlation. Activists between 45 and 53 years old are in fact more participative than the others, while if white and blue collars, especially working in the private sector, are more participative, professionals of the associative sector are more prone to accept delegation (see Table 6.5). Even though the association is not statistically significant, less educated activists are a little more pro-delegation than the average: 68 per cent of those holding no or a compulsory degree of education versus about 74 per cent of those with a post-compulsory education value full participation in any kind of decision making as a democratic ideal.

As for the last item, which opposes those preferring voting to those preferring consensus as a method of decision making, least consensual appear to be men, more than 54 years old, especially belonging to the upper class; while more consensual are teachers, between 45 and 53 years old. In none of these cases, however, is the difference statistically significant (Table 6.5).

Table 6.5 Democratic ideals by sociographic profiles

Socio-graphic variables	Deliberative ideals items (% of those who agree with...)			
	Arguments	Acceptance	Full participation	Consensus
Gender				
Men	90.4	86.6	72.0	43.4
Women	91.4	89.9	73.5	47.4
Total	90.8	87.7	72.7	45.1
(N)				
Cramer's V	n.s.	n.s.	n.s.	n.s.
Age groups				
Up to 29	89.4	87.7	69.9	45.2
30–44	88.9	86.4	74.2	46.7
45–53	91.7	88.5	82.7	49.4
54+	96.7	89.5	69.7	39.5
Total	90.7	87.7	72.7	45.3
(N)	(1,062)	(1,061)	(1,060)	(1,060)
Cramer's V	0.09*	n.s.	0.10**	n.s.
Employment status				
Blue and white collars	89.6	84.3	65.3	47.8
Upper class (professionals, managers, employers)	91.3	90.4	72.6	40.8
Teachers	91.6	89.3	77.1	53.1
Unemployed	91.7	89.8	81.6	41.7
Retired	95.7	97.9	80.9	43.5
Students	91.2	88.6	72.0	46.6
Total	91.2	88.5	71.9	46.2
(N)	(857)	(858)	(855)	(846)
Cramer's V	n.s.	n.s.	0.10*	n.s.
Working sector				
Private sector	85.7	84.6	78.1	43.4
Public sector	91.8	87.4	74.4	45.2
Associative sector	90.6	88.2	62.5	45.2
Total	89.8	86.8	72.6	44.7
(N)	(537)	(537)	(537)	(528)
Cramer's V	n.s.	n.s.	0.13**	n.s.

If, then, sociographic variables seem to distinguish participants at the ESF in terms of their degree of involvement in protest activities and decision making, besides playing a relevant role in the leadership making, the democratic ideals that the GJM is fighting for tend to be internalized across social groups. Although the dilemma between voting and consensus still divides GJM activists (reflecting the cleavage between horizontals and verticals), this does not depend on sociographic factors.

The social bases of the GJM: which kind of inclusion?

We started this chapter by picturing the GJM self-description, according to which social inclusion and heterogeneity are not only distinctive features of the movement but also the democratic principles it most values. Those claims do not resonate with some basic academic findings on political participation, starting from the old theory of social centrality; our findings suggest that the 'centrality' hypotheses remain valid also for GJM mobilization, but only as far as some dimensions are concerned. In fact, participants in the European Social Forum are characterised by the relatively high presence of the youngest generation. These results support the description of the global justice movement as involving a new generation of activists. The gender ratio is also rather balanced, suggesting a normalisation of protest in terms of the participation of women. However, the comparison between the general population and the ESF samples points out in general a huge difference in the educational level. As in other studies on political participation, education continues to be the best predictor for political involvement. Additionally, non-manual workers are clearly over-represented among participants, especially those working for the public or associative sectors. Our analysis has also detected, as a most relevant trend along the different European social forums, an increasing presence of professional activists. This result can be interpreted as an indicator of professionalization or institutionalisation of the ESF, which clearly suggests, together with the other findings, the need to take with caution the GJM claim of inclusivity.

When we look at what we called 'sustained activism', the selective process of political participation is even more evident. Our findings confirm Downton and Wehr's argument that once activism is available for the individual, sustained activism is more a function of collective factors (interactions within organized groups, interactions with leadership, and collective identification) than of individual social profiles. Yet, more educated and older males, especially working in the associative and the public sectors, are more likely to be leaders of their groups and to participate more in GJM events and decision making. Similarly, those well integrated in the labour market show a higher percentage of involvement in the movement (decreasing among those with a temporary job or the unemployed). In brief, we could speak of two types of participants. Some participants who could be situated in a more peripheral social position (especially in terms of age and labour market situation) tend to show lower levels of involvement in movement activities (in some cases despite their high level of identification and trust in the movement). On the other hand, we find a group of activists that could be portrayed as occupying more central social positions (especially highly educated people working for the associative sector), who also take part to a greater extent in the movement's activities, especially in movement decision making. The impact of a particular sociographic variable, namely age, suggests an alternative interpretation to the classic 'centrality' argument: 'sustained activists' are more likely to be those whose previous experiences date back to the 1960s and 1970s waves of protest in Europe.

Notwithstanding the mentioned level of social exclusion in social forums and decision making, however, the activists of the ESFs seem to have internalized social inclusion as far as their democratic attitudes are concerned. Contrary to what some scholars have argued, the deliberative ideal that the movement advocates is widely accepted among ESF participants, with basically no sociographic differences. Indeed, the GJM and its social forums seem to create a space where people share normative conceptions of democracy and experiment with a new model of democracy; arguments are valued more than resources and power; recognition is considered as more important than conflict; and full participation in decision making more democratic than delegation. Only the consensus rule is not dominant, since slightly more than half of the participants continue to prefer the old voting procedure to choose between different options; but in any case, an inclusive dialogic ideal has been internalized as the most legitimate democratic norm among most activists, regardless of social profile.

Notes

1 Massimiliano Andretta is the principal author of 'The social bases of participation and democracy: an introduction', 'Who does what, how much and for how long', 'The social bases of GJM sustained activism', and 'The social bases of activist's democratic views'. Isabelle Sommier is the principal author of 'Who are those people in the forum?' and 'The social bases of professional activists'. Finally, 'The social bases of GJM: which kind of inclusion?' were written by both authors. We thank Ilhame Hajji for her help in the analysis of some data reported in the chapter, and Donatella della Porta for her very useful comments.
2 This analysis compares the results of three surveys: the survey conducted by the group Grace, co-ordinated by Donatella della Porta during the first ESF in Florence (N = 2,579); the survey conducted by the Center of Political Research of the Sorbonne, co-ordinated by Isabelle Sommier during the second ESF in Paris (N = 2,198); and the survey conducted by the DEMOS project during the fourth ESF in Athens (N = 1,058). For the results of the first ESF, see della Porta et al. 2006a; for those of the second, see Agrikoliansky and Sommier (2005).
3 Our data on the general population stem from three databases: the European Social Survey, the World Values Surveys (WVS, but only the European sample), and the last available Eurobarometer. Because of the lack of compatibility between the ESF variables and those of the main surveys on the population, we had to choose three of them to ensure comparability.
4 This may be because there was no such distinction in the questionnaire translated into Italian; in the German version, the distinction was used only at the university level, while the technical secondary school was in the same category as the other kind of diploma.
5 The original variable varies from 0 to 4: 0 = never before; 1 = once; 2 = 2–5 times; 3 = 6–10 times; 4 = more than 10 times. We recoded the variable by assigning to each

activist the median of the range attached to her value (for instance, we attached to category 2 (range 2–5 times) the value 3.5, while we decided somewhat arbitrarily to attach the value 12 to category 4 (range: more than 10 times). Moreover, we built another variable (dummy) where 0 stands for none or little previous participation (less than 6 events) and 1 for '6 or more events' (see Table 6.4).

6 The variable is built on a 0–3 scale, where 0 stands for 'not at all', 1 'a little', 2 'quite a lot' and 3 'very much'.

7 Each of these statements were presented in a polarized form; activists could position themselves on a scale ranging from 0 (argument, equal discussants, delegation, and voting) to 3 (resources, no mutual acceptance, full participation, and consensus). To give a clearer idea on the opinions of the activists based on their sociographic features, we dichotomized each item.

7 The organizational dimension[1]
How organizational formality, voice, and influence affect mobilization and participation

Clare Saunders and Massimiliano Andretta

Introduction

To mark the G8 summit of July 2005, over 200,000 people took to the streets of Edinburgh in the largest protest march the city had ever witnessed, united by their goal to 'Make Poverty History'. Make Poverty History (MPH) was an impressive, if short-lived, campaign coalition, established, organized, and dominated by 'NGOs' – the label that Rootes and Saunders (2007: 139) used to define 'hierarchically structured, formal organizations'. At its peak, it brought together over 500 NGOs. These formally structured organizations contrast significantly with more informal networks of activists present in 'disorganizations' like Dissent! – a network that scorned MPH for being too reformist. Although MPH organized an impressive one-off protest march, it did not provide activists with the opportunity to intrinsically participate in global justice movement (GJM) protest and decision making, beyond participating in the hierarchically organized protest march on the day. In contrast, Dissent! offered myriad opportunities for participation in both actions and decision making: it organized a variety of autonomous protest events, was non-hierarchical and participatory, and made decisions by consensus. As such, it allowed activists to engage much more directly in the internal politics of the GJM.

The contrast between MPH and Dissent! suggests that we should expect to find differences in the extent of activists' participation in formal and informal organizations in the GJM. In this chapter, drawing on data from the Athens European Social Forum (ESF) survey (see Chapter 2 for details of methodology), we explore whether informal organizations do generally encourage wider activist participation in GJM activities and decision making than their more formal counterparts. We also explore whether activists belonging to formal organizations seem less satisfied with the more hierarchical decision making structures to which they are subjected, and we compare activists' ideals of democracy with their perceptions of how internal democracy works within organizations.

Before addressing these questions, we discuss the term NGO, arguing that it cannot accurately be used to refer to 'hierarchically structured, formal organizations' in the manner that Rootes and Saunders (2007: 139) suggest. This is because it is a slippery term that is defined in various ways by different scholars within and between schools of thought. Instead of supporting the sometimes forced and artificial bifurcation between SMOs and NGOs, we instead offer a new typology of organizational types that avoids the definitional chaos surrounding the term NGO. We move on to use theoretical insights from social movement and political science theories to help us determine the effect of varying degrees of organizational formality, voice, and influence on mobilization and participation in the GJM. We hypothesize that informal social movement organizations are more likely than their more formal counterparts to directly involve their members and supporters in decision making and are also more likely to offer them direct and meaningful involvement in campaign actions. Informal organizations should also be viewed by their members as more inclusive and participative than other types of groups, which in turn should produce a wider diffusion of deliberative norms.

NGO: a tired, abused, and misused term?

To avoid replicating mistakes often made by other scholars of NGOs – selectively using examples of NGOs to generalize, ignoring structures, degrees of influence, and levels of operation – we first set out to discuss competing definitions of NGOs. As William Fisher rightly concludes:

> The term 'NGO' is shorthand for a wide range of formal and informal associations. There is little agreement about what NGOs are and perhaps even less about what they should be called. The generalizations about the NGO sector obscure the tremendous diversity found within it. Varying terminology, ideological biases, and unanalysed assertions contribute to an obfuscation of widely varied functions and forms of organizations.
>
> (Fisher 1997: 447)

Because the term NGO has been used in so many different ways, we believe that, if it is to be used at all, it is most useful to take an 'inclusive' approach, viewing it as a generic term covering all types of GJM organizations. All such organizations do, after all, meet the minimum requirement of being 'non-governmental' and work for the general good. However, as William Fisher (1997: 449) states, 'the trick is to differentiate among various forms of organizing while avoiding reified and reductionist uses of the concept of NGO'.

The term NGO is notoriously difficult to define and operationalize, not least because both scholars and activists determine the boundaries of the category in different ways. Although some of the confusion is due to the theoretical lenses through which scholars frame NGOs – such as the 'civil society', 'social movement' and 'international relations' frames – there is also a lack of clarity within these schools of thought. At its origin, the concept may have had greater clarity as used by international relations scholars to illustrate the point that there was more to politics than national governments. But time and interpretation has certainly done much to warp the concept. At the two main poles, we can identify 'inclusive' and 'exclusive' approaches to the definition of NGOs. The 'inclusive' approach has few criteria for inclusion in the category: simply being non-governmental may be enough to qualify. In contrast, the 'exclusive' approach lays down a set of much stricter criteria resulting in a more restricted pool.

Mansbach and Rafferty (2008: 393) provide a perfect example of an inclusive definition: 'NGOs are organizations whose members are individuals who do not represent the government of any state'. Apart from its insistence upon individual membership,[2] this definition has very broad terms of reference. It could allow for consideration of informally structured organizations, private organizations, multinational corporations (Griffiths and Callaghan 2002: 216), and even front groups of corporations (Rootes 2001: 466). Others, taking a slightly more restrictive but still relatively inclusive approach, stress that the non-state organizations be not-for-profit and that they must be concerned with political, humanitarian, or economic purpose (deMars 2005: 32) or be non-violent (Griffiths and Callaghan 2002). In a similar vein, the World Bank defines NGOs as 'private organizations that pursue activities to relieve suffering, promote the interests of the poor, protect the environment, provide basic social services, or undertake community development' (World Bank 2001). In these definitions, there is no mention of structures and levels of operation that would help us to distinguish an NGO from a social movement organization (SMO). As Rootes (2001: 446) suggests, 'the chief difficulty in discussing NGOs is the increasing vagueness and inclusivity of the term and the difficulty of distinguishing NGOs from other types of association'. Some commentators using the inclusive approach, for example, go so far as to suggest that NGOs are social movements (Mingst 1999: 205). According to these commentators, we should view *all* GJMOs as NGOs.

However, this is not how many movement activists view the term, nor how it is applied in other literature, particularly by activists and in literature critical of NGOs' alleged cumbersome hierarchies, bureaucratic nature, and support for the neoliberal state. Focusing on development NGOs in poor countries, for example, Petras launches a critique of NGOs, claiming that they destroy left movements, co-opt their strategies, and 'provide[d] a thin stratum of professionals with income in hard currency to escape the ravages of the neo-liberal economy that affects their country' (1999: 431). Petras makes two common mistakes in his (undefined) conception of an NGO: first, by emphasizing that they are formal entities with professional staff, he overlooks the variety of structures that NGOs can have; and second, by focusing exclusively upon development organizations, he attenuates the variety of issues on which NGOs can work.

Petras is by no means the only scholar to focus his lens on a particular type of NGO. Much of the scholarly work on NGOs has tended to look almost exclusively at humanitarian, relief, and development organizations (e.g. Aaal *et al.* 2000, Edwards 1997, Duben 1994, Mitlin *et al.* 2007, Salamon and Anheier 1996: 12–13). And it is commonly assumed that NGOs have a formal structure, professional staff (Howes 1997), membership, a budget, and power (Griffiths and O'Callaghan 2002: 215) with 'insider status' (Reese *et al.* 2006), and a less contentious nature than SMOs (Tarrow 2001: 12). Some even stress that NGOs must have a relationship with the UN system or have network links across countries (Heater and Berridge 1992: 127; Keck and Sikkink 1998).

Although relying upon an exclusive definition of NGOs would allow us to use the term to emphasize the differences between formal (NGOs?) and informal (SMOs?) organizations, such would fail to clarify the muddy definitional waters of NGOs and leave us accused of selecting a definition that befits our hypotheses. Besides, definitional chaos in the study of associations neither begins nor ends with the term NGO.[3] There have been similar levels of disagreement over what constitutes an SMO – is it a 'complex or formal organization' (e.g. McCarthy and Zald, 1977: 1218), or is it a 'nebulous loose network' (Melucci 1999)? And where do we draw the boundaries between an SMO and an NGO? Lowi (1971), for example, suggests that once they become highly institutionalized, SMOs become 'interest groups', a term equating roughly with some of the 'exclusive' definitions of NGOs.[4] But how do we classify organizations that engage in a mixture of institutional and non-institutional protest, as do many so-called NGOs *and* many so-called SMOs?

As Dana Fisher *et al.* (2005) demonstrate, so-called NGOs may participate in international negotiations such as IMF meetings and the COP (Conference to Parties, United Nations Framework Convention on Climate Change) negotiations; but the number of delegates allowed within the meetings is limited, and representatives remain locked out of many key negotiations even when they have official observer status. As a result, these so-called NGOs are often instrumental in organizing protests *outside* of the event, in a realm traditionally regarded as being that of the 'social movement'. As Fisher *et al.* (2005: 105) state, 'SMOs, some of which would classify themselves as NGOs, have played a significant role in large-scale protests targeting international organizations and multi-lateral regimes'.

So when Reese *et al.* (2006) tell us that SMO participants are more inclined to participate in GJM events and are more radical than NGO participants, does this actually mean anything to us? Probably not. This exploration of definitions has demonstrated that an NGO can be an SMO and an SMO can be an NGO, but that definitions may vary according to the analytical or empirical framework the analyst has in mind. Of course, an NGO can only be an SMO if it is networked, if it shares the concerns of the movement and engages in collective action (Saunders 2007); but nevertheless, many so-called NGOs can still be called SMOs.

Thus, we agree with several other commentators (Rootes 2001; Mitlin *et al.* 2007) that the term NGO is lacking in analytical and descriptive value; it is, indeed, a tired, abused, and misused term. If it has any value at all, that value lies in the inclusive approach – as a means of distinguishing the governmental from the non-governmental. Beyond that, competing definitions conflict, confuse, and serve to corrupt the term further. Therefore, to get an analytical handle on the organizational dynamics of the GJM, a new typology of organizations is required that is more meaningful than the false bifurcation between NGOs and SMOs.

Organizational types in the GJM

In order to differentiate among the types of organizations in the GJM, we have identified five organizational types on the basis of their structures and territorial levels of influence: *informal organizations*, *ITOs* (Influential Transnational Organizations), *formal trade unions, political parties*, and *other formal organizations* (see Figure 7.1).

ITOs, sometimes misleadingly labelled 'international NGOs' (INGOs) (cf. Keck and Sikkink 1998) are globally oriented and formally structured non-profit organizations, with consultative status in international governance institutions such as the WTO, World Bank, EU, IMF and UN and/or Council of Europe.[5] They engage in 'routine transactions with states, private actors *and* international institutions' (Tarrow 2001: 21) and are networked with other organizations around the globe.

Trade unions are mainly nationally oriented organizations that support the rights of workers, via formal membership. They engage in collective bargaining on behalf of their members and/or broader social constituency and have a formal organizational structure – something required by the nature of their work. The more traditional ones have stable relationships with institutions and companies.

Political parties generally have a much broader focus than the other organizational types we discuss here (Baggot 1995); yet they are mainly nationally oriented, even if they do sometimes seek power at federal and/or local levels. Political parties are political organizations that participate in electoral campaigns seeking power or rights of governance at the federal or state level. As Rose (1974: 3) states, a political party is:

> An organization concerned with the expression of popular preferences in contesting control of the chief policy-making offices of government ... Parties are concerned with the expression of popular preferences; their activities are thus

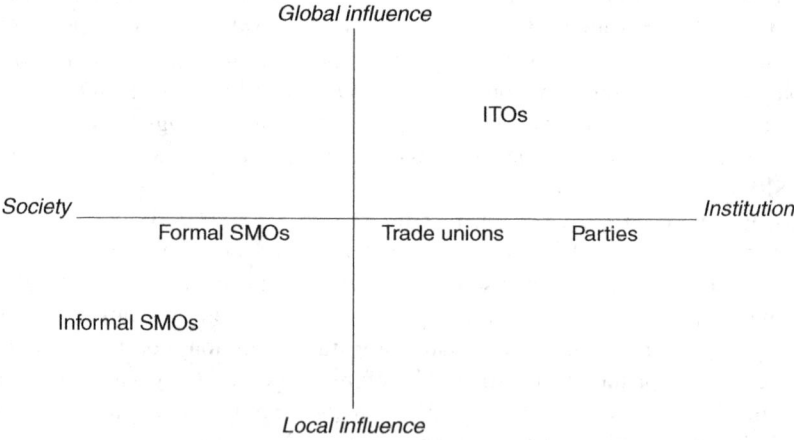

Figure 7.1 Typology of organizations in the GJM.

related to the mass of society as well as government. Parties are concerned with controlling policy-making office in government. Thus they differ from pressure groups such as trade unions and industrial associations, which seek to influence policies without taking official responsibility.[6]

Formal SMOs are *mainly* nationally oriented (they lack the transnational consultation status of ITOs), but they are, in any case, generally closer to society than to political institutions. They are formally organized, having formal roles and a recognized organizational structure, and they usually have a legal identity (for example, in the UK they might be registered as a charity or as a limited company) (cf. Staggenborg's 1988 distinction between formalized and informal organizational types).

Finally, *informal SMOs* are *mainly* local/urban and are very distant from political institutions. They may be far from institutions as a matter of choice, or because they are at an early stage of development and have yet to gain resources and status or access. Those that are distant from institutions as a matter of choice are often radical and explicitly reject any kind of internal formal structure, practising pre-figurative politics as a matter of principle (see della Porta and Reiter 2006a). Both types are informally organized, having no formal roles and no explicit organizational structure. They will usually not have a legal identity.

Now we shall ask how we might expect these different types of organization to impact upon the mobilization and participation of their supporters or members in the GJM.

Organizational formality, voice and influence and mobilization and participation in movements

Academic literature strongly stresses the tendency of formal organizations to become bureaucracies that organize hierarchically and limit public participation to the opportunity to pay membership fees or to otherwise make financial contributions. The chief proponents of such arguments in the social movement literature are Michels, who long ago developed the well known 'iron law of oligarchy' (1959 [1915]); resource mobilization theorists who talk of 'professional social movement organizations' (especially McCarthy and Zald 1973); and other authors who discuss the similar notion of a 'protest business' (Jordan and Maloney 1997).

The 'iron law of oligarchy' predicts that once formal organizational structures take root, power will inevitably become concentrated in few hands. This can be related to Jordan and Maloney's notion of a 'protest business', which they view as a way of doing politics that leads to 'anticipatory oligarchy'. In a 'protest business', members have minimal obligation (usually just a financial contribution), professionals run the organization, and members can influence organizational policy only by exit, not by voice (Jordan and Maloney 1997: 190). An antecedent of the concept of 'protest business' is the 'professional social movement organization', an organization that, as it professionalizes, witnesses a shift away from dependence on volunteers to dependence on professional full-time staff (McCarthy and Zald 1973).

Also in the resource mobilization tradition, Zald and Ash (1966) noted that bureaucratic organizations are good at effecting institutional change but poor at grassroots mobilization, whereas decentralized and informal organizations are effective at grassroots mobilization but offer little by way of institutional success.

In the political science literature, a distinction is made between 'insiders' and 'outsiders' (Grant 1987; Baggot 1995). Once they become 'insiders', working within the government behind closed doors, organizations increasingly refrain from grassroots mobilizations so as to avoid tarnishing their reputations. The predicted outcome in both schools of literature is the same: a tendency to employ professional staff and to favour organizational maintenance and reputation over grassroots participation in decision making and grassroots mobilization. Thus it seems that there is an inevitable trade-off: formal organizations with hierarchical decision making strategies are able to exert strategic influence but fail at grassroots mobilization, whereas informal organizations that are more participatory can effectively mobilize the grassroots but fail to exert strategic influence.

How might this theoretical implication play out in each of our organizational types? Of course, the situation is complicated because many organizations work in the grassroots and institutional worlds simultaneously. We also have to consider the resources that organizations have available in order to mobilize for GJM protest events. Whilst informal organizations might be expected to be more participatory, they will certainly have fewer funds available to support members at overseas protests than their more formal counterparts. And whilst ITOs might be like 'protest businesses' in many ways, they are sometimes locked out of negotiations and resort to protest (see discussion of Dana Fisher *et al.*'s 2005 work, above). Taking a 'protest business' view of ITOs is also problematic because it precludes discussion of ITOs' ability to use resources to fund or support activists to attend demonstrations from outside of their local area.[7] Considering the theoretical insights and caveats mentioned above, we have developed a set of expectations of the mobilization and participation potential of the various types of organizations in the GJM (Table 7.1).

In what follows, we shall address these issues using the empirical evidence provided by the survey at the fourth ESF in Athens. We have operationalized 'organizational types' based on participants' responses to the request 'now please think of the [voluntary/campaigning] group that is most important to you'. This was initially a string variable that we have recoded according to our new typology. Of our respondents, 489 did not name their most important organization, and for a further 41 we were unable to classify the organization because of illegible handwriting, translation difficulties, or the organization's obscurity.

Global justice movement organizations: mobilization and participation in decision making

Involvement in the ESF and the global justice movement

Political parties are the most prominent in ESF participants' 'most important organization of which they are a member', mentioned by over one-third of the

Table 7.1 Expectations of types of organizations' extent of activist participation in mobilization, action repertoires, and decision making

	Mobilization	Action repertoire	Decision making
ITOs	Mobilization for participation of a few in international demonstrations (especially staff)	'Insider' consultation, with carefully managed public demonstrations	Low participation from activists
Trade unions	Possibility of high rates of mobilization, especially on labour issues	Traditional trade unions have moderate actions (radical ones might put the organization's survival in jeopardy). Grassroots unions may be more adventurous	Traditional trade unions tend to have low participation from activists, but grassroots ones may be more participatory
Political parties	Low rates of mobilization	Moderate actions (radical ones might put the organization's survival in jeopardy)	Nominal participation from many activists
Formal SMOs	Seeking consultation status at the national level. Mobilization for participation in national demonstrations	Moderate actions (radical ones might put the organization's survival in jeopardy)	Generally low participation from activists because formalized decision making procedures place decision-making in the hands of an elite cadre
Informal SMOs	Mobilization of grassroots at all levels (but resource constraints)	A range of techniques, but always 'outsider'. Sometimes violent	High participation from activists

activists who named an organization, followed by formal SMOs (29.2 per cent), informal SMOs (18.7 per cent), and trade unions (13.8 per cent). ITOs were mentioned only infrequently, in 4.1 per cent of valid cases. Thus, although ITOs may be accustomed to attending international conferences and summits, and play a key role in many GJM protests (Fisher et al. 2005), they are not generally regarded as important to ESF participants, who seem to assign greater importance to political parties and formal SMOs. Although the insignificance of ITOs may be surprising, it is less unexpected to find that formal organizations are important to ESF participants; after all, theory and empirical work on movements (cf. Klandermans 1993) lead us to expect that formal organizations would have high mobilization potential: they are, for example, able to provide funding or logistical support to make their supporters' or staff members' attendance possible.

The (still somewhat surprising) importance of political parties can be explained by reference to the nature of civil society in Greece, where over one-fifth of those participants mentioning an organization formally reside. Nearly two-thirds of the organizations mentioned by the Greek activists were political parties, whereas in most other countries the proportion of political parties was less than one-third, and in the UK it was less than 6 per cent. The prevalence of political parties in Greek civil society is well documented and is frequently given as a reason for the overall weakness of civil society there. Many Greek campaigning groups and voluntary associations are reliant upon major political parties for funding, or have been heavily influenced by them (Sotiropoulos and Karamagioli 2006). Even if we remove the Greek influence, though, political party supporters are much more active than Michel's 'iron-law' of a passive rank and file would lead us to believe.

Other cross-national differences are important to mention too. For example, in Spain, over one-third of the 'important' organizations mentioned are informal. This is an expected result given that 'in comparison with other European countries, we notice a minor role played by large NGOs as well as more difficulties in establishing stable alliances with left-wing groups like in Italy ... or France' (Jiménez and Calle 2007: 98). In Germany, the fact that the GJM is strongly rooted in NSMs (Rucht et al. 2007: 180) may explain the prevalence of informal organizations, which, as in Spain, were mentioned by over one-third of German participants. In comparison, only 5.7 per cent of British activists mentioned an informal organization, with formal organizations seeming especially important. Of the 35 organizations mentioned by British activists, 12 are socialist (League for the Fifth International, Socialist Workers Party, Revolution and Globalise Resistance are each mentioned by at least two activists). The prevalence of socialist organizations as a favoured type of organization for British activists is perhaps evidence of the energetic and persistent attempts of some British socialist organizations to hegemonize the movement, in turn deterring involvement of activists from other movement sectors unwilling to associate with socialists (Rootes and Saunders 2007: 154).

In addition to feeling sidelined by socialist organizations and marginalized by the prevalence of political parties in Greek civil society, informal SMOs may be underrepresented at the Athens ESF for other reasons. Activists involved in these SMOs may have lacked the resources needed to attend. Certainly, informal organizations had the lowest proportion of paid staff attending the forum,[8] meaning that participants of informal organizations required greater commitment in order to take time off work and pay for travel from their own pockets. In contrast, paid staff members from formal organizations were most likely provided with free transport and accommodation courtesy of their organizations and were, in effect, being paid for their attendance at the Athens ESF.

Although few of the ESF participants who listed an organization claimed to be 'not actively involved' in it, most of these few tended to be members of formal organizations (7.1 per cent of those listing an ITO, 2.2 per cent political parties and 3.6 per cent formal SMOs). In contrast, only one of the 126 ESF participants listing an informal organization was not actively involved in it. This demonstrates that although ITOs and other formal organizations seem to be far from the archetype of a 'professional social movement organization' (McCarthy and Zald 1973) or a 'protest business' (Jordan and Maloney 1997), they certainly have lower participation rates.

We have a second take on the question of participation derived from our data on ESF participants' extent of involvement in the GJM, both generally and abroad (Table 7.2). When looking at the most committed participants in the GJM (those involved in at least ten GJM protests), we can see that those from informal organizations are the most involved (40.5 per cent of those mentioning an informal organization, compared to 10.7 per cent of those mentioning an ITO). Despite the likelihood that they are paid staff members who may have travel budgets for such events, ESF participants favouring ITOs and other formal organizations are actually less likely to travel abroad for a GJM protest than their counterparts from informal SMOs. It is clear, then, that formal organizations are more than marginally less participatory than their more informal counterparts. But is it true that the forms of action in which their sympathizers engage are more moderate?

Engagement in different types of movement activity

To determine whether ESF participants from formal organizations engage in more moderate types of actions than those from informal SMOs, we have classified action types as 'moderate' (party politics, encouraging people to sign petitions, attending demonstrations, and handing out leaflets), 'unconventional' (strikes,

Table 7.2 ESF participants' involvement in GJM protest at home and abroad by organizational type[1]

Types of most important group	Involved in GJM protest at least twice (%)	Involved in GJM protest at least ten times (%)	Involved in a GJM protest abroad (%)
Informal SMOs	79.4	40.5	68.3
Formal SMOs	79.9	33.0	63.2
among which ITOs	60.7	10.7	39.3
Political parties	73.9	34.3	52.4
Trade unions	73.4	35.6	64.1
Total	188	236	406
Cramer's V	0.235***	0.204***	0.126***

Note
1 Due to the few cases of ITOs, the measures of association are calculated for the variable in which ITOs are included in the Formal SMOs category.

non-violent direct action, boycotts, and cultural events) and 'radical' (civil disobedience, occupying buildings or land, blockades, and violence against property). Moderate and unconventional forms of participation are ubiquitous for ESF participants from all organizational types, possibly because they constitute a low-risk form of activism. However, there are starker differences in the extent to which radical actions are pursued. Only just over one-third of activists listing an ITO as their preferred organization claimed to have engaged in radical actions, compared to over 70 per cent for those listing other types of organizations.[9] The figure is actually highest for trade unions, which, despite having a formal organizational structure, tend to have a radical nature, at least in continental Europe. In contrast, British trade unions tend to be moderate, mostly due to the Thatcherite legacy that curtailed the scope of activities in which they could legally engage (Rootes and Saunders 2005). However, the critical unions that have developed in continental Europe have been much more overtly political, mobilizing their rank and file to participate in radical actions against the deregulation of the market and cuts in the welfare state.

By looking specifically at types of actions for which there were significant differences among organizational types (Table 7.3), we can confirm that ITO supporters have a more restrained action profile: they are less inclined to work for political parties, to hand out leaflets, engage in strikes, and especially to become involved in the occupation of buildings and blockades – perhaps, as staff members, feeling the need to uphold the reputation of their organizations and any 'insider' status they may have gained, as Grant (1987) would predict.

Somewhat surprisingly, though, ESF participants listing other formal SMOs, trade unions, and political parties seem no less radical than informal SMOs. Although they are formal organizations that could risk tarnished reputations, this

Table 7.3 Significant differences in ESF participants' action repertoires by organizational type

Types of most important group	Engagement in types of movement activity				
	Worked for a political party (%)	Handed out leaflets (%)	Engaged in strikes (%)	Temporary occupation of buildings (%)	Blockade (%)
Informal SMOs	28.6	84.9	61.1	45.2	42.1
Formal SMOs among which	34.7	77.8	50.2	31.1	32.0
ITOs	17.9	60.7	32.1	14.3	14.3
Parties	78.8	90.6	71.6	42.9	36.8
Trade unions	53.8	90.3	84.9	53.8	52.7
N	346	574	433	276	259
Cramer's V	0.428***	0.166**	0.258***	0.172***	0.156***

has not stifled their action profiles. Under conditions of political acceptance or 'openness', we would more readily expect formal SMOs to seek consultation status at the national level. However, many GJM protesters likely view the political system as unaccepting or 'closed' to their interests. Furthermore, many formal SMOs, radical unions, and political parties within the GJM probably consider themselves as being faced with a 'critical' campaign moment – one with imminent and irreversible consequences in the progressive roll-out of the neoliberal agenda. Such a critical moment is likely to spark a radical reaction as a consolidated attempt to alter the current state of affairs and as illustrated by moments such as the 'Battle of Seattle'; organizational reputations may become less important than attempts to bring about meaningful change.

Democratic norms and practices within GJMOs

How democracy works within activists' most important groups: a 'new institutionalist' approach?

As we have mentioned many times, the GJM has been seen as a promoter of democracy from below (della Porta *et al.* 2006a). Consensus practices are reported to be widespread in the meetings of the networks that support it (della Porta 2005a; Andretta 2005b, 2007), and most of the World Social Forums have been held in Porto Alegre, a city known for experimenting with new democratic practices and considered by the GJM as a symbol of how democracy should work (Allegretti 2001; Baiocchi 2005). The question is now to what extent different types of GJMOs are perceived by their members as 'prefiguring' this new form of democracy within their decision making. To investigate how democracy is perceived as working within GJMOs, let us start by elaborating a few expectations that can be derived from the 'new institutionalist' approach (Hall and Taylor 1996).

First, we should expect activists primarily involved in political parties and trade unions to conceive of democracy according to the 'associational model', as delegation and voting are the traditional tools through which mass organizations have implemented their internal democracy. However, although political parties have scarcely modified this institutional democratic design, some trade unions emerging after the 1960s protest wave began to implement a more participative model. Mostly SMOs within the left-libertarian family, they not only challenged liberal democracies by criticizing the principle of delegation, but also tried to apply direct participation – a basic element of the democracy of the 'ancients' (Kitschelt 1993) – in their internal decision making, considering the assembly as the only legitimate 'space' for decision making. Eventually, the myth of the 'assembly' was overcome by the institutionalization of important social movement organizations working in the fields of women's and human rights, the environment, and international solidarity. Moreover, with the process of transnationalization of social movement activities, ITOs had to centralize many decisions in order to become effective and to implement projects generally funded by governments, but also by donors and members. Delegation was seen as the only way to solve collective action problems – although since the members of such organizations' executive bodies are usually experts, they could probably take decisions through deliberation, choosing among different options on the basis of rational arguments (Majone 1989). Contrary to (both national and international) formal SMOs, some informal SMOs have survived the decades of institutionalization, attempting to reproduce the assembleary model of decision making. In the course of GJM mobilization, new formal and informal SMOs have emerged, such as Attac,[10] Indymedia, local social forums, and other networks. Some have tried to implement the consensus rule within their organizations, focusing on the communicative, deliberative aspect of their decision making. One would then expect formal SMOs to rely upon either an 'associational' or a 'deliberative representative' model (see Chapter 4). In any case, respect between opponents and quality of the arguments should be supported and actually perceived as prevailing practices among activists. Finally, informal SMOs should perceive their group's prevailing practices as more participative, but also more deliberative, since 'consensus' and 'direct participation' are two of the most important keywords of the movement struggling for 'another world'.

In Table 7.4, we summarize the results on each of the items we used to identify the perception of decision making practices at the group level according to activists' most important group. Political parties and trade union members describe the internal decision making as a bit less sensitive to the quality of the arguments than do the activists of formal and informal SMOs; among the members of formal SMOs, those belonging to ITOs seem to perceive their decision making as even more open to the contribution of arguments (but the differences are not statistically significant). The acceptance of opposing views seems to be the rule in case of disagreement in (both formal and informal) SMOs, and even more so in ITOs, slightly less so in trade unions, and even less so in political parties.

Those patterns of democratic perceptions change slightly for the other two items, namely degree of participation in internal decision making and method of decision making: here, informal SMO members tend to describe their decision making as more participative and consensus-oriented than formal SMO members do; the distance from parties and unions, described as less participative and vote-oriented, is now more notable; and ITOs are described as being more similar to the latter than to the former.

Using a similar index of deliberativeness to that of Chapter 4,[11] we tend to find a linear relationship between this index and the degree of formalization of the group, assuming the informal SMOs as the least structured and trade unions and political parties as the most structured organizations, with formal SMOs in between (see Figure 7.2).

Thus, in general, we have confirmed the expectations drawn from the argument, as SMOs are seen as more participative and deliberative than political parties and trade unions, and informal SMOs are the most deliberative overall. However, there are some important novelties: support for the quality of the arguments and the extent to which opponents accept one another's arguments seem to be widespread even within parties and unions; the latter are also perceived as practising more

Table 7.4 Perceptions of democracy working within the group (row %)

Types of most important group	Perceptions of how internal democracy works within one's group							
	Item 1 Quality of arguments		Item 2 Acceptance bet. opp.		Item 3 Participation		Item 4 Consensus	
	%	Cr. V	%	Cr. V	%	Cr. V	%	Cr. V
Informal SMOs	76.8		85.6		72.1		75.0	
Formal SMOs	73.2		85.9		62.7		53.6	
among which ITOs	77.3		90.9		57.1		42.9	
Political parties	65.1	n.s.	74.8	0.13***	56.6	0.12***	34.4	0.31***
Trade unions	68.2		80.2		54.2		35.3	
Total valid cases %	70.3		81.3		61.1		48.2	
(N)	(613)		(613)		(606)		(606)	

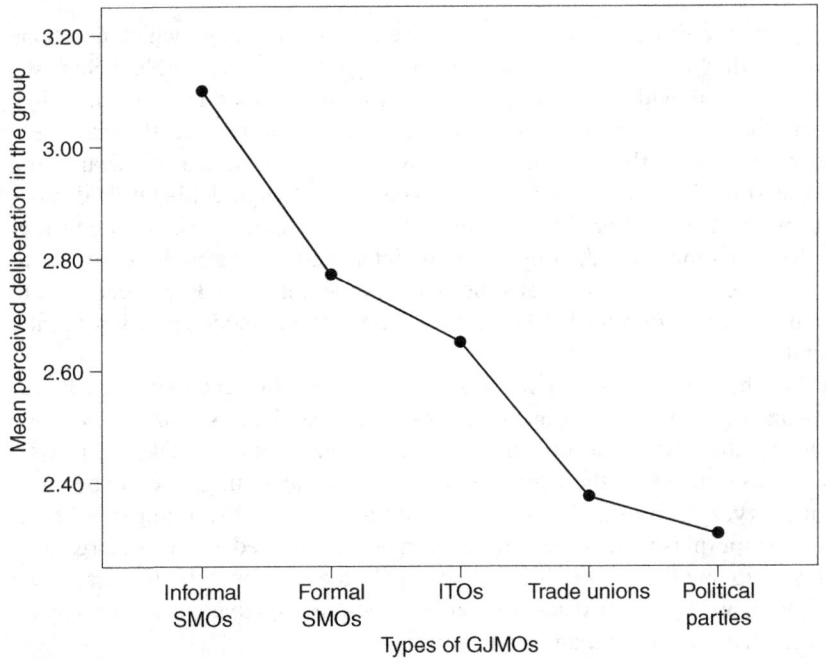

Figure 7.2 Level of perceived deliberativeness within one's most important group.

Notes
a ETA = 0.27, significant at 0.001 level.
b Assuming the degree of structuration of the groups: linearity, F = 44,171, significant at 0.001 level.
c Statistics are calculated for the variable in which ITOs are included in the Formal SMOs category.

inclusive decision making than expected, sometimes bypassing the voting procedure in the search for consensus; institutionalized SMOs are mostly perceived as adopting a deliberative-participative model of decision making; and informal SMOs are applying deliberation to their older assembleary model.

There are two possible explanations for the greater than expected degree of participation: first, activists may have described the decision making process at the local level in which they are actively involved, where full participation and even consensus may be experimented with. Second, in this chapter we do not distinguish between types of parties and trade unions, and, as anticipated for the latter, the different ideological traditions (e.g. traditional leftist, radical leftist, green, centralized or grassroots, etc.), which may have a role in explaining the variation in the perceptions of the activists.[12] Similar considerations, especially the territorial level addressed by the activists in their responses, may apply for the formal SMOs, and particularly for the ITOs, that appear to be less 'deliberative' but also more participative than expected. In any case, there are signs that more participative and deliberative practices are diffusing beyond the boundaries that path-dependent theory would draw.

Democratic ideals: organizational patterns or diffusion?

It is one thing to describe the procedures or the process through which decisions are taken within one's group; it is another to judge them as preferable. ESF participants, as any individuals, bear democratic ideals and values against which they contrast the actual democratic practices they see in social movement contexts (but also in the broader political system). These normative ideals were investigated in Chapter 4, where it was noted that although deliberative democracy is one of the most preferred normative ideals – about 37 per cent consider those decisions that are taken by everyone interested and through consensus to be democratic – it is by no means the only one: as many as 36 per cent would prefer an assembleary model, 19 percent an associational model, and 8 per cent a deliberative representative one.

In this chapter we want to see if such divergence of democratic ideals can be explained by activists' organizational experiences. Here, we can contrast two hypotheses: the first would take the neoinstitutional argument that ESF participants' ideals depend on the democratic organizational settings they experience in their everyday activism. The second would instead take the argument of sociological isomorphism, that legitimized norms are diffused from one organizational site to another through organizational interactions.[13] In this case, we should find an equal diffusion of deliberative-participative ideals among all activists, whatever their organizational affiliation.

Table 7.5 shows that some norms are widely accepted by all activists. Almost nobody believes that resourceful or even more representative groups or individuals should have more weight than the quality of the arguments. Equally, almost everybody thinks that in case of disagreement, opponents should treat each other as 'equals'. However, some differences can be identified, where procedures are

Table 7.5 Normative ideals of democracy

Types of most important group	Normative ideas of democracy							
	Item 1 quality of arguments		Item 2 acceptance bet. opp.		Item 3 participation		Item 4 consensus	
	%	Cr. V	%	Cr. V	%	Cr. V	%	Cr. V
Informal SMOs	93.9		90.4		74.3		66.7	
Formal SMOs among which	88.9		87.8		69.9		48.8	
ITOs	80.8		88.5		70.4		34.6	
Political parties	89.4	0.11***	88.0	n.s.	74.8	n.s.	41.6	0.22***
Trade unions	97.7		89.4		71.8		30.6	
Total valid cases %	91.2		88.6		72.7		47.1	
(N)	(620)		(621)		(622)		(614)	

concerned: is delegation a legitimate device to solve decision making problems, or should the inclusion of everyone interested always be a priority? Should decisions be taken by voting or consensus? Data reported in Table 7.5 show that the proportion of members who support full participation is higher for informal SMOs than for formal SMOs, but almost the same as for parties and only slightly more than for trade unions (the differences are not statistically significant). The proportion of informal SMO members supporting consensus (rather than voting) is much higher than in any other kind of organization, with formal SMOs', but not ITOs', members following them.

Those findings would suggest accepting the diffusion argument according to three of the four items considered. This is also confirmed by the high degree of deliberative attitudes at the group level, for the members of each type of the most important group considered here: Figure 7.3 shows that although deliberativeness is much more widespread among informal SMO members, those activists whose primary membership is in parties and unions are as deliberative as those belonging to formal SMOs, and even more deliberative than ITO members.

We can go into more depth by correlating the four items that describe democracy at the group level with the four items that discriminate among democratic ideals. In addition, we can correlate the degree of deliberativeness attributed by the activists to their most important group with the degree of deliberativeness of their democratic ideals.

According to our data, activists who declare themselves active in groups that they perceive as deliberative and participatory (quality of arguments is considered more than resources, acceptance between opponents is the rule, full participation is assured, and consensus is the main decision making method) bear a congruent democratic ideal.[14] Particularly evident is the correlation between the voting/consensus items, suggesting a real democratic procedural cleavage

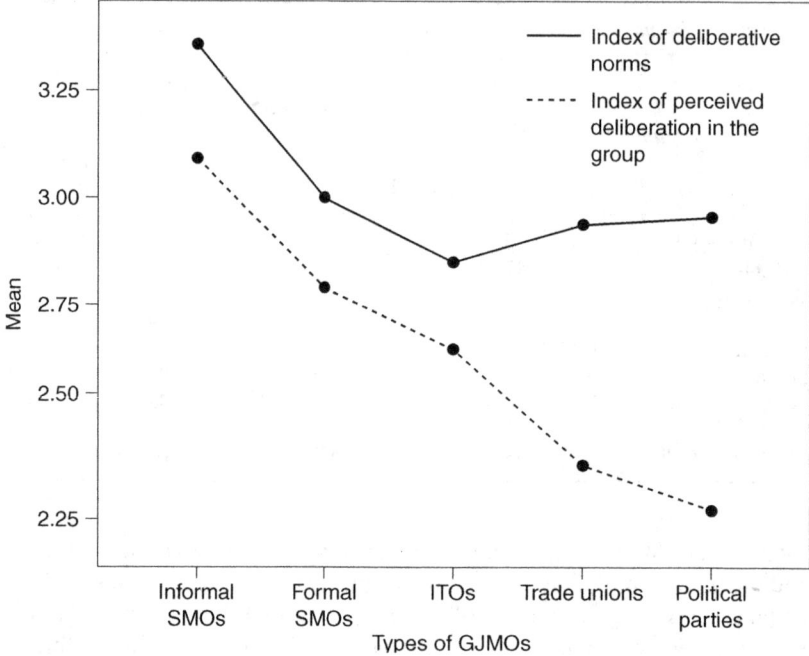

Figure 7.3 Deliberation as normative models among members.

between activists accustomed to counting preferences and consequently seeing voting as is the most democratic way to decide, and those used to integrating preferences consensually and consequently valuing consensus. This dichotomy corresponds to the conflict between 'horizontals' and 'verticals' in the preparations for the London Social Forum – each side saw the other as undemocratic, but saw its own side as exemplifying democracy. However, data show that there are normative ideas of democracy, based on the principles of direct participation, equality, and rationality (the importance of the arguments), that are spread beyond the sites in which they seem to be applied.

Satisfaction with democracy: comparing norms and practices

So far we have focused on how activists describe democracy for the group in which they are primarily active. We have also tried to understand activists' democratic ideals by comparing different organizational affiliations. In this section, we raise the question of how satisfied activists are with democracy in their group. After all, satisfaction with democracy should favour sustained involvement in collective action, be it within one particular group or in the GJM mobilization overall. Our data indicates that such satisfaction within one's group (the one considered most important) is very high: about 85 per cent on average declare themselves moderately or very satisfied with the group – although when we isolate only those activists who are 'very' satisfied with their group's democracy, the percentage decreases to 30 per cent.

In which type of group do members declare themselves more satisfied, and in which less? We can suppose that if the most legitimate ideals of democracy are based on full deliberation, activists should be less satisfied with democracy in the group when they perceive a democratic setting which is less so. As shown in a previous section, this would more likely apply within ITOs, political parties, and trade unions. Actually, satisfaction with democracy is higher in informal SMOs (45.3 per cent of their members being very satisfied), slightly less in formal SMOs (about 33 per cent), and lowest in parties and trade unions (27 and 23 per cent, respectively).[15]

As can be noted in Figure 7.4, satisfaction with democracy within groups highly correlates with the deviation between perceived practices and ideal standards. Incongruence is, in fact, higher among political parties and trade union members where, actually, satisfaction with democracy is less. It is lower in formal and

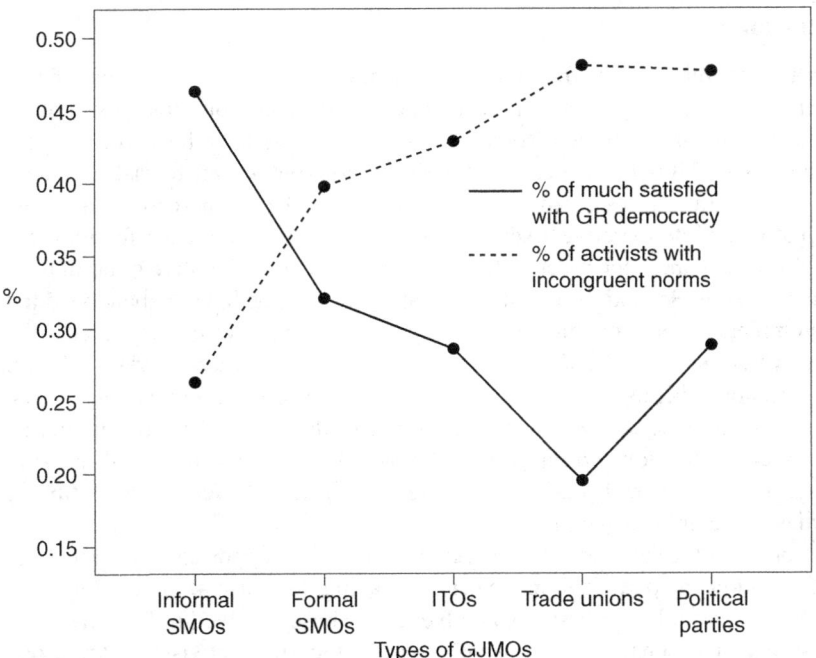

Figure 7.4 Comparing satisfaction with groups' democracy and incongruence* between perceived practices and norms.

Note
* The index of incongruence varies from 0 (fully congruent) to 3 (fully incongruent). Percentage refer to activists who score at least 0.75 on the index (see Chapter 4 for the operationalization).

informal SMOs, which are relatively more satisfied: the percentage of activists holding incongruent ideals with their groups' perceived practices is 26 per cent among informal SMOs' activists; 40 per cent in formal SMOs (but 43 per cent in ITOs); and about 50 per cent in parties and unions.[16] Simple correlations show that the lower the incongruence between perceived practices at the group level and democratic ideals, the higher activists' satisfaction with democracy in their most important group.[17] On the other hand, the higher the degree of deliberativeness activists attribute to their most important group, the higher their satisfaction.[18]

These findings confirm that decisions are more legitimate when they are perceived to be taken fairly (congruence with norms): when participation of all members is guaranteed, arguments are seriously considered, and participants are tolerant. In such a democratic setting, consensus as a procedure seems to be less important, at least in satisfying the democratic needs of the activists. If this is true, formal organizations have to solve the trade-off between effectiveness and internal democracy by improving their decision making settings if they want their members to be fully and happily involved in their activities. Political parties and trade unions should be more concerned with this, but formal SMOs and especially ITOs may also want to learn from the former organizations' mistakes.

Conclusion

There are several findings that are worth mentioning in the conclusions of this chapter. With respect to democratic practices and ideals, our findings show a complicated picture. Although some of our expectations have been confirmed – with informal SMOs being perceived as more horizontal than formal organizations, and with parties, trade unions and ITOs being perceived as least participative and deliberative – some important novelties have been found. First, many formal organizations' activists seem to indicate a deliberative trend in their decision making. Second, informal SMOs are perceived as having abandoned the old assembleary model to embrace a deliberative-participative model. Finally, the way in which activists see their organizations does not always correspond with their democratic ideals, especially for political parties, trade unions, and ITOs. This leads us to conclude that there is a process of diffusion of democratic norms that may create tensions within groups that adopt a 'vertical' model of decision making. Satisfaction with internal democracy is, in fact, lower among members of parties, trade unions, and ITOs.

Not only do formal organizations seem to offer less opportunity for rank and file deliberation and participation in decision making; they also seem to offer fewer opportunities for radical grassroots involvement. Those involved in ITOs have the greatest tendency to harbour a 'passive' rank and file: their activists tend to travel abroad less to participate in protest, to be less committed to protest, and to disproportionately engage in moderate rather than radical actions. Yet, it would be too harsh a judgement to brand ITOs as archetypal of 'protest businesses' or 'professional movement organizations', for they appear to allow a much greater degree of participation in movement activity than Michels (1959) or Jordan and Maloney

(1997) would concede. ITOs have also managed to avoid becoming the 'prisoner groups' that could be expected by virtue of their insider status. Although they may be careful to steer their staff and activists clear of riots, they do engage in protest on the streets in addition to participation in formal international financial institutions' conference proceedings (Dana Fisher *et al.* 2005). Formally organized political parties and trade unions buck the tendency towards exclusive decision making and passivity of membership to an even greater extent – by having introduced more participatory decision making styles, and encouraging, or at least condoning, participation in GJM events. In conclusion, we have found that there is less of a tendency towards oligarchy and passive membership in the GJM than has been both predicted by theory and witnessed in other social movements.

Notes

1. Clare Saunders is the principal author of 'Introduction', 'NGOs: a tired, abused and misused term?', 'Organizational formality, voice and influence and mobilization and participation in movements', 'Global justice movement organizations: mobilization and participation in decision making', and 'Engagement in different types of movement activity'. Massimiliano Andretta is the principal author of 'Democratic norms and practices within GJMOs', 'Democratic ideals: organizational patterns or diffusion?', and 'Satisfaction with democracy: comparing norms and practices'; while 'Organizational types in the GJM' and 'Conclusions' were co-authored. We would like to thank Donatella della Porta for her very useful comments on an earlier version of this chapter. We are also grateful to Christopher Rootes and Herbert Reiter for helping us to improve our categorization of organizational types.
2. The insistence upon non-political individual membership is problematic because some NGOs might have members who are affiliated with or even represent a political party. It also seems an odd distinction to make because many organizations, particularly in the GJM, have collective members because they are protest coalitions or solidarity networks.
3. William Fisher (1997: 448), for example, stresses that the related acronyms GSO, ISO, GRSO, MSO, QUANGO, DONGO, etc. are also applied in a variety of manners.
4. There is also a long-standing definitional muddle over the meaning of 'interest group' and its relationship to similar terms: pressure groups, cause groups, promotional groups, and sectional groups (see Kimber and Richardson 1974: 1–3).
5. For our operationalization of this category of organizations, we checked consultative status using two search engines, (online, available at: http://esa.un.org/coordination/ngo/new/index.asp?page=searchPage (UN) and http://coe-ngo.org/WebForms/NgoList.aspx?L=en (Council of Europe)). If the international branch of a national organization had consultation status but the national branch did not, then the national branch was *not* considered an ITO.
6. Thus, although the British Socialist Worker's Party (SWP) calls itself a party, it does not participate in elections or attempt to take government power for itself and is instead classified as a formal organization.
7. Dana Fisher *et al.* (2005), for example, found that SMOs gave support to just over 30 per cent of the non-local attendees at the five globalization protests that they surveyed. On the other hand, Klandermans' (1993) research, which compared participation in various Dutch social movements, found that the loose, participation-oriented network of the women's movement, which is broadly comparable to the organizational structure of informal SMOs, was the least effective at mobilizing activists. The centralized, federal, and power-oriented trade union he studied fulfilled its mobilization potential much more significantly.

8 Of those mentioning a political party, 11.7 per cent claimed to be a paid staff member, and 29.9 per cent claimed a leadership role. For trade unions, 12.9 per cent claimed to be staff members and 40.9 per cent to be part of the leadership. If we assume that leadership is often a paid role in these organizations, over half of the trade union representatives were paid for their attendance. In comparison, only 4 per cent of those from informal organizations claimed to be a staff member, and 24.6 per cent were part of the leadership. However, we can assume that most informal organizations do not have paid staff, and so the proportion of unpaid volunteers is much larger.
9 The measure of association between engagement in radical action – recoded as a dichotomous variable (radical actions engaged in, yes or no) – against organizational types was statistically significant at the 0.001 level. The Cramer's V score was 0.169.
10 While Attac has adopted top-down decision making in France and Germany, in Italy the association adopted a horizontal and consensual practice in which the Assembly of all members is the main decisional body.
11 We dichotomized each of the four items and added them up. The index varies from '0' (activists perceive that individuals are more important than arguments, in case of disagreements there is no acceptance, only a few people decide, and voting is the main decision making procedure), to '4' (maximum deliberativeness, the quality of arguments prevails, opponents treat each other as equals, full participation is more or less guaranteed, and consensus is the method).
12 The differences between traditional and radical leftist organizations will be explored in a separate chapter (Chapter 9).
13 According to Powell and DiMaggio (1991), organizations are embedded in a complex interorganizational system that pushes toward a sort of homogenization. Each relational system generates myths that legitimate organizational models: for instance, the 'bureaucratic rationality' or, in other contexts, the myth of the 'assembly' (Meyer and Rowan 1977). In our case, the GJM is supposed to have generated the 'myth' of consensus in democratic practices.
14 The relative Kendall's tau-b figures are respectively 0.207, 0.181, 0.131, and 0.401, while for the correlation between the two indexes of deliberation (perceived practices and normative ideals) it is 0.265 (all significant at 0.001 level).
15 The degree of satisfaction varies from 0 (very unsatisfied) to 3 (very satisfied); percentages refer to activists declaring themselves 'very satisfied'. Cramer's V = 0.15, significant at 0.001 level.
16 Cramer's V = 0.170, significant at 0.001 level.
17 Kendall's tau-b = – 0.295, significant at 0.001 level.
18 Kendall's tau-b = 0.316, significant at 0.001 level.

8 Novel characteristics of the GJM[1]
A (latent) network analysis approach

*Massimiliano Andretta, Iosif Botetzagias,
Moses Boudourides, Olga Kioufegi, and
Mundo Yang*

Latent networks in the fourth ESF: an introduction

According to academic research as well as activists' descriptions, the GJM exhibits a constellation of characteristics supporting the notion that something new has emerged since the protests in Seattle (della Porta *et al.* 2006a). In this chapter, we will review these assessments, focusing on activists' latent networks at the fourth European Social Forum in Athens. We will first enumerate the assumptions made so far in the literature, relate them to the study of the European Social Forum, and finally elucidate which empirical patterns confirm or challenge these notions of a unique occurrence.

First, specific network characteristics support the notion of the GJM as a 'movement of movements'. In contrast with earlier times, when activists tended to adhere to either one or another strictly defined ideological current, GJM activists seem to hold tolerant identities, allowing openness to a wide array of themes, social perspectives, and political stances. Rather than loose networking between clearly segmented currents with exclusionary membership, what have emerged are rhizomes and complex entanglements not only between but also within single activists of the GJM. A volunteer working within a trade union and at the same time in an environmental group, for example, can broaden and connect both social perspectives. As a result, the GJM is highly inclusive: a wide array of thematic niches, political traditions, and issue types are at home in their complex network structures. These network patterns blur conventional distinctions. For example, within the GJM the 'old' or 'traditional' left, namely bureaucratized trade unions or socialist parties, does not necessarily shy away from cooperation with radical grassroots (see Chapter 9 in this volume).

Second, the network metaphor not only grasps the characteristics of inclusiveness and tolerance, but also the transnational character of the GJM. While cross border activities of social movements are not entirely new, the current mobilizations exhibit a pattern of mass participation of individuals in transnational efforts. Thus, in contrast to earlier times, both rank and file activists and leaders of social movement organizations are active at the transnational level.

Third, notwithstanding, or because of, this heterogeneity, the GJM must establish some commonality regarding procedures for their joint principles of cooperation. If participants work in traditional trade unions and at the same time in radical grassroots groups, the GJM must provide a common understanding of how decisions are made, or at least, should be made. Many activists of the GJM interpret social forums as the attempt to offer such commonality by providing a discursive space guided by the ideals of consensus-oriented communication and full participation. In this vein, della Porta (2005a) concludes that the GJM provides a fertile ground for practising what scholars of normative political theory term 'deliberative democracy'.

In attempting to empirically assess these statements, scholars face the problem of where to start, since social movements – especially those as broad as the GJM – are difficult to observe at all. Our approach of looking at the participants of the European social forums not only updates past research on these questions and accommodates to practical restrictions, such as scarce resources and time. It can also be justified in two regards. On the one hand, these social forums serve as the 'infrastructure' of the GJM (Rucht 2008), meaning that these events are of high importance for internal coordination and opinion formation. While we cannot assume that the picture shown here is widely representative for the whole GJM in Europe, we can nonetheless estimate the adequacy of scholars' descriptions for one of these major events, namely the fourth ESF in Athens.

On the other hand, activists try to apply normative standards within the social forum. According to the charter of Porto Alegre, the bylaws of the social forums, the event is explicitly open to all kinds of social movements from all over the world. It should serve as a 'context for interrelations', thereby building a transnational discursive space. The use of the concept of 'space' rejects the notion of being an actor and stresses the need to shield egalitarian, participative discourses oriented towards consensus from the assaults of power politics. The charter clearly proposes a horizontally and egalitarian networked space for deliberative democratic practices and forbids voting and representative politics in the name of the forum (see also Chapter 1 and Chapter 2 in this volume).

Indeed, deliberative and participative values and practices are quite popular among the participants of the ESF in Athens (see Chapter 4), and these findings align well with our participant observation of sessions and workshops. But conflicts between 'verticals' and 'horizontals' still play a role (see Chapters 2, 4, and 9), indicating that this normative claim is not undisputed by all participants. Over the last several years, key activists have repeatedly lamented some characteristics of social forums as prescribed in the charter, urging reform. For example, Walden Bello,[2] a prominent intellectual figure of the GJM, asked for more action orientation of the World Social Forum, suggesting that the original concept of the forum as a space rather than an actor/movement may hinder activists from speaking with a partisan voice. In his response, Chico Whitaker[3] judged that such an opportunity for expression was always available from within the open space methodology and thus, for him, the World Social Forum can both incubate contentious movements and foster the principles of horizontality and openness.[4]

We can also question whether the normative claim stated in the charter actually worked in the case of the fourth ESF in Athens, given that in practice, it is difficult to mobilize such a diverse, well networked, and democratically oriented mass. If we look at the number of participants from the different countries, we might observe huge differences in attendance related to factors such as support for the forum by some major national social movement organizations or simply logistical costs. As a result, some became suspicious that participation in social forums largely consists of paid professionals who are not as engaged in other activities of the GJM.

Since participant observation does not allow us to fully answer these questions, in what follows we will investigate the degree to which both normative standards and scholarly descriptions are in accord with empirical observations obtained through the survey at the social forum. Using methods of network analysis, we will approach the question from another perspective by going one step further: While the questionnaire data cannot inform us about the actual materialization of *transversal, transnational, and trans-hierarchical* networking at the forum, it allows us to look at potential organizational interconnections, through individuals. In this perspective, we asked activists about their multiple memberships in different types of political organizations. In contrast with earlier studies, we use only information about organizational contexts in which activists were actively involved at the time of our research. Thus, we gained access to the micro-level of individual participation in different organizational contexts and to the networking practices that are likely to occur if one respondent is active in two or more different organizational (sometimes also ideological) contexts.

Looking at patterns of multiple memberships thus opens up an alternative view on organizational structure: the formal and official networks between organizations are not analysed; instead, currents and traditions, such as trade unionism, anarchism, or socialism are conceptualized as types that build up network nodes. Each single activist may use one or more of them as spaces for activities and can thereby connect different issue types. For our research question, these patterns of multiple memberships elucidate something invisible to most participants. For example, if two activists meet and discuss at the forum and each is active in three different political groups, they can compare nine times different experiences from their activities in these six groups. On the other extreme, if both activists belong exclusively to the same political current, their ability to exchange different political perspectives would be limited.

For this kind of analysis, we can rely on existing methods for multiple membership data (Cornwell and Harrison 2004; Gulati and Gargiulo 1999). Rather than focusing on the visible relations between organizations, we apply this perspective on the organizational relations that emphasize activists' contribution and agency. Activists in fact build a latent network of relations among various organizations via multiple memberships. As Cornwell and Harrison write in their study on embeddedness of US trade unions, which applies the same methodology: 'By maintaining voluntary associations, individuals link the organizations in their lives ... to community and, ultimately, to organizational culture', activists build 'organizational connectivity' which can be considered a 'latent embeddedness' (2004: 863).

One important limitation of this method is that the understanding of organizational and ideological contexts like environmentalism or trade unionism is quite context specific: for instance, a socialist type reflects a very moderate organizational context in Italy, while quite radical in the UK. In addition, when an activist declares membership in two types, it is likely that she refers to her country's organizations. Thus, given that the meaning of data is nationally bounded, we will conduct this type of analysis at the country level for respondents from Italy, France, Germany, and Greece.

In the next section, we will develop our method of analysis by describing our approach, clarifying the operationalization of the network-based indicators, and providing a justification of our cases' selection. We will then sketch out the latent networks' properties by showing differences and similarities in the selected countries' network structures, testing the connection between the position of the types in the national network and their members' participation in the broader GJM mobilization, and differentiating between network integration through leaders' or rank and file members' multiple affiliations. Finally, we will focus on the potential diffusion of deliberative ideas through the integration of the activist into the network. We will summarize our empirical findings in the last section.

Method: a non relational analysis

As mentioned, we will base our network analysis on activists' multiple memberships. Let us first describe what such a network analysis consists of. As we know, what distinguishes social network analysis from traditional social science methodologies is that in network analysis the focus is on dyadic data – that is, relations among the individually studied entities – while in traditional social science it is on monadic (personal) attributes of individuals (Wellman 1988; Borgatti and Everett 1997). One talks in social network analysis of two types of dyadic or relational data among individuals, and two types of respective social networks. First, we have the 1-mode data, which are composed of homogeneous dyads among all studied individuals, called actors, giving rise to 1-mode networks. Second, assuming that the studied entities may break into two parts, one part of individuals and another part of more general categories in which individuals may partake in some sense, then we have the bipartite, or 2-mode data, composed of heterogeneous dyads (or pairs) among an individual and an associated category and, thus, the so-called 2-mode networks. In the latter case, typically, individuals might be individual actors (i.e. persons) or collective actors (i.e. organizations and so on), and the more general categories might be affiliations of actors into more general groups or participations of actors in various events (Breiger 1974).

Operatively, in the Athens ESF survey data, each respondent declares affiliation with one or more among 24 types of organizations, mostly based on the issue (environment, human rights, anti-racist, etc.) listed in the questionnaire. Therefore, for each country, we obtain a 2-mode data matrix composed of N rows (where N is the number of respondents in the questionnaire from that country) and 24 columns (the issue types – for the sake of brevity, we will often use 'types' from now on) – that is, an N-by-24 matrix. Such 2-mode data may create a 1-mode network among types, whose adjacency matrix is a 24-by-24 matrix (Breiger 1974). The value in any cell in this adjacency matrix represents the number of respondents who declare affiliation with both types in the intersecting row and column that corresponds to this cell. Such an adjacency matrix (as symmetric and valued) gives rise to a 'social network' among 24 actors (i.e. the considered types in the questionnaire), which are related to each other by overlaps in the specific organizational affiliations (or co-affiliations) the respondents declare among the totality of these types. The social network analysis of such affiliation data is often used in structural multi-organizational studies (Cornwell and Harrison 2004). Following this method, one could compute a number of indicators, which measure different relational (network) properties of the types in the induced 1-mode network from the affiliation data. Among the most important of these network indicators are the two indicators of embeddedness, which measure the degree to which a type in the induced 1-mode network is tied and bound with all the other types with whom they compose a given multi-organizational community (Gulati and Gargiulo 1999; Cornwell and Harrison 2004).

The first of these indicators of embeddedness is *structural embeddedness*, which evaluates the similarity or commonness among members of types. The underlying idea is that the more common members two or more types share, the more prone they are to form strategic alliances and to become institutionally isomorphic (Maggio and Powell 1983; Gulati and Gargiulo 1999). A type has a high structural embeddedness when it has many co-memberships with many other types.

To operationalize the computation of the structural embeddedness for type i, we first measure the co-memberships between this type and any other type j. Then, dividing by the number of members in the smaller of the two types i and j, we obtain the number of co-memberships between the two types as a proportion of all the individuals who could possibly have been in both. Taking the average value of the latter proportion for all other types j gives the indicator of structural embeddedness for type i. Finally, after computing the structural embeddedness for each one of the 24 types, one usually normalizes this indicator by dividing it for its maximum value, so that its range lies between 0 and 1.

A second indicator of embeddedness is *positional embeddedness*, calculated through Bonacich's power centrality index for each type. This indicator measures the centrality of a type, or how advantageous its connections with other more central types (Bonacich 1987; Borgatti and Everett 1997). When a type has a high positional embeddedness, this type has many co-memberships with many other types, which in their turn have a few co-memberships with a few other types (Hanneman and Riddle 2005). This is because positional embeddedness, as measured by Bonacich's power index, is based upon the intuitive idea that a powerful actor is one that is connected with other weak actors (as 'my strength is your weakness and the other way around').

To compute positional embeddedness, we used the UCInet software, after first having normalized the induced 1-mode network adjacency matrix by both rows and columns in order to get rid of marginals (Borgatti et al. 2002). The computed indicators become conceptually distinct from membership rates, and we avoided the occurrence of high values of these indicators simply because of high membership rates (Cornwell and Harrison 2004: 867). As before, normalizing over the maximum indicator among the 24 types restricts the range of positional embeddedness in the interval from 0 to 1.

The above definitions suggest that both structural and positional embeddedness depend increasingly on membership rate. This is because the more members a type has, the more shared co-members it might have with other types.[5]

Furthermore, from concrete computations, one might observe that for a given type, its positional embeddedness tends to be higher than its structural embeddedness, unless the type's membership rate is low. Why is this happening, and how can such a tendency be interpreted? The underlying idea is that a powerful type is not necessarily at the same time highly central – it only has to have co-memberships with other less powerful (that is, weaker) types. But for low membership rates, power seems to wither (together with co-memberships), although centrality can still be sustained (although at moderate levels).

For each type, we have considered the following four indicators (Cornwell and Harrison 2004):

Membership rate: This is just the proportion of a type's members (i.e. respondents who have answered that they are affiliated with that type) over the whole number of respondents who have completed the questionnaire. Obviously, this indicator (ranging from 0 to 1) describes how popular a certain type is among all respondents.

Members' average number of memberships in other organizations (AverNo): To compute this indicator for type i, we have added the number of co-memberships between this type and any other type j and divided the result by the number of the type's i members. Thus, if this indicator is more (or less) than 1, then membership in a type is lower (or higher) than co-memberships in other types.

This/other: This represents the proportion of members of a certain type who are in other types too (with respect to all co-memberships). To calculate this indicator for each type, we first counted the number of its members who are also affiliated with other types and then divided by the total number of respondents who are affiliated with at least two types. Theoretically, this number is at most 1; the higher is the number, the more multi-affiliated members belong to the given type.

Other/this: The proportion of members of other types who are members of a certain type. To calculate this indicator for a type, we counted the number of its members who are also affiliated with other types, and then divided the result by the total number of its members. Again, this number is at most 1; the higher the number, the more members of *other* types are affiliated with *this* type too.

Let us restate that with this type of analysis, we do not say anything about the real concrete organizations that actually participate in the making of the GJM in Europe: organizations appear as types (unions, parties, environmental types, anarchist groups, and so on) and the types are our main units of analysis. The network measures of the different types will be calculated by country by comparing four national organizational communities created by activists' multiple memberships:

German, Greek, Italian, and French. The selected countries vary in terms of political culture and domestic opportunity structure, as well as domestic configuration of the GJM (della Porta 2007b). The cross-country comparison helps us to understand the different configurations of potential networks and makes us more confident in generalizing the similarities we find. Also, due to the low numbers of other nationalities' respondents, our analysis has to be restricted to the aforementioned four countries.

In each country, types with less than ten members were excluded from the analysis. Those are: for Germany, Women's groups, Gay/lesbian, Development aid, Human rights, International solidarity, Consumerist, Trotskyite, Communist, Anarchist, Autonomist, Peasants, Charity, and Unemployed; for Greece, Gay/lesbians and Anarchist; for France; Peasants and Unemployed; for Italy, Socialist, Trotskyites, Anarchists, Peasants, and Trade unions. Religious groups are excluded in all selected countries.

Latent networks in the four countries

In this part, we describe the network structure of the different national organizational communities, built through the activists' multiple affiliations for each national delegation that participated at the fourth ESF in Athens.

The ESF, a context for interrelations?

If, indeed, a diverse and densely interconnected network has assembled at the ESF in Athens, there should be few or no marginalized and highly peripheral types. At least marginalization and peripheral network positions should be distributed in a stable pattern, which for example could point at non-egalitarian structures. In order to address this question, we can analyse the networks in different ways, the most meaningful being crossing the two dimensions of embeddedness: positional and structural.

To give an idea of how a type is structurally or positionally embedded in our four cases, we can correlate the positional and structural indicators with the other indicators we presented in the previous section. The results in Table 8.1 show that in each country, a type is both structurally and positionally embedded when it has a relatively high number of members (rate), who are also members of other types (this/other). Embeddedness is not always correlated with the members' average number of memberships in other organizations (AverNo), which means that members of an embedded type do not necessarily have to also be members of as many other types as possible. Finally, in each country, positional and structural embeddedness are highly correlated.

Comparing structural with positional embeddedness for types with variable membership rates (note that both indices of embeddedness are normalized), we can have one of the following four results:[6]

1 Both structural embeddedness and positional embeddedness are high.
2 Positional embeddedness is high and structural embeddedness is low.

Table 8.1 Bivariate non parametric correlations (Kendall's tau-b) between network indicators in each country network.

Net indicators	Italy		Germany		France		Greece	
	Posit.	Struct.	Posit.	Struct.	Posit.	Struct.	Posit.	Struct.
Rate	0.436**	0.412*	0.659**	0.644**	0.783***	0.684***	0.706***	0.631***
AverNO	n.s.	n.s.	n.s.	n.s.	n.s.	n.s.	n.s.	n.s.
This/Other	0.493**	0.468**	0.644**	0.658***	0.789***	0.690***	0.725***	0.651***
Other/This	n.s.	n.s.	n.s.	n.s.	n.s.	n.s.	n.s.	n.s.
Positional	–	0.915***	–	0.989***	–	0.765***	–	0.852***

Notes
Levels of significance as follows:
*significant at 0.05 level, **significant at 0.01 level, ***significant at 0.001 level, n.s. not significant.

3 Structural embeddedness is high and positional embeddedness is low.
4 Both structural and positional embeddedness are low.

Roughly speaking, in mode 1, a type would be both central and powerful (in the relational sense); in mode 2, it would be more powerful than central; in mode 3, it would be more central than powerful; and in mode 4, it would be weak and marginal. In our four countries, we have examples of modes 1, 2, and 4, while mode 3 is an empty category (see Table 8.2). We then classified the types in each country in three categories: category 2, both positionally and structurally embedded; category 1, positionally but not structurally embedded; and category 0, weak and marginal. Table 8.2 summarizes the results by classifying each type in each country accordingly.

Starting from the Italian types, we can then distinguish between very embedded types (such as international solidarity, human rights, anti-racism, alternative consumerism, political parties); and less structurally embedded but positionally well integrated ones (such as student, charity, unemployed, anti-neoliberal, autonomist, communist, and local social forums [LSF]); while marginal groups (such as Trotskyite, peasant, anarchists, socialist, religious, gay/lesbian, and trade unions) all have less than ten members, then not shown in the table.

As we can see, the embeddedness of the various types does not depend on their organizational structure. In the ESF, and for the Italian activists, very formal and structured organizations such as political parties are as well integrated as others of a less formal type – such as peace, international solidarity, consumerist, and human rights groups – but also very informal types, such as the groups belonging to anti-racist movements. In contrast, formal and large organizations such as trade unions are marginal, as are anarchist and Trotskyist ones. Unemployed, LSF, student, and anti-neoliberal and charity groups, which are only half integrated, also differ in terms of formalization.

In Germany, the situation is slightly different, the most embedded types being trade unions, political parties, anti-neoliberal types, LSF, and peace movements; the most marginal are alternative media.

Table 8.2 Level of embeddedness for each type in each country*

Level of embeddedness	Italy	Germany	France	Greece
High structural and positional	*Peace, Develop. aid, Human rights, Intern. solidarity, Anti-racist,* Consumerism, Communist, *Anti-neoliberal,* Alternat. media, *Political party*	Environment, *Peace, Anti-neoliberal, LSF,* Socialist, Trade unions, *Political Party*	Women, *Peace, Develop. aid, Human rights, Intern.solidarity, Anti-racist,* Consumerism, *Anti-neoliberal, LSF,* Peasant-farmers, Trade union, *Political party*	Women, Environment, *Peace, Develop. aid, Human rights, Intern. solidarity, Anti-racist, Anti-neoliberal, LSF, Political party*
High positional and low structural	Women, Environment, Student, *Autonomist, LSF,* Charity, Unemployed	Anti-racist, Student	Environment	Gay, Lesbian, Student, Socialist, Communist, *Autonomist,* Trade Unions
Low structural and positional		Alternat. media	Student, Socialist, *Trotskyite,* Communist, Autonomist, Alternat. media, Charity, Unemployed	*Trotskyite,* Anarchist, Alternat. media, Charity, Consumerist

Note
* We reported in italic the types that result in a similar position in different countries and that we thought worth commenting upon in the text.

The French organizational community is still different. Political parties and trade unions are very well embedded as in the German case (while for the Italians this is true only for political parties), but they are less embedded than the anti-racist groups, which are very active in French contemporary mobilizations (Sommier and Combes 2007). The most marginal are student, socialist, Trotskyist, communist, autonomist, alternative media, and unemployed types.

Finally, in Greece, as in the other countries, political parties are very well embedded; but trade unions are less so. Women, anti-neoliberal, environmental, peace, international solidarity and other internationally oriented types are very embedded, while together with trade unions, socialist, communist, autonomist, student and gay/lesbian groups are only positionally embedded. The most marginal are Trotskyist and anarchist, as well as consumerist, charity, and alternative media types.

As can be noted, cross-national differences are considerably fewer than similarities: political parties, peace, development aid, human rights, international solidarity, anti-neoliberal groups, LSF, and anti-racist groups perform similar functions of network integration in at least three of the selected countries; while alternative media, Trotskyist, anarchist, religious, and charity types are either excluded from the analysis (because they have less than 10 members) or very marginal in at least three countries.

Yet, we do observe some important differences. For one, we see a high positional embeddedness in Italy and Greece of autonomist groups,[7] which in France and Germany are marginal or excluded from the analysis. This difference could be accounted for by different factors: first, in France those groups are very weak, since in the French anti-capitalist field Trotskyites largely prevail, among which the LCR party has a clear hegemony (Sommier and Combes 2007); second, in Italy, the autonomist groups have transformed their practices and frames and invested a lot in the GJM mobilization (della Porta *et al.* 2006a), while in Germany and in Greece they remained linked to an old style of mobilization that is difficult to combine with the perceived reformist style of the social forums. Arguably, for the Greek autonomists the stake of having a European Social Forum in Athens was very high and the cost of mobilization at that level relatively low – which was not the case for the German autonomists, who probably decided to stay home.

A second difference is the weakness of trade unions in Italy, in contrast to their embeddedness in the other three countries. This relative weakness could be explained by the growing distance between the Italian trade unions themselves and the rest of the domestic branch of the GJM, due to competitiveness between the big confederations and the radical grassroots unions. In addition, large Italian trade unions are traditionally linked with party politics (the so-called *collateralismo*). At the time of the forum in Athens, Italy was about to vote in national elections in which the centre-left was called to challenge the incumbent government coalition lead by the tycoon Berlusconi: a very polarized electoral campaign that absorbed most of the energy of the traditional leftist activists.

Despite those differences, our data indicate that at the core of the organizational populations in each of the considered countries is the 'strange alliance' between old and new social movements that has been underlined by other scholars (Levi and Murphy 2006; della Porta *et al.* 2006a). Also central are groups born with the rise of the GJM, especially local social forums and anti-neoliberal groups (basically Attac). Meanwhile, the radical, anti-capitalist groups are at the periphery of the movement, with the reported exception of autonomist groups in Italy and Greece.

In general, the (self-)description of the GJM as an open space for interrelation for a wide range of types is quite adequate. This would not be the case if one assumed that every type should perform the same function in the latent network, in terms of size (number of activists declaring membership) and embeddedness. But this would be an unrealistic measure, since specific types, such as gay/lesbians or alternative media, tend by definition to be smaller in size and consequently relatively less embedded. Instead, the self-proclamation of transversal character would be a contradiction in terms, if specific types were to systematically occupy peripheral and marginal positions in the network due to ideological reasons. But as we have shown, the cleavages between old and new, or between formalized and spontaneous, could not be backed up by our data. In addition, the differences among types are quite small and can be largely explained by the size of the membership: this fact points to the principle that types tend to gain importance based on the number of mass activities that take place. The thematic fields for major mobilizations by the GJM are therefore generally central in the ESF: peace, environment, global social justice, and LSF. The high importance of peace activism, for example, can be connected to the mass mobilizations that have taken place since the war against Iraq broke out in early 2003.

While there are consistently marginalized types (such as religious, charity, Trotskyite, anarchist, and alternative media movements), other currents known to be small in size are quite well embedded – for example, anti-racism or consumerism. If we consider that certain types, for example anarchists or autonomists, tend to parallel the forum activities with alternative events,[8] then we can indeed support the finding that the forum is open in principle, while not yet an ideal transversal place.

The ESF as main part of GJM

So far, we have classified the types according to their latent embeddedness in the national organizational communities participating in Athens; but to what extent does their position in the networks predict their (members') active involvement in the broader GJM mobilization?

Theoretically, this aspect can be related with the 'social capital' argument that connection with the social environment is important for political participation. According to Teorell (2003: 51), for instance: 'one thing the social environment surrounding an agent might attempt is to *persuade* him or her to take part in political action'. By overlapping arguments derived from the social capital theory elaborated by Putnam (especially, 2000), the 'weak ties' approach by Granovetter (1973), and the 'structural holes' metaphor by Burt (1992), this author concludes that:

> We should expect people having access to large but loosely coupled networks – in other words, 'bridging' social capital – to get more requests for participation. This follows from the idea that such networks link people to a wider context, and thus increase the probability of being exposed to appeals for political action. According to this logic, then, the power of voluntary associations to promote political action hinges on their ability to develop weak ties (or bridge structural holes).
>
> (Teorell 2003: 52)

In the language of the network analysis we use here, to control the accuracy of this prediction we should answer the following question: is embeddedness in the organizational communities of the fourth ESF related to higher participation in the GJM?

The involvement in the GJM varies by country: members of our types participated on average more than seven times (7.4) in other GJM events before Athens,[9] the means varying from 5.9 in Greece, to 5.8 in France, to more than 8 in Italy and Germany (8.9 and 8.3 respectively). About 64 per cent of members on average did participate transnationally: 43 per cent in Greece, 62 per cent in

160 M. Andretta et al.

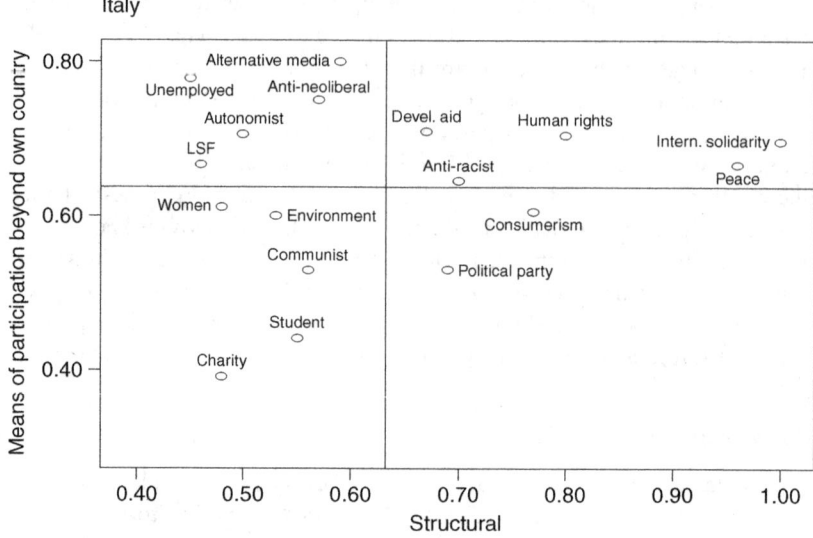

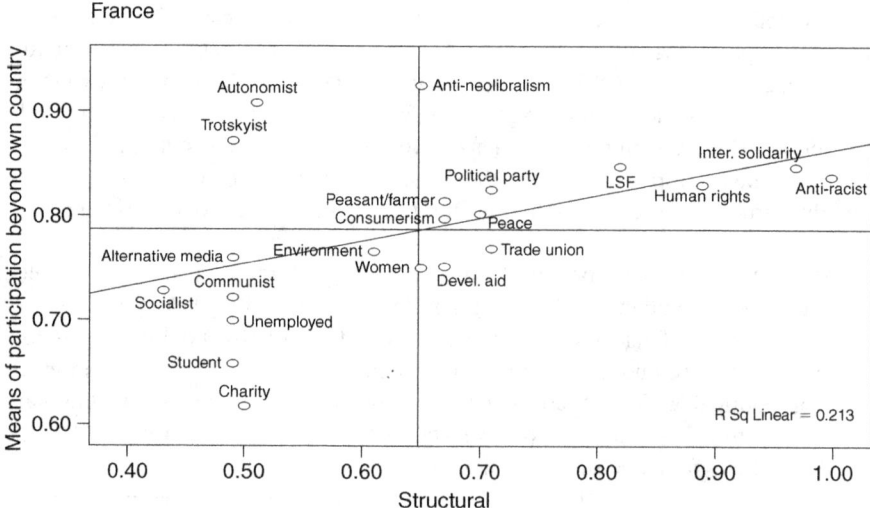

Italy, 71 per cent in Germany, and 79 per cent in France. Finally, the identification with the GJM is on average very high, being always more than 'enough' (that is, between 2 and 3) in each country.[10]

If we isolate participation in GJM events abroad and cross it with structural embeddedness in each country, we notice that the picture is less clear than we would expect (see Figure 8.1). Only in France is the relation quite linear: most of the embedded types are also more transnationally active, and most of the

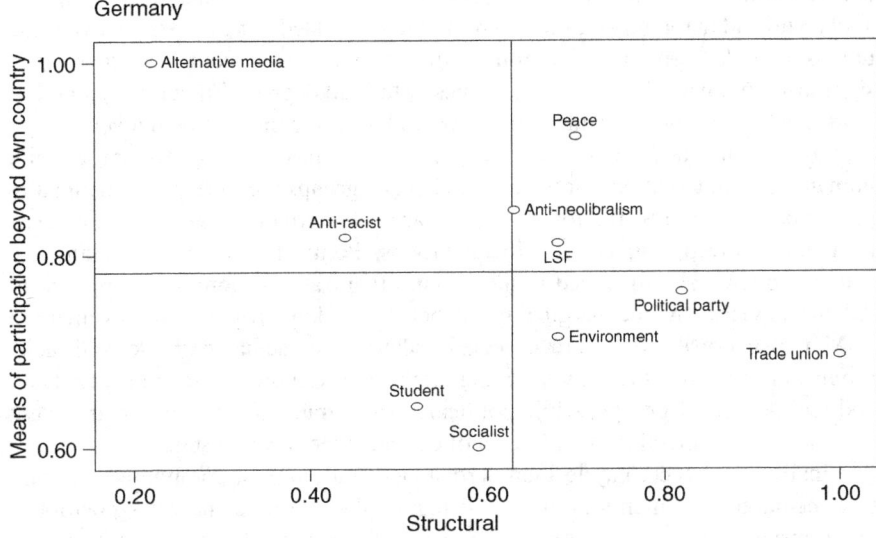
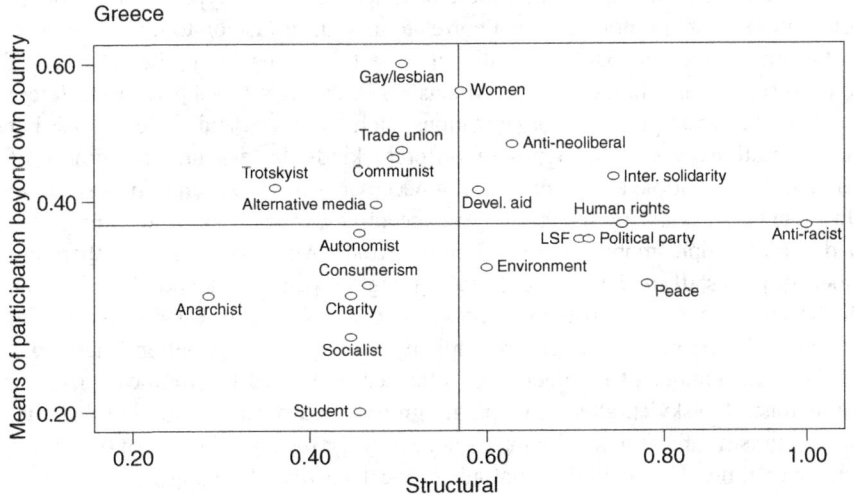

Figure 8.1 Crossing structural embeddedness and participation in GJM events abroad.[1]

Note
1 The lines show the mean points embeddedness and the percentage of members who participated in a GJM protest events in country other than her own before Athens.

marginal types are less so (the non-parametric Kendall's tau-b correlation is 0.420, significant at 0.01 level). Exceptions are, on the marginal side, the active Trotskyite and autonomist groups and, on the embedded side, the less active trade unions and development aid groups. In the other three countries, there is a significant number of both marginal types with high degree of involvement and of embedded types whose members participated less at the transnational level.

To start with Italy, the members of embedded types such as development aid, human rights, international solidarity, and peace groups are indeed transnationally active; but the same is true for the more marginal alternative media, LSF, autonomist, unemployed, and anti-neoliberal groups. Political party members are less active, though well embedded in the Italian organizational community present in Athens. In Germany, the marginal types that show a high degree of involvement in GJM transnational events are especially alternative media, but also anti-racist groups; the embedded types whose members are also more active are peace, LSF, and anti-neoliberal groups; while political parties, trade unions, and environment types are less involved than their level of embeddedness would suggest.

Finally, in Greece, gay/lesbian, Trotskyist, trade union, communist, alternative media, and women's groups – all marginal in terms of network position – are transnationally more active than the well embedded environment, peace, political party, anti-racist and LSF types.

Our findings, then, suggest that the embeddedness of the types in the national organizational communities does not correlate in a linear fashion to their members' level of involvement in GJM transnational protest. It seems that in the networks of the GJM (or, at least, in those at the Athens ESF), different types perform different functions. For example, mass organizations such as parties and trade unions, but also internationally oriented types of different kinds, have a greater number of members with multiple affiliations but not necessarily always keen to participate in GJM events. After all, by using selective incentives, mass organizations may rely on different people mobilized in different periods. Many of those members are leaders or paid staff members (see 'Elite meeting or open to rank and file?', below), which testifies to the resources those organizations mobilize for GJM activities. On the other hand, more informal groups – relatively marginal in the national networks, with a small number of members, and often characterized by a radical ideology (autonomist, Trotskyist, alternative media groups, and others) – provide that sustained activism (of a few people) that is necessary for the reproduction of the movement over time. This partially contradicts the idea that 'bridging social capital' would produce more participation than 'bonding social capital', the latter lacking the ability to overcome the 'structural holes' of a network, as Teorell contends.

It is indeed a finding of social movement research that sustained activism is (also) a function of a radical view of society (Downton and Wehr 1998). Sometimes the relatively low degree of connection with other groups may reproduce sustained activism over time, simply by isolating some groups from the environmental changes: 'Groups that are not well linked to other segments of society may find themselves at an advantage when it comes to organizing for collective action' (Oberschall 1973: 118–24).

Marginal groups might also tend to participate more in events abroad because they have fewer opportunities at home: thus, the transnational arena may provide the 'free space' where they can try to find the visibility and legitimacy they lack in their domestic contexts. To be sure, the absence of significant ties with other national organizations – that is, low embeddedness in domestic networks – qualifies this point.

Another line of interpretation, which can be combined with the previous ones, would suggest that besides the new types emerging with the birth of the GJM (anti-neoliberal, alternative media, or LSF types), the most transnationally active types are those that have been long characterized by an international mission, such as international solidarity, peace, human rights, and so on. Exceptions to this rule are often radical groups, which seem to be very active (autonomists or Trotskyites), though one can argue that those groups too have a traditional international mission: the proletarian revolution.

To conclude, if embeddedness is correlated to a *high proportion* of members with *multiple affiliations* participating in a transnational context such as the ESF in Athens, marginal groups, lacking these characteristics, seem to make an effort to assure their presence by instead promoting the *sustained participation* of their (few) members in events abroad.

Regarding our initial questions, we can conclude that the social forum indeed gathers activists from the GJM who had participated to an extraordinarily high degree in transnational protests. In contrast to earlier movements, the GJM converts their commitment to international solidarity into mass actions on the transnational level. But in line with Bello's (2007) criticism of the social forum as being good for 'talking' but more and more distanced from 'action', there is indeed a certain gap between activity in transnational protest and high embeddedness in the Athens Social Forum. In relation to their importance in transnational protests, radical types are slightly less embedded, while more professionalized and formal types (parties, trade unions, and other types like environmental and human rights groups) tend to take more crucial positions in the network.

Elite meeting or open to the rank and file?

The various types are differently integrated if we consider only the multiple affiliations of leaders and staff, or only those of ordinary and voluntary members. This distinction is important for two reasons. First, if leaders connect different types through their multiple affiliations, this should lead to a much more 'concrete' embeddedness, which would overcome the simple 'latentness': if a leader of a trade union is also a member of, say, a charity type, she will be more able than a simple member to reinforce and reproduce the cooperation between the two types. On the other hand, a mere elite meeting would highly question the notion of the intensified transnational character of the GJM, present at the ESF. It is possible that certain currents just send some high officials, quite well known and interconnected for sending solidarity notes, while most rank and file members abstain from transnational actions.

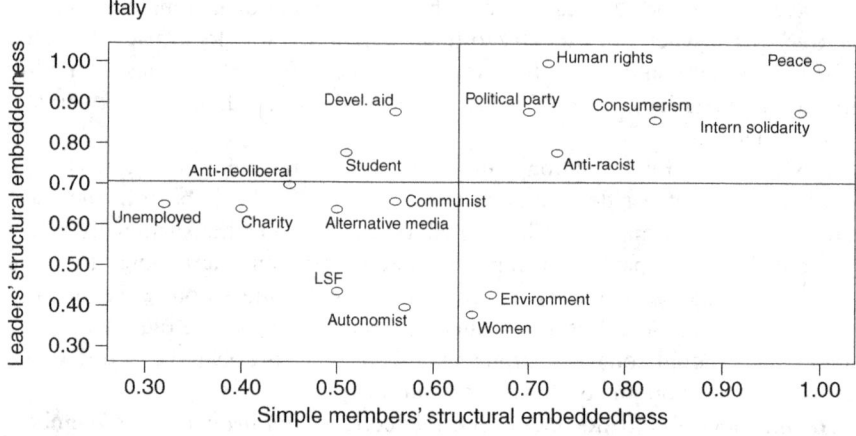

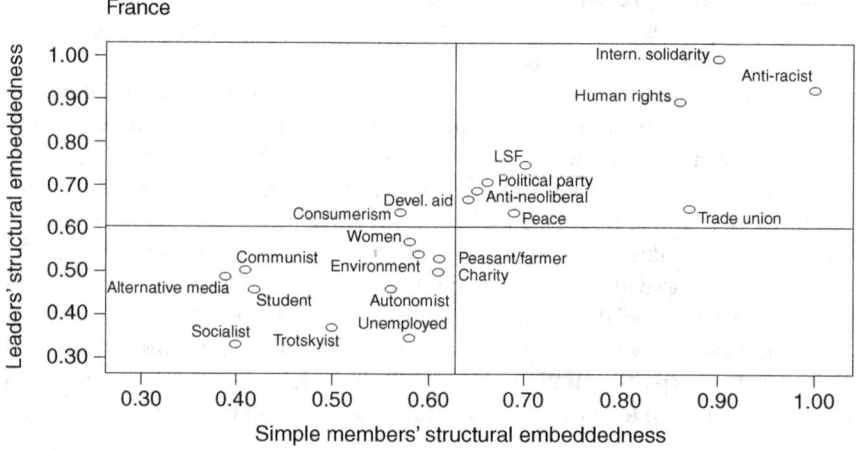

It follows that for a network to be both integrated and open to mass participation, the types should be mostly embedded through both leaders and members. If we calculate the same measures of embeddedness separately for each country, we have two networks for each country: a network of leaders and a network of simple members. We thus produced a two-dimensional space/plot where every type can be placed according to structural embeddedness, showing the different degrees of importance of each type within the respective network of leaders and members.

In order to operationalize this typology, we constructed two indexes of ordinary and voluntary members and leaders and staff embeddedness. For both leaders' and simple members' embeddedness, we use only structural embeddedness. Figure 8.2 shows the visualizations for the different countries.

We can distinguish among:

Novel characteristics of the GJM 165

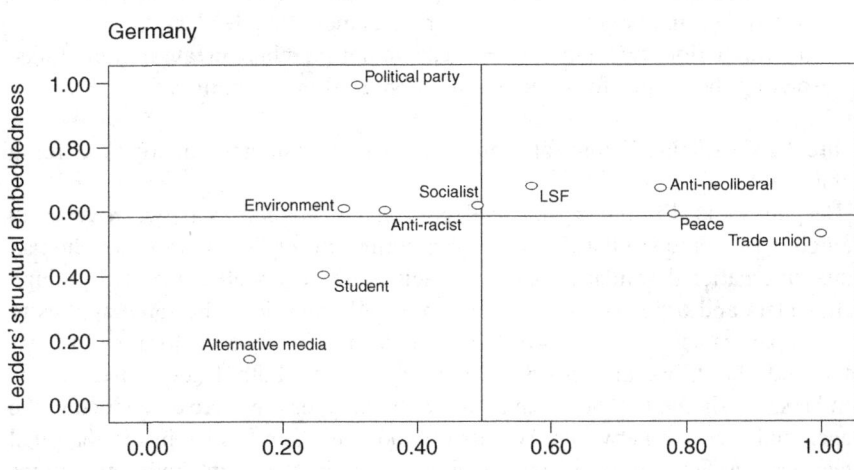

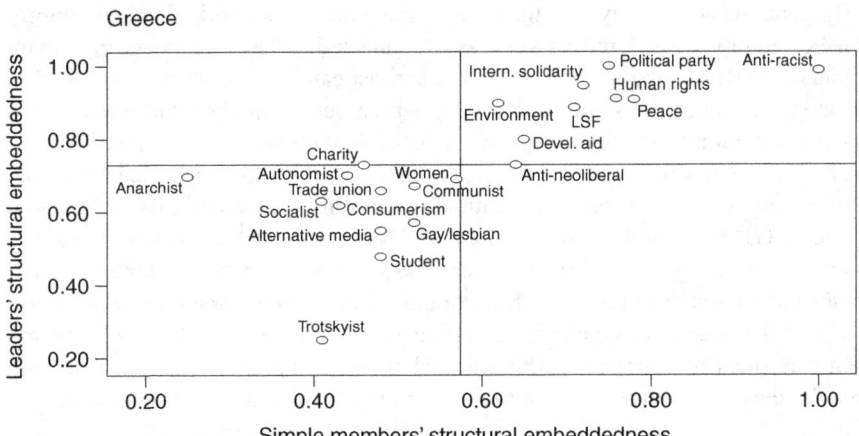

Figure 8.2 Latest networks according to leaders and simple members (structural) embeddedness.[1]

Note
1 The lines show the means points on leaders and simple member's structural embeddedness

- Types embedded through both leaders and simple members, where both leaders and ordinary members contribute to create indirect links through multiple memberships;
- Types embedded only through leaders, where leaders (more than simple members) create indirect links with other types;

- Types embedded only through simple members, where ordinary members overlap their memberships with other types more than leaders do;
- The true periphery: where neither leaders nor members create indirect links, isolating their types from the broader organizational community.

Figure 8.2 shows the finding for each type in each considered country, according to this typology.

Despite some differences in the degree of embeddedness between types in each country, some similarities are worth noting. SMOs active in peace, human rights, international solidarity, and anti-racism are very well embedded through both leaders and ordinary members in almost all countries. The same applies to political parties and other types of the GJM, such as local social forums. In Italy, Attac and the LSFs are marginal, with respect to both leaders and simple members.[11] It should be noted that anti-neoliberal types are more embedded in the French and German networks. We also found some similarities in the marginal categories: gay/lesbian, socialist, Trotskyite, anarchist, peasant, religious groups and alternative media are not embedded, either through leaders or through rank and file, in the relative organizational communities in almost all countries.

In general, we can say that the core of the national networks in each country can be reliably considered as very well connected. These are types that share leaders or staff members. Obviously, one activist can be a leader or staff member of one type and at the same time a simple member of another; but even in this case the function of sharing information, ideas, and resources this type of activist may perform is quite strong. At the same time, this does not mean that the ESF is only a matter of elite integration, confirming the beliefs of scholars who conceive GJM as simple coalition (Levi and Murphy 2006). On the contrary, our data show an integration of both leaders and simple members, a clear sign that a social movement formation, with a complex but common identity, is at work. The fact that marginal types are often marginal at the level of both leaders and members does not contradict this picture: those groups are connected, though weakly: even small groups are participating in network and identity building.

The ESF as space for deliberation

Although it has been stressed that one important novelty of the GJM is its activists' emphasis on consensus practices and ideas (Ceri 2003; della Porta 2005a; della Porta *et al.* 2006a), it was noted in Chapter 4 of this volume that activists share different normative ideas on how democracy should work in general; there are many who still think that delegation and voting are legitimate principles upon which democracy should be organized. In this section, we try to assess to what extent the latter constitutes a challenging faction visible within the latent networks, one that clearly withstands the tendency to accept participation and consensus as normative ideals.

In order to measure the deliberativeness of activists' ideas, in this section we use only two out of four items included in the questionnaire: (*a*) the statement separating those whose normative idea of democracy is compatible with *delegation of power* from those who think that the *participation of all* interested persons should always be a priority; and (*b*) the statement distinguishing those who believe that decisions should be taken by *voting* from those who are convinced that they should be taken by *consensus*. We then calculated (by country) the percentage of members of each type who value both full participation and consensus in ideal decision making, that is, those who favour deliberative participation as a model (see Chapter 4). The percentage of deliberative-participative activists is on average 24 per cent in Greece, 42 per cent in France, 45 per cent in Germany, and 49 per cent in Italy.

We shall now look at the relation between embeddedness and deliberative values within each national network. Figure 8.3 shows those relationships by means of scatter plots. If we look at the Italian network, we see that with the exception of consumerism, none of the structurally embedded organizations has a percentage of members above the average, while this happens in five of the ten non-embedded types: autonomist, anti-neoliberal, women's, students', and alternative media movements. Surprisingly, the local social forums' members are less deliberative than the average. The peace, human rights, and international solidarity types, which are fully embedded in the Italian network, show a percentage of members valuing both full participation and consensus a little below the average (always more than 40 per cent), while not surprisingly, political parties' members are the least deliberative.

In the German organizational community, in contrast, four of the six embedded types have many deliberative members (more than the average), as do three of the four marginal types. Especially interesting is the high deliberativeness of trade union members, and on the other side the fact that the local social forums have the lowest percentage of deliberative members. It comes as no surprise that among the German participants, those associated with political parties are also less deliberative than the average.

Within the French network, too, degree of embeddedness is not associated with deliberativeness: four of nine marginal types have many deliberative members, as well as six of 12 embedded types. Here, members of political parties, trade unions, women's, peasants', and peace organizations, but also LSF, though very embedded in the network, are less deliberative than the average, while members of the other embedded types such as anti-neoliberal, consumerist, development aid, international solidarity, anti-racist, and human rights are more deliberative. Among the marginal types, members of unemployed, autonomist, alternative media, and students' groups are more deliberative, while members of environment, charity, Trotskyist, socialist and communist types are less so.

Finally, for the Greek network, among the embedded types, only anti-neoliberal, women and, in contrast to other countries, LSF members are more deliberative than the average – but the proportion of deliberative members is always less than 30 per cent, while the only types with a proportion of deliberative members higher than 40 per cent are the anarchists and autonomists, which

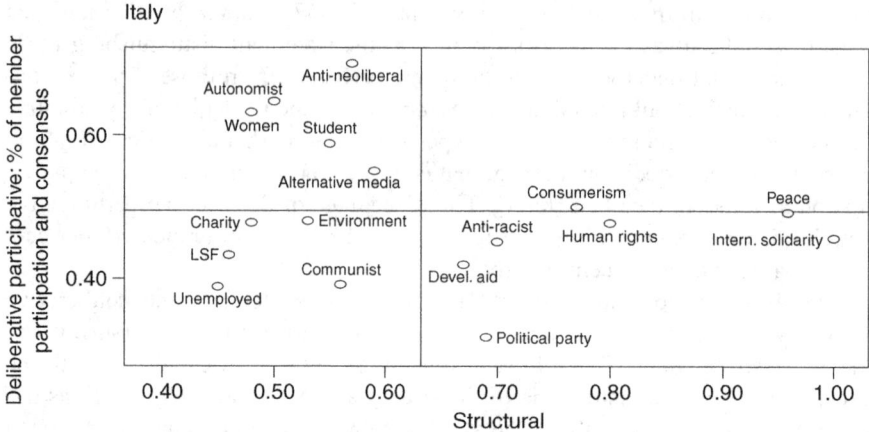

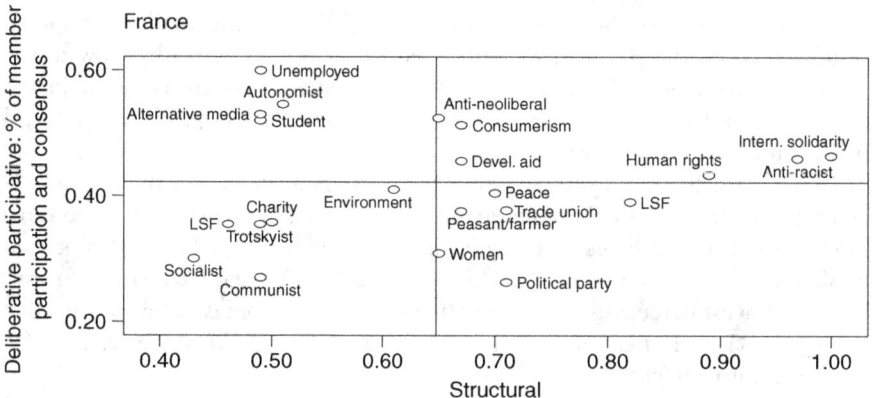

are not embedded in structural terms. Other marginal types with a percentage of deliberative members above the average (which is approximately 24 per cent) are communist, consumerist, alternative media, trade unions, and student groups.

In general, we can say that in the Italian and Greek networks, the members of marginal types are more oriented towards deliberative views, while in the French and German networks, the (low) embeddedness is not a predictor of deliberative attitudes: deliberation is widespread among both marginal and embedded types' members.[12] It is quite reasonable that small and marginal groups' members would prefer a consensual and participative model of democracy in which they, too, could have a say; but the data show that the members of mass organizations like trade unions and internationally oriented types are also understanding democracy in a different light, sometimes very different from the kind of democracy they are used to within their own organization. However, this

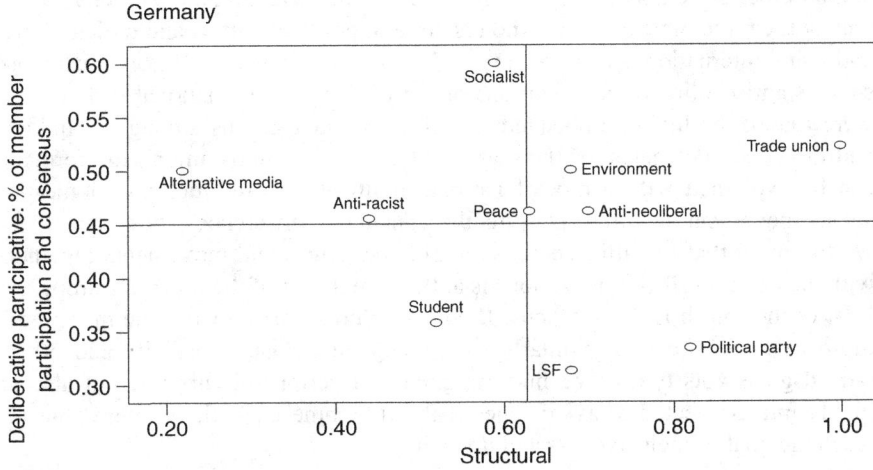

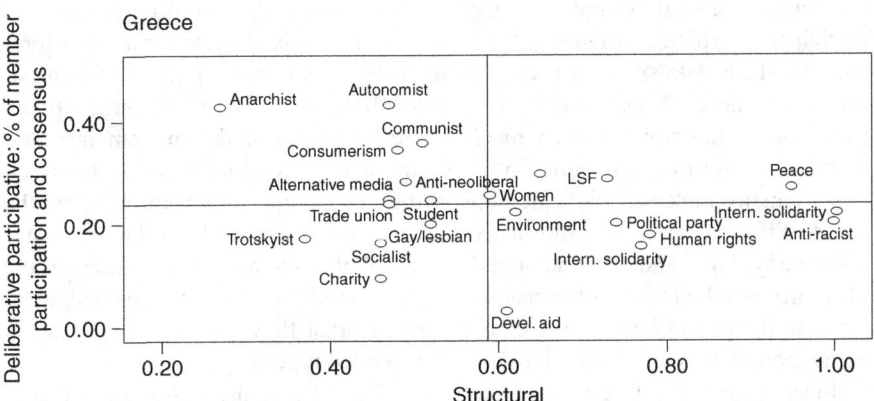

Figure 8.3 Crossing structural embeddedness and deliberative participative values.[1]

Note
1 The lines show the means points on positional embeddedness and the percentage of members valuing both participation and consensus.

- process of diffusion of democratic ideas is more visible in some countries (Germany and France) than in others (Italy and Greece), and it applies little to political parties.

Conclusion: (latent) networks and democracy in the GJM

The aim of this chapter was to analyse the multiple affiliation patterns of activists (of four national delegations) participating in the fourth ESF.

The simple description of the latent network structures revealed that many similar types are embedded in a similar way in the different national networks – among them the most powerful and resourceful political parties and trade unions and many internationally oriented types, but also the newest GJM organizations such as anti-neoliberal organizations or the LSF. Very few national differences were found: the higher embeddedness of autonomist groups among the Italian and the Greek delegates, or the marginality of trade unions among the former, can be explained with a mix of national political opportunities and domestic social movement features. Despite these national differences, however, it is worth noting that the alliance between old and new social movements together with the newest GJM organizations is at the core, if not of the GJM in Europe, at least of the fourth ESF in Athens. It comes as no surprise that at the margin of those networks we find, similarly by country, anarchist, Trotskyite and other radical grassroots types. We find marginal and peripheral currents, but also a highly interconnected array of types that, with some exceptions, seem able to reach the goal of inclusiveness and diversity.

In addition, it seems that the ESF indeed assembles activists who are highly active within transnational protests and who identify highly with the GJM. Also, seemingly marginal currents nonetheless entail a high share of quite committed participants, which strengthens the picture of a dense, diverse network. Moreover, the ESF data shows a picture of the GJM as a specific pattern of transnational activism. Though there are types where this degree of transnational participation has not yet been reached, the backbone of the movement's networking seem to be constituted not only by paid professionals and leaders, but also by many rank and file. The networking process is surely reinforced by the effort to use an open and consensual method of decision making that resonates with many rank and file members' ideals. Although deliberative democratic ideals seem to be more widespread among the members of those types that are at the margins of the latent networks, we noticed that they are also supported by many members of large, structured, and embedded types.

In sum, the current descriptions of scholars as well as the self-descriptions of the GJM align – mainly – with the latent structures of multiple membership of the respondents attending the ESF. But there are minor deviations from this picture that are worth mentioning. While, in general, participatory and deliberative ideals are accepted as practical common standards over procedures, there are differences among countries; and among members of political parties, these attitudes are relatively less widespread. Additionally the latter, though quite embedded, are less actively involved in transnational activities. Even the regular character of social forums cannot change the volatile and fluid character of mass mobilization within every social movement. There still are types that remain marginal due to the ebbs and flows in the various fields of activism. Finally, the social forum concept does not encompass the whole of the GJM. Anarchists and autonomists, for example, though present in remarkable numbers, stand aside, paralleling the social forum in Athens with autonomous transnational spaces (see Chapter 2). This points to another aspect of the study of social movements' networks that could not be taken into account here: namely, the tension between cooperation and competition that could result either in the deepening of the network integration or in a more visible cleavage within the network between reformists and radicals (Reese *et al.* 2006) or, alternatively, between verticals and horizontals (Waterman 2005).

Notes

1 Massimiliano Andretta is the principal author of 'Latent networks in the four countries' and 'The ESF as space for deliberation'; Iosif Botetzagias of 'The ESF as main part of GJM'; Moses Boudourides of 'Method: a non relational analysis'; and Mundo Yang of 'Latent networks in the fourth ESF: an introduction' and 'Elite meeting or open to rank and file?'; while 'Conclusion: (latent) networks and democracy in the GJM' is co-authored. We thank Olga Kioufegi, who was responsible for the inputting and the computation of the network data, and Donatella della Porta for her useful comments.
2 Walden Bello is executive director of Focus on the Global South, professor of sociology and public administration at the University of the Philippines, and a fellow of the Transnational Institute. On this topic, see Bello 2007.
3 Chico Whitaker is a Brazilian Catholic activist, awarded the Right Livelihood Annual Prize for his commitment to peace and social justice. On this topic, see Whitaker 2007.
4 See also Thomas Ponniah's (2007) synthesis and reply.
5 In fact, Cornwell and Harrison (2004) have presented positive statistical evidence for this occurrence (at least with respect to high membership rates).
6 The classification is made by dichotomizing both structural and positional embeddedness according to the means in each country.
7 We translate with the English term 'autonomist group' or 'social centre', the Italian term 'gruppo autonomo' or 'centro sociale' (squatted social centre), the German term 'autonomen grouppen', the French term 'centre autonome' or centre social or squats, and the Greek term 'Αυτόνομοι χώροι και στέκια'. To get an idea of this movement, the definition of the Wikipedia online encyclopaedia (online available at: http://en.wikipedia.org/wiki/Autonomism) is sufficient here:

> Autonomism refers to a set of left-wing political and social movements and theories close to the socialist movement. Autonomism (*autonomia*) emerged in Italy in the 1960s from workerist (*operaismo*) communism.... Those who describe themselves as autonomists now vary from workerist Marxists to post-structuralists and (some) anarchists... Unlike other forms of Marxism, autonomist Marxism emphasises the ability of the working class to force changes to the organisation of the capitalist system independent of the state, trade unions or political parties.

8 There at least have been three 'autonomous spaces' paralleling the forum. (See blog re Athens autonomous spaces, online, available at: www.athensautonomousspaces.blogspot.com/).
9 The original variable varies from 0 to 4: 0 = never before; 1 = once; 2 = 2–5 times; 3 = 6–10 times; 4 = more than 10 times. We recoded the variable by assigning to each activist the median of the range attached to her value (for instance, we attached the value 3.5 to category 2 (range 2–5 times), while we decided somewhat arbitrarily to attach the value 12 to category 4 (range: more than 10 times). We then measure the means for each type by country.
10 The original variable varies from 0 (no identification) to 3 (much identification). We calculated the means for each type by country.
11 Attac has never gained in Italy the political visibility that the association has in France, where it was born, or in Germany where it met unexpected success (Kolb

2005). LSFs had initially mushroomed in Italy just after the Genoa protest in 2001, but after some years, especially because of internal conflicts, they substantially disappeared from the political scene (Andretta 2005b).
12 This is already visible in the scatter plots shown in Figure 7.3. No correlation has been found between the degree of embeddedness and the propensity for deliberation in any of the selected national organizational communities.

9 Parties, unions, and movements[1]
The European Left and the ESF

Massimiliano Andretta and Herbert Reiter

Introduction

When it entered the public arena in November 1999 with the protests against the third World Trade Organization conference in Seattle, the global justice movement (GJM) presented itself as an unusual coalition of traditional organizations, new social movements, and emerging groups contesting neoliberal globalization. The organizers of the Seattle protests included 'turtles and teamsters' – activists of the Sea Turtle Restoration Project and trade unionists – ranging from the People for Fair Trade/Network opposed to the WTO (PFT), to the Direct Action Network (DAN) and the American Federation of Labor–Congress of Industrial Organizations (AFL–CIO) with its local affiliates (Levi and Murphy 2006: 652).

Similar alliances developed on the old continent, although with one important difference: while organizations of the socialist or communist tradition, including political parties, are largely absent from the GJM in the US, they are quite central to the European GJM, where the large European trade unions are historically closely intertwined with these parties and organizations (Bartolini 2000). Alongside this block of parties, trade unions, and collateral organizations that we consider as the 'traditional Left', we find a 'radical Left' sector of parties, grassroots trade unions, and groups of an autonomous, anarchist or Trotskyite tradition with their roots in the 'New Left' of the 1970s (della Porta and Rucht 1995; Tarrow 1989). In the following we will analyse the involvement of traditional left and radical left organizations and activists in the GJM, their integration into GJM decision making, and in particular the democratic models that their activists promote.

In the first part of the chapter, dedicated to the involvement of organizations of both the traditional and radical Left in the social forum process, we use documents of left-wing organizations as sources (we conducted a search of their websites for documents related to the rise of the GJM and to the ESF process), as well as the programmes of the ESFs and material related to the organization of the successive forums. We will first briefly sketch some national differences in the traditions of the Left, which may have contributed to differences in organizational involvement in the GJM. We will then discuss the reactions of the European Left (particularly party families and trade unions) to the GJM and the social forum process, characterized by a protracted diffidence by socialist and social democratic organizations – whereas organizations with a communist and left socialist past, together with groups of the radical Left, embraced the movement from early on. We will further sketch the role played by traditional and radical left organizations within the European Social Forum process, looking at the furnishing of logistical support for the forums in Florence, Paris, London, and Athens; the visibility of left organizations in the programmes of the ESFs; and the involvement of their activists in the European Preparatory Assemblies (EPA).

The second part of this chapter is devoted to an analysis of the activist survey conducted by the Demos research team at the 2006 ESF in Athens (see Chapter 1 in this volume). We will first present some indicators of the presence of the European Left in the successive ESFs from Florence to Athens. Singling out the activists who declared a traditional left or radical left group as most important to them, we will present the sociographic and national characteristics of these activists, indicate differences in the patterns of political activism, and analyse their involvement in GJM activities and decision making. In the final part of our chapter we will concentrate on activists' perceptions of the democratic practices in their group of reference, comparing them with their ideals of democracy. Our findings seem to indicate processes of diffusion, although filtered through existing organizational cultures. While the ideal of direct participation is overwhelmingly supported – also by activists of the traditional Left – deliberation, although also supported by large sectors, only emerges as the most popular form of democracy among activists of the newest social movements directly connected with the rise of the GJM. In addition to showing the greatest incongruence between perceived democratic practices and ideals, traditional left activists are the most unsatisfied with democracy within their group.

The involvement of European leftist organizations in the social forum process

The traditional and the radical Left in Europe: cross-national differences

For our analysis, we divided European left-wing organizations and groups into two broad categories. The first consists of the traditional Left, including socialist or social democratic and communist or post-communist parties and organizations, as well as traditional trade unions; the second is made up of the radical Left, including grassroots unions as well as political parties and organizations with their roots in the New Left of the 1970s. While trade unions and communist or post-communist parties and organizations dominate among the traditional Left, for the radical Left Trotskyite groups emerge as the most numerous component.

In our analysis, we did not specifically consider the national differences in left-wing political culture, which can only be briefly indicated. As far as the traditional Left is concerned, in some of the countries (like Germany or the UK) a socialist or social democratic tradition has historically dominated, including in the trade unions. In other countries (like Italy or France) the Communist Party had a far greater or even dominant influence, also within the trade union movement. Regarding the radical Left, in some countries (like Italy) grassroots unions and autonomous groups prevail, while in others (like France) it is the Trotskyites. In still other countries, like Greece, the Left is particularly fragmented. It can be assumed that these national characteristics contribute to differences in the importance the social forum process seems to have for organizations, in particular of the traditional Left, in the various countries.

Reflecting the strength of the GJM in the respective countries, the self represented role of social forums on leftist organizations' websites varies considerably among the various countries: Italian websites, for instance, are richer in material than German sites. This phenomenon can also be observed for political parties of the same party family, for example the German social democrats (SPD) and the Italian Democratici di sinistra (DS; Democrats of the Left),[2] both members of the Party of European Socialists.[3] These results seem to reflect participation in the ESFs: of the circa 1,000-strong delegation of ECOSY (the federation of European socialist party youth organizations) at the ESFs in Florence and Paris, for instance, only five were representatives of the German Jusos (Burger 2002; 2003).

Notable differences also emerge for trade unions: numerous documents on the ESF and the social forum process in general can be found on the web pages of the Italian trade union confederation CGIL (traditionally dominated by communists) and especially of some of its member unions like the metalworkers of the FIOM. In contrast, such material is practically non-existent for the German federation DGB, dominated by social democrats. It is also rare on the pages of those of its member unions most closely involved in the social forum process, like the metalworkers of the IG Metall or the services union Ver.di. On the latter's site, for instance, the section on the ESF contains only a short report on Ver.di's participation in the Paris 2003 forum, but no material on the Athens ESF, where the international campaign against the retailer Lidl was presented – a campaign that was started by Ver.di and figures prominently on its site.

A similar picture emerges if we look at the trade unions mentioned as organizers of seminars or workshops in the printed programme of the Athens ESF: international union organizations, global or EU level, appear eight times in this role. Concentrating on the countries covered by the Demos project, neither British nor Swiss trade unions are mentioned. The Spanish presence is limited to two traditional and two radical unions, while German traditional unions (Ver.di and IG Metall) appear nine times as co-organizers of seminars. In contrast, we find a large presence of Italian and French trade unions, including traditional federations like the CGIL and the CGT: for Italy, we counted 22 references to traditional unions and 21 to grassroots unions; for France, 32 references to traditional unions and 15 to grassroots unions. In addition, while the German unions appear only in connection with seminars reflecting specific trade union concerns, French and especially Italian unions, both traditional and grassroots, are also mentioned as co-organizers for seminars covering other themes like peace, migration, or (in the case of grassroots unions) 'repression'. We can hypothesize that this reflects a traditionally stronger political conception of a union's role within the (communist dominated) French and Italian left-wing trade union movement.

As we have already underlined, in the following we will not discuss these national differences in detail. Where possible, examples that illustrate the attitudes of the European Left towards the GJM and the ESF process will be taken from the transnational level, for example the Socialist International. Moreover, the German and Italian cases will be used specifically to illustrate broader trends.

The European Left and the GJM

According to the World Social Forum Charter of Principles, the forum is an open space for groups and movements of civil society opposed to neoliberal globalization.[4] At the same time, it is described as a 'non-governmental and non-party context'. Alongside military organizations, in fact, party representations are excluded from participation, while government leaders and members of legislatures who accept the commitments of the charter may be invited to participate in a personal capacity. Social movement theory, however, stresses the role of political allies – especially left-wing political parties – in favouring mobilization. During the protest cycle of the late 1960s and early 1970s, while the emerging New Left criticized the institutional left for the alleged betrayal of their original 'revolutionary' values (Pizzorno 1996), traditional left-wing parties channelled many of the emerging demands into the representative institutions. During the 1980s, a de facto division of tasks developed: social movements 'retreated' to the social sphere, and political parties 'represented' them in political institutions.

When the GJM emerged, political opportunities appeared as far more closed. The acceleration of the evolution from mass parties to 'base-less' or 'professionalized' parties (Katz and Mair 1992; della Porta 2001) had reduced the potential for contacts and alliances between the GJM and left-wing parties, particularly those from the socialist or social democratic tradition. In fact, the effects of the crisis of Keynesian economic policies and the hegemony of neoliberal ideology were especially felt by these parties. In contrast, communist and post-communist parties, which after the fall of the Berlin wall were seen as doomed to a more or less rapid demise, saw an opportunity for mobilization in the globalization process, along with those groups that we classified as being part of the radical Left. In addition, the threat to the European welfare state model posed by neoliberal policies opened the possibility of at least partial alliances between the GJM and even moderate trade unions. The attraction of the GJM, however, was especially felt where social conflict was strong and in countries where, since the 1980s, grassroots unions had grown in competition with the established trade union organizations.

The traditional Left and the social forum process

The relationship between the GJM and the dominant moderate left-wing European parties of the socialist or social democratic tradition, especially when in government, has been strained. This diffident if not conflictual relationship developed despite the fact that the European socialist parties had discussed problems of global development and global governance early on, significantly shaping important UN reports (Independent Commission on International Development Issues 1980; Commission on Global Governance 1995). Starting in the 1980s, they had also opened the (previously largely European) Socialist International to parties from the developing world, including progressive parties outside the socialist party family in the strictest sense. The 'Declaration of principles of the Socialist International' adopted by the XVIII congress (Socialist International 1989) contains a specific section on globalization, affirming the principles of freedom, justice, and solidarity and calling for 'the creation of a pluralist and democratic world, based on consensus and cooperation'.

When in government in the 1990s, however, European socialist parties adapted to neoliberal policies in response to the challenges of globalization. They paid scarce attention to the emerging GJM, in particular to the criticism of policies implemented at home in Europe, reducing the significance of the movement to a mobilization for the world's poor. For a long period during the preparatory phase of the Genoa anti-G8 protests in 2001, conducted largely under an Italian centre-left government, authorities concentrated their efforts on convincing the movement to hold the counter-summit a week before the G8 (della Porta *et al.* 2006a: chapter 6). This attitude cannot be explained exclusively by the fear of public disorder as occurred in Seattle or, just a short time before, at the EU summit in Gothenburg. In the discussion that took place in the aftermath of the Genoa counter-summit, in fact, divergent views of the European socialist parties and of the GJM emerged not only on responses to the challenge of globalization, concerning both social justice and democratic governance, but also on the role of civil society and particularly that of social movements (ibid.: chapter 7).

While the GJM promoted participatory and deliberative forms of democracy, criticizing the dominant representative models, the socialists in fact remained sceptical of the role of civil society, defending the predominance of parliamentary representative democracy and the role of political parties also at the global level. The Socialist International's report 'Governance in a Global Society – the Social democratic approach', adopted at the XXII congress in Sao Paolo in October 2003, affirms:

> Civil society participation must be complementary to, not a substitute for, the role of parliaments. Participatory democracy goes hand in hand with representative democracy ... The goal of the SI must be to parliamentarise the global political system – with the representation of political parties that offer alternative global political values, theories and projects.
> (Socialist International 2003)

In this scenario, the role of civil society and social movements is restricted to being a marker for emerging problems, the solutions for which are to be provided by parliaments and political parties. This is also true for the sectors of

European socialist parties directly and closely involved with the GJM, for instance the youth organizations or thematic groups specifically working on global justice themes. In a resolution approved at the second bureau meeting of the European federation of socialist youth organizations (ECOSY), the social forums were defined as 'valuable platforms', advocating participation on both a regional and an international level (ECOSY 2003). The role of the Young European Socialists was seen as offering political formulations to the issues raised by the GJM, forming a bridge between civil society and politics:

> Our priority should be to convince the new grassroots activists of the social movement of the relevance of politics in the strategy for the overall reforms needed (inclusion of the reformed WTO, IMF, WB, into a transparent and democratic global governance through a more political UN) in the pursuit of a world based on the principles of Liberty, Equality, Solidarity and Justice.
>
> (Ibid.)

Similarly, a document approved at the first national congress of 'Altrimondi', the thematic group of the Italian DS, defines the idea of a party being part of the movement as instrumental and invasive:

> The Democrats of the Left have to know how to listen to their demands, and especially to criticism, but as a party their specific task is a propositive one: knowing how to give political answers to the questions posed by the movements.
>
> (Altrimondi 2002)

The sectors of the socialist and social democratic parties closest to the movement in fact follow a 'double strategy': they see themselves as part of both the GJM and their parties, acting as a bridge between the two realities. However, as the above quote from the ECOSY Bureau resolution on the ESF shows, whereas the activities of parties are considered as constituting politics, the activities of the GJM are not. As a German member of the ECOSY bureau put it in an article on the ESF in London: 'The ESF will never be our main topic, but it would be wrong not to accompany it politically' (Burger 2004).

If we compare the attitudes of European socialist parties with those of the traditional trade union confederations, differences emerge: many unions, in fact, including the European federation ETUC, have participated in the ESF since its first edition in Florence in 2002. In contrast to political parties, caught up in the aforementioned evolution from mass parties to 'base-less' or 'professionalized' parties, trade unions are generally dependent on the support of their members, without whom they risk losing influence and negotiating power. As has already been mentioned, in countries where trade union confederations have traditionally been strongly intertwined with social democratic parties (like in Germany), the pursuit of neoliberal policies by socialist or social democratic governments provoked friction between unions and the ruling parties, finding expression in different attitudes towards the GJM. In 2002, for instance, the German trade union confederation DGB elaborated a joint resolution on globalization with Attac and the Association of German Development NGOs (DGB, VENRO and Attac 2002).[5] Some of its member unions also called for broader cooperation with NGOs and civil society actors against neoliberal globalization (Ver.di 2003). Within the German trade unions, however, other voices called for a concentration of activities on the core tasks, leaving political mediation to the social democratic party. For critics of this position – like the IG Metall liaison office for social movements – the GJM also seems to remain one of many possible allies of the union, with the ecology and the peace movements mentioned separately, alongside churches and other social initiatives.

In countries where the Communist Party historically had a strong position within the trade union movement, unions showed a greater openness towards the GJM, in particular towards the claims for participatory democracy. In Italy, the traditional left-wing trade union confederation CGIL initially displayed a cautious attitude. In contrast with some of its member unions, like the metalworkers of the FIOM, it did not officially participate in the Genoa Social Forum or the anti-G8 counter-summit of 2001. In declaring its participation in the first ESF in Florence, it continued to underline a clear distinction between trade unions and social movements but acknowledged that the GJM had put the theme of the unjust effects of globalization on the agenda of world politics. Moreover, it declared that the movement had objectively assumed responsibility, proposing civic participation as a politically relevant act (CGIL 2002). In the introduction to the international section of its website, the FIOM, associated with the CGIL, declares its participation in a larger anti-neoliberal movement that continues to develop in the social forums.[6] This participation, however, is only one of the international commitments of the union, the other being international trade unionism, to which a separate part of the international section of the site is dedicated.

Within the traditional Left, an open attitude towards the GJM was displayed, especially by communist and post-communist parties. Recently federated as the European Left, they declared at the first congress in Athens in 2005:

> The European Left and its member parties are committed to fight together with social movements, trade unions, and political left forces for another Europe, which is possible. In this context, we fully support all European mobilisations and initiatives against neo-liberalism and war, particularly the Fourth European Social Forum to be held in Athens.
>
> (European Left 2005a)

In the executive board motion 'Yes, we can change Europe – Political theses', the European Left defined the emergence of new movements and their capacity to link up in a collective drive forward as the real novelty of the new millennium. It affirmed:

Our task is to contribute to generate a popular left and social majority that is, and must be, bigger than us: with other political parties, with the European Social Forum and social movements, with feminists, trade unions, popular associations and individuals. A popular majority will grow with alliances and convergences with all who want to build with us another Europe.

(European Left 2005b)

However, while the parties of the European Left highlighted their openness to equal participation in the GJM without hegemonic intentions, their original agenda remained clearly visible in the framing of the GJM as anti-capitalist. This is also the case for the Italian Rifondazione Comunista (RC), probably the European political party most closely connected with the GJM, especially through its youth organization Giovani Comunisti (GC).[7] In its constitution, adopted in April 2002, it affirms the autonomy of the organisms of the alternative left and of the social movements, with which the party collaborates on an equal footing and in which its members participate in democratic and non-sectarian ways (Rifondazione 2002). In October 2003, a document approved by the National Political Committee of RC affirmed: 'The participation of RC in the movement against war and neoliberal policies, which effectively has been defined as a "movement of movements", is an essential element of its political initiative, moreover, it constitutes the basis of its inspiration' (Rifondazione 2003).

The very role of a party, however, risks clashing with the participative and deliberative democratic ideals of the movement, as well as with the more antagonistic strategies of the radical Left.[8] Increasingly, in fact, RC's moves into the institutional political arena created tension both within the party and with sectors of the GJM. Faced with the upcoming elections in April 2006, party secretary Bertinotti presented a motion at RC's 2005 congress defining the construction of a participative democracy as a fundamental challenge in which the critique of social movements could transform itself into a left-wing political and programmatic alternative, a process of transformation of capitalist society. In this context, he posed the problem of participation of an antagonist force in government, not as a decision of value but as a necessary phase to liberate Italy from the Berlusconi administration. The construction of participative democracy was seen as the primary objective of a future government coalition.

As one of the Greek organizers of the Athens ESF underlined, the participation of RC in the centre-left government, which emerged victorious from the 2006 Italian elections, created a sentiment of disappointment in a large number of activists, especially among radical youth (see Almpanis 2006). This move created particular problems for the youth organization GC, deeply involved in the GJM and more so than the youth organizations of other European communist or post communist parties.[9] In the document they presented at the 2005 party congress, the GC had already asserted: 'today the idea that the revolution coincides ... with the taking of one or more places of power is unsustainable.... Revolution is not the exercise of counter-power but the construction of another kind of power' (Giovani Comunisti 2005). Participative democracy was defined as a new space in which politics (and the GC) were called to transform themselves into conflictuality rather than representation in institutions. A motion presented at the GC's third national conference in September 2006 likened entering the government to entering a cage and spoke of the decision as weighing like a stone on the GC, significantly narrowing their space of autonomy and initiative (Giovani Comunisti 2006). The majority document that was passed asserted:

> It is the critique of power which permits us to live the decision of the party to contribute to the government of the country, not as an end, but as an instrument to construct a season of rights, breaking with the dynamic conflict – repression: ...we chose the government with which to enter in conflict, knowing that the construction of an alternative passes through society.[10]

The radical Left and the social forum process

The radical Left that is involved in the social forum process presents a far more variegated picture than the traditional Left, ranging from grassroots unions developing in various national contexts (particularly Italy and France) since the 1980s, to political parties stemming from various traditions of the 1970s New Left, to autonomous and anti-imperialist groups of more recent years. From early on, grassroots unions like the French Union Syndicale Solidaires or the Italian COBAS played an important role in the GJM and the European Social Forum process. Bearers of a conception of trade unionism that sees the union as a political (and cultural) subject, they are critical of the mainstream traditional unions in Europe, accused of having followed a policy of condoning neoliberalism. A point of contention in this context is the EU Constitutional Treaty, opposed by the grassroots unions but accepted by the traditional ones, albeit with reservations. Advancing an anti-capitalist and autonomous interpretation of globalization, both COBAS and Solidaires see themselves as part of the GJM and encourage their members to actively take part in the struggles against neoliberal globalization (see Solidaires 2004; COBAS 2002). Some differences do need to be underlined: Solidaires has a more state-centred approach and is more concentrated on a social agenda, while COBAS follows a stronger autonomous line, with greater emphasis on self-organization.

Concerning the ESF process, both unions see the forum as a place to construct a GJM with common action strategies and to agree upon common European campaigns and mobilizations.[11] In fact, Solidaires laments the fact that the forums have not yet succeeded in elaborating common action strategies, despite the potential of the assembly of social movements to unite those movements willing to act together. Beyond imposing GJM themes on the public debate, it calls for a supplementary phase in the construction of a social movement at the European level, capable of creating the necessary balance of power for imposing the movement's alternatives (Solidaires 2004). In a similar vein, COBAS pushes for a 'synthesis between discussion and action', applauding the fact that in Athens the ESF had no longer presented itself as a show event, but as a relevant passage in the continuous process of European self-organization. COBAS expressed satisfaction with the evident radicalization in terminology – for example, the dominance of terms like anti-capitalism and anti-imperialism over terms like anti-neoliberalism – as well as in themes, content, and objectives.[12]

Other organizations of the radical Left, for example Trotskyite parties and groups, also push for a more radical and action oriented stance of the GJM and in particular of the ESF process. In France, the Ligue communiste révolutionnaire (LCR) – which follows a strategy of building a 'Left–Left pole', mostly based on movement activism – plays a central role because of its activists' commitment in several families of the movement (Sommier and Combes 2007: 115). LCR underlines the function of the ESF to define the common action programme at the European level, which the trade unions alone were incapable of defining during the last 40 years.[13] At its fifteenth world congress in 2003, the Fourth International (with which LCR is affiliated) declared: 'We continue to support and build the "movement against neo-liberal globalisation" around imperialist summits, so as to denounce neo-liberal international policies, de-legitimise the "new institutions" of global capitalism and build an anti-capitalist/anti-imperialist, internationalist pole.'[14]

To varying degrees, these groups appear less open to inclusiveness and 'contamination' than the grassroots unions, arguing for more organization and less 'movement'. In this context, the role of political parties in the social forum process takes on special importance. After the Florence ESF, LCR called for an acceptable solution allowing for the presence of political parties in the preparation and the course of the forum, respecting the independence of social movements. LCR, in fact, criticized the Socialist Workers' Party (SWP; affiliated with the International Socialist Tendency) for having failed to respect this independence by shouting their slogans and displaying their banners at the assembly of social movements that concluded the Florence ESF.[15] At the London ESF, Phil Hearst, a British Trotskyite, insisted that the Left needed institutions for continuous politics. According to him, the plurality of movements alone did not develop a solid strategic convergence of positions, and a party – not simply the sum of social movements – might still be the best agent of a conscious 'unification' in a 'worker's state'.[16]

At the borders of the ESF process, the position that the ESF should be more strictly organized for the task of directing the struggles of the GJM is particularly emphasized by the League for the Fifth International, organizer of a seminar on 'A charter of citizens rights or programme of action – From the ESF to a world party of social revolution' at the Athens ESF.[17] The League expressed its content with the fact that 'the reactionary Principles of Porto Alegre, which ban the participation of parties and the taking of decisions' were largely ignored in Athens (League 2006). Proposing to throw off the tutelage of the WSF, it underlined that since Florence it had argued that

> The ESF must turn itself into a permanent organising centre of struggle against neoliberalism and imperialism. We believe it is vital to break the logjam in how the movement operates, particularly the wretched and

hypocritical 'consensus principle', which effectively amounts to a veto, whereby the most right wing forces can paralyse indefinitely the whole movement, and indeed prevent the Assembly of the Social Movements debating any political or tactical differences.

(Ibid.)

As a solution, the League proposed a decision making process (majority vote on resolutions presented and debated) and organizational changes (election of a standing committee or council of the ESF to respond to 'urgent tasks arising from the class struggle' and to develop a political action programme for the movement) (ibid.). These proposals run counter to the debate within the ESF, centred on participative and deliberative practices. In the eventuality of a stalling of the ESF, the creation of 'a forum of struggle' by those forces 'who do not place unity with the neoliberal parties above the needs of the working class' is envisaged.[18]

The European Left and the organization of the ESF

Turning to the direct involvement of European left-wing organizations in the ESF process, we will look at three aspects: the furnishing of logistic support, visibility in the ESF programme, and participation in the European Preparatory Assemblies (EPA). Notwithstanding the exclusion of political parties from participation, indispensable material resources for the organization of all ESFs was provided not only by well established left-wing organizations – particularly trade unions – but also by government representatives and agencies, including those of social democratic or socialist leaning (see Chapter 2 in this volume). In addition, associations or personalities identifiable as close to political parties, if not clearly representing them, appear in the programmes of the ESFs; traditional and radical left groups, including party youth organizations (to whom the ban on political parties does not apply) also figure prominently as organizers of seminars and workshops. Finally, activists of traditional and radical left organizations, including trade unions but also political parties, form an important component of the EPAs. Within the traditional Left represented in the ESF programmes and the EPAs, the moderate social democratic or socialist component remains a minority.

The furnishing of logistical support for the ESFs

For the first ESF in Florence, the resources provided by local government institutions (all led by the DS, of social democratic leaning) were of great importance for the success of the meeting. These resources included general assistance for the accommodation of the forum participants and the Fortezza da Basso, the ESF venue, placed at the disposal of the organizers by the regional government – led by a president, Claudio Martini, who had shown more attention to the GJM than his party did. The participation of well established traditional left organizations, in particular the Italian (CGIL) and the European (ETUC) trade union confederations, helped overcome diffidence and resistance of state institutions (including the police) and local government agencies.[19]

The material resources provided by local government agencies and established left-wing organizations were again fundamental for the following ESFs and, in contrast to Florence, included direct contributions – the ban on direct contributions by third parties for the first ESF had led to a deficit of about €80,000. For the Paris ESF, resources and support were provided above all by the communist-led municipalities of the *banlieues*. In the case of the London ESF, two of the principal organizers were the SWP and the Socialist Action group – Socialist Action had supported Ken Livingstone's successful campaign as an independent for mayor of London in 2000, and some of its members became advisors in his administration. The Greater London Authority is said to have put an estimated £400,000 towards the event. For the Athens Social Forum, the Greek trade union federations GSEE and ADEDY provided €350,000, with a further €30,000 contributed by other Greek trade unions. GSEE provided the entire infrastructure necessary for the accommodation and function of the Greek Organising Committee (Stratoulis 2006). The importance of the support and involvement of well established organizations is further testified by the fact that, at Athens, the German and Austrian candidacies for holding the next ESF evaporated because of the unwillingness of the major trade unions to become involved in the process (see COBAS 2006). Such contributions are also central to national social forums.[20]

The visibility of the European Left in the ESF programmes

Numerous organizations of the traditional and radical Left, many of them well established, also appear in the official social forum programme as organizers of seminars or workshops. The programme of the ESF in Florence saw the participation of major traditional trade unions, starting with the European confederation ETUC and including the Italian confederation CGIL, the Italian metalworkers union FIOM, the French confederation CGT, and the German service union Ver.di. From the traditional Left, we also find party youth organizations like the Sinistra giovanile, close to the DS or the GC, while other party representatives were identified under their respective internal currents.[21] In addition, important DS figures like regional president Martini and Florence mayor Domenici took part in their institutional roles. Also present were foundations like the French Espace Marx (PCF) and the German Rosa-Luxemburg-Stiftung (PDS), with clear and direct links to political parties. However, clear identification of participants as party figures seems to have been given only for the plenary on movements and political parties.[22] Similarly, for the radical Left, grassroots trade unions (like COBAS, Sin.COBAS, and CUB or Solidaires) were directly identified, while exponents of parties like the SWP were presented under their professional identities (for example, university professor) or appeared as representatives of SMOs (for example, Globalise Resistance).

In subsequent editions of the ESF, the presence of established traditional and radical left organizations in the official programme seems to have consolidated.

At Athens, the European Trade Union Confederation (ETUC) and 40 other European confederations and sector federations participated in the seminars or had a stand (Stratoulis 2006). Although many of these activities dealt with core trade union issues – 30 seminars were dedicated to the implications of neoliberal policies in the field of employment and 12 to privatization and civil services – traditional unions (particularly from Italy and France) also addressed other themes: representatives of the Italian CGIL spoke in 24 seminars ranging from the Bolkestein directive to self-determination in the Western Sahara.[23] Of the grassroots unions, the Italian COBAS were involved in about 25 seminars and thematic assemblies, apart from core union issues covering themes like peace, education, health, migrants, women, ecology, and repression (COBAS 2006).

As far as left-wing political parties are concerned, apart from the seminar on 'Basic democratic agreement for the resolution of the Basque political conflict', for which several Basque parties are mentioned as organizers, only in one case does the Athens ESF programme directly mention a party (the Communist Party of Great Britain) as co-organizer of an event, while in other cases party youth organizations (e.g. the Greek Youth of Synaspismos, the Italian Sinistra giovanile and GC, the German Solid) are indicated. The ban on political parties is also reflected in the fact that the printed programme rarely indicates speakers' party allegiance, even for members of parliament. As in previous editions, however, actors more or less directly linked to political parties can be identified, for example in foundations like the Rosa-Luxemburg-Stiftung (PDS) or in party newspapers like *Liberazione* (RC). Athens also saw the indirect participation of the traditional European socialist parties in the form of the Global Progressive Forum, co-organizer of a seminar ('The role of Europe and of the social forces in the peace process in the Middle East').[24] Radical left parties, particularly the SWP, as in previous editions of the ESF, did not appear directly but under the name of connected organizations like Globalise Resistance.[25]

It must be stressed that the different sectors we singled out do not necessarily appear separately. Many seminars on the themes of social justice and workers' rights were co-organized by traditional and grassroots unions – in some national cases, like Italy, signing jointly as a campaign together with other SMOs (for example against the Bolkestein directive). In addition, other seminars were organized by ESF networks: the European network of education of the ESF, the ESF network against security policies and repression, the European network for the right to health, the ESF migrations network, and so on. Athens saw the creation of a European network to provide an alternative trade union response to the Lisbon criteria for employment and working relations, as well as a European network for the defence of civil services.

Notwithstanding this increased networking, a look at the groups listed as organizers of seminars and workshops in the programme of the Athens ESF can give some indication of the presence of the traditional and radical Left within the ESF process (see Table 9.1). About 50 per cent of the entries concern new social movement organizations (NSMOs) with their roots in the 1970s, non governmental organizations (NGOs), and other groups; the traditional Left counts in with

Table 9.1 Groups indicated as organizers of seminars or workshops at the Athens ESF[1]

Type of group	No. of mentions as organizer	%
Traditional Left	280	25.3
Radical Left	126	11.4
NSMOs, NGOs, and others	533	48.1
Newest movements	169[2]	15.3
Total	1,108	100.0

Notes
1 We based our count on the printed programme of the Athens ESF, taking into account 277 seminars and workshops – excluding the seminar on the solution of the Basque problem, which mentioned numerous Basque parties and movements. In correspondence to the other sectorial assemblies (anti-imperialist, etc.), the women's assembly was counted with only one organizer. Due to lack of information, in particular on the Turkish organizations, not all groups mentioned in the printed programme me could be classified.
2 Of these 169 mentions, 39 concern ESF networks.

around one-quarter of the entries; and the radical Left was just as present as an organizer as the newest movements directly connected with the rise of the GJM.

The European Left and the EPA

A final indicator of the role of the European Left in the ESF process is constituted by the presence of its activists in the EPAs. However, information on the organizational provenance of EPA participants is available on the Web only for the March 2002 EPA in Vienna (see Table 9.2).[26] These data indicate that while activists of the organizations with greater resources (of the traditional Left) play an important role within the preparatory process of the ESFs, those of groups more committed to the ESF process (of the radical Left and of the newest movements) show a comparatively strong representation.

It must be added that there are also critical voices from within the movement concerning the composition of the EPA. According to the Attac European Network, participation in the EPA is still limited to the individuals and organizations present from the beginning; in particular, the representation of unions, environmental, development and human rights NGOs is too limited.[27]

Activists of organizations of the European Left at the ESF: involvement in the social forum process and conceptions of democracy

The presence of activists of the European Left at the ESFs

Turning from the organizations of the European Left to the activists, some of the original variables used in three surveys conducted in Florence, Paris, and Athens can give us indications about the importance of the presence of left activists in the various ESFs.

Table 9.2 Participants EPA Vienna, 10–12 May 2002 (only countries covered by Demos project)

	Traditional Left	Radical Left	NSMOs, and others NGOs	Newest movements	Not indicated	Total
Italy	11	8	9	7	3	38 (32.8%)
France	6	6	9	8	2	31 (26.7%)
Germany	6	4	4	3	1	18 (15.5%)
UK	3	7	4	1	1	16 (13.8%)
Spain	2	2	1	3	1	9 (7.6%)
Switzerland	2	0	1	1	0	4 (3.4%)
Total	30 (25.9%)	27 (23.3%)	28 (24.1%)	23 (19.8%)	8 (6.9%)	116 (100%)

Asked to place themselves on a left–right scale, an average of 75 per cent of the activists surveyed in the three ESFs placed themselves on the left or the radical left of the political spectrum. In fact, European GJM activists can be considered an important electoral constituency for leftist parties: about 68 per cent in Florence and 82 per cent in Athens declared having voted in the last elections, while in Paris as many as 90 per cent declared 'always' or 'often' voting in general elections. Regarding electoral preferences, one part of the left party spectrum is especially dominant among GJM activists. In Athens, 48.5 per cent of the surveyed activists declared having voted for a communist or a left socialist party in the last national election in their home country, 12.3 per cent for a socialist or centre-left party, 8.9 per cent for an ecologist party, and 7.6 per cent for a Trotskyite or new left party. A further 11.3 per cent declared that they had been unable/not entitled to vote, while 11.5 per cent can be considered convinced non-voters – that is, they did not vote or cast a blank or spoilt ballot because no party reflected their political ideas, or because they do not approve of representative democracy.[28]

In the following, we are concerned with those GJM activists who identify above all with two areas of the European Left: the traditional Left of social democratic, socialist, or communist inspiration; and the radical Left with its roots in the New Left of the 1970s. In order to isolate activists of these two areas, we recoded the variable of our Athens questionnaire that asked ESF participants to indicate the full name of the group most important to them. Concentrating on the fourth ESF, we can thus isolate the members who attach more meaning to traditional left or radical left organizations than to other groups. For the recoding, we considered traditional left organizations as established leftist political parties of the communist or socialist/social democratic party family; established trade unions of the same tradition (such as the Italian CGIL, French CGT, or German Ver.di); student and youth groups linked to the established leftist parties; and communist or socialist non-party organizations (such as the Italian ARCI or French Espace Marx). There are 260 activists in this category, representing about 22 per cent of the full sample, 28.2 per cent if we exclude the missing cases (activists who are members of an organization but who did not specify the group most important to them or specified a group that we were unable to classify – 23.5 per cent of the sample), and about 33.5 per cent if we also exclude activists with no membership (about 16 per cent of the sample). As radical left organizations we considered anarchist, autonomist or Trotskyite groups or parties, and grassroots trade unions such as the Italian COBAS or the French Sud. The activists of the radical Left number 142 and represent 12 per cent of the full sample, 15.4 per cent if we do not consider the missing cases, and about 18 per cent if we also exclude the non-members.

In our analysis, we compare the two types of leftist activists with the members of those newest social movement organizations (such as Attac, Indymedia, local social forums, and so on) that emerged with the GJM. In this category we find 97 activists – that is, 8 per cent of the full sample, about 11 per cent if we do not consider the missing cases, and 18.3 per cent if we also exclude the non-members. In addition, we grouped together members of new social movement organizations (NSMOs), NGOs, and any other organization that did not fall into one of the previous categories. These activists number 278 (23 per cent of the full sample, 30 per cent if we do not consider missing cases, and about 36 per cent if we also exclude non-members). Here we find above all environmental organizations and NGOs, but also non leftist parties like the Greens, and some Catholic trade unions. Finally, we will also consider the 145 activists (12 per cent of the full sample and about 16 per cent if we exclude missing cases) who are not members of any organization.

The data confirm the importance of the organizational components of both the traditional and the radical Left within the ESF process: taken together, the activists of these two areas of the European Left represent the most numerous component of the ESF in Athens. If we compare the presence of activists with the visibility of organizations in the programme of the Athens ESF (see Table 9.1), we see that both the traditional and radical Left are more present in terms of activists than visible in the programme. In contrast, NSMOs, NGOs, and others, as well as the newest movements, are more visible in the programme than in terms of numbers of activists.

Our data indicate that the voters of different types of parties are differently attracted by the types of organizations we defined. For 43.9 per cent of the voters of communist/left socialist parties an organization of the traditional Left is particularly close, and for 26.4 per cent an NSMO or NGO. Of the socialist/centre-left voters, 36.4 per cent declare an NSMO or NGO as closest to them and 29.5 per cent an organization of the traditional Left. Among the voters of ecologist parties, 55.9 per cent feel particularly close to an NSMO or NGO and 14.6 per cent to a newest movement. Voters of Trotskyite and new left parties clearly favour organizations of the radical Left (51.5 per cent) and, to a lesser extent, NSMOs and NGOs (17.6 per cent). Convinced non-voters are particularly attracted by organizations of the radical Left (34.2 per cent) and by NSMOs and NGOs (24.7 per cent). Of those unable/not entitled to vote, 30.1 per cent are not members of an organization, while 25.3 per cent consider an organization of the traditional Left and the same percentage an NSMO or NGO as closest to them.[29]

If we were to summarize the socio-demographic features of the average traditional and radical left activists present at the Athens ESF, they would be male (respectively 63 and 57 per cent) and young (48 and 42 per cent respectively are under 30 years old). They are well educated (about 50 per cent of both traditional and radical leftists have a university education), although less so than the other organized participants (the percentages of graduated or post-graduated activists increase to 60 per cent among NSMs and 70 per cent among newest social movement members). They are especially students and non manual workers (40 and 23 per cent for traditional leftists and 34 and 26 per cent for radical leftists), and employed above all in the public sector (38 per cent for the traditional leftists but as much as 66 per cent for the radical leftists).

The only relevant difference between traditional and radical leftists is that of those who are not students, 31 per cent of the former (36 per cent of members of NSMO and NGOs) but only 6 per cent of the latter are employed in the associative sector – that is, they can be classified as 'professionals'. More precisely, many members of the traditional Left present at the Athens ESF are directly employed by their own organizations as leaders or paid staff, something that the radical Left has traditionally criticized as a sign of bureaucratization – one of the most important radical leftist principles being the refusal of delegation and professional politics. In fact, while about 46 per cent of the traditional left activists declared themselves as leaders or paid staff members of their group, for the radical Left this percentage falls to 29 per cent (NSMOs and NGOs: 37 per cent; newest movements: 31 per cent; Cramer's V = 0.13***). Correspondingly, the percentage of radical leftists who declared themselves voluntary activists/campaigners (29.7 per cent) is considerably higher than for the traditional Left (19.5 per cent), although lower than for NSMOs and NGOs (34.1 per cent) or for the newest movements (39.8 per cent). However, both the radical Left (34.1 per cent) and the traditional Left (27.3 per cent) were represented at the Athens ESF with a far higher percentage of ordinary members than both NSMOs and NGOs (17.6 per cent) and newest movements (18.3 per cent). This indicates that the decision of the left leadership to attend the ESF is sustained by the mobilization of its rank and file members.

National opportunities for transnational participation?

Some national differences – connected with the different traditions of the Left in the various countries that we briefly indicated in the first part of this chapter – become apparent when looking at the activists surveyed at the Athens ESF. The results for the single countries seem to only partially confirm the hypothesis based on the literature (Kriesi *et al.* 1995) that the Left will be less present in protest in the consensual and corporatist countries where the old cleavages are pacified. If the radical Left is particularly strong in majoritarian countries (especially true for French and UK activists: respectively 30 and 38 per cent, while Greek radical leftists are only 22 per cent), the re-emergence of social cleavages is also reflected in a stronger involvement of organizations of the traditional

Left in consensual countries: German traditional leftists are 29 per cent, Italians 40 per cent, and traditional leftists from other Western European consensual countries 23 per cent (Cramer's V = 0.20, significant at 0.001 level). We can hypothesize that the traditional Left of the consensual countries is more involved in the mobilizations of the GJM, because on the one hand it is trying to defend a social model threatened by neoliberalism, while on the other hand its organizations risk losing the power gained through corporatist practices.

In a further step, we used two indicators elaborated by Lijphart (1999): the executive-parties dimension, which classifies countries based on whether decisions are taken by majority or by compromise (majoritarian versus consensual); and the interest groups pluralism index, which classifies them based on the type of interest representation (pluralist versus corporatist).[30] Regarding participation in the Athens ESF, our results confirm that radical left activists from majoritarian and pluralist countries are particularly numerous; but that traditional left activists also show strongly for consensual and corporatist regimes, where both NSMOs and NGOs and the newest social movements are particularly strong (see Table 9.3).

Leftist patterns of political activism

Political activism and attitudes

In various respects, the traditional and radical Left show differences in their patterns of political activism. Although it seems to have successively incorporated new emerging themes, the traditional Left, in fact, remains anchored in patterns of political activism consonant with representative democracy. The radical Left, on the contrary, shows a greater distance from the established and institutionalized forms of political participation.

The activists participating at the ESF in Athens are characterized by multiple memberships in various types of organizations. This characteristic is even more

Table 9.3 Traditional and radical left activists by type of democratic regime (%)

	Type of organization considered most important					
	Non-members	Traditional Left	Radical Left	NSMOs, NGOs, and others	Newest social movements	Valid cases
Type of democratic regime						
Majoritarian	18.8	24.6	21.0	25.3	10.2	499
Consensual	10.5	35.2	7.7	34.9	11.6	352
Cramer's V = 0.24***						
Type of interest representation model						
Pluralist	16.5	28.5	17.9	26.9	10.2	666
Corporatist	11.4	30.8	7.0	37.8	13.0	185
Cramer's V = 0.16***						

pronounced for leftist activists than for others: members of both traditional and radical left organizations declared on average to be members of another 4.5 groups (for NSMOs/NGOs the figure is 3.9 and for newest social movements, 3.8). Thus, our traditional and radical left organizations share their members with various types of NSMOs and NGOs such as women's rights organizations (23 per cent for the traditional Left, 22 per cent for the radical Left), peace organizations (both about 34 per cent), gay and lesbian groups (10 and 11 per cent), human rights organizations (35 and 37 per cent), and international solidarity groups (40 and 38 per cent). If traditional leftists seem to be more inclined towards consumerism and fair trade (20 versus 12 per cent), development aid organizations (18 versus 11 per cent), and charity organizations (15 versus 6 per cent), radical leftists tend to favour anti-racist organizations (50 versus 37 per cent), student groups (33 versus 27 per cent), environmental groups (22.5 versus 18.8 per cent), and unemployed organizations (13 versus 10 per cent).

We can therefore conclude that the traditional and radical left activists are expressions of a new politics – postmaterialist, postmodern, postfordist, whatever we may want to call it – just like other GJM activists: they have multiple and open identities that make it possible to bridge old and new social movement frames (Andretta 2005a; della Porta 2005a; della Porta *et al.* 2006a: chapter 4). Activists of the traditional and radical Left are, in fact, also involved in newest social movement organizations, for example in local social forums (36 and 29 per cent, respectively), in groups against the neoliberal economic agenda (6 and 9 per cent), and in alternative media (14 and 11 per cent).

However, activists of the traditional and radical Left show distinctive patterns of action repertoires. The traditional Left, in particular, shows party related repertoires: 77.8 per cent persuaded someone to vote for a political party (versus 58.1 per cent for the radical Left, 53.7 per cent for NSMOs and NGOs, 48.4 per cent for newest social movements, and 29.9 per cent for non-members); 75.5 per cent worked in a political party (versus 56.6 per cent for the radical Left, 30.1 per cent for NSMOs and NGOs, 29.5 per cent for newest social movements, and 5.2 per cent for non-members). For trade union activity, the differences between the traditional and the radical Left narrow considerably: 66.5 per cent of the former and 68.4 per cent of the latter had participated in a strike, while for NSMOs and NGOs and newest social movements the percentage is, respectively, 51.5 and 66.3 per cent, and for non-members 35.1 per cent. Finally, at 36.7 per cent, the traditional left activists showed the lowest propensity to visit the autonomous spaces at the Athens ESF (versus 45.5 per cent for the radical Left, 59 per cent for NSMOs and NGOs, 48.8 per cent for newest social movements, and 60.7 per cent for non-members).

All organized activists of the ESF regularly practise more conventional participative forms of action like attending a demonstration, signing a petition, or handing out leaflets (with NSMOs and NGOs showing a lower percentage for the latter). The radical Left, however, far more than the traditional Left, favours unconventional and antagonistic forms of action like civil disobedience (59.6 versus 47.5 per cent), non-violent direct action (64 versus 61.5 per cent), blockades (53.7 versus 37 per cent), occupying public buildings (56 versus 42.8 per cent) or abandoned homes (19 versus 11 per cent), and violence against property (13.2 versus 5.4 per cent). Regarding the strategies of the GJM, the radical Left with 31.3 per cent (versus 19.7 per cent for the traditional Left, 10.3 per cent for the newest movements, and 9.3 per cent for NSMOs and NGOs) attributes the greatest importance to the option 'take to the streets to express dissent publicly'.[31]

A greater closeness of the traditional Left to institutionalized representative politics also emerges from the data on trust in political actors: 40.4 per cent of traditional leftists trust political parties at least a fair amount, versus 17.6 per cent of the radical Left, 19 per cent of members of NSMOs and NGOs, 14.6 per cent of members of newest social movements, and 7.6 per cent of non-members. Trade unions are trusted by 63.4 per cent of the traditional Left, versus 41.1 per cent of the radical Left, 45.8 per cent of NSMOs and NGOs, 47.7 per cent of newest movements, and 38.5 per cent of non-members.[32] With 33 and 28 per cent, respectively, the traditional Left also shows comparatively high trust in local government (average: 28 per cent; radical Left: 10 per cent) and in the national parliament (average: 22 per cent; radical Left: 6 per cent). In contrast, of all our categories (including non-members), the radical Left shows the lowest trust in all political actors, with the exception of political parties and trade unions (although trust remains low in these two cases), confirming their distance from institutional politics as practised in Western democracies.

Finally, about 42 per cent of traditional leftists place themselves in a radical leftist position and about 46 per cent in a more moderate but still leftist position; for the radical leftists these percentages are respectively about 66 and 26 per cent, for NSMO members 31 and 41 per cent, and for the newest social movements, 30 and 54 per cent.

Leftist activists and the GJM: which kind of involvement?

In the first part of our chapter, based on the organizational affiliation of participants in the EPAs, we noted that the traditional Left plays an important role within the preparatory process of the ESFs, although the groups most committed to the ESF process (the radical Left and newest movements) show comparatively strongly (see Table 9.2). These results seem to be confirmed by our survey of participants at the Athens ESF.

First, our data show that identification with the GJM is highest among activists of newest social movements and of the radical Left but also remains high for those of the traditional Left (see Table 9.4).[33] Both traditional and radical leftists identify with the GJM on average more than 'enough'; but in this respect, no difference emerges with the full sample.

Analysing the degree of involvement in the GJM, we notice that the activists of newest social movements show the highest degree of participation in GJM activities. Leftist activists, however, also show a strong involvement: if activists generally participated in more than five GJM events prior to Athens, traditional leftists did so more than six times and radical leftists about seven times, while the participation of activists of NSMOs and NGOs remains below average.

Table 9.4 The involvement of leftist activists in the GJM

	Identification with GJM		General participation in GJM activities		Only national participation in GJM		Transnational participation		Participation in GJM decision making	
	Means	ETA	Means	ETA	Means	ETA	Means	ETA	Means	ETA
Non-members	1.8		2.3		1.3		0.22		.27	
Traditional leftists	2.3	0.336***	6.2	0.348***	4.0	0.322***	0.53	0.282***	0.73	0.356***
Radical leftists	2.4		6.6		2.8		0.65		0.81	
NSMOs, NGOs, and others	2.3		5.0		2.7		0.52		0.64	
Newest movements	2.6		8.0		5.9		0.70		0.74	
Total	2.3		5.5		2.9		0.51		0.65	

Interestingly, if we isolate the activists who (prior to Athens) had participated only in national events but not in GJM activities outside their countries of residence, the level of participation of the traditional Left is significantly higher than that of the radical Left and NSMOs and NGOs, though it remains lower than that of the newest social movements. Regarding transnational participation, traditional leftists (53 per cent) show a level of participation similar to NSMOs and NGOs, while activists of the radical Left (65 per cent) and especially of the newest social movements (70 per cent) participated far more in GJM activities outside their own countries. Unsurprisingly, at all levels, non-organized activists are far less involved than activists with some kind of membership.

The results on participation in GJM decision making do not mirror those on participation in GJM activities. Here, organizational commitment and available resources come into play. As presented in the example of the May 2002 EPA in Vienna in the first part of this chapter (see Table 9.2), both the traditional and radical Left seem to play an important role in GJM decision making, as important as, or even more so, than the one played by the newest social movements. In fact, 73 per cent of traditional leftists and as much as 81 per cent of radical leftists declared having been involved in GJM decision making, as compared to 65 per cent of the total. The involvement of activists of newest social movements (74 per cent) mirrors that of the traditional Left, while NSMOs and NGOs (64 per cent) remain slightly below the average of 65 per cent.

Concluding, both of our categories of left-wing activists, notwithstanding the closer proximity of those of the traditional Left to institutional forms of political participation, are clearly and strongly involved in GJM activities, playing a prominent role in GJM decision making.

Democratic practices and ideals of leftist activists in the GJM in Europe

The GJM has reactivated a reflection on 'radical democracy' by emphasizing a 'new' model of democracy based on consensus and direct participation. Most of the activists surveyed at the Athens ESF share a normative democratic ideal that we called 'deliberative-participative democracy', based on consensual decision making and the refusal of delegation (see Chapter 4 in this volume). This model of democracy is advanced in particular by the newest and most innovative sector of the movement.

The question is, then, whether specific traits of traditional left and radical left activists emerge regarding perceived democratic practices and democratic ideals. Two competing hypotheses can be advanced and tested. According to a 'path dependency' argument (Mahoney 2000; Pierson 2000), activists associated with the traditional Left should be more likely to support the 'associational model' of democracy, based on delegation and majority decision making, traditionally implemented in the organizations of the workers' movement. Considering the critique of delegation and bureaucratization advanced by the 1970s New Left, activists of the radical Left should support what we have called the 'assembleary model', combining direct participation with majority decision making. Following a sociological institutionalism approach (March and Olsen 1989; Maggio and Powell 1991), one could instead hypothesize that the involvement of leftist activists in the GJM led to 'contamination' with the deliberative-participative democratic ideal advanced by the new movement, and the acceptance of a model that is deliberative-representative (combining consensus and delegation) or deliberative-participative (based on consensus and direct participation). In this case, a process of diffusion of new ideas and practices through intense and sustained networking could be seen at work (McAdam *et al.* 2001). We can test the two hypotheses by correlating our typology of left GJM activists with perceived democratic practices within the group of reference and with normative ideals of democracy.

Perceived democratic practices in traditional left and radical left groups

Regarding the perception of democratic practices within the group of reference (see Table 9.5), our data give conflicting results. If the relative majority of traditional leftists perceive the practices of their own group as being associative (with a clear majority indicating decision making by vote, but slightly more than 50 per cent the participation of all members), the relative majority of radical leftists characterize their group not as 'assembleary' but as 'deliberative-participative' (with a clear majority indicating the participation of all members and slightly more than 50 per cent consensus as a decision making method). Further elements are added by taking a separate look at the original variables of our Athens survey, that is, participation of members in decision making and decision making methods, measured on a four digit scale. If we concentrate on the extremes of the scales, regarding participation, traditional leftists and activists of NSMOs and NGOs show the highest frequencies for the option that only few

Table 9.5 Typology of activists and perceived organizational democratic practices (%)

Typology of activists	Perceived organizational democratic practices				
	Associative	Deliberative representative	Assembleary	Deliberative participative	Valid cases
Traditional Left	32.4	16.2	29.6	21.9	247
Radical Left	15.9	9.5	31.0	43.7	126
NSMOs, NGOs and others	23.6	20.0	21.4	35.0	220
Newest movements	15.5	14.3	23.8	46.4	84
Total sample row	24.4	16.0	26.4	33.2	677

Note
Cramer's V = 0.14***

members participate in decision making and the lowest for the option that all members do so. Concerning consensus, the traditional and radical Left show the highest frequencies for the option that decisions are always taken by vote and the lowest for the option that they are always taken by consensus.

Our findings seem to indicate processes of diffusion, although constrained by specific organizational cultures. In fact, contradictory results emerge for the traditional Left for participation and for the radical Left for decision making method, that is, consensus. In this respect we can advance the hypothesis that activists' perceptions reflect tension between the organizational practices and the particular original democratic values of the two types of leftist organizations, exposed by the participatory and deliberative claims of the GJM. For organizations of the traditional Left, in fact, participation remains a fundamental value that is repeatedly stressed in key documents but increasingly problematic in its translation into practice (della Porta and Reiter 2006a). Similarly, the ideal of unanimity of the radical Left, in organizational practice often translated into provisions of qualified majorities, is particularly challenged by the deliberative forms of decision making usually advanced by the GJM.

Finally, the fact that activists see their organizations as increasingly practising participation and deliberation – about 21 percent of even the traditional leftists perceive the practice of their group as 'deliberative-participative' – indicates that (regardless of whether these perceptions correspond to real practices or not) something 'new' is happening in the internal democracy of both traditional and radical Left, at least in terms of activists' aspirations.

Democratic ideals of traditional left and radical left activists

In order to isolate the aspirations of activists – that is, their democratic ideals – we also asked them to indicate how they think political decisions should be taken in general (see Chapter 4 in this volume). Our results show that traditional left and radical left activists to a very large extent share the same democratic ideals with other types of activists. In fact, no significant differences emerge concerning the importance of the quality of arguments and of mutual respect of opponents in a political conflict. Concentrating on the ideals of direct participation in decision making and of consensus as a decision making method, both are most clearly accepted by the activists of the newest movements that emerged with the rise of the GJM. Whereas a clear overall preference for the ideal of direct participation emerges, the use of the consensus method in political decision making is a far more divisive issue: 85 per cent of activists of the newest movements, 73 per cent of traditional leftists, 72 per cent of members of NSMOs and NGOs, and 68 per cent of radical leftists believe that direct participation should be a priority in decision making; but with the exception of the newest movements (46 per cent of whose activists, however, are also favourably disposed towards at least sometimes using the vote), an overall preference for voting emerges, from non-members (66 per cent), to traditional leftists (57 per cent), radical leftists (54 per cent), and members of NSMOs and NGOs (54 per cent).

If we cross-tabulate our results for the ideals of direct participation and consensus, we obtain the four-fold typology of democratic models that we used in the previous section to discriminate among perceived democratic practices in the groups of reference, with the associational, deliberative-representative, assembleary, and deliberative-participative models now representing different ideal types of democracy (see Table 9.6). Surprisingly, as many as 38 per cent of the traditional leftists prefer an assembleary model – the model of the new left-libertarian movements of the 1960s and 1970s – compared to 36 per cent of the whole sample, and, more importantly, 31 per cent of the radical leftists themselves. Moreover, few traditional leftists are inclined to see an associational setting as an ideal type of decision making: only members of newest social movements refer to such a model less often. Activists who mentioned a radical leftist organization as their most important group are relatively more inclined to see the associational model as an ideal of democracy. Activists who most favour a deliberative-participative ideal are, not surprisingly, those of the newest social

Table 9.6 Typology of activists and normative democratic models (%)

Typology of activists	Normative democratic models				
	Associative	Deliberative representative	Assembleary	Deliberative participative	Valid cases
Non-members	26.4	5.4	39.5	28.7	129
Traditional Left	18.6	8.9	38.1	34.4	247
Radical Left	21.7	10.1	31.8	36.4	129
NSMOs, NGOs, and others	20.1	7.9	33.9	38.1	239
Newest movements	8.4	7.2	37.3	47.0	83
Total sample row	19.7	8.1	36.0	36.2	827

movements (47 per cent as compared to about 36 per cent on average); but neither the traditional nor the radical leftists are less inclined towards deliberative participation than the average. Finally, the deliberative-representative model is the least popular ideal option for all types of activists.

To summarize, traditional leftist activists show considerable distance from the old associative model and appear far closer to a more participative type of democracy, be it assembleary or deliberative-participative. At the same time, activists involved in radical left groups generally support either their traditional assembleary model or the new deliberative-participative one. However, within the radical groups, a democratic model based on delegation and voting seems to hold an unexpected appeal.

The diffusion model is compatible with our findings; but as underlined before, processes of diffusion are filtered through existing organizational cultures. This is particularly visible regarding the issue of voting, with consensus emerging as minoritarian for both traditional and radical leftists. However, even activists of the traditional Left – also by reappropriating and reinterpreting the original participatory values of their organizations – show considerable distance from a democratic model based on the delegation of power. It remains difficult to explain why radical leftists show comparatively higher support for the traditional leftist practice of delegating power.

Internal democratic practices challenged

Comparing the results of the normative models of democracy with those of the perceptions of democratic practices at the group level, we notice visible signs of incongruence between the two (see Tables 9.4 and 9.5). For instance, although 33 per cent of the activists primarily involved in traditional left organizations perceive their groups as practising an associational model, only 18 per cent support this model as a democratic ideal. Similarly, while 41 per cent of the activists primarily involved in radical leftist organizations perceive their groups as 'deliberative-participative', only 34 per cent bear a congruent ideal of democracy.

We can more precisely analyse the degree of congruence between perceived democratic practices of the group of reference and democratic ideals by calculating the differences between the respective scores.[34]

The results show that for both delegation/participation and voting/consensus, activists who declared their primary involvement in traditional left organizations show a higher degree of incongruence than radical leftists between perceived democratic practices in their group and democratic ideals (see Table 9.7). The differences in the index of total incongruence (considering also arguments/resources and mutual acceptance) are statistically significant. If we dichotomize the index and distinguish between a high and low/degree of incongruence[35], we see that as many as 51.5 per cent of traditional left activists show real incongruence, as compared to only 31 per cent of radical leftists, 37 per cent of activists of newest social movements, and 43 per cent of members of NSMOs and NGOs (the average is 43 per cent).

Table 9.7 Typology of activists and level of incongruence and satisfaction with democracy in the group

Typology of Activists	Incongruence between group democratic practices and democratic ideals and (dis)satisfaction with democracy in the group							
	Inc. in deleg./partic.		Inc. in voting/ consensus		Index of total incongruence		Dissatisfaction with group democracy	
	Means	ETA	Means	ETA	Means	ETA	Means	ETA
Traditional Left	1.00		0.87		0.94		1.04	
Radical Left	0.80	0.122*	0.64	n.s.	0.67	0.182***	0.58	0.236***
NSMOs, NGOs, and others	1.12		0.81		0.87		0.80	
Newest movements	0.92		0.68		0.76		0.74	
Total	0.99		0.78		0.85		0.83	

Not surprisingly, the level of incongruence is correlated with dissatisfaction with democracy within the group of reference (see Chapter 4 and Chapter 7 in this volume).[36] Traditional leftists emerge as those less satisfied with democracy in their own groups: 21 per cent declare being moderately or very unsatisfied, versus only 6 per cent of radical leftists (10 per cent for NSMOs and NGOs, 12 per cent for newest movements, and 14 per cent on average). If we isolate this 21 per cent of unsatisfied traditional leftists, we notice that 83 per cent perceive that decisions are not taken by all (or almost all) participants, while 77 per cent highly value direct participation in democratic decision making; 69 per cent perceive that decisions are taken by voting, while 47 per cent value consensus as an ideal method; 60 per cent perceive decision making in their group as following the associational model, while as many as 76 per cent indicate a participatory ideal, preferring either an assembleary (39 per cent) or deliberative-participative model (37 per cent). Only 10 per cent describe their group as assembleary and only 8 per cent as deliberative-participative. In general, if we extend the analysis to the full sample, 47 per cent of those activists describing their group as associational would prefer an assembleary model and 24 per cent a deliberative-participative one, while only 21 per cent of those activists describing their group as assembleary and as few as 8 per cent of those describing it as deliberative-participative would prefer an associational model.

To conclude, the organizational model of the traditional Left, based on delegation and voting, is still perceived as a valid model, not only by traditional leftists. The radical leftist model, based on direct participation and voting, is even more widely indicated as an ideal by activists, and not only among radical leftist activists. These findings suggest that the presence of the traditional and radical Left in the GJM is felt not only in terms of their organizations and activists, but also in terms of their democratic traditions and ideals. At the same time, however, we have seen evidence of the diffusion of a new model of democracy, based on direct participation and deliberation, among both traditional and radical leftists. The 'contamination' of these activists with a new democratic model could become particularly important for members of organizations adopting an associational model: strongly favouring direct participation, they could choose to leave if they do not see their aspirations satisfied. However, disillusionment might also mount with regard to the GJM. In the perception of the activists, even GJM decision making does not (yet?) conform to the ideal of deliberative participation, and while a relative majority concedes that deliberation takes place, most activists (with the exception of those belonging to the newest movements) believe that direct participation is not actually practised.

Conclusion

As we argued in the first part of this chapter, different sectors of the European Left showed divergent reactions to the rise of the GJM. Among social democratic and socialist parties, diffidence dominated. For these parties, differences with the GJM about the answers needed to adapt to the challenges of globalization are particularly evident. In fact, regarding the question of (global) democratic governance, the socialists defend representative democratic practices and a dominant role for political parties, including in the transnational political arena. The threat to the European welfare model posed by the neoliberal economic agenda led the traditional European trade unions, instead, to greater openness, particularly for those unions with a historically strong communist influence. Communist and post-communist parties, in fact, saw an opportunity for mobilization in the globalization process. For these parties, however, tension developed with the GJM and with those of their own members active in the movement because of the very role of political parties in the institutional political arena. This issue became particularly acute when the question of sustaining a government arose. Grassroots unions and radical left political groups with their roots in the New Left of the 1970s were instead deeply involved in the GJM from the very beginning. Some of these groups, however, argued for a structured organization of the social forum process, aimed at uniting and leading resistance to 'the system', at odds with the deliberative and participative ideals of the GJM and its open network character.

Analysing the involvement of traditional left and radical left organizations in the social forum process, we have highlighted the fact that the traditional Left in particular contributed important resources to the organization of the successive ESFs. In addition, both traditional and radical left organizations emerge as important contributors to the ESF programmes, organizing numerous seminars and workshops. However, comparing participation of activists in the ESF with visibility in the programme, both sectors of the European Left are characterized more by participation than visibility. Finally, as the example of representation in the EPAs shows, activists of both traditional and radical left organizations are prominently involved in the preparatory process of the ESFs.

Turning to the results of our activist survey, we underlined the strong and sustained presence of activists of the European Left in the successive ESFs from Florence to Athens. Regarding socio-demographic characteristics and occupational status, the most important results to underline are that, surprisingly, the traditional Left shows the highest percentage of young activists, probably due to the involvement of their youth organizations. At the same time, traditional left activists are more likely to be employed by their own organizations as paid staff or leaders and can therefore be seen as professional politicians. On the other hand, the traditional Left, together with the radical Left, was most present in terms of ordinary members at the ESF, signifying that any decision of the leadership to attend was sustained by mobilization of its rank and file members. Looking at national differences, we find the activists of the radical Left most strongly represented in majoritarian and pluralist regimes, but both the traditional left activists and those of NSMOs and NGOs in consensual ones.

Differences between the traditional and the radical Left emerged in the patterns of political activism. If the former, remaining anchored in forms of political activism consonant with representative democracy, show greater proximity to conventional and particularly party related action forms, the latter promote more radical and disruptive action repertoires, showing a greater distance from the established and institutionalized forms of political participation. Regardless of these differences, both the traditional and the radical Left show a high level of involvement in GJM activities, particularly in decision making

In the final part of our chapter, we concentrated on democratic ideals and on perceived democratic practices within the group of reference. Our findings seem to indicate processes of diffusion, although filtered through existing organizational cultures. In fact, while the ideal of direct participation emerges particularly strongly, deliberation, although making important inroads into the traditional and particularly the radical Left, is shared as a value only by a minority. Especially for activists of the traditional Left, however, we saw a considerable distance between their democratic ideals and the perceived model of democratic decision making in their own group. This incongruence between ideals and perceived practices corresponds to decreased satisfaction with democratic practices in the group of reference. The 'contamination' of activists with a new democratic model could create particular problems for organizations adopting a traditional model of decision making combining delegation and voting, as they risk alienating activists who strongly favour direct participation. However, the GJM might run a similar risk: activists in fact perceive GJM decision making as not (yet?) conforming to the ideal of deliberative participation, and in particular as not achieving the goal of direct participation.[37]

Notes

1 Herbert Reiter is the principal author of 'Introduction' and 'The involvement of the European leftist organizations in the social forum process'; Massimiliano Andretta of 'Activists of organizations of the European Left at the ESF: involvement in the social

forum process and conceptions of democracy' and 'Conclusion'. We are grateful to Donatella della Porta for her useful comments on previous versions of this chapter.
2 The fall of the Berlin wall led to the decision to reform and rename the Italian communist party (PCI), a move opposed by a minority, which founded Rifondazione Comunista. The DS, the largest successor party, are of a social democratic orientation, and a member of the Socialist International as well as the Party of European Socialists. In 2007, the DS merged with their centre ally Margherita and formed a new party (Partito Democratico – Democratic Party), which is not a member of the Party of European Socialists and, according to its leader Walter Veltroni, not a left-wing party.
3 A Google search for 'Sozialforum' on the website of the SPD yields no results, while the same search for 'forum sociale' on the DS website gives 329 hits. Except when indicated differently, all web documents were accessed in February 2007.
4 The Charter of Principles (WSF 2002) refers to

> Groups and movements of civil society that are opposed to neo-liberalism and to domination of the world by capital and any form of imperialism, and are committed to building a planetary society directed towards fruitful relationships among Mankind and between it and the Earth.

5 'Globalisierung gerecht gestalten' was the DGB motto for the Labour Day celebrations on 1 May 2002 (see also DGB 2006).
6 A document of the political commission for the twenty-third congress (FIOM 2004) explicitly called for the continuation of the union's participation in the mobilizations of the movement.
7 Up to 2007, RC contained a small Trotskyite minority, which split in disagreement with the policies of the centre-left government backed by RC and formed its own party.
8 At the London ESF, RC secretary Fausto Bertinotti was criticized from an autonomous position for an 'atrophied perspective' in which 'self-organization' and the reinvention of politics (as party politics) are the same. John Holloway questioned the use of a party to construct the revolutionary subject as the building of hierarchies, decision making in the name of others, rather than the self-construction of the subject: 'Our power is no counter-power but anti-power.' See Candeias 2004.
9 Solid, the youth organization of the German sister party of RC, is not as closely connected with the GJM as the GC. As for other German organizations, the GJM is at the moment the most important movement for Solid, although only one of many movements in which it seeks to root itself.
10 The synthesis of the majority document ('Rigenerazioni: l'autonomia di una generazione che diserta, disobbedisce, ama') published by the party newspaper, online, available at: www.liberazione.it/giornale/060922/LB12D6AB.asp.
11 Mainstream unions also criticize the ESF's weakness in coordinating action (for example, for the IG Metall Verbindungsbüro soziale Bewegungen, see the November 2006 minutes of the Frankfurt EPA: Online, available at: www.fse-esf.org/IMG/pdf/Minutes_from_EPA_Nov4_06.pdf). For grassroots unions, however, this criticism is embedded in a larger political strategy.
12 In this context, particularly underlined are the difficulties of RC, characterized as a sustainer of the term 'against war and terrorism' (see COBAS 2006).
13 See LCR-rouge article, online, available at: www.lcr-rouge.org/article.php3?Id_article=1110.
14 'Role and tasks of the Fourth International' (online, available at: www.isg-fi.org.uk/spip.php?Article100).
15 See 'Mouvement altermondialist. Retour sur Florence'. Online, available at: www.lcr-rouge.org/archives/121902/controv.html. The participation of political parties also remained an important theme for LCR at subsequent ESFs, up to Athens. See 'Forum Social d'Athènes. Réussite incontestable'. Online, available at: www.lcr-rouge.org/article.php3?Id_article=3997.

16 Candeias 2004. As was pointed out, this position ignores the current weakness of workers' resistance, as well as concrete relations between movements and party.
17 The League for the Fifth International is an international grouping of revolutionary Trotskyite organizations founded in the 1980s as the Movement for a Revolutionary Communist International, later renamed the League for a Revolutionary Communist International.
18 See League 2006. According to the document 'European Social Forum: A Crisis of Direction' (online, available at: www.fifthinternational.org/index.php?Id=14,585,0,0, 1,0), the European Left parties, in particular RC, consciously and deliberately try to prevent the ESF from becoming a fighting body due to the desire to enter into coalitions with the socialist parties.
19 Interview with a spokesperson of the Florence ESF, conducted 24 April 2004.
20 According to Angela Klein (2005), the first German social forum at Erfurt would not have materialized without the support of the regional organization of the trade union confederation DGB and of the post-communist party PDS.
21 This is the case, for instance, for Cesare Salvi of the left wing of the DS, whose 'Socialismo 2000' figures as a co-organizer of a seminar. ECOSY, the European federation of socialist youth organizations, presented four seminars and was present in Florence with more than 900 participants from 18 member organizations and 15 countries (see information online, available at: www.ecosy.org/uploads/media/Reports_Activities_2001-2002.PDF pp. 109ff.).
22 This plenary saw the participation of Elio di Rupo (Belgian Socialists), Rosi Bindi (Margherita, identified as democratic Catholic), Fausto Bertinotti (RC), Christian Ströbele (German Greens), and a representative of the French Trotskyite party LCR.
23 Information regarding initiatives of the CGIL, online, available at: www.cgil.it/internazionale/Tematiche/rapportoconmovimenti/forumsocialeeuropeo/fseateneseminari.htm.
24 The Global Progressive Forum (since March 2006 a member of the International Council of the WSF) is an initiative of the PES (Party of European Socialists), the Socialist group in the European Parliament, and the Socialist International. It is aimed at creating a space for cooperation and dialogue on globalization between progressive politicians, NGOs, and trade unions. The GPF vice president attended the ESF in London and in Athens.
25 Recognizing that in Athens party speakers were advertised as such, rather than pretending they spoke for a movement, Tina Becker of the UK Communist Party considered it unsurprising that groups like the SWP and the ISP continued to hide behind covers like Globalise Resistance. Article online, available at: www.euromovements.info/upload/Extremely%20pleasant%20Tina%20Becker.rtf?PHPSESSID=09f9823603eb2e245ef2c1f28fdd362c.
26 List of participants, online, available at: www.euromovements.info/e-library/autorsview.php?Id_autore=677. Detailed online information could be found only for the Vienna assembly in preparation of the first ESF. Regarding the preparatory process for the Athens ESF, 211 Greek delegates, 71 delegates of 29 European associations, and 23 delegates of trade unions participated at the first EPA (Athens, February 2005; online, available at: www.fse-esf.org/spip.php?Article15). At the EPA in Istanbul (October 2005), 450 delegates from 34 countries were present, representing 106 European and 61 Turkish organizations (online, available at: www.fse-esf.org/spip.php?Article105). Monetary contributions were given by the Confederation of Revolutionary Workers Union, Chamber of Electrician Engineers, Chamber of Doctors of Istanbul, Confederation of Public Workers Union, Chamber of Engineers and Architects, and other Turkish organizations (ibid.).
27 Contribution to the European Preparatory Assembly of the ESF in Frankfurt, 3–5 November 2006 (online, available at: www.euromovements.info/upload/attacnetworkinfranckfurt.doc?PHPSESSID=94032928677863b8b34b64cf834d2b2a). In the

same document, Attac lamented that Athens saw confirmation of the high influence and visibility of political parties, which it defined as a clear breach of the WSF charter. Attac underlined the urgent need to discuss the place of political parties in the ESF process and spoke of the danger that their visibility might lead to a reduction of the scope of potential participating groups.

28 For these figures we excluded, from a total of 1,205 cases, 12.2 per cent missing, 2.9 per cent who voted for centre/right parties, and 3.7 per cent who voted for other parties (e.g. regional) or for parties that we were unable to place.
29 The cross tabulation of our typology of organizations declared as closest with party voted at the last national election gives a Cramer's V of 0.261***.
30 Covering 1,104 activists, i.e. 91.6 per cent of our sample, we applied the scores attributed by Lijphart for each country present both in his research and in our sample (Austria, Belgium, Colombia, Denmark, Finland, France, Germany, Greece, Ireland, Israel, Italy, Netherlands, Portugal, Spain, Sweden, Switzerland, UK, and US).
31 The option 'promote alternative social and economic models', instead, is favoured especially by the newest movements with 43.2 per cent, versus 39.8 per cent for NSMOs and NGOs, 36.8 per cent for the traditional Left, and 26.4 per cent for the radical Left.
32 Only a low percentage of radical leftists, who are involved in grassroots trade unions, declare trust in unions in general. This can be explained by the fact that radical leftists might not want to express trust for a category that also includes the established unions they criticize.
33 The original variable 'Identification with GJM' varies from 0 (no identification) to 3 (much identification). If the mean is more than 2, on average activists of the relative category declare that they identify with GJM more than 'enough'. The original variable 'General participation in GJM activities' varies from 0 to 4: 0 = never before; 1 = once; 2 = 2–5 times; 3 = 6–10 times; 4 = more than 10 times. We recoded the variable by assigning to each value the median of the attached range (for instance, we attached to value 2, the value 3.5, or to value 3, the value 8). For the variable 'Only national participation in GJM' we used the variable 'General participation in GJM activities', selecting those activists who prior to Athens had never participated in a protest/demonstration other than in their country of residence. The original variable 'Transnational participation' was a dichotomy: 0 = No, I did not participate in a country other than my own; 1 = Yes, I did. We calculated the mean for each type of activist, reflecting the proportion of members participating at the transnational level (i.e. a mean of 0.53 for the traditional leftists means that 53 per cent of them participated at the transnational level). The original variable 'Participation in GJM decision making' was a dichotomy: 0 = No, I did not participate in GJM decision making; 1 = Yes, I did. The means represent the proportion of activists having participated in GJM decision making (for instance, 0.71 for the traditional leftists means that 71 per cent of them have participated in such decision making settings).
34 The synthetic index varies from 0 (no incongruence) to 3 (full incongruence); see Chapter 4 and Chapter 7 for the operationalization.
35 We considered such a score of incongruence to be up to 0.75, which means an average of less than 1 point on the 0–3 scale for each item.
36 The Kendall's tau-b of the correlation between the two variables is 0.29, significant at 0.001 level.
37 For this chapter we considered events up to the Athens ESF. For further developments see in particular the Labour and Globalization network (http://openesf.net/projects/labour-and-globalization).

10 Protest and the forum
Forms of participation in the global justice movement

Marco Giugni, Alessandro Nai, and Herbert Reiter

The European Social Forum (ESF) is an open space for debate but also a space for protest. Its participants not only attend workshops and discuss alternatives to neoliberal globalization and ways to build another Europe, but also use their broad repertoires of protest within and around the forum. This chapter discusses the use of various forms of action within the global justice movement (GJM), tackling the issue at two distinct levels of analysis. In the first part, we look at the relationship between protest and the arena we chose for our analysis, that is, the ESF. We first discuss the forum as a form of protest in its own right, or more precisely as a space where multiple and heterogeneous forms of protest against neoliberal globalization are planned and practised. The acceptance of variegated action repertoires with the one condition of nonviolence emerges as a distinct common aspect of the protest activities connected with the ESF. Notwithstanding this acceptance, tension in connection with specific protest events and certain forms of action also reveals the forum as a contested protest space. This tension mirrors general strains within the social forum process, concerning in particular the boundaries of the movement and internal decision making. However, the common basis within the ESF also proved to be solid with regard to forms of action.

In the second part, we analyse the use of various forms of action by individual participants in the May 2006 ESF in Athens, based on the survey we conducted there in the context of the Demos project. Here, we follow the research tradition on political participation (Barnes and Kaase 1979; Dalton 2002; Milbrath 1965; Verba and Nie 1972; Verba et al. 1978) to inquire into the differences in the forms of participation by those who attended the Athens ESF, distinguishing among three general forms: party related activities, demonstrative protest, and confrontational protest. Although we treat these general forms as three distinct ways of engaging in politics, they can be seen as increasingly demanding in terms of commitment and as increasingly radical in their expression.

We first look into the relationship among the three general forms of participation and their connection with the different areas of the GJM. We argue that the overlapping use of action forms by the various movement areas constitutes a factor contributing to the solidity of the ESF protest space, notwithstanding its characteristic as a contested space. We then examine how the use of these forms of participation is influenced by three sets of factors: the structural characteristics of the people involved (gender, age, social status (being a student), and position within the group most important to the respondent); their attitudes towards politics (as indicated by degree of identification with the global justice movement, being a radical leftist, degree of political and institutional trust, and level of satisfaction with decision making processes); and their views about democracy as well as globalization. In other words, we aim to look at how certain social, political, and cultural characteristics and values of participants in the ESF influence their political activities.

The latter factor is of particular interest for us, as it allows us to study the relationship between forms of action and the democratic views of participants in the ESF and more generally in the global justice movement. The focus here will be on three aspects that give us a broad picture of how activists place themselves vis-à-vis democracy and globalization: their views about how collective decisions should be taken, about strategies to enhance democracy, and about strategies to tame globalization. Concerning the first aspect, we shall focus more specifically on four key features of deliberative democracy (see Chapter 4 in this volume): whether the quality of arguments (rather than resources) should primarily make the difference in decision making; whether mutual acceptance is always important in a political conflict; whether participation (rather than delegation) should always be a priority in decision making; and whether political decisions should be taken by consensus (rather than voting). The latter two aspects, in particular, define the deliberative-participative model of democracy (della Porta 2005a) often stressed by the movement.

The arena: the ESF as a protest space

The ESF: a multiple and heterogeneous protest space

Social forums in general, and the ESF in particular, have been described as communicative spaces and also as an organizational form typical of the highly networked nature of the GJM. The organization and holding of social forums at the global, regional, and local levels can also be considered as a form of protest. In fact, the first edition of the World Social Forum (WSF) in January 2001 was conceived as a counter-event to the World Economic Forum in Davos. It was meant to intercept media attention, but also to propose a counter-model to the dominant ways of discussing and practicing global governance. At the first ESF in Florence in November 2002, its character as a protest event found expression in the slogan, 'Against war, racism and neoliberalism'. The 'Call of the European Social Movements' published on that occasion explicitly states: 'We have gathered in Florence to express our opposition to a European order based on corporate power and neoliberalism' (ESF 2002). In addition, the call locates the ESF in a series of protest events: 'We have come together through a long process: the demonstrations of Amsterdam, Seattle, Prague, Nice, Genoa, Brussels, Barcelona' (ibid.). Similar statements have also characterized the subsequent editions of the ESF.[1]

More than a clearly defined form of protest, however, the ESF is a space where different forms and conceptions of protest against neoliberal globalization may be planned and practised. As often underlined, in fact, the ESF is not a homogeneous actor; according to the WSF Charter of Principles adopted in 2001, to which the ESF also refers, it is not an actor at all. The charter defines the social forum as 'an open meeting place for reflective thinking, democratic debate of ideas, formulation of proposals, free exchange of experiences and interlinking for effective action, by groups and movements of civil society that are opposed to neo-liberalism' (WSF 2002). At the same time, the charter underlines that the WSF does not intend to be a body representing world civil society. In fact, the meetings of the WSF and ESF do not deliberate on behalf of the forum as a body, and no one is authorized to express positions claiming to be those of all its participants.

The protest space provided by the ESF is in fact populated by organizational actors engaging in multiple and heterogeneous protest activities. An analysis of organizations involved in the European Social Forum process, based on fundamental documents of these organizations and interviews with their representatives, has shown that they employ different strategies to reach their goals: protest, lobbying, constructing concrete alternatives, promoting political education, trying to raise citizens' awareness (see della Porta and Mosca 2006; della Porta and Reiter 2006a). Most of these groups do not limit themselves to a single strategy but employ and mix various approaches. Contrary to the assumption that lobbying and protest are opposite strategies used by different actors, we found evidence for the use of both by a significant percentage of the sampled groups.

Within the protest space provided by the ESF, different organizations, but also the same organization, may therefore express their opposition to neoliberal globalization in different ways: by organizing seminars or workshops, leafleting, circulating petitions, organizing demonstrations or vigils, participating in the concluding demonstration of the ESF, and so on. These variegated action repertoires are not only tolerated within the social forum framework, but are seen positively as part of the diversity that the GJM considers one of its strengths, rather than a weakness. In fact, the WSF and the ESF encourage the acceptance of diversity in forms of action, with the one condition of non-violence. The WSF charter speaks of openness to 'the diversity of activities and ways of engaging of the organizations and movements that decide to participate in it'. In this context, it stresses transparency, the sharing of experiences, and the encouragement of 'understanding and mutual recognition amongst its participant organizations and movements', by strengthening and creating new national and international links with the aim of increasing 'the capacity for non-violent social resistance to the process of dehumanization the world is undergoing and to the violence used by the State' (WSF 2002).

The principles contained in the WSF charter – in particular the acceptance of diversity in forms of action with the condition of non-violence – found their first European expression in the protests against the G8 summit in Genoa in 2001, that is, more than a year before the first ESF. Agreed upon at the WSF, the counter-summit was organized by a light ad hoc structure, the Genoa Social Forum (GSF), which stipulated a 'work agreement' (echoing the WSF charter elaborated roughly at the same time) binding the signatories to 'respect all forms of direct, peaceful, nonviolent expression and action declared publicly and transparently' (GSF 2001). At the Florence ESF (and at subsequent editions of the forum), a work agreement similar to the one in Genoa was not formally signed, but informally applied.[2]

An important function of the ESF as a protest space consists in the planning and promotion of protest events beyond the forum itself. The very fact that such protest events were perceived as being promoted by the WSF or the ESF jars with a strict definition of the forum as an open space for debate, that is, limited to providing an opportunity for organizations, groups, and networks to meet, exchange ideas, and discuss and co-ordinate future common action (Whitaker 2004). In fact, the assembly of social movements, which does in its calls promote specific protest events, is convened after the official end of the WSF or ESF, albeit implicitly part of these events. Strictly speaking, the role of the assembly is limited to being an instigator or catalyst of protest events, and any concrete planning is conducted by those networks and organizations willing to collaborate on that task.

Considering this tenuous connection between the ESF (and even the assembly of social movements) and protest events beyond the forum, it must be underlined how successful it has been as an instigator of protest events. This is particularly true for the first of these events, the 15 February 2003 demonstrations against the imminent war in Iraq, considered to have been the largest ever mobilization of the peace movement. The demonstration held in Rome, said to have involved three million people, is listed in the 2004 *Guinness Book of World Records* as the biggest anti-war rally in history.

The February 15th Global Day of Action was promoted by the assembly of social movements at the Florence ESF in November 2002, which called on the movements and citizens of Europe to organize 'massive opposition to an attack on Iraq' and 'to start organizing enormous anti-war demonstrations in every capital on February 15'. One month later, this call was confirmed by the European Preparatory Assembly (EPA) in Copenhagen, which also saw the presence of the newly founded US umbrella organization United for Peace. In January 2003, a specific February 15 preparatory workshop was conducted at the third WSF in Porto Alegre. Temporary national coalitions were set up containing a whole range of organizations and national social movements. Although the originally planned worldwide website never materialized, the websites of the national coalitions were linked to each other. An intensive e-mail circuit was set up, connecting all of the European and eventually also the US peace movements. A worldwide symbol of the protests (a missile crossed out by the words 'Stop the War') and identical slogans to be used at all demonstration sites ('No war in Iraq', 'Not in my name', and 'No blood for oil') were agreed upon (see Verhulst forthcoming).

As an instigator and catalyst of protest events, the ESF was successful not only in terms of the number of participants in these events, but also in permeating them with its spirit. As mentioned above, the principles defined in the WSF charter – acceptance of diversity in the forms of action with the condition of non-violence – were taken up in the 'work agreement' of the GSF, which bound the signatories to 'respect all forms of direct, peaceful, nonviolent expression and action declared publicly and transparently'. Similar formulas in general characterize the demonstrations promoted by the ESF and also by the national movements promoting the ESF.[3]

However, in spite of the successful February 15 demonstrations, the ESF's capacity to build a frame for mobilizations was judged as insufficient by parts of the GJM. Attac France (2004), for instance, criticized that decision making on common actions had largely been reduced to setting the dates of common global events, underlining that this was obviously important but clearly insufficient.[4] Specific criticism has been raised in connection with the politically ambitious common mobilization of the movement and the European Trade Union Confederation (ETUC) on 19 March 2005, called for by the assembly of social movements at the London ESF.[5] Criticizing the ESF's weakness in co-ordinating action, groups of the radical Left in particular called for the forum to become a space for the construction of a GJM with common action strategies and the organization of common European campaigns and mobilizations (see Chapter 9 in this volume). In this context, some of these groups questioned the consensual decision making within the social forum process, revealing tension between certain types of political radicalism and deliberative democratic models.

The ESF: a contested protest space

The acceptance and encouragement of diversity in forms of action by the ESF has not been unproblematic, as a look at specific protest events organized during the days of the forum shows. The main such event, the big concluding demonstration, is part of the official forum programme and directly organized by the ESF. In addition, single components of the forum stage specific protest events as a part or continuation of their forum activities. Some of the protest events organized during the days of the forum led to friction not only with state authorities,[6] but also within the ESF. Concentrating on the latter, tension has been provoked by disagreement about appropriate action forms, by the presence of groups considered external to the ESF, and by dissatisfaction with the decision making process – that is, by aspects intimately connected with the identity of the movement. This tension can be seen as mirroring general strains within the ESF process. In fact, the WSF and ESF have increasingly been recognized as plural and contested rather than simply as open spaces (Osterweil 2004b: 187). Processes both of dialogue and collaboration, and of criticism and competition develop not only between the forum and external groups and forces, but also within the forum itself.

Divergences within the GJM about acceptable forms of action had already become apparent before the first ESF in Florence. In the preparatory phase for the Genoa G8 counter-summit, the acceptance of diversity in forms of action was an evident straining factor between the movement and its potential allies. Notwithstanding the work agreement mentioned above, preoccupation with violent action repertoires was an argument in the refusal to participate, not only by moderate catholic groups, but also by the traditional Left trade union confederation CGIL.

In the aftermath of Genoa, self-critical reflection within the movement saw a more fundamental opposition to violence gaining ground. At the mass demonstration concluding the first ESF in Florence, the self-critical reflection as a result of the Genoa events found expression in a partial revision of the movement's attitudes (della Porta and Reiter 2004, 2006b). The organizers paid closer attention to the self-policing of the demonstration, introducing a steward service, which had been rejected for the anti-G8 counter-summit on grounds of principle. In addition, the autonomous sector downgraded its action repertoires, with the 'disobedients', for instance, abandoning their traditional habit of wearing protective gear. The enormous success of the demonstration concluding the Florence ESF (between 500,000 and 1,000,000 participants, according to police, and twice as many according to the organizers, without a single act of violence) made any tension remaining after the Genoa anti-G8 protests evaporate. However, at protest events organized by single sectors of the movement during the days of the forum – for example, at the US military base Camp Derby – preoccupation about possibly escalating forms of action had signalled the persistence of differences between more moderate and more radical areas of the movement.[7] At the same time, however, preoccupation emerged around the tendency to label as violent certain effective, high-profile forms of direct action internally accepted as legitimate (della Porta *et al.* 2006a: 142ff., 191ff.).

At subsequent editions of the ESF, tension and difficulties (re)emerged in relation to the concluding demonstrations, on the one hand connected with the boundaries of the movement, on the other hand with internal decision making. In Paris, some participants protested against the participation of a bloc of French Socialists, seen as an intrusion of outside forces. In Athens, the provocations of radical groups external to the ESF, using the demonstrators as human shields for attacks on the police, led to incidents partly involving also the official march. On this occasion, a lack of debate within the ESF on the modalities of the demonstration, and resulting lack of decision making, was lamented (see Bersani 2006).

With antagonisms, differences, and tensions developing within the social forum process, the ESF itself became the target of protest. In fact, protest against official forums, or certain of their aspects, has been present from early on and has continued up to the most recent editions. For example, at the 2002 WSF, a group of radical grassroots activists marched to the official forum site and occupied the VIP room, chanting 'We are all VIPS, we are all VIPS!' As a result, no VIP room was provided the following year. The 2007 WSF in Nairobi saw protests against the high prices for food.

The autonomous spaces organized during the forum days can be seen as a particular (albeit ambiguous) form of protest against the ESF. In the preparatory phase of the first ESF in Florence, many autonomous and radical groups remained ambivalent towards the forum, criticizing the support given by local authorities as well as the prevalence of large and bureaucratic organizations. This protest potential found an outlet in the autonomous spaces, permitting the pursuance of a 'one foot in, one foot out' strategy by being independent from the official forum but present on the official programme, by maintaining at the same time a critical attitude towards the forum process and close contacts with it (see Chapter 2 in this volume).

A significant part of the protest directed against the ESF and organized during the forum days was aimed at its decision making processes, criticized by so-called horizontals as top-down and dominated by traditional established organizations (verticals). If shared experiences of protest (especially the Genoa G8 counter-summit) had generated mutual trust between 'verticals' and 'horizontals' in Italy (see Chapter 4 in this volume), this relationship had already become more strained by the second ESF. Reflecting a particularly conflictual preparatory phase, with a number of more horizontal groups withdrawing from the official forum, autonomous spaces reached their fullest expression during the 2004 London ESF. On this occasion, the accumulated tension erupted in several protest events specifically targeting the ESF. At the Iraqi plenary, the representative of the Iraqi Federation of Trade Unions, in favour of the Anglo–American occupation but invited because of strong support from many British trade unions, was shouted down. At the anti-racism plenary, autonomous horizontal groups rushed the stage where the city of London Mayor, Ken Livingstone, was supposed to speak. These groups protested against the 'verticals', in particular the Socialist Workers' Party and Socialist Action,[8] as well as against the influence of the Greater London Authority on ESF decision making.

At the London ESF, the decision making process in connection with the concluding demonstration also came under particular attack. The European Preparatory Assembly (EPA) in Brussels (4–5 September 2004) had turned down the UK proposal to aim the march against war and (US President) Bush.[9] Instead, the demonstration was intended to refer to the spirit of the ESF, that is, lasting peace and a Europe of progressive social development. The slogans, therefore, were to be against social cuts and war and for a Europe of social justice, with the 'No to Bush' slogan used by the British delegation only. The UK co-ordinating committee was accused of failing to implement the EPA's decision, resulting in a demonstration primarily against Bush. This outcome was attributed to a structural problem inherent in the ESF decision making: without a system of accountability to ensure the implementation of decisions taken at the EPA, local organizers retain de facto power over most decisions (see Maeckelbergh 2004; Cobas 2004; Bohn 2004). During the concluding demonstration, additional tension erupted over several arrests and the fact that instead of the agreed upon concert, speeches were given, monopolized by the English to the exclusion of all other European delegations.

Notwithstanding its contested character, the common basis of the ESF protest space proved to be solid. Divergences about acceptable action forms did not lead to irreconcilable conflicts. The attempts of horizontal groups to 'have a positive effect by creatively engaging the forum from outside' (Juris 2004a) were largely successful. In general, they were able to organize their own horizontal projects, while at the same time challenging commonly accepted ideas and making conflicts visible at the official Forum. In addition, their actions had long term effects. The conflicts at the London ESF, for instance, contributed to the elimination of plenary sessions privileging VIP luminaries at the Athens ESF (2006) in an attempt to reduce internal struggle between horizontals and verticals and to leave more space for more horizontal activities such as workshops and seminars (see also Chapter 2 in this volume).

The use of forms of action by ESF participants

Overlapping action repertoires and movement areas

One of the factors contributing to the overall solidity of the multiple, heterogeneous, and contested ESF protest space can be found in the use of forms of action by ESF participants. If activists from the different areas of the GJM show preferences for more conventional or more unconventional tactics and forms of participation, they do not use these exclusively. We argue that the overlapping action repertoires of activists from different movement areas have contributed to preventing irreconcilable conflicts in and around the ESF protest space.

Repeated surveys conducted at the ESFs have shown the activists attending the various forums to be highly involved with protest (see Table 10.1).[10] Along with the organizations active in the social forum process, the individual activists of the GJM also show variegated past and present action repertoires, combining more conventional forms (like working in a political party or signing a petition) with more unconventional ones (like participating in non-violent direct action or in cultural performances as a form of protest). Although 'attending a demonstration' emerges as the most frequent form of action in our activist survey conducted at the Athens ESF, unconventional forms of action seem at least as widespread as conventional ones. At the same time, a clear rejection of violence emerges: only 6.3 per cent of the activists surveyed at the Athens ESF declared having used violent forms of action against property.[11]

In the following, we focus on three general forms of action that we recoded on the basis of the more specific political activities respondents declared having used:[12] party related activities (voted in last national election, tried to persuade someone to vote for a political party, worked in a political party); demonstrative protest (signed a petition/public letter, boycotted products, attended a demonstration, handed out leaflets, participated in cultural performances as a form of protest, took part in a strike); and confrontational protest (practised civil disobedience, took part in non-violent direct action, took part in an occupation of a public building, took part in an occupation of abandoned homes and/or land, took part in a blockade, used violent forms of action against property). The latter two can be considered as forms of protest, while the former is a more institutional way of doing politics.

Table 10.1 Past and present action repertoires of ESF participants in Florence, Paris, and Athens (percentages, total N)

	Florence 2002	Paris 2003	Athens 2006
Attended a demonstration	–	95.5 (2,080)	92.6 (1,194)
Signed a petition/public letter/call for referendum	88.8 (2,509)	96.3 (2,102)	84.2 (1,194)
Participated in an assembly/congress/discussion group	91.3 (2,512)	83.3 (2,010)	–
Handed out leaflets	73.4 (2,498)	74.0 (1,970)	70.9 (1,194)
Boycotted products	65.8 (2,494)	74.7 (2,003)	68.8 (1,194)
Participated in cultural performances as a form of protest	–	–	58.2 (1,194)
Symbolic action	–	64.9 (1,885)	–
Took part in a strike	86.0 (2,507)	71.2 (1,950)	56.7 (1,194)
Took part in non-violent direct actions	–	–	54.7 (1,193)
Tried to persuade someone to vote for a political party	51.8 (2,494)	–	54.1 (1,193)
Practiced civil disobedience	–	–	42.5 (1,193)
Worked in a political party	33.5 (2,496)	–	41.2 (1,193)
Took part in an occupation of a public building	68.0 (2,509)	39.2 (1,904)	33.5 (1,193)
Took part in a blockade	67.9 (2,480)	47.7 (1,865)	31.2 (1,193)
Took part in an occupation of abandoned homes and/or land	25.9 (2,488)	–	12.1 (1,193)
Used violent forms of action against property	8.4 (2,494)	6.0 (1,830)	6.3 (1,193)

Let us look first at the distribution of the three general forms of participation in our sample (1,205 respondents) (Figure 10.1). The bars show the relative frequency of use. As we can see, all three forms are widespread among the respondents, with the share of people having used them ranging from 73 to 99 per cent. These are important figures, especially for demonstrative protest, but not so surprising if we consider that most of the attendants at the ESF are strongly committed activists or at least people often involved in politics.

Given these distributions, for the analyses below we have computed an alternative, more conservative measure that takes into account the average use of the three forms of participation, calculated based on the number of tactics in each form a respondent declared using (standardized to vary between 0 and 1). For each form, we distinguish between those who have used it above the average from those who have done so below the average (including no use at all). The dotted line in Figure 10.1 shows the distribution of this alternative measure across the three forms. It suggests that fewer people have used confrontational protest above the average (31.8 per cent of valid cases) as compared to party related activities (56 per cent) and demonstrative protest (52.4 per cent). Clearly, the latter form of protest is more demanding in terms of commitment and sometimes, as in the case of the most radical activities, in terms of the risk involved as well.

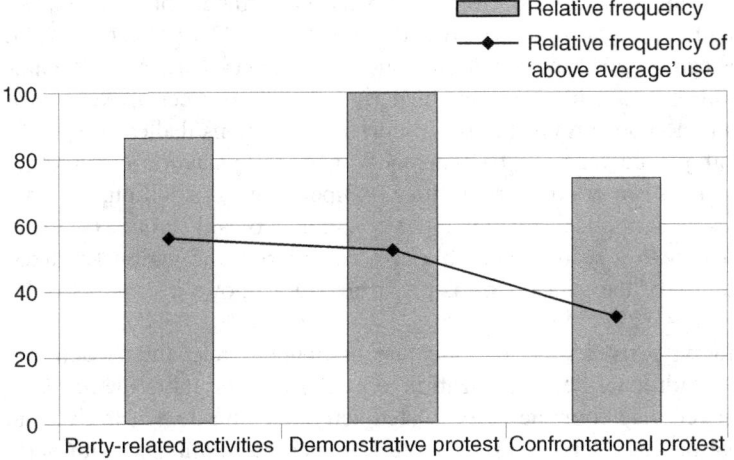

Figure 10.1 Use of general forms of participation (percentages).

Most activists do not show an exclusive preference for above average use of one of the three general forms of action, but mix them in various ways. Only 17.5 per cent, in fact, engaged above the average only in party related activities, 8.5 per cent only in demonstrative protest, and 4.1 per cent only in confrontational protest. Further, 19.3 per cent mixed above average use of party related activities and demonstrative protest, 7.4 per cent of demonstrative and confrontational protest, and 3.5 per cent of party related activities and confrontational protest. As many as 23 per cent of those surveyed at the Athens ESF did not engage above the average in any of the general forms of action, whereas 16.4 per cent did so in all three of them.

Looking at respondents' country of permanent residence indicates that our sample reflects more the characteristics of the specific segment of movement activists that travelled to Athens to attend the ESF, than the characteristics of the GJM in the various countries (della Porta 2007b) or national social movement traditions in general. This seems particularly evident in the case of the German respondents who privilege confrontational protest, either exclusively or in combination with party related activities or with demonstrative protest, and for the Spanish respondents who show a relatively high response rate only for demonstrative protest. Like in previous surveys of the ESF, respondents from the host country stand out as a special case, characterized also by the presence of people visiting the forum more out of curiosity than because of political activism (see also Bédoyan *et al.*2004). In fact, the percentage of those registering as 'low' for all three general forms of action is particularly high for Greek attendants of the ESF.

In light of these results, the correlation between the action forms of movement activists attending the Athens ESF and the movement area to which they feel the strongest connection seems particularly significant. Based on a variable asking respondents to name the group that was most important to them, we distinguished among organizations of the traditional Left (27.7 per cent of valid cases), groups centring on new social movement themes (14.1 per cent), organizations working on solidarity/peace/human rights (13.3 per cent), New Left, anarchist or autonomous groups (12.6 percent), organizations dedicated specifically to global justice themes (10.7 percent), and groups working on other themes like regionalism or ethnic minorities (6.3 per cent). In addition, 15.3 per cent of the respondents declared not to be a member of any group. Crossing movement areas with a recoded variable also considering the variously mixed above-average use of the general forms of participation shows a strong correlation (Cramer's $V = 0.223^{***}$).

Unsurprisingly, party related activities are particularly relevant for activists that declared a traditional Left organization to be most important to them. These activists, however, also combine party related activities with demonstrative and confrontational protest. Demonstrative protest, sometimes combined with party related activities, is important above all for activists of new social movement and solidarity/peace/human rights groups. Activists working specifically on global justice themes also concentrate on demonstrative protest, but some of them mix it with confrontational protest instead. Confrontational protest, also in combination with demonstrative protest and with party related activities, is privileged above all by activists of New Left, anarchist, or autonomous groups.

Our results seem to confirm that differences in the action repertoires of the activists at the Athens ESF mirror general tensions within the GJM, in particular between a more or less institutional alignment and between more or less radical attitudes. At the same time we notice an overlapping of action repertoires among the different movement areas that can explain the solidity of the ESF protest space, notwithstanding these tensions.

ESF participants and their action repertoires: structural characteristics and attitudes towards politics

We have described the ESF as a multiple and heterogeneous, and also as a contested protest space, and we have argued that the solidity of this protest space, notwithstanding repeatedly emerging tension, can be explained at least partly by the overlapping of action repertoires among the different areas of the GJM. The question now is how the position of participants in the Athens ESF with regard to the forms of protest relates to their structural characteristics, their attitudes towards politics, and especially their views about how decisions should be taken in general.

Although we may think of democratic visions as influenced by political engagement and more specifically by the very use of certain forms of participation, it seems more plausible to look at how values impinge upon action rather than the other way around. Therefore, we consider form of participation as our dependent variable. The main goal of our analysis is to inquire into some of the potential explanatory factors for the use of each of the three general forms of participation by ESF activists. We focus on three sets of factors. The first two have often been studied in the political sociology research tradition, which has stressed the role of individual resources for political participation (Verba and Nie 1972; Verba et al. 1978): the structural characteristics of individuals as well as their location both in society at large and in the more specific social groups to which they belong, on the one hand, and their political attitudes and orientations, on the other.

Concerning the first set of factors, we focus more specifically on the following aspects that we consider as relevant for the present analysis: gender, age, social status (being a student), and position within the group most important to the respondent.[13] Concerning the second set of factors, we look at the following aspects: degree of identification with the global justice movement, being a radical leftist, degree of trust towards various political and institutional actors (the United Nations, European Union, national government, national parliament, local government, judiciary, police, political parties, trade unions, non-governmental organizations, social movement organizations, churches, and mass media), and level of satisfaction with the decision making process on different levels (one's own group, groups and networks taking part in the global justice movement, the national political system, European Union, and United Nations).[14] Most importantly, we look at the impact of respondents' views about democracy and the GJM. Specifically, we examine their views about how decisions should be taken, the strategies the GJM should use to enhance democracy, and appropriate strategies to tame neoliberal globalization. Concerning the first aspect, the focus will be on four key features of deliberative decision making: the quality of arguments (as opposed to the importance of resources), mutual acceptance among opponents, participation of all interested persons (as opposed to delegation), and decision by consensus (as opposed to decision by voting).

Our analysis proceeds in two steps. First, we look at the presence of bivariate relationships between views about democracy and the GJM and the three general forms of participation we distinguished earlier (party related activities, demonstrative protest, and confrontational protest). Second, we run a series of logistic regressions (one for each form of participation) in order to examine the net effect of each explanatory factor under control of the other factors. Here, we will also include as controls the movement area to which the respondents belong and the effect of the other two general forms of participation.

In our bivariate analysis, we look at how views about decision making processes, about the strategies the GJM should use to enhance democracy, and about what should be done to tame neoliberal globalization impact upon the three general forms of participation (Tables 10.2, 10.3, and 10.4). In general, greater scepticism towards deliberative and participative decision making processes and strategies relying more on institutional actors seem more strongly connected with party related activities. Support for deliberative and participative decision making processes seems to channel political participation more towards demonstrative and confrontational protest. The different degrees of scepticism towards institutional actors and of the importance of taking protest to the streets appear as distinguishing elements between demonstrative and confrontational protest.

Table 10.2 Relationship between views about decision making processes and general forms of participation

	Party related activities		Demonstrative protest		Confrontational protest	
	% of above average use	N	% of above average use	N	% of above average use	N
Quality of arguments (versus resources)	n.s.		$V = 0.083^+$		n.s.	
Arguments rather than resources	57.3	756	55.2	748	32.5	748
More arguments than resources	55.2	221	45.7	221	32.6	221
More resources than arguments	56.1	66	48.5	66	34.8	66
Resources rather than arguments	48.6	35	60.0	35	40.0	35
Mutual acceptance (versus no acceptance)	n.s.		n.s.		n.s.	
Acceptance always important	55.9	740	54.3	735	32.1	735
Acceptance sometimes important	57.8	206	48.1	206	35.9	206
Acceptance scarcely important	60.5	76	52.7	74	25.7	74
Acceptance not important	55.4	56	60.0	55	41.8	55
Participation (versus delegation)	n.s.		$V = 0.110^{**}$		n.s.	
Participate always important	55.7	503	58.7	501	33.9	501
Participate sometimes important	54.8	279	47.8	276	30.8	276
Delegate sometimes important	62.2	188	52.7	188	37.2	188
Delegate always important	54.7	106	43.7	103	26.2	103
Consensus (versus voting)	n.s.		$V = 0.122^{***}$		$V = 0.167^{***}$	
Always consensus	52.0	225	63.6	225	47.6	225
Sometimes consensus	53.4	253	52.2	252	31.0	252
Sometimes voting	58.1	267	52.7	262	29.0	262
Always voting	59.9	309	46.4	317	26.8	317

Notes
$^+ p \leq 0.10$, $^* p \leq 0.05$, $^{**} p \leq 0.01$, $^{***} p \leq 0.001$, n.s. non significant.

Regarding views about decision making processes, the quality of arguments (versus resources) and mutual acceptance (versus no acceptance) do not give significant results, although with a surprisingly high percentage of demonstrative and confrontational protestors among those for whom arguments and acceptance are less important. Those who see delegation as at least sometimes important and those who are more sceptical towards consensus as a decision making method are more drawn to an above average use of party related activities, that is, a more institutional form of political participation. In contrast, the percentage of activists with above average use of demonstrative protest is particularly high among those who see participation and above all consensus as always important in democratic decision making. Among those who see consensus as always important in decision making, above average use of confrontational protest is also particularly widespread. However, many confrontational

Table 10.3 Relationship between views about strategies to enhance democracy and general forms of participation

	Party related activities		Demonstrative protest		Confrontational protest	
	% of above average use	N	% of above average use	N	% of above average use	N
Contact political leaders	n.s.		V = 0.155***		V = 0.161***	
Most important	55.8	78	46.1	76	25.0	76
Second most important	51.8	112	37.8	111	23.4	111
Third most important	64.4	99	46.5	99	18.2	99
Fourth most important	59.9	147	45.5	145	25.5	145
Fifth most important	55.8	624	58.8	622	38.0	621
Practice democracy in group life	n.s.		n.s.		n.s.	
Most important	51.4	296	54.8	294	31.3	294
Second most important	59.8	194	55.2	194	32.0	194
Third most important	55.7	230	52.4	229	33.2	229
Fourth most important	60.9	243	53.5	241	33.8	240
Fifth most important	59.6	109	43.5	108	27.8	108
Take to the streets	n.s.		V = 0.115**		V = 0.169***	
Most important	62.5	168	50.6	168	40.5	168
Second most important	59.5	163	53.1	162	38.5	161
Third most important	57.0	235	59.0	234	36.8	234
Fourth most important	51.4	321	55.6	320	30.0	320
Fifth most important	55.4	177	41.4	174	16.7	174
Spread information to the public	n.s.		V = 0.121**		V = 0.133***	
Most important	56.4	287	44.3	287	24.1	286
Second most important	54.4	338	55.1	336	29.5	336
Third most important	55.4	267	53.6	263	38.4	263
Fourth most important	59.1	149	63.1	149	40.3	149
Fifth most important	68.8	32	50.0	32	31.3	32
Promote alternative models	n.s.		n.s.		n.s.	
Most important	60.1	386	55.6	383	32.1	383
Second most important	57.0	293	52.4	290	32.1	290
Third most important	52.3	199	49.7	199	26.8	198
Fourth most important	54.1	146	50.3	145	37.9	145
Fifth most important	53.6	56	50.0	56	30.4	56

Notes
$^+p \leq 0.10$, $*p \leq 0.05$, $**p \leq 0.01$, $***p \leq 0.001$, n.s. non significant.

protestors can also be found among those who see delegation as sometimes important.

Turning to the strategies the GJM should use to enhance democracy, activists with above average use of party related activities are particularly numerous among those who give some credit to contacting political leaders. In contrast, the percentage of demonstrative and confrontational protestors is particularly high among those who see this strategy as least important. Practising democracy in

Table 10.4 Relationship between views about strategies to tame globalization and general forms of participation

	Party related activities		Demonstrative protest		Confrontational protest	
	% of above average use	N	% of above average use	N	% of above average use	N
Strengthen national government	n.s.		n.s.		V = 0.172***	
Strongly disagree	52.3	421	57.0	419	42.5	419
Disagree	60.2	372	53.3	368	29.2	367
Agree	56.6	244	50.4	242	24.8	242
Strongly agree	51.7	29	53.6	28	14.3	28
Strengthen EU	V = 0.111**		V = 0.103**		V = 0.171***	
Strongly disagree	55.2	359	58.4	356	43.5	356
Disagree	54.1	340	46.7	338	28.8	337
Agree	55.4	298	55.3	295	25.1	295
Strongly agree	76.3	76	46.7	75	25.3	75
Strengthen UN	V = 0.133***		n.s.		V = 0.177***	
Strongly disagree	47.3	283	56.7	282	45.4	282
Disagree	57.6	262	49.6	258	30.2	258
Agree	58.6	355	54.3	352	29.0	352
Strongly agree	67.9	156	52.3	155	21.3	155
Build new institutions to involve civil society at EU level	V = 0.115**		V = 0.094*		n.s.	
Strongly disagree	37.8	45	48.9	45	35.6	45
Disagree	51.9	81	41.8	79	31.6	79
Agree	53.7	438	49.8	434	32.6	433
Strongly agree	61.8	557	57.0	554	31.8	554
Build new institutions to involve civil society at international level	0.86*		n.s.		n.s.	
Strongly disagree	62.5	24	58.3	24	41.7	24
Disagree	47.5	61	42.6	61	32.8	61
Agree	52.3	375	50.8	370	27.6	369
Strongly agree	60.0	667	54.6	663	33.8	663

Notes
†$p \leq 0.10$, *$p \leq 0.05$, **$p \leq 0.01$, ***$p \leq 0.001$, n.s. non significant

group life and promoting alternative models sees particular support among demonstrative and (to a lesser extent) confrontational protestors. The percentage of confrontational protestors is particularly high among those for whom taking to the streets is the most important strategy to enhance democracy.

Regarding strategies to tame neoliberal globalization, activists with an above average use of party related activities see the strengthening of existing institutions like the EU and the UN as adequate, albeit at the same time advocating the building of new institutions to involve civil society at the EU and international levels. To the contrary, the percentage of demonstrative protestors is particularly high among those who disagree strongly with strengthening institutions like the EU and the UN. Many demonstrative protestors, however, can also be found among those advocating the building of new institutions to involve civil society at the EU and international levels, an option that does not seem to find significant support among confrontational protestors.

Next, we discuss the results of multivariate analyses with statistical controls (Table 10.5). We run three separate logistic regression models, one for each of the three general forms of participation (party related activities, demonstrative protest, and confrontational protest), and show the odds ratios for their occurrence under the effects of the selected indicators of structural characteristics, political attitudes, and views about decision making.[15] Each regression also includes an indicator of respondents' belonging to a specific movement area. Finally, we

Table 10.5 Effects of selected independent variables on general forms of participation (odds ratios)

	Party related activities	Demonstrative protest	Confrontational protest
Woman	0.79	1.48	0.94
Age	0.99	1.03**	0.98
Student	0.74	1.34	1.03
Leader in the group	1.34	1.53	1.41
Identification with the movement	1.71**	1.48*	1.27
Radical Left	1.35	1.24	1.69*
Political and institutional trust	1.56***	1.01	0.75*
Satisfaction with decision making processes	0.99	0.90	0.54**
Quality of arguments (versus resources)	1.22	1.10	0.89
Mutual acceptance (versus no acceptance)	0.88	1.02	1.00
Participation (versus delegation)	1.02	1.22+	0.88
Consensus (versus voting)	0.89	1.15	1.31*
Movement area (ref.: other)	***		**
NSM themes	1.46	1.00	0.51
Solidarity/peace/human rights	1.37	1.01	0.19**
New global themes	0.98	1.26	0.37+
Traditional Left	5.81***	1.06	0.70
New Left/anarchism/autonomy	2.64+	0.82	1.06
Party activities	–	2.14**	0.89
Demonstrative protest	2.10**	–	4.74***
Confrontational protest	0.86	4.39***	–
Nagelkerke R^2	0.23	0.27	0.32
–2 log likelihood	468.254	468.674	464.795
Degrees of freedom	19	19	19
N	428	428	428

Notes
+$p \leq 0.10$, *$p \leq 0.05$, **$p \leq 0.01$, ***$p \leq 0.001$.

control for the effect of multiple activities by including in each model two variables that measure the usage of the other two forms of participation.

To begin with party related activities, we observe that none of the structural characteristics seems to increase the probability of engaging in party activities, at least not in a statistically significant way. In other words, the above average use of this form of participation does not seem to be related to gender, age, professional status, or position within the group most important to the respondent. Among the indicators of political attitudes, however, two have a significant effect: identification with the movement, and political and institutional trust. Activists who identify with the movement and those who trust political and institutional actors are more likely to be involved in party related activities. While a strong identification with the movement is probably a requirement for participating in any type of political activity, political and institutional trust is especially needed for more institutional participation such as involvement with political parties. In addition, confirming what we found in the bivariate analyses, none of the indicators of democratic views shows a statistically significant effect.

The two control variables have a significant and strong effect on party activities. On the one hand, activists belonging to the traditional Left are far more likely to use party related activities than activists from other movement areas. A similar impact can be seen for those who are in the movement area close to the New Left, anarchism, or autonomy. For both the institutional and the radical Left, party related activities remain more important than for other movement areas. On the other hand, we observe an overlapping participation in party activities and demonstrative protest, as the latter have a significant and positive effect on the former. In other words, the use of demonstrative protest makes the use of party related activities more likely (or vice versa).

Turning to demonstrative protest, we find a statistically significant effect of age, but the strength of the effect is extremely weak. All other structural characteristics are not significant, although they all increase the likelihood of being involved in demonstrative protest. The same applies to the indicators of political attitudes, with the exception of identification with the movement, which makes this form of participation more likely. In contrast, political and institutional trust no longer has an impact. Among the four indicators of views about decision making, only the one relating to the importance of participation as opposed to delegation shows a statistically significant and positive effect (at the 10 per cent level).

Unlike for party related activities, movement area does not influence respondents' involvement in demonstrative protest. The use of this kind of political activity is independent from belonging to a specific area of the movement. It is, however, strongly dependent on involvement in both party activities and confrontational protest. Both forms of participation strongly increase the likelihood of being involved in demonstrative protest, but especially the latter.

Finally, the use of confrontational protest is not associated with the structural characteristics of respondents. It is, however, influenced by three of the indicators of political attitudes, although in opposing directions. On the one hand, quite understandably, radical left activists are more likely to use confrontational protest. On the other hand, activists who trust political and institutional actors and those who are satisfied with decision making processes in general are less likely to be involved in this form of participation. Thus, the resort to more radical forms of protest is also a result of lack of trust in political and institutional actors as well as a lower degree of satisfaction with decision making processes. We also observe a significant and positive effect of one of the indicators of democratic views, namely the one concerning the importance of consensus as opposed to voting in decision making. The search for consensus and a radical action repertoire do not necessarily exclude each other, and we can assume that a combination of both can be found in particular among the so-called 'horizontals'.

In addition, movement area displays a statistically significant effect. Activists who belong to the area of solidarity, peace, and human rights are much less inclined to make use of confrontational protest than are activists in other areas. The very issues raised by organizations active in this field seem to lead to a more peaceful way to engage in protest politics. Similarly, but perhaps more surprisingly, activists close to the movement area stressing new global themes are also less likely to be involved in confrontational protest. Finally, we observe once again the overlapping between forms of action, as using demonstrative protest increases the likelihood of using confrontational protest.

In sum, looking at the impact of the various explanatory factors across the three general forms of participation, the structural characteristics of respondents have little or no effect; identification with the movement has a positive effect on party related activities and demonstrative protest, but not on confrontational protest; political and institutional trust increases the chances of being involved in party activities but diminishes the likelihood of using confrontational protest; the latter depends in particular on leftist radicalism and on a lower degree of political and institutional trust as well as of satisfaction with decision making processes; democratic views have little impact, with the exception of the stress on participation (for demonstrative protest) and consensus (for confrontational protest); movement area plays a significant role, especially insofar as traditional left activists are more involved in party related activities, while activists belonging to the area of solidarity, peace, and human rights as well as those who are close to the area stressing new global themes are less involved in confrontational protest; finally, we have observed a multiple activities effect between party related activities and demonstrative protest, on the one hand, and between demonstrative protest and confrontational protest, on the other.

Conclusion

Our analysis of the relationship between the forms of protest used by participants in the 2006 ESF in Athens and their conceptions of democracy has proceeded in two steps. In the first part, we discussed the ESF as a multiple, heterogeneous, and contested protest space. More than a clearly defined form of protest, the forum is in fact a space where different forms and conceptions of protest against neoliberal globalization may be practised and planned. The acceptance of diversity in forms of action with the one condition of non-violence, which emerged as a distinct common aspect of the protest activities connected with the ESF, has not been unproblematic. Increasingly, in fact, the ESF has emerged as a plural and contested space, with the forum itself also becoming the target of protest. Notwithstanding the tension emerging in connection with certain forms of action and specific protest events, related in particular with factors concerning the identity of the movement like internal decision making, the protest space provided for by the ESF proved to be solid.

In the second part of our chapter, we analysed the forms of participation of global justice movement activists on the basis of the survey we conducted at the Athens ESF in 2006. The results of our survey show the specificity of this population as very deeply engaged in political activities. The large majority of the respondents have been involved in all three general forms of participation that we have defined (party related activities, demonstrative protest, and confrontational protest). Moreover, most respondents show an above average use of more than one of the three general forms of participation. In fact, we have argued that the overlapping use of different forms of participation by movement activists from various areas of the GJM at least partly explains the solidity of the ESF as a protest space.

Yet, some participants of the Athens ESF are more deeply involved in certain forms of participation than in others. Such variations are hardly explained by the different structural characteristics of the respondents in terms of gender, age, social position, social status, and position within the group of which they are part. More can be predicted about the use of the three forms of participation we have distinguished by looking at political attitudes. Specifically, we found that identification with the global justice movement increases the chances to become involved in party related activities and demonstrative protest (a positive effect can also be observed on confrontational protest, but it is not statistically significant). We also found an effect of political and institutional trust. However, while more trustful activists tend to be more involved in party activities, they are generally less active in confrontational protest. Finally, the latter, which is the most radical form of participation, also depends on self-placement on the extreme left side of the political spectrum (being radical leftists).

While the role of political attitudes is in line with mainstream research on political participation (Verba and Nie 1972; Verba et al. 1978), we found little evidence of an impact of activists' views about democracy or about globalization on the form of their participation – be it their views about the decision making process, strategies to enhance democracy, or strategies to tame globalization. Some effects were found in the bivariate analyses, but they are generally not very strong and, moreover, they disappear when controlled in multivariate analyses, except for the impact of consensus on confrontational protest and partly for the impact of participation on demonstrative protest. Thus, while most of those who attend the ESF and perhaps other global justice movement events embrace a wide range of political activities, it appears that their social profile, but above all the way in which they situate themselves vis-à-vis the movement and its organizations, account for differences in the intensity of commitment and participation, more than the ways in which they view the decision making process in politics. These findings suggest a more nuanced picture than the distinction between 'verticals' and 'horizontals'.

Notes

1 The 'about' section of the Athens 2006 website (online, available at: http://athens.fse-esf.org/4th-european-social-forum-athens-may-2006) states:

> The European Social Forum is, alongside Genoa and Seattle, one of the major events of the movement against neo-liberal globalization and war, deregulation of labor and poverty, climate change and environmental destruction, violation of democratic rights and sexism, racism and the threat of the far right.... We have marched together against the G8, the International Monetary Fund and the World Bank in Prague, in Genoa, in Evian. We took part, all together, in the siege of the European Union Summits in Thessalonica, Nice, Seville, Brussels. We met during the huge antiwar rallies on the 15th of February 2003, in the mass demonstrations against racism, in working class mobilizations defending pensions, public health and education, in rallies against the destruction of the environment, the 'anti'terrorist laws and repression.

Except when indicated differently, all web documents were accessed in February 2007.
2 Interview with a spokesperson of the Florence ESF, conducted 24 April 2004.
3 A press release of the Italian movements promoting the ESF, published on the occasion of mobilizations against the war in Iraq in 2003, talks of 'valorising and respecting the many and different practices of the movement', underlining specifically non-violence and civil disobedience. Online, available at: www.fiom.cgil.it/internazionale/forum/cs_forum.htm.
4 In its collective appraisal of the London ESF, the French Initiative Committee for the ESF underlined that the ESF's capacity to build a frame for mobilizations was still problematic, especially concerning the follow-up of thematic campaigns, and proposed the creation of a specific place to centralize and diffuse information (newsletter online, available at: www.euromovements.info/newsletter/french_committee.htm).
5 In particular, it was lamented that after the setting of the date, no European team was put together to build a mobilization campaign or to establish contacts with ETUC (see Slegers 2005). Especially in those countries with closer connections between the GJM and trade unions, the common character of the mobilization was in fact far more visible than at the European level. Whereas the press release of the joint campaign for the March 19 demonstration of the Italian trade unions and movements (press release online, available at: www.fiom.cgil.it/uff_inter/europa/bolkestein/appello.htm) speaks of 'the anti-neoliberal movement, in all its associative and trade union components', the ETUC call for participation in the demonstration (ETUC document online, available at: www.etuc.org/a/485) does not mention the social movements or the ESF.
6 On the particular question of the policing of transnational protest, see della Porta *et al.* (2006a: chapter 5); della Porta *et al.* (2006b).
7 The only moment of tension with the police was caused by an unannounced protest event.
8 Socialist Action, a small Trotskyite group, had supported Livingstone's campaign as an independent in the election for Mayor of London in 2000, and some of its members became key advisors in his administration.

9 The minutes of the Brussels EPA are online, available at: www.ukesf.net/downloads/9d dec3f280478d6f93933eaff10149d5/mins_brussels_preparatory_assembly_4_5_Sept.rtf.
10 For the survey conducted at Paris, see Agrikoliansky and Sommier 2005; for the survey conducted at Florence, see della Porta *et al.* (2006a). An initial survey of GJM activists had been conducted at the Genoa G8 counter-summit in 2001 (see Andretta *et al.* 2002).
11 A different picture emerges for violence as a reaction to police intervention. According to the Paris survey (Agrikoliansky and Sommier 2005: 139), only 2.8 per cent declared having exercised physical pressure on a person, whereas 25.8 per cent declared having resisted police forces. Of the Florence activists, 29.2 per cent declared violence as self-defence necessary in the event of repression of a protest demonstration, another 46 per cent as justifiable. Experiences like participation in the Genoa anti-G8 demonstrations significantly strengthen this response (della Porta *et al.* 2006a: 170f.).
12 In the original variables, respondents had been asked whether they had engaged in certain political activities within the last five years. To these activities, we added electoral participation, based on a variable asking whether respondents had voted in the last national elections in their home countries. Respondents mentioning at least one of the specific political activities included in one of the general forms of action were considered as having used that general form.
13 Education is another important individual resource stressed in the literature. We initially included this aspect in our analyses. However, we eventually decided to exclude it as it gave very poor results, probably because we are dealing with a population of highly educated people.
14 Being a radical leftist is based on self-placement on the left/right scale. We take this measure instead of the whole scale, as the large majority of ESF participants are on the left-hand side of the political spectrum. To measure satisfaction with the decision making process, we first created an additive variable based on the five different levels on which respondents expressed their level of satisfaction. To measure political and institutional trust, we first created an additive scale on the declared trust for each actor (two missing data allowed). The resulting scale was then recoded into an ordinal five-point variable.
15 Odds ratios represent the strength of a given effect and can be interpreted as follows: when the odds ratio is greater than 1, the independent variable has a positive impact on the dependent variable; when the odds ratio is smaller than 1, the effect is negative; finally, when the odds ratio equals 1, there is no effect (although it might be statistically significant). The effect can be considered to be multiplicative. For example, a coefficient of 2 means that having the characteristics described by the independent variables doubles the likelihood of having the characteristics described by the dependent variable (in this case, having participated in party activities, demonstrative protest, or confrontational protest). The same reasoning applies to coefficients lower than 1, but in the opposite direction. For the sake of parsimony, we excluded from the multivariate analyses all the variables, discussed earlier, concerning the strategies to enhance democracy and the strategies to tame neoliberal globalization. Models including these variables, furthermore, did not yield interesting results (not shown).

11 Another Europe
Some conclusions

Donatella della Porta

The focus of this volume has been on visions and practices of democracy in the European Social Forum, combining attention to the organizational level of the 'forum process' and the individual characteristics of its participants. In our work, we started from a paradox. Although social movements have traditionally been said to propose alternative visions of democracy (by and large the 'ancient' forms of participatory and direct democracy), social movement studies have only rarely addressed the issue of democracy in movements, from either the empirical or the normative point of view. True, there are very important exceptions: Francesca Polletta's (2002) influential work on practices of democracy in social movements as well as Ferree *et al.*'s (2002) inspiring research on the debate on abortion law in the public sphere are among the most relevant. These exceptions notwithstanding, when we started our comparative project on the global justice movement and reviewed the social movement studies for support and inspiration, we found much less than we expected.

However, some of the reasons for this limited focus on democracy in movements were part of our interest in focusing on this issue. First, we were aware of a 'hyper-normalization' of research on social movements. During the low ebbs of mobilization – such as the 'terrible 1990s', to use the expression of an activist we interviewed – social movements were increasingly described as 'single issue' (e.g. Kitschelt 2003), NGO-ized, politics-as-usual. At the national level, the routinization of protest and the institutionalization of 'movements-without-protest' and 'protest-without-movements' were stressed (della Porta 2003b). Transnationally, a 'global civil society' has been described as developing from the 'taming of the social movements' (Kaldor 2003). These statements tended to reflect some real trends in social movements in Northern societies and at the transnational level, but also to hide other, emerging trends.

In parallel, another element that has pushed attention away from the research on democracy in movements has been a focus in political science on 'minimalistic', procedural conceptions of democracy. Increasingly in mainstream political science, democracy has been identified with representative institutions and assessed against narrow criteria of electoral accountability. While the number of countries counted as democratic increased after the fall of the Berlin Wall, the criteria used to assess democracy are limited and formal (but for the debate on democratic qualities, see Diamond and Morlino 2005).

Other reasons for this limited attention to democracy are built into dominant rationalist visions, which have stressed the instrumental role and functioning of social movements, with limited focus on their normative content. In a certain sense, a hyper-normalized vision of social movements has driven research towards objects and methods that tended to confirm that vision. The mainly empirical orientation of social movement studies has deflected attention from normative reflections, and the focus on the behaviour (protest, lobbying, etc.) of social movement organizations vis-à-vis institutional politics has discouraged the research on their prefigurative politics (but see Polletta 2002; Leach and Haunss 2009). Finally, a sort of conservatism (or path-dependency) encouraged a 'new-wine-in-old-bottles', sceptical view on any emerging trend in social movements. Within it, a seemingly widespread assumption is that social movement organizations and their activists continue to be as capable (or incapable) as they always were of conceiving and implementing alternative democratic models.

Going from 'constraints' to 'opportunities', a move toward increased attention to democracy in movements seems to be supported by some general trends in the social sciences, as well as the reality of social movement mobilizations. To mention just a few, a 'cultural turn' in social movement studies pushed towards a recognition of the symbolic and emotional dimension of social movement politics. This did not imply a denial of the instrumental role social movements play in normal politics, or the role that concerns for efficiency have in their choice of internal forms of organization as well as external strategies of protest. However, it opened the way to considering the 'passionate' (and normative) dimension of social movement politics. At the same time, especially in normative theory, the debate on deliberative forms of democracy – the polisemy of the term notwithstanding – offered many potential instruments for a fresh look at the visions of democracy inside and outside social movements.

In parallel to these conceptual (if not paradigmatic) shifts, some stimuli for studying democracy in movements come from the transformations in action in our societies. Empirical research on institutional politics has identified many challenges to representative democracy. Power shifted from politics to the market, with neoliberal economic policies increasing the power of multinational corporations and reducing the capacity of traditional state structures to control them. Additionally, the increasing power of some international institutions, primarily financial (WB, IMF, WTO) as well as some macro-regional (mainly the EU), has challenged the (image of) nation-states' autonomy. Even supporters of the 'new-wine-in-old-bottles' vision should admit that the effects of these changes on social movements are hard to overestimate. This does not mean that nation-states no longer play a role, but it pushes us to enrich our analytic tools especially where we are weaker: for example, in the analysis not of national polities, but of the transnational dimensions of politics.

Since social movements seem to respond to these transformations – even though our knowledge of how they do so is still scarce – some additional challenges to address the (emerging and changing) conceptions of democracy in social movements come from observed internal changes in social movements, and especially in the characteristics of the global justice movement addressed in this volume. Among them are its dimension as a movement of movements, with intense (and innovating) forms of networking; the related development of tolerant identities, with acknowledgment of diversity and subjectivity as positive elements; the presence of multiple repertoires, with a pragmatic acceptance of both protest and lobbying, but also a focus on the experimentation of 'possible utopias' (della Porta 2007b).

In this conclusion, while summarizing some of our main empirical results in light of the questions discussed in the introductory chapter, I will discuss the potential for generalizing our findings beyond our case study to broader tendencies in contemporary social movements. I shall do this especially by looking at some existing research on the global justice movement in other parts of the world. This will also allow for some reflections on what is 'European' and what is not in the development of the transnational protest events we have observed.

Our case study is typically European. Although attending to global phenomena, the focus of much debate at the ESF has been European, as most of its participants have been. Previous research has indicated that notwithstanding global appeal and transnational networking, the global justice movement inherited, in each country and continent, specific organizational configurations and traditions (della Porta 2007b). Although symbolically influenced by several processes underway in the global South (among them the Zapatistas' peaceful revolution in Mexico) as well as the World Social Forum in Porto Alegre, the European Social Forum remained a Northern phenomenon. A comparison with the WSF, where the ESF story started, can help us to reflect on the similarities and differences in the global justice movement of the North and the South of the world.

Our research confirmed, that democracy is important for movements, and movements are important for democracy. By and large, even if the normative assumptions of social movement activists are far from being fulfilled in their own movement, the ESF represents an arena for self-reflexive experimentation with different solutions to the tensions between participation or representation and consensual or majoritarian decision making – tensions that are acknowledged by the activists themselves. In terms of intervention in the broader society and political system, the movement we have observed represents a fundamental criticism of existing institutions, but also a determined search for alternatives. Although not aiming at conquering power, it does not renounce engagement in multiple repertoires in order to influence institutional power-holders. In this sense, a search for another politics (not for 'antipolitics') is visible, once again, in a participatory and discursive democratic emphasis. Looking at conceptions about democracy inside movements, decision making is discussed not only in instrumental, but especially in normative terms. Looking at the external dimension of democracy, social movement activists simultaneously interact with public institutions and advance a fundamental critique of representative democracy.

Democracy within

Starting from the internal dimension of democracy, some common elements emerged in the conception of the forum: mainly, attention to communication in an open space, focus on networking, respect for diversity, equal participation, and inclusiveness. Our aim has been to reconstruct the activists' conceptualizations, but also to assess the movements' practices on these dimensions.

As emerged repeatedly, the ESF took inspiration from the WSF in its conception of the forum as a space for *communication*. From the normative point of view, the ESF presents itself as an open space for discussion. The main effort, during the meeting – but also before and after – is to stimulate dialogue in different settings, using various channels in order to improve communication among participants (see Chapter 3 and Chapter 9 in this volume). In this sense, it follows the WSF charter:

> The meetings of the WSF do not deliberate on behalf of the WSF as a body ... it does not constitute a locus of power to be disputed by the participants ... nor does it constitute the only option for interrelation and action by the organizations and movements that participate in it.

Similarly, the ESF works as a setting for encounters of activists from different localities and with different ideologies. Beyond communication inside the ESF, the memory project as well as the forum's websites, press office, and media centre aim at informing the broader public.

Shared in this setting is the idea of the forum as a place for *networking*, with a positive emphasis on diversity. In its normative self-conception, the ESF is an inclusive public sphere. The main organizational challenge is indeed to combine co-ordination – through structures such as the EPA but also via the informal role played by a network of cosmopolitan activists – with respect for the autonomy of the various organizations and activists that participate in the forum process (Chapter 2 in this volume). Moving from norms to practices, the forum appears capable of mobilizing thousands of groups, networking them in various combinations. The activists we interviewed had individual experiences of multiple memberships in various kinds of organizations and on various issues. The functioning of the forum allowed for the production and reproduction of specific networks and campaigns, combining the various interests and identities of participants in multiple ways. The networks in the forum emerged as dense, with a particularly high embeddedness of those activists sharing a long tradition of attention to transnational issues, nurtured in previous mobilizations on issues such as solidarity with the South and peace (Chapter 8).

Our data on previous involvement of participants confirms such a plurality of backgrounds. It indicates that about one-third of participants in the fourth ESF were members of parties, unions, or pacifist, international solidarity and pro-migrant rights organizations; the same proportion were from the more specifically alterglobalist local social forums and organizations against neoliberal globalization.

Additionally, about one-fifth had been members of feminist, ecologist, and student organizations and about 10 per cent of charities, pro-unemployed, and gay-lesbian-transgender groups (Chapter 7). ESF participants were members of many organizations focused on different issues: only 6 per cent of participants at the ESF in Athens did not declare membership in any of the types of organizations listed; just 19 per cent were members of only two, while one-half of the sample declared more than four memberships and one-quarter declared seven or more. A similar capacity for networking has been stressed for the WSF. According to the UC-Riverside survey at the WSF 2005, about 70 per cent of WSF participants claimed that they were 'actively involved' in at least one social movement and about 40 per cent in three or more types of social movements. However, the identification with traditional ideologies is limited in both the ESF and the WSF: at the fourth ESF, 16 per cent declared membership in socialist groups, 17 per cent in communist, 3 per cent in anarchist (versus respectively 14 per cent, 5 per cent, and 3 per cent at the WSF in 2005) (Smith *et al.* 2007: 63–4).

More broadly, our research stressed the importance of a networking logic that has been said to reflect, and at the same time contribute to, the spreading of a 'cultural logic', as embedded sets of values oriented towards the building of horizontal ties, decentralized coordination of autonomous units, and the free circulation of information allowed by the Internet (Juris 2004b). Perceived by the activists as a 'new way of doing politics', networking implies reliance on non-hierarchical structures, open access to information, direct participation, and consensual methods of decision making (ibid.). In contrast to 'old politics' based upon unitary strategy and a logic of representation, this 'new politics' invokes the creation of open spaces, with limited convergences of diverse actors that are connected but with a respect for their individuality (ibid.). Calls for democracy tend to be particularly lively in network structures – in the words of activists (cited in Juris 2004b), 'Participatory democracy is not only a transversal theme in our work, it constitutes our model of ... operation'; the 'building of these networks is the world we want to create'. Networks are in fact perceived as structures that allow organizations to 'balance freedom with coordination, autonomy with collective work, self-organization with effectiveness'.

Nurtured in the ESF, but not limited to it, is the strong *transnational* dimension of networking. The social forum processes develop from the convergence of different movements with previous experiences of common transnational mobilizations. The first Intercontinental Encounter for Humanity and Against Neoliberalism in Chiapas in 1997, along with the campaigns against the Multilateral Agreement on Investment in 1998, were important steps in the process of globalization of protest. In the year 2000, 'protest intensifies and spreads geographically to every continent; the social arc of organizations participating in them appears to have expanded and enriched itself in terms of demands and proposals' (Seoane and Taddei 2002: 110). Together with the Zapatistas in Mexico, the peasants protesting the privatization of water in Cochabamba, the World Women's March, the Peasant Way meeting in Bangalore, and the EU counter-summit in Nice all converged in the year 2000 into a common path of contestation of IGOs.

Although internationalism is not new for social movements of the Left, the share size of an ESF (or, especially, a WSF) is much bigger than similar international meetings of the labour movement or even of new social movements. Moreover, notwithstanding the large (and growing) institutionalization of the social forum process, we saw that those travelling to and participating in them are far from being only national leaders. The results of our research point at the permanence of national levels of organization, evident in the role of the national organization committees of the ESFs' host countries, but also in the national delegations that take part in the EPA. However, they also highlight the role of informal networks of cosmopolitan actors that feel and are felt as developing a primary loyalty to the transnational nature of the process (see Chapter 3).

Networking involves different and diverse actors, particularly at the transnational level. In the ESF, as in the WSF, this has been nurtured under the conception of an 'open space method' that should make strength from diversity. Our research confirms that this value is widespread among activists across ideological and national borders. Beyond the social forum process, common to the global justice movement seems to be the emphasis on *respect for diversity*, including its own internal diversity, based on recognition of the history of the different organizations that converge in it. The activists of the WSF, as those of the ESF, stress multiculturalism and respect for diversity, stating that 'everybody has to understand that each organization has its qualities, its history, and must be respected' (cited in Pleyers 2007: 111). Not by chance, the Call of the Social Movements at the 2002 WSF defined 'the cultures and identities of the peoples' as a 'patrimony of the humanity' (cit. in ibid.: 104). The positive stress on the encounter of diverse people open to mutual understanding is deeply rooted in the movements that contributed to the forum process. Often quoted is 'subcommandante' Marcos' greeting to the activists participating in the first Intercontinental Encounter in the Lacandon Rainforest:

> Some of the best rebels from the five continents came to the mountains of the Mexican South-East. All brought things, brought words and ears, brought their ideas, their hearts, their worlds. To meet with other ideas, with other hearts, with other worlds ... A world made of many worlds is to be met these days ... A world made of many worlds opens its space and conquers its right to be possible.... A world of all worlds that rebel and resist the power.
>
> (in Schultz 1998: 602)

Together with respect for diversity, *horizontality*, or lack of vertical power, is a founding value of the ESF as well as the WSF. Although the lack of acknowledgment of the presence of power inside the forum is considered risky by some activists, as a value it has in fact a mobilizing and legitimizing effect. Although the ESF per se does not take decisions, the European Preparatory Assembly and the Assembly of the European Social Movements make decisions by consensus and refuse delegation (including a permanent steering committee).

The degree to which these norms are implemented in practice is often debated in the movement itself. Most contested is the capacity to overcome vertical power in the social forum process. As we observed, the differential weight of different individuals is in fact (informally) recognized in the ESF assemblies, according to their reputation within a sort of 'complex representation' (Chapter 2). Similarly for the ESF, the activist Teivanen stresses that although 'it is strategically and morally desirable that movements that want to radically democratize the world apply democratic principles to themselves', 'pretending that there is no relations of power that should be made visible within the WSF process is the most harmful of these depoliticizing elements' (2004: 2–3). Although reflected in grassroots workshop activities, the ideal of horizontality is little represented in the governing body of the WSF (Pleyers 2005: 512). Testifying to these tensions between norms and practices, the ESF organizational structure has in fact often been reformed on such issues as the plenaries with invited speakers or the division of tasks between the national organizing committees of the different ESF editions and the EPAs. Similarly, the WSF process has also been often reformed, recognizing some of the criticisms and appeals for more participatory and transparent decision making (Teivanen 2002; Smith 2004: 417, 419; Pleyers 2007: 61).

We can add that diversity is itself a source of tensions. The ESF, as the WSF, emerged in fact as 'a plural and contested space' (Osterweil 2004a: 187) where different forms of power play a role in the preparatory process as well as during the forum. In both, 'ideological differences were largely coded as disagreement over organizational process and form' (Juris 2005a: 264; see also Juris 2005b). Differences are especially visible in conceptions of democracy that contrast horizontal and vertical visions. If from the normative point of view the forum stresses 'horizontality,' the participating organizations as well as the activists favour different organizational models. Our research confirmed that, in various moments (especially around the third edition of the ESF), the image of 'vertical' versus 'horizontal' cleavages dominated. The same conceptualization has been used for the WSF, where:

> The 'horizontals' favor more decentralized, loosely knit movement networks and organizations with flat, open, non-hierarchical, and more directly democratic decision making processes. They often are self conscious about prefiguring the type of society they want to create. However, they often lack mechanisms to ensure that those actually participating are accountable to, or represent the concerns of, constituents. The 'verticals', on the other hand, accept the need for hierarchy, institutionalism, professionalism, and representative structures. They include larger professional NGOs, trade unions, and affiliated parties. While some of these organizations, such as unions and parties, include mechanisms, such as elections or formal decision making processes, to try to keep leaders accountable to their members or constituents, larger professional NGOs often lack these mechanisms.
>
> (Smith *et al.* 2007: 27–8)

These positions have been described as going beyond the preferred internal decision making, aligning along two different registers: 'Whereas one side (the horizontals) sees culture itself as a political terrain – a site where real change is effected – the other (the verticals) believes that culture, form and structure are subservient to real politics' (Osterweil 2004a: 501).

Although this distinction overlaps in part with the two polar types in our typology of democratic types, our conceptualization of the controversies around democracy pointed at a more complex, and at the same time nuanced, image than that of two rigid blocs. As Juris observed, 'the broadest convergence spaces, including the social forums, involve a complex amalgam of diverse organizational forms' (Juris 2005a: 257). We have in fact noted a number of controversies, with shifting alliances. Taking the example of communication, we noted the conflicts of grassroots versus professional conceptions, as well as centralized versus decentralized ones, with contestation inside the media center as well as on the organization of the press work (Chapter 3). The tension between the EPA and national organizing committees reflected the cleavage between cosmopolitan and nationally rooted conceptions of mobilization. The main cleavages we identified, between participation versus delegation and consensus versus majority vote, produce various conceptions and (perceived) praxes of democracy – what we have termed associational, deliberative-representative, assembleary, and deliberative-participative (Chapter 4).

Within a common challenge to representative democracy, different democratic qualities are stressed by participants belonging to different organizational and ideological traditions (Chapters 4, 7, 10). As we saw, activists tend to evaluate consensus and participation more than their organizations practice them (Chapter 4). Satisfaction, and then identification and mobilization, increase with the degree of congruency between normative conceptions and actual organizational practices (Chapter 4), with activists of more formal organizations and of the traditional Left more likely to resent the lack of coherence between their ideals and the perceived practices of their own organizations (Chapters 7 and 10). Members of parties and international formal organizations (sometimes called NGOs) tend to have lower levels of participation, while informal SMOs are more participatory and use a broader repertoire of collective action, defending a more participatory and consensual vision of democracy. However, conceptions of consensus and participation are widespread among all organizational types and ideologies (Chapters 7, 10). We also noted that some basic values of participation and consensus building are widespread among activists belonging to different ideological and organizational types.

One way to assess the normative claims of inclusion is related to the social, generational, and geographical background of the activists. Regarding the ESF with its European appeal, an important dimension of inclusion refers to the participation of Eastern Europeans. This involvement is, for instance, difficult to realize for the EPA – given the need for hosts to ensure enough resources for the meeting – but also for the ESFs in general, due to travel costs as well as the selective effects of organizational memberships. Solidarity funds aim to increase the participation of Eastern Europeans, which nevertheless remains low (Chapter 2). Similarly, research on the WSF has stressed its limited capacity to cover some geographical areas. Notwithstanding that 'there is little doubt that an important degree of the prestige and legitimacy of the WSF derives from its effort to reach out and include "all the countries in the world" ', and although the official registration data for the 2005 edition indicate participants from 135 countries, the numbers of participants from each area are uneven, with Asia and Africa most under-represented (Institute for Research on World-Systems 2006).

From the point of view of social background, according to our data, although gender is relatively balanced and young people tend to participate a great deal, women's presence is lower among professionals, and the cohort of participants younger than 25 declines from 48 per cent in the first ESF to 29 per cent in the fourth edition. Additionally, among participants, students and employees (especially in the public sector) are very over-represented in comparison with the total population, while blue-collar workers and unemployed are under-represented. In particular, the level of education is much higher among ESF participants than in the population at large.

Research on the WSF has confirmed various levels of selectivity. Although a high 42 per cent of respondents were under 26 years old, WSF participants tended to be white and well-educated (Institute for Research on World-Systems 2006). As many as 70 per cent of respondents were either students (about one-third) or employed in middle class occupations (about 15 per cent as professors or teachers), while less than 10 per cent were part of the working class or peasantry and only about 3 per cent were unemployed or retired (Smith *et al.* 2007). Results from other surveys conducted among WSF participants have confirmed this profile (Ibase 2006; Brunelle 2006). Additionally, the number of young people, although not low in absolute terms, is declining from one edition to the next.

Beyond geographical and social background, another dimension of inclusion/exclusion emerged as relevant in assessing the extent to which the ideals of the forum are put into practice. The forum emphasizes individual participation – 'we women and men'. However, as in other instances of collective action, individuals often participate in an organized fashion. Our data indicate that members of organizations tend to have more sustained paths of participation, particularly at the transnational level. Additionally, 'professional activists', as staff members of various types of social movement organizations, are increasingly present among ESF participants, almost doubling (from 21 to 38 per cent) from the second to the fourth edition (Chapter 6). Similarly, the UC-Riverside survey at the WSF confirms some concerns about the 'NGOization of social movements'. The largest share of respondents (39 per cent) was in fact affiliated with an NGO; a similar 37 per cent belonged to a social movement organization, about 21 per cent were affiliated with unions, and almost 17 per cent with political parties (Smith *et al.* 2007: 61–2). The data from the Ibase (2006) confirm that participants express high rates of participation in organizations (24 per cent to parties, 55 per cent to SMOs); moreover, comparing Brazilians with other participants, it emerged that the percentage of members of NGOs increases for those coming from abroad, although those belonging to social movement organizations are more likely to have participated in the preparatory events of the forum, as well as other local, national, and world social forum editions (Ibase 2006: 59). Indeed, in both the WSF and the ESF, a growing involvement of formalized NGOs has been noted and discussed (Pleyers 2007: 88).

Democracy outside

The above-mentioned values on internal democracy, as well as the related cleavages, are linked to those on the external dimension of democracy. Our data testify that ESF activists have a strong interest in producing political change, confirming that globalization 'at one and the same time creates a growing process of social exclusion within and between nations but also the social movements that will contest it and seek to democratize it' (Munck 2002: 10). Activists' repertoires of action, in particular, demonstrate the importance given to the development of 'another democracy' outside the movement (Chapters 5 and 9).

One widespread element in the conception of 'another politics' proposed by ESF participants is the appeal for the development of a civil society autonomous from the state. The often-mentioned Zapatistas continued on the path of a 'self-limited' revolution, which had been developed in Eastern Europe, with the explicit object not of seizing power but of strengthening the civil society vis-à-vis the state (Schultz 1998: 596). Similar positions are especially prevalent in the autonomous spaces that developed around the ESF and in the 'horizontal' groups within it. The repertoire of action used by our interviewees testifies to a focus on the prefigurative (and not only or mainly instrumental) role of political participation. In fact, among the preferred strategies to reach the movement's goals, contacting politicians is considered the least important. Protest is considered as relevant, but even more valued strategies are the promotion of concrete alternative as well as the information to the public and the prefigurative role of group life (Chapter 5). Similarly, as many as 90 per cent of participants at the 2005 WSF perceived the strengthening of the mobilization of the civil society at the global, continental, national, and local levels as the road for building another world – versus 72 per cent mentioning democratization of governments (Ibase 2006: 52). Politics is in fact perceived as a direct commitment (Chapter 5). As observed in the WSF, the forum can be defined as a 'foundation for a more democratic global polity', which enables citizens of different countries to develop shared values and preferences, exchanging information and dialogue (Smith 2004: 420). In this sense, 'The WSF not only fosters networking among activists from different places, it also plays a critical role in supporting what might be called a global counter-public' (ibid.: 3–4).

Some actors, however, push for a more direct political role for the forum, as noted with regard to the radical Left and the critical unions. Whether the ESF (or the WSF) will remain an open space or develop into a collective actor, although of a special sort, is a contested choice. According to a survey of participants at the 2005

WSF, respondents were evenly split over the question of whether or not the forum should take positions on issues or remain an open space for discussion (Chase-Dunn et al. 2007). As for the ESF, some of its organizational characteristics – such as the presence of an Assembly of movements only partially integrated into the official programme of the ESF – testify to this tension.

Although the ESF is formally a nongovernmental and non-party space, the complex relationship with politics is reflected in a complex relation with parties. Compared to the WSF, the ESF has recognized more spaces for political parties: their representatives can participate in national delegations, they can register as delegates, and they can organize workshops – despite the focus on avoiding the 'competitive politics' identified with party behaviour (Chapter 2). Through the Socialist International, the traditional Left has played a relevant role in starting the criticism of globalization, and ECOSY (the Socialist European Youth) had a 1,000 member delegation at the first ESF (Chapter 10). Although the traditional Left has contributed important logistic resources by hosting and/or financing the various editions of the forum, left-wing parties in the socialist tradition have been particularly lukewarm in their support for the forum, stressing at best a division of labour between parties and civil society. The exception are, in some countries, the organizations coming from the communist tradition, which saw in the ESF a window of opportunity and were sometimes open to it. In addition, a high percentage of the participants in the EPA as well as the ESF are activists of organizations of the traditional Left, and left-wing activists are involved in ESF decision making more than the average (Chapter 10). Traditionally linked to left-wing parties, unions, being more sensitive to their bases, have since the beginning been more open to participation (notably, the largest Italian trade union, the CGIL, was quite visible in Florence, and 40 union federations were present in Athens). Unions are also very observable in the programme of the forum (in Athens, the Italian unions organized 33 seminars, the French 47), not only on labour issues. At the same time, political parties are strongly mistrusted, by ESF participants (73 per cent have no or little trust) even more than by WSF participants (where 59 per cent distrust parties).

Similarly complex are relations with political institutions. Our research identified a widespread mistrust for representative institutions, not much more pronounced for IGOs than for national institutions (with somewhat less mistrust for local governments). While mistrust is also widespread in the WSF, specific to the ESF is attention to Europe. The EU is mistrusted in particular for its perceived neoliberal stance, as well as for its democratic deficit. However, almost all activists perceive the need to construct alternative supranational institutions of governance, and only a few want to strengthen national governments. Additionally, Europe is not rejected: far from it, there are constant appeals for the construction of a Europe of rights, a Social Europe, a Europe from below. The activists not only feel quite attached to Europe, but perceive themselves as promoters of a cosmopolitan vision, part of which is an open European identity (Chapter 5). The strength of a European dimension is testified by the presentation of the forum as addressing EU issues in a global perspective and not, in contrast, of addressing global issues in a European perspective – a position that developed into the refusal to present the fourth ESF as part of the polycentric edition of the WSF in 2006 (Chapter 2). While level of trust is influenced by ideological position, identification with the movement increases the belief in the need to produce alternative institutions of supranational governance (Chapter 5).

Different positions are also present in the forum concerning diagnostic, prognostic and motivational frames, with anti-capitalists opposing the (more moderate) anti-neoliberals, reformists opposing those expecting more fundamental change, and supporters of more conventional means opposing the promoters of direct action. Similarly for the WSF, a distinction was observed between those who believe in the abolition of global governance institutions and those who would be content with reforming them. However, here as well, 'many see the WSF as an important instrument for preparing the public to participate actively within, and influence the decisions of, such institutions' (Smith *et al.* 2007: 76). In both, in fact, the discussion on democracy acquires a transnational dimension, with a simultaneously strong criticism of existing IGOs and recognition of the need for building new international institutions.

The emerging properties of the forum process

If protests at the transnational level are rare, we have shown that they can nevertheless be especially 'eventful' (Sewell 1996; also Chapter 1 in this volume), in the sense of producing social change. Our research emphasizes the emergent nature of the forum, with the activation of relational, cognitive, and affective mechanisms.

First, the forum is a product of *networking* that, in turn, produces other networking. Beyond the actual meeting, the months from one ESF to the next are filled by the continuous EPA processes that help in fostering personal relations of trust among participants. Meetings at the forum produce new campaigns and smaller networks among groups and individuals that share concerns. As was noted for the WSF, using a jazz ensemble metaphor,

> The performance itself represents just a fraction of the effort and capabilities of participating musicians, and time spent practicing and preparing for a given performance can itself generate new relationships while inspiring new ideas and initiatives. This continued activism assures that future social forums are new iterations revisiting the concerns established in earlier meetings but moving the agenda of the social forum forward.... As people gain more experience with the WSF process, they have learned to make better use of the networking possibilities therein, and more people are beginning to use the process to launch new and more effective conversations and brainstorming sessions about how to improve popular mobilizing for a more just and peaceful world.
>
> (Smith *et al.* 2007: 108)

Similarly, an increasing geographical as well as typological diversity of participant organizations as observed in the evolution of the WSF (Pleyers 2007) can also be noted from one ESF edition to the next.

As repeatedly mentioned, the forum has also a strong *cognitive* dimension, implying sustained and complex communication across thematic and ideological perspectives, with activists coming from different ideologies and concerns, classes, and nationalities confronting their discourses and increasing mutual understanding. From the normative point of view, the ESF stresses the need to communicate in an open, transparent, and inclusive way. Various instruments are developed for internal communication, with extensive use of new technology and alternative media. Websites, mailing lists, and memory projects all testify to a focus on communication that takes a particular tune in multilingual environments (Chapter 3). Both the WSF and the ESF can be described as:

> A setting where activists can meet their counterparts from other parts of the world, expand their understandings of globalization and of the interdependencies among the world's peoples, and plan joint campaigns to promote their common aims. It allows people to actively debate proposals for organizing global policy while nurturing values of tolerance, equality, and participation. And it has generated some common ideas about other visions for a better world.
>
> (Smith *et al.* 2007: 3)

Communication has sustained the forum process, through many editions, supporting change within continuity. Again, as observed with the WSF, the forum process not only promotes a democratic globalization but also produces political globalization

> By enabling people to imagine themselves as part of a global human community, even when the contexts within which people live reinforce local and national identities. Through the staging of local social forums that are linked to a globally integrated process, the WSF process fosters global identities and values while serving as an incubator for new ideas about how to address the world's problems.
>
> (Smith *et al.* 2007: 129–30)

As for the ESF, we observed a strong European dimension, a Europeanization of social movements that contests but also accompanies the development of European institutions (della Porta and Caiani 2009).

Finally, the *emotional* content of the forum has been stressed by several authors, who present 'the forum's lively sounds and colors; the exhilarating mix of different languages and cultures; and even the uncanny and ubiquitous presence of a sense of magic and possibility' (Osterweil 2004a: 495). Seating arrangements favour non-confrontational relations, while the final march stresses the feeling of common belonging (Chapter 3). Activists have presented the forum as an epistemology of the South, stressing the 'power of open, free and horizontal structures' and the 'different kind of movement'. The forum is defined as 'an opportunity for diverse networks to physically converge, generate affective ties, communicate alternative messages and physically represent themselves to each other and the public' (Juris 2005a: 260). Participation in the forum is described by activists as 'an amazing experience. You really felt part of a huge global movement' (in Juris 2005a: 261). It is 'an intense experience and an opportunity to meet activists of different horizons and continents' (Pleyers 2007: 15). The various forms of protests within the forum (Chapter 9) tend in fact to produce 'high-powered social dramas' such as those described for the powerful images of the samba-dancer of the pink blocs or the protective shield and turtle tactics of the White Overalls (Juris 2004b). Informal linkages of trust and solidarity and the building of a common identity are indeed at the basis of the continuation of the history of the forums, beyond and behind the challenges that we have identified.

Appendix
Questionnaire for participants of the European Social Forum in Athens 2006

This questionnaire is part of the project *Democracy in Europe and the Mobilization of Society* (Demos) which is being carried out by scholars from six European countries. The Demos project focuses upon the movement that developed in opposition to neo-liberal globalization and in favour of more democratic, political practices. If you want to learn more about the research group, please visit the project website at http://demos.iue.it and/or write to us at demos@iue.it. On the website you will find information on our project and intermediate results of our research. We thank you in advance for helping us and for the time spent filling in this questionnaire.

– The data will be treated anonymously –

1. **Have you ever participated in any protest/demonstration of the global movement (global justice movement, for a globalization from below, for another globalization, *from now only global movement*) prior to this European Social Forum?**

No	Once	Between 2 and 5 times	Between 6 and 10 times	More than 10 times
$_0\square$	$_1\square$	$_2\square$	$_3\square$	$_4\square$

2. **If so was at least one of them a protest/demonstration in a country other than your country of residence (prior to this ESF)?**

    $_1\square$ Yes $_0\square$ No

3. **To what extent do you identify with the global movement?**

Not at all	Little	Quite a lot	Very much
$_0\square$	$_1\square$	$_2\square$	$_3\square$

4. **Have you been or are you planning to go to the Autonomous Spaces in the city centre?**

    $_1\square$ Yes $_0\square$ No $_9\square$ I have not heard of Autonomous Space

5. **Have you engaged in any of the following activities within the last five years?**
    (please tick all that apply)

a. Tried to persuade someone to vote for a political party   ₁☐
b. Worked in a political party   ☐
c. Signed a petition/public letter   ☐
d. Attended a demonstration   ☐
e. Handed out leaflets   ☐
f. Took part in a strike   ☐
g. Practiced civil disobedience   ☐
h. Took part in non-violent direct actions   ☐
i. Boycotted products   ☐
j. Participated in cultural performances as a form of protest   ☐
k. Took part in an occupation of a public building   ☐
l. Took part in the occupation of abandoned homes and/or land   ☐
m. Took part in a blockade   ☐
n. Used violent forms of action against property   ☐
 ₉ Other *(please specify)*   ☐
 ₉ₐ..

6. **Have you ever been a member of any group or organization?**

    ₁☐ Yes
    ₀☐ No → *please go to question 10.*

7. **Have you ever been involved in any of the following kinds of voluntary/campaigning groups?**
    *M*ultiple answers possible. (Please tick only one box for each group you are, or have been, involved in and distinguish between present and pas*t membership)*

	Present	Past
a. Women's rights	₁☐	₂☐
b. Environmental/anti-nuclear	☐	☐
c. Peace	☐	☐
d. Gay/lesbian/transgender	☐	☐
e. Development aid	☐	☐
f. Human rights	☐	☐
g. International solidarity	☐	☐
h. Anti-racist, immigrants rights or pro-immigrants group		
i. Consumerism/fair trade	☐	☐
j. Student group	☐	☐
k. Socialist	☐	☐
l. Trotskyist	☐	☐
m. Communist	☐	☐
n. Anarchist	☐	☐
o. Autonomist/social centre	☐	☐
p. Against neo-liberal economic agenda	☐	☐
q. Local social forum	☐	☐
r. Alternative media	☐	☐
s. Peasant/farmer	☐	☐

Appendix 241

t. Charity organization/social voluntary ☐ ☐
u. Religious group/religious community ☐ ☐
v. Trade union ☐ ☐
w. Unemployed ☐ ☐
x. Political party ☐ ☐
₉ Other (please specify) ☐ ☐

9a..

8. **Now please think of the group that is most important to you. What is its name?**
   (if there isn't one please go to question 10)

   ....

9. **What is the position you have in this group? (please tick only the most relevant box)**
   ₄☐ Member of the leadership
   ₃☐ Paid staff member
   ₂☐ Voluntary activist/campaigner
   ₁☐ Ordinary member
   ₀☐ Not actively involved in the group
   ₉☐ Other *(please specify)*

   9a..

10. **To what extent are you satisfied with the decision making processes in each of the following?**

	Very satisfied	Moderately satisfied	Moderately unsatisfied	Very unsatisfied	I'm not part of a group
a. Your group	₀☐	₁☐	₂☐	₃☐	₉₉☐
b. The groups and networks taking part in the global movement	☐	☐	☐	☐	
c. Your national political system	☐	☐	☐	☐	
d. The European Union	☐	☐	☐	☐	
e. The United Nations	☐	☐	☐	☐	

Now please think about the meetings/assemblies of your group during the last few months. If you do not belong to any group, or have never attended such meetings, or if your group does not have them, please go to question 12.

11. **Which of the opposing statements below better describes the meetings of your group?**
    Please tick the appropriate box, depending on which pole comes closer to your own experience.

A	In case of disagreement, it is primarily the quality of arguments that makes a difference regardless of who produces them.	or	In case of disagreement, arguments have a different weight depending on who produces them.
	high importance of arguments ₀☐——₁☐——₂☐——₃☐		**high importance of individuals**
B	When there is disagreement, the opponents usually accept each other as equal discussants.	or	When there is disagreement, the opponents rarely accept each other as equal discussants.
	usually equal discussants ☐——☐——☐——☐		**rarely equal discussants**
C	Most decisions are taken by a few people.	or	Most decisions are taken by all participants.
	few participants ☐——☐——☐——☐		**all participants**
D	Decisions are taken by voting, raising hands or similar.	or	Decisions are taken by consensus.
	voting ☐——☐——☐——☐		**consensus**

12. **In your opinion, which of the opposing statements below better describe decision making within networks and campaigns of the global movement?**
    Please tick the appropriate box depending on which pole comes closer to your opinion.

A	In case of significant disagreement in the discussion, it is primarily the quality of arguments that makes a difference regardless of who produces them.	or	In case of significant disagreement in the discussion, arguments have a different weight depending on who produces them.
	high importance of arguments ₀☐——₁☐——₂☐——₃☐		**high importance of individuals**
B	When there is disagreement, the opponents usually accept each other as equal discussants.	or	When there is disagreement, the opponents rarely accept each other as equal discussants.
	usually equal discussants ☐——☐——☐——☐		**rarely equal discussants**
C	Most decisions are taken by a few people.	or	Most decisions are taken by all participants.
	few participants ☐——☐——☐——☐		**all participants**
D	Most decisions are taken by voting, raising hands or similar.	or	Most decisions are taken by consensus.
	voting ☐——☐——☐——☐		**consensus**

E	Have you ever participated in such network/campaign meetings?	₁☐ Yes	₀☐ No

13. **Which of the opposing statements below better describes how you think political decisions should be taken in general?** *Please tick the appropriate box.*

A	In decision making, it should be primarily the quality of arguments that makes a difference regardless of who produces them. **arguments** ₀☐——— ₁☐——— ₂☐——— ₃☐	or	In decision making, the arguments of more resourceful and active groups / individuals should have more weight. **resources rather than arguments**
B	In a political conflict, it is always important that the opponents accept each other as equal discussants. **acceptance always important** ☐——— ☐——— ☐——— ☐	or	In political conflict, there are situations in which mutual acceptance is not important. **acceptance not always important**
C	In many cases it is right to delegate political decisions to others. **delegation** ☐——— ☐——— ☐——— ☐	or	The participation of all interested persons should always be a priority in decision making. **participation**
D	Political decisions should be taken by voting. **voting** ☐——— ☐——— ☐——— ☐	or	Political decisions should be taken by consensus. **consensus**

14. **To what extent do you trust the following types of institutions and organizations?**

	Not at all	A little	A fair amount	A lot
a. The United Nations	₀☐	₁☐	₂☐	₃☐
b. The European Union	☐	☐	☐	☐
c. National government	☐	☐	☐	☐
d. National parliament	☐	☐	☐	☐
e. Local government	☐	☐	☐	☐
f. The judiciary	☐	☐	☐	☐
g. The police	☐	☐	☐	☐
h. Political parties	☐	☐	☐	☐
i. Trade unions	☐	☐	☐	☐
j. NGOs (Non governmental organizations)	☐	☐	☐	☐
k. Social movement organizations	☐	☐	☐	☐

l. Churches ☐ ☐ ☐ ☐
m. Mass media ☐ ☐ ☐ ☐

15. **In your opinion, what strategies should the global movement use to enhance democracy?**
 Please rank these activities; 1 = most important, 2 = second most important, etc.

 please rank strategies
 a. Contact political leaders to influence their decisions
 b. Practice democracy in group life
 c. Take to the streets to express dissent publicly
 d. Spread information about global problems to the public
 e. Promote alternative social and economic models

16. **In your opinion, what should be done to tame neoliberal globalization?**

	Strongly disagree	Disagree	Agree	Strongly agree
a. Strengthen national governments	$_0$☐	$_1$☐	$_2$☐	$_3$☐
b. Strengthen the EU	☐	☐	☐	☐
c. Strengthen the United Nations	☐	☐	☐	☐
d. Build new institutions that involve civil society on the European level	☐	☐	☐	☐
e. Build new institutions that involve civil society on the international level	☐	☐	☐	☐

17. **Now please think of public decisions taken on national issues in your home country over the last year or so. To what extent do you agree with the following statement?**

	Strongly disagree	Disagree	Agree	Strongly agree
When politicians in my own country take decisions, they sometimes consider the demands of groups with less power.	$_0$☐	$_1$☐	$_2$☐	$_3$☐

18. **Some people believe that the involvement of citizens in decision making processes implemented by local governmental institutions (e.g. Agenda 21, participatory budget, etc.) improves the quality of political decisions. Do you agree?**

Strongly disagree	Disagree	Agree	Strongly agree	Don't know
$_0$☐	$_1$☐	$_2$☐	$_3$☐	$_9$☐

19. **Have you ever participated in such a process?**

    ₁☐ Yes   ₀☐ No

20. **If you use the Internet, have you:** *(If you don't use the Internet go to question 21)*

	At least once a week	At least once a month	Less frequently	Never
a. Signed online petitions or participated in campaigns through e-mail and/or mailing-lists/chat?	₃☐	₂☐	₁☐	₀☐
b. Expressed political opinions (in mailing-lists, forums, blogs, chat, etc.)?	☐	☐	☐	☐
c. Participated in a net-strike and/or other forms of radical online protest?	☐	☐	☐	☐
d. Exchanged information online within your political group?	☐	☐	☐	☐

    Finally, please tell us something about yourself:

21. **Sex:**   ₁☐ Female   ₀☐ Male

22. **Year of birth:**   19 ☐☐

23. **Country of permanent residence:** ....

24. **Size of the town in which you live:**

    ₀☐ Smaller than 20,000 inhabitants
    ₁☐ Between 20,000 and 100,000 inhabitants
    ₂☐ More than 100,000 inhabitants

25. **What is your employment status?**

    Tick where appropriate. If you have any doubt, please specify your profession in the box 'other'.

Manual worker	₁☐
Non-manual worker	₂☐
Employer/manager	₃☐
Professional (doctor, lawyer, etc.)	₄☐
Teacher	₅☐
Unemployed, looking for a job	₆☐
Retired/early retired	₇☐

Homemaker, no paid work for family reasons/caring work 8☐
Student → **go to question 28** 9☐
Other (*please specify*) 99☐

9a..

26. Do you have a temporary job? 1☐ Yes 0☐ No

27. In which sector do you work?

Industry 1☐
Private service sector 2☐
Public education 3☐
Public sector, other 4☐
Associative sectors (charities, parties, NGOs) 5☐
Other sector (*e.g. agriculture/fishery, please specify*) 9☐

9a ....

28. What is your highest educational qualification?

None 1☐
Completed primary school 2☐
Completed secondary school 3☐
Passed examinations at undergraduate level 5☐
First degree 7☐
Higher degree 8☐

29. 'Left' and 'Right' are notions used to describe political positions. Where do you place yourself on this scale?

Left   **Right**

| 0☐ | 1☐ | 2☐ | 3☐ | 4☐ | 5☐ | 6☐ | 7☐ | 8☐ | 9☐ |

99☐ I cannot/don't want to place myself on this scale.

30. Did you vote in the last national election in your home country? (*if you did not vote please go to question 32*)

1☐ Yes 0☐ No

31. Which political party did you vote for? —————

32. ... I did not vote/cast a blank or spoilt ballot because

I was unable/not entitled to vote 1☐
There is no political party that reflects my ideals/interests 2☐

I do not approve of representative democracy	3☐
For another reason *(please specify)*	9☐

9a..

If you want to add something about your commitment, or if you want to comment on this questionnaire, please go ahead!

....

....

....

....

....

....

....

....

....

....

....

....

....

THANK YOU FOR YOUR COLLABORATION!

References

Aaal, Pamela, Migenberger, Daniel T., and Weiss, Thomas G. (2000) *Guide to IGOs, NGOs and the Military in Peace and Relief Opportunities*, Washington: USIP Press.

Agrikoliansky, Eric and Cardon, Dominique (2005) 'Un programme en débats: forums, formes et formats', in Eric Agrikoliansky and Isabelle Sommier (eds), *Radiographie du mouvement altermondialiste: le second forum social européen*, Paris: La Dispute, pp. 45–74.

Agrikoliansky, Eric and Sommier, Isabelle (2005) *Radiographie du mouvement altermondialiste: le second Forum social européen*, Paris: La Dispute.

Agrikoliansky, Eric, Mayer, Nonna, and Fillieule, Olivier (2005) *L'altermondialisme en France, la longue histoire d'une nouvelle cause*, Paris: Flammarion.

Aguiton, Christophe and Cardon, Dominique (2005) *Le Forum et le Réseau: une analyse des modes de gouvernement des forums sociaux*, paper prepared for the Colloque 'Cultures et pratiques participatives: une perspective comparative', 20–21 January, Fondation Nationale des Sciences Politiques, Paris. Online, available at: http://mokk.bme.hu/centre/conferences/reactivism/FP/fpDC accessed 3 September 2007.

Alberoni, Francesco (1981) *Movimento e istituzione*, Bologna: IL Mulino.

Allegretti, Giovanni (2001) 'Bilancio partecipativo e gestione urbana: l'esperienza brasiliana di Porto Alegre', in Massimo Carli (ed.), *Il ruolo delle Assemblee elettive*, vol. I, Torino: Giappichelli Editore, pp. 551–79.

Almpanis, Yannis (2006) 'A Report on Athens ESF'. Online, available at: http://lists.fse-esf.org/pipermail/fse-esf/2006-May/000962.html accessed 30 January 2007.

Altrimondi (2002) 'Documento congressuale approvato dal primo Congresso Nazionale di Altrimondi – Firenze 12 ottobre 2002'. Online, available at: www.dsonline.it/autonomie/altrimondi/documenti/dettaglio.asp?id_doc=8153 accessed February 2007.

Andretta, Massimiliano (2005a) 'Il "framing" del movimento contro la globalizzazione neoliberista', *Rassegna Italiana di Sociologia*, 2: 77–97.

—— (2005b) 'Movimenti e democrazia tra globale e locale: il caso di Napoli', in Francesca Gelli (ed.), *La democrazia locale tra rappresentanza e partecipazione*, Milano: FrancoAngeli, pp. 281–318.

—— (2007) 'Democrazia in azione: modelli decisionali e ideali democratici degli attivisti globali', in Fabio De Nardis (ed.), *La società in movimento: i movimenti sociali nell'epoca del conflitto generalizzato*, Roma: Editori Riuniti, pp. 111–40.

Andretta, Massimiliano and Doerr, Nicole (2007) 'Imagining Europe: Internal and External Non-state Actors at the European Crossroads', *European Foreign Affairs Review*, 12(3): 385–400.

Andretta, Massimiliano and Mosca, Lorenzo (2003) 'Il movimento per una globalizzazione dal basso: forze e debolezze di un'identità negoziata', in Donatella della Porta and Lorenzo Mosca (eds), *Globalizzazione e movimenti*, Roma: Manifestolibri, pp. 21–47.

Andretta, Massimiliano, della Porta, Donatella, Mosca, Lorenzo, and Reiter, Herbert (2002) *Global, noglobal, new global: la protesta contro il G8 a Genova*, Roma-Bari: Laterza.

—— (2003) *Global, New Global: Identität und Strategien der Antiglobalisierungsbewegung*, Frankfurt am Main: Campus Verlag.

Assembly of the Movements (2006) 'Declaration of the Assembly of the Movements of the 4th European Social Forum', Athens, 7 May. Online, available at: www.athens.fse-esf.org/ workgroups/press-office/declaration-of-the-assembly-of-the-4th-european-social-forum.

Attac France (2004) 'The European Social Forum: Appraisal and Future Perspectives'. Online, available at: www.euromovements.info/upload/attac_france.doc accessed 25 January 2007.

Baggott, Robert (1995) *Pressure Groups Today*, Manchester: Manchester University Press.

Baiocchi, Gianpaolo (2002) 'Synergizing Civil Society, State–Civil Society Regimes in Porto Alegre, Brazil', *Political Power and Social Theory*, 15: 3–52.

—— (2005) *Militants and Citizens: The Politics of Participatory Democracy in Porto Alegre*, Stanford, CA: Stanford University Press.

Barnes, Samuel and Kaase, Max (1979) *Political Action: Mass Participation in Five Western Democracies*, Beverly Hills, CA: Sage.

Bartolini, Stefano (2000) *The Political Mobilization of the European Left, 1860–1980: The Class Cleavage*, Cambridge and New York: Cambridge University Press.

Becker, Tina (2002) 'Greek Left Divisions', *Weekly Worker*, no. 441 (18 July): 9. Online, available at: www.cpgb.org.uk/worker/441/ww441.pdf accessed 20 November 2007.

—— (2004a) 'Bureaucratic Grip Tightens: The London Mayor is in Control of Preparations for the European Social Forum', *Weekly Worker*, no. 512 (22 January): 10. Online, available at: www.cpgb.org.uk/worker/512/ww512.pdf accessed 20 November 2007.

—— (2004b) 'Bad Methods Slammed', *Weekly Worker*, no. 525 (22 April): 10. Online, available at: www.cpgb.org.uk/worker/525/11esf.html accessed 25 January 2008.

Bédoyan, Isabelle and van Aelst, Peter (2003) 'Limitations and Possibilities of Transnational Mobilization: The Case of the EU Summit Protesters in Brussels, 2001', paper presented at the conference 'Les mobilisations altermondialistes', Paris: GERMM, November.

Bédoyan, Isabelle, van Aelst, Peter, and Walgrave, Stefaan (2004) 'Limitations and Possibilities of Transnational Mobilization: The Case of EU Summit Protesters in Brussels, 2001', *Mobilization*, 9(1): 39–54.

Bello, Walden (2007) 'The Forum at the Crossroads', Silver City, NM and Washington, DC: International Relations Center, 4 May. Online, available at: www.fpif.org/ fpiftxt/4196 accessed 2 April 2008.

Benhabib, Seyla (1996) 'Toward a Deliberative Model of Democratic Legitimacy', in Seyla Benhabib, *Democracy and Difference: Contesting the Boundaries of the Political*, Princeton: Princeton University Press, pp. 67–94.

Bernhagen, Patrick and Marsh, Michael (2007) 'Voting and Protesting: Explaining Citizen Participation in Old and New European Democracies', *Democratization*, 14: 44–72.

Bersani, Marco (2006) 'L'altra Europa c'è'. Online, available at: www.carta.org/cantieri/ forumAtene2006/060518Bersani.htm.

Böhm, Steffen, Sullivan, Sian, and Reyes, Oscar (2005) *Ephemera*, 5(2). Online, available at: www.ephemeraweb.org/journal/5-2/5-2ephemera-may05.pdf accessed 11 November 2007.

Bohn, Lars (2004) 'ESF: Addressing the Democratic Deficit', in Oscar Reyes, Hilary Wainwright, Mayo Fuster I Morell, and Marco Berlinguer (eds), *The European Social Forum: Debating the Challenges for its Future*, Euromovements Newsletter 1. Online, available at: www.euromovements.info/newsletter/lars.htm accessed 11 November 2007.

Bonacich, Phillip (1987) 'Power and Centrality: A Family of Measures', *American Journal of Sociology*, 92: 1170–82.

Borgatti, S.P. and Everett, M.G. (1997) 'Network Analysis of 2-mode Data', *Social Networks*, 19: 243–69.

Borgatti, S.P., Everett, M.G., and Freeman, L.C. (2002) *Ucinet 6 for Windows: Software for Social Network Analysis*, Cambridge, MA: Analytic Technologies.

Bourdieu, Pierre (1979) *La distinction*, Paris: Minuit.

—— (1986) 'The Forms of Capital', in J.C. Richardson (ed.), *Handbook of Theory and Research for the Sociology of Education*, Westport: Greenwood Press, pp. 241–58.

Breiger, Ronald L. (1974) 'The Duality of Persons and Groups', *Social Forces*, 53: 181–90.

Breines, W. (1989) *Community and Organization in the New Left: 1962–1968: The Great Refusal*, New Brunswick, NJ: Rutgers University Press.

Brunelle, Dorval (2006) 'Le Forum social mondial: origine et participants', *Observatoire des Amériques*. Online, available at: www.ieim.uquam.ca/IMG/pdf/chro_brunelle_06_03_pdf.

Burger, Simone (2002) '"No global" oder "New global"', Bericht vom 1. Europäischen Sozialforum in Florenz vom 06 – 10 November 2002'. *Update (Informationsdienst des Juso Bundesvorstands)* 2(7): 13–15. Online, available at: www.jusos.de/servlet/PB/show/1168409/249%20update2.7%23rz.pdf accessed February 2007.

—— (2003) 'Europäisches Sozialforum – Reloaded', *Update (Informationsdienst des Juso Bundesvorstands)* 3(5): 20–1. Online, available at: www.jusos.de/servlet/PB/show/1477580/update3.5_P03.pdf accessed February 2007.

—— (2004) 'Contra und pro zum Europäischen Sozialforum vom 15–17 Oktober in London', *Update (Informationsdienst des Juso Bundesvorstands)* 4(5): 16–17. Online, available at: www.jusos.de/servlet/PB/show/1536340/bund_update_4_5.pdf accessed February 2007.

Burt, Ronald S. (1992) *Structural Holes: The Social Structure of Competition*, Cambridge, MA: Harvard University Press.

Candeias, Mario (2004) 'Antinomies: Relations between Social Movements, Left Political Parties and State: Reflections on the European Social Forum in London and Beyond'. Online, available at: www.moviments.net/euromovements/tiki-download_file.php?fileId=97 accessed February 2007.

Cardon, Dominique and Haeringer, Nicolas (2008) 'Formes politiques et coopération digitale, les usages d'internet par les forums sociaux', in Isabelle Sommier, Olivier Fillieule, and Eric Agrikoliansky (eds), *Généalogie des mouvements altermondialistes en Europe, une perspective comparée*, Paris: Karthala, pp. 247–68.

Ceri, Paolo (ed.) (2003) *La democrazia dei movimenti: come decidono i noglobal*, Cosenza: Rubbettino.

CGIL (Confederazione Generale Italiana del Lavoro) (2002) 'Forum Sociale Europeo: perché la CGIL partecipa', press release 6 November. Online, available at: www.cgil.it/ufficiostampa/ufsta/ht/notizia_large.asp?stato=archivio&ref=1669 accessed February 2007.

Chase-Dunn, Christopher, Reese, Ellen, Herkenrath, Mark, Giem, Rebecca, Guttierriez, Erika, and Petit, Christine (2007) 'North–South Contradictions and Bridges at the World Social Forum', in Rafael Reuveny and William R. Thompson (eds), *North and South in the World Political Economy*, Cambridge, MA: Blackwell.

Clemens, Elisabeth S. and Minkoff, Debra C. (2003) 'Beyond Iron Law: Rethinking the Place of Organizations in Social Movement Research', in David A. Snow, Sarah H. Soule, and Hanspeter Kriesi, *The Blackwell Companion to Social Movements*, Oxford: Blackwell, pp. 155–70.

COBAS (Commissione internazionale) (2002) 'Un nuovo modello di autoorganizzazione sociale: dal rifiuto della delega alla costruzione dei movimenti di lotta contro la globalizzazione capitalista'. Online, available at: www.cobas.it/Sito/Commissione%20 Internazionale/Presentazione/Cobas%20presentazione.doc accessed February 2007.

—— (2004) 'Il Forum sociale europeo a Londra'. Online, available at: www.euromovements. info/newsletter/cobas.htm accessed July 2008.

—— (Delegazione della Confederazione COBAS al Forum sociale europeo di Atene) (2006) 'Relazione generale sul 4° Forum Sociale Europeo di Atene'. Online, available at: www.cobas.it/Sito/Documenti/Forum%20Sociale%20Mondiale/Atene_2006/ Relazione%20FSE%20Atene.doc accessed February 2007.

Cohen, Joshua (1989) 'Deliberation and Democratic Legitimacy', in Alan Hamlin and Philip Pettit (eds), *The Good Polity: Normative Analysis of the State*, Oxford: Basil Blackwell, pp. 17–34.

Coleman, James S. (1988) 'Social Capital in the Creation of Human Capital', *American Journal of Sociology*, 94: 95–120.

Commission on Global Governance (1995) *Our Global Neighbourhood: The Report of the Commission on Global Governance*, Oxford: Oxford University Press.

Corinto, Arturo di (2001) 'Don't Hate the Media, Become the Media', in Mario Pianta, Christian Marazzi, Andrea Fumagalli, Marco Bascetta, Antonio Negri, Guido Caldiron, Andrea Colombo, Bendetto Vecchi, Arturo di Corinto, Lanfranco Caminiti, and Guido Caldiron (eds), *La sfida al G8*, Roma: Manifestolibri, pp. 157–80.

Cornwell, Benjamin and Harrison, Jill Ann (2004) 'Union Members and Voluntary Associations: Membership Overlap as a Case of Organizational Embeddedness', *American Sociological Review* 69: 862–81.

Coy, Patrick G. (2003) 'Introduction', in Patrick G. Coy (ed.), *Research in Social Movements, Conflicts and Change: Consensus Decision Making, Northern Ireland and Indigenous Movements*, vol. 24, Stamford, CT: JAI Press, pp. vii–xiv.

Cristante, Stefano (ed.) (2003) *Violenza mediata: il ruolo dell'informazione nel G8 di Genova*, Roma: Editori Riuniti.

Crouch, Colin (2004) *Post-democracy*, Cambridge: Polity.

Dalton, Russell J. (1996) *Citizen Politics: Public Opinion and Political Parties in Advanced Industrial Democracies*, Chatham, NJ: Chatham House Publishers.

—— (2002) *Citizen Politics: Public Opinion and Political Parties in Advanced Industrial Democracies*, 3rd edn, New York: Chatham House Publishers.

Dekker, Paul, Koopmans, Ruud, and van den Broek, Andries (1997) 'Voluntary Associations, Social Movements and Individual Political Behaviour in Western Europe', in Jan van Deth (ed.), *Private Groups and Public Life: Social Participation, Voluntary Associations and Political Involvement in Representative Democracies*, London and New York: Routledge, pp. 220–40.

Della Porta, Donatella (1995) *Social Movements, Political Violence and the State*, Cambridge and New York: Cambridge University Press.

—— (1996) *Movimenti collettivi e sistema politico in Italia (1960–1995)*, Bari: Laterza.
—— (2001) *I partiti politici*, Bologna: Il Mulino.
—— (2003a) 'Politica, antipolitica e altra politica: concezioni della democrazia e movimento per la globalizzazione dal basso', in Emidio Diodato (ed.), *La Toscana e la globalizzazione dal basso*, Firenze: Chari-Firenze Libri, pp. 127–54.
—— (2003b) 'Social Movements and Democracy at the Turn of the Millennium', in Pedro Ibarra (ed.), *Social Movements and Democracy*, New York: Palgrave Macmillan, pp. 105–36.
—— (2005a) 'Deliberation in Movement: Why and How to Study Deliberative Democracy and Social Movements', *Acta Politica*, 40: 336–50.
—— (2005b) 'Multiple Belongings, Tolerant Identities, and the Construction of "Another Politics": Between The European Social Forum and the Local Social Fora', in Donatella della Porta and Sidney Tarrow (eds), *Transnational Protest and Global Activism*, Rowman and Littlefield, pp. 175–202.
—— (2005c) 'The Social Bases of the Global Justice Movement: Some Theoretical Reflections and Empirical Evidence from the First European Social Forum', Civil Society and Social Movements, paper no. 21, United Nations Research Institute for Democracy, December.
—— (2007a) 'The Global Justice Movement: An Introduction', in Donatella della Porta (ed.), *The Global Justice Movement: Cross-national and Transnational Perspectives*, Boulder, CO: Paradigm.
—— (ed.) (2007b) *The Global Justice Movement: Cross-national and Transnational Perspectives*, Boulder, CO: Paradigm.
—— (ed.) (2009) *Democracy in Movements*, London: Macmillan, forthcoming.
—— forthcoming, 'Paths to the February 15th Marches: Structural Or Cultural Determinants?', in Stefaan Walgrave and Dieter Rucht (eds), forthcoming, *Protest Politics: Antiwar Mobilization in Advanced Industrial Democracies*, Minneapolis: The University of Minnesota Press.
Della Porta, Donatella and Andretta, Massimiliano (2006) *Global Activists: Conceptions and Practices of Democracy in the European Social Forums*, WP5 report, Democracy in Movement and the Mobilization of the Society – DEMOS, European Commission.
Della Porta, Donatella and Caiani, Manuela (2009) *Social Movements and Europeanization*, Oxford: Oxford University Press, forthcoming.
Della Porta, Donatella and Diani, Mario (2006) *Social Movements: An Introduction*, 2nd edition, Oxford: Basil Blackwell.
Della Porta, Donatella and Mosca, Lorenzo (eds) (2003) *Globalizzazione e movimenti sociali*, Roma: Manifestolibri.
—— (2005) *Searching the Net*, WP2 report, Democracy in Movement and the Mobilization of the Society – DEMOS, European Commission.
—— (2006) *Organizational Networks in the Global Justice Movement*, WP4 report, Democracy in Movement and the Mobilization of the Society – DEMOS, European Commission.
—— (2007) '*In movimento*: "Contamination" in Action and the Italian Global Justice Movement', *Global Networks*, 7(1): 1–27.
Della Porta, Donatella and Reiter, Herbert (eds) (1998) *Policing Protest The Control of Mass Demonstrations in Western Democracies*, Minneapolis: The University of Minnesota Press.
—— (2004) *La protesta e il controllo: movimenti e forze dell'ordine nell'era della globalizzazione*, Milano: Altraeconomia and Piacenza: Berti.

—— (2006a) *Organizational Ideology and Vision of democracy in the Global Justice Movement*, WP3 report, Democracy in Movement and the Mobilization of the Society – DEMOS, European Commission.

—— (2006b) 'The Policing of Global Protest: The G8 at Genoa and its Aftermath', in Donatella della Porta, Abby Peterson, and Herbert Reiter (eds), *Policing Transnational Protest*, Aldershot: Ashgate, pp. 13–41.

Della Porta, Donatella and Rucht, Dieter (1995) 'Left-libertarian Movements in Context: Comparing Italy and West Germany (1965–1990)', in J.Craig Jenkins and Bert Klandermans (eds), *The Politics of Social Protest: Comparative Perspectives on States and Social Movements*, Minneapolis: University of Minnesota Press, pp. 229–72.

—— (eds), forthcoming, *Meeting Democracy: Power and Decision-making in Global Justice Movements*.

Della Porta, Donatella and Tarrow, Sidney (2005) 'Transnational Processes and Social Activism: An Introduction', in della Porta, D. and Tarrow, S., *Transnational Protest and Global Activism*, pp. 1–17.

Della Porta, Donatella, Andretta, Massimiliano, Mosca, Lorenzo, and Reiter, Herbert (2006a) *Globalization from Below: Transnational Activists and Protest Networks*. Minneapolis. University of Minnesota Press.

Della Porta, Donatella, Peterson, Abby, and Reiter, Herbert (eds) (2006b) *The Policing of Transnational Protest*, Aldershot: Ashgate.

Della Porta, Donatella, Valiente, Celia, and Kousis, Maria (forthcoming) 'Women and Democratisation: The Women's Movement and their Outcomes in Italy, Greece, Portugal, and Spain', in N. Diamantouros, R. Gunther, and H.-J. Puhle (eds), *Democratic Consolidation in Southern Europe*, Washington, DC: The Johns Hopkins University Press.

DeMars, William (2005) *NGOs and Transnational Networks: Wildcards in World Politics*, London: Pluto Press.

DeNardo, James (1995) *Power in Numbers: The Political Strategy of Protest and Rebellion*, Princeton, NJ: Princeton University Press.

DGB (Deutscher Gewerkschaftsbund) (2006) 'Eine neue internationale Gewerkschaftseinheit – bessere Chancen, die Globalisierung sozial zu gestalten', resolution passed at the 18th federal congress. Online, available at: www.dgb.de/dgb/kongress2006/beschluesse/internationale_politik_globalisierung.pdf accessed February 2007.

DGB (Deutscher Gewerkschaftsbund), VENRO (Verband Entwicklungspolitik deutscher Nichtregerungsorganisationen) and Attac (2002) 'Globalisierung gerecht gestalten – gemeinsame Erklärung von DGB, VENRO und ATTAC'. Online, available at: www.dgb.de/themen/themen_a_z/abisz_doks/g/globalisierung.pdf/view?showdesc=1 accessed February 2007.

Diamond, Larry and Morlino, Leonardo (eds) (2005) *Assessing the Quality of Democracy*, Baltimore: The Johns Hopkins University Press.

Diani, Mario (1995) *Green Networks. A Structural Analysis of the Italian Environmental Movement*, Edinburgh: Edinburgh University Press.

DiMaggio, Paul J. and Powell, Walter W. (1983) 'The Iron Cage Revisited: Institutional Isomorphism and Collective Rationality in Organizational Fields', *American Sociological Review*, 48: 147–60.

—— (1991) *The New Institutionalism in Organizational Analysis*, Chicago: University of Chicago Press.

Doerr, Nicole (2006a) 'Public Discourse, Deliberation and Gender – a Critical Analysis from the Perspective of "Women Without" in the European Social Forum Process', paper presented at UCLA Graduate Student Research Conference Thinking Gender, Los Angeles, 3 March.

—— (2006b) 'Thinking Democracy and the Public Sphere beyond Borders. Language(s) and Decision-Making in the European Social Forum Process', Paper presented at the XVI ISA World Congress of Sociology, Durban, 23–28 July.

—— (2007) 'Is "Another" Public Sphere Actually Possible? The Case of "Women Without" in the European Social Forum Process as a Critical Test for Deliberative Democracy', *Journal of International Women's Studies*, 8(3): 71–87. Online, available at: www.bridgew.edu/SoAS/jiws/April07/Doerr.pdf accessed 12 July 2007.

Doerr, Nicole and Haug, Christoph (2006) *Public Spheres in Movement(s): Linking Transnational Social Movements Research and the (Re)Search for a European Public Sphere*, paper presented at the international colloquium 'Crossing Borders: On the Road toward Transnational Social Movement Analysis', Social Science Research Center, Berlin, 5–7 October.

Downton, James and Wehr, Paul (1998) 'Persistent Pacifism: How Activist Commitment is Developed and Sustained', *Journal of Peace Research*, 35(5): 531–50.

Dryzek, John S. (2000) *Deliberative Democracy and Beyond*, New York: Oxford University Press.

—— (2004) 'Handle with Care: The Deadly Hermeneutics of Deliberative Democracy', paper presented at the conference on 'Empirical Approaches to Deliberative Politics', European University Institute, Florence, 22–23 May.

Duben, Alan (1994) *Human Rights and Democratization: The Role of Local Governments and NGOs*, Istanbul: WALD.

ECOSY (Young European Socialists) (2003) 'European Social Forum: Resolution Adopted at the 2nd Bureau Meeting of the European Federation of Socialist Youth Organizations (ECOSY) in Perugia (9–12 October 2003)'. Online, available at: www.ecosy.org/uploads/media/031012_BM_Italy_RESOL_ESF.PDF accessed February 2007.

Edwards, Michael (1997) *NGOs, States and Donors: Too Close for Comfort*, Basingstoke: Palgrave.

Eggert, Nina and Giugni, Marco (2007) 'The Global Justice Movement in Switzerland', in Donatella della Porta (ed.), *The Global Justice Movement: Cross-national and Transnational Perspectives*, New York: Paradigm.

EPA (2005) *Istanbul Report from the Logistics European Working Group*. Online, available at: www.fse-esf.org/spip.php?article111 accessed 28 August 2007.

ESF (European Social Forum) (2002) 'Call of the European Social Movements'. Online, available at: www.resist.org.uk/reports/archive/esf/esfcall.html accessed February 2007.

—— (2003a) 'For a Europe of Citizens' Rights, Democratic Rights, Analysis and Critical Assessment of the Convention: Role of the Institutions, Participative and Representative Democracy'. Online available at: http://workspace.fse-esf.org/mem/Act2223 accessed 20 December 2006.

—— (2003b) 'Presentation of the Seminar'. Online, available at: http://workspace.fse-esf.org/mem/Act2303/doc448 accessed 4 January 2007.

—— (2003c) 'Compte-rendu du séminaire'. Online, available at: http://workspace.fse-esf.org/mem/Act2106/doc295, accessed 20 December 2006.

—— (no date) 'Debating the Challenge for its Future'. Online, available at: www.euromovements.info/newsletter/index.htm accessed 24 December 2006.

European Left (2005a) 'Athens Declaration of the 1st Congress of the European Left Party in Athens'. Online, available at: www.european-left.org/press/pressreleases/pr/pressrelease.2005-11-23.8395199335 (accessed February 2007).

—— (2005b) 'Yes, we Can Change Europe – Political Theses', executive board motion to the first congress of the Party of the European Left, Athens. Online, available at: www.european-left.org/press/pressreleases/pr-fr/pressrelease.2005-10-14.7592296840 accessed February 2007.

Favre, Pierre, Fillieule, Olivier, and Mayer, Nonna (1997) 'La fin d'une étrange lacunae de la sociologie des mobilisations. L'étude par sondage des manifestants: fondaments théoriques et solution techniques', *Revue Française de Science Politique*, 47: 3–28.

Fennema, Meindert and Tillie, Jean (1999) 'Political Participation and Political Trust in Amsterdam: Civic Communities and Ethnic Networks', *Journal of Ethnic and Migration Studies*, 25: 703–26.

Ferree, Myra Marx, Gamson, William, Gerhards, Juergen, and Rucht, Dieter (2002) *Shaping Abortion Discourse: Democracy and The Public Sphere in Germany and the United States*, Cambridge and New York: Cambridge University Press.

Fillieule, Olivier (1997) *Stratégies de la rue: les manifestations en France*, Paris: Presses de Sciences Po.

Fillieule, Olivier and Blanchard, Philippe (2006) 'Individual Surveys in Rallies (INSURA): A New Eldorado for Comparative Social Movement Research?', paper presented at the conference on 'Crossing Borders: On the Road towards Transnational Social Movement Analysis', WZB Berlin, 5–7 October.

Fillieule, Olivier, Blanchard, Philippe, Agrikoliansky, Eric, Bandler, Marko, Passy, Florence, and Sommier, Isabelle (2004) 'L'altermondialisme en réseaux', *Politix*, 17: 13–48.

FIOM (Federazione Impiegati e Operai Metallurgici) (2004) 'Documento conclusivo. Proposta unanime della commissione politica', XXIII Congresso, Livorno 5 June. Online, available at: www.fiom.cgil.it/eventi/2004/xxiii_con/doc_pol.htm accessed February 2007.

Fisher, Dana R., Stanley, Kevin, Berman, David, and Neff, Gina (2005) 'How do Organizations Matter? Mobilization and Support for Participants at Five Globalization Protests', *Social Problems*, 52(1): 102–21.

Fisher, William F. (1997) 'Doing Good? The Politics and Anti-Politics of NGO Practices', *Annual Review of Anthropology*, 26: 439–64.

Flam, Helena (1994) 'Political Responses to the Anti-Nuclear Challenge: (2) Democratic Experiences and the Use of Force', in Helena Flam (ed.), *States and Antinuclear Movements*, Edinburgh: Edinburgh University Press, pp. 329–54.

Freeman, Jo (1974) 'The Tyranny of the Structureless', in Jane Jaquette (ed.), *Women in Politics*, New York: Wiley.

Fruci, Gian Luca (2003) 'La nuova agora: i social forum fra spazio pubblico e dinamiche organizzative', in. Paolo Ceri (ed.), *La democrazia dei movimenti: come decidono i noglobal*, Soveria Mannelli: Rubbettino, pp. 169–95.

Fung, Archon and Wright, Erik Olin (2001) 'Deepening Democracy, Innovations in Empowered Participatory Governance', *Politics and Society*, 29(1): 5–41.

Gamson, William (1990 [1975]) *The Strategy of Social Protest* (2nd edition), Belmont, CA: Wadsworth.

—— (1992) *Talking Politics*, Cambridge and New York: Cambridge University Press.

George, Susan (2004) 'Taking the Movement Forward', in Vittorio Agnoletto, *Anticapitalism: Where Now?*, London: Bookmarks Publications.

Gerlach, Luther and Hine, Virginia (1970) *People, Power and Change*, Indianapolis: The Bobbs-Merrill Company.

Giovani Comunisti (2005) 'Emendamento integrativo del documento "alternativa di società" – perché 'alternativa di società', offline document.

—— (2006) 'Giovani comunisti di lotta o di governo: per una sinistra anticapitalista globale', motion presented at the third national conference. Online, available at: www.giovanicomunistiancona.it/downloads/documenti/gc/terzaconferenza/Terzo%20doc%20-%20giovani%20comunisti%20di%20lotta%20o%20di%20governo.rtf accessed February 2007.

Giugni, Marco (2004) *Social Protest and Policy Change*, Lanham, MD: Rowman and Littlefield.

Giugni, Marco, McAdam, Doug, and Tilly, Charles (eds) (1998) *From Contention to Democracy*, Lanham, MD: Rowman and Littlefield.

—— (eds) (1999) *How Movements Matter*, Minneapolis: The University of Minnesota Press.

Gosselin, Sophie (2005) 'Nomad', in *Euromovements Newsletter 4 – Learning from Practice*. Online, available at: www.euromovements.info/newsletter/nomad_sophie.htm accessed 28 August 2007.

Granovetter, Mark (1973) 'The Strength of Weak Ties', *American Journal of Sociology*, 78: 1360–80.

Grant, Wyn (1987) *Pressure Groups, Politics and Democracy in Britain*, London: Philip Alan.

Griffiths, Martin and O'Callaghan, Terry (2002) *International Relations: The Key Concepts*, Abbingdon: Routledge.

GSF (Genoa Social Forum) (2001) 'Work Agreement'. Online, available at: http://spazioinwind.libero.it/rfiorib/genova/manifesto_gsf.htm accessed February 2007.

Gulati, Ranjay and Gargiulo, Martin (1999) 'Where do Interorganizational Networks Come From?', *American Journal of Sociology*, 104(5): 1439–93.

Gutmann, Amy (1996) 'Democracy, Philosophy, and Justification', in Seyla Benhabib, *Democracy and Difference: Contesting the Boundaries of the Political*, Princeton: Princeton University Press, pp. 340–7.

Hall, Peter A. and Taylor, Rosemary C.R. (1996) 'Political Science and the Three New Institutionalisms', *Political Studies*, 44(5): 936–57.

Hanneman, Robert A. and Riddle, Mark (2005) 'Introduction to Social Network Methods'. Online, available at: http://faculty.ucr.edu/~hanneman/nettext/ accessed 29 June 2008.

Haug, Christoph (2006) 'The European Social Forum and Democracy', paper presented at the international conference on 'Transnationalization and Social Movements', Fondazione Feltrinelli, Cortona, November.

—— (2007a) 'Meta-democracy? Practices of Public Decision-Making in the Preparatory Process for the European Social Forum 2006', paper prepared for the ECPR Joint Sessions of Workshops, 7–12 May, Helsinki. Online, available at: www.wzb.eu/zkd/zcm/pdf/haug07_helsinki_metademocracy.pdf accessed 29 October 2007.

—— (2007b) 'Decision-making at the European Preparatory Assemblies', paper prepared for the European Preparatory Assembly, 15–16 September, Stockholm. Online, available at: www.openelibrary.info/upload/770/epa_decisionmaking.pdf accessed 20 September 2007.

—— (2008) 'Public Spheres within Movements: Challenging the (Re)Search for a European Public Sphere', RECON working paper 2008/02, Oslo: ARENA, Centre for European Studies. Online, available at: www.reconproject.eu/main.php/RECON_wp_0802.pdf?fileitem=5456060 accessed 29 January 2008.

Heater, Derek and Berridge, G.R. (1992) *Introduction to International Relations*, Contemporary Political Studies Series.

Held, David and McGrew, Anthony (2000) *The Global Transformation Reader: An Introduction*, Cambridge: Polity Press.

Hooghe, Mark (1999) 'Voluntary Associations and Social Capital: An Empirical, Survey-Based Test of the Putnam Hypothesis', paper presented at the American Political Science Association meeting, Atlanta.

Howes, Mick (1997) 'NGOs and the Development of Local Institutions', *Journal of Modern African Studies*, 35: 17–35.

Ibase (Brazilian Institute of Social and Economic Analyses) (2006) 'Study of participants at the 2005 WSF'. Online, available at: www.ibase.org.br/userimages/relatorio_fsm2005_INGLES2.pdf accessed 5 January 2007.

Independent Commission on International Development Issues (1980) *North–South: A Program for Survival*, Cambridge, MA: MIT Press.

Inglehart, Ronald (1977) *The Silent Revolution, Changing Values and Political Styles among Western Publics*, Princeton, NJ: Princeton University Press.

Institute for Research on World-Systems (2006) 'Alliances and Divisions within the "Movement of Movements". Survey Findings from the 2005 World Social Forum', University of Riverside, paper irow29.

Jiménez, Manuel and Calle, Angel (2007) 'The Global Justice Movements in Spain', in Donatella della Porta (ed.), *The Global Justice Movement: Cross National and Transnational Perspectives*, Boulder: Paradigm Press, pp. 79–102.

Jones, Dave (2004) 'ESF Media and Communications Strategies', in *Euromovements Newsletter 4 – Learning from Practice*. Online, available at: www.euromovements.info/newsletter/dave–jones.htm accessed 28 August 2007.

Joppke, Christian (1993) *Mobilizing against Nuclear Energy: A Comparison of Germany and the United States*, Berkeley, LA: University of California Press.

Jordan, Grant and Maloney, William (1997) *The Protest Business*, Manchester: Manchester University Press.

Juris, Jeffrey S. (2004a) 'The London ESF and the Politics of Autonomous Space'. Online, available at: www.euromovements.info/newsletter/jeff.htm?SectionID=41&ItemID=6552.

—— (2004b) 'Networked Social Movements: The Network Society', in Manuel Castells (ed.), *The Network Society*, London: Edward Elgar, pp. 341–62.

—— (2005a) 'Social Forums and their Margins: Networking Logics and the Cultural Politics of Autonomous Space', *Ephemera*, 5(2): 253–72. Online, available at: www.ephemeraweb.org/journal/5-2/5-2juris.pdf accessed 9 November 2007.

—— (2005b) 'The New Digital Media and Activist Networking within Anti-corporate Globalization Movements', *The Annals of the American Academy of Political and Social Sciences*, 597: 189–208.

Kaldor, Mary (2003) *Global Civil Society: An Answer to War*, Cambridge: Polity Press.

Katz, Richard and Mair, Peter (eds) (1992) *How Parties Organize: Change and Adaptation in Party Organizations in Western Democracies 1960–1990*, London: Sage Publications.

Kavada, Anastasia (2005) 'Exploring the Role of the Internet in the "Movement for Alternative Globalization": The Case of the Paris 2003 European Social Forum', *Westminster Papers in Communication and Culture*, 2(1): 72–95.

—— (2007) 'The "Horizontals" and the "Verticals": Competing Communicative Logics in the 2004 European Social Forum', paper prepared for the ECPR conference, panel 'Horizontals, Verticals and the Left in Transnational Social Movements', Pisa.

Keck, Margaret and Sikkink, Kathryn (1998) *Activists beyond Borders*, Ithaca, NY and London: Cornell University Press.

Kimber, Richard and Richardson, J.J. (1974) *Pressure Groups in Britain: A Reader*, London: Dent.

Kitschelt, Herbert (1986) 'Political Opportunity Structures and Political Protest: Anti-nuclear Movements in Four Democracies', *British Journal of Political Science*, 16: 57–85.

—— (1993) 'Social Movements, Political Parties, and Democratic Theory', *The Annals of The AAPSS*, 528: 13–29.

—— (2003) 'Landscape of Political Interest Intermediation: Social Movements, Interest Groups and Parties in the Early Twenty-first Century', in Pedro Ibarra (ed.), *Social Movements and Democracy*, New York: Palgrave Macmillan, pp. 105–36.

Klandermans, Bert (1984) 'Mobilization and Participation: Social–Psychological Expansions of Resource Mobilization Theory', *American Sociological Review*, 49(5): 583–600.

—— (1989) 'Introduction: Social Movement Organizations and the Study of Social Movements', in Bert Klandermans (ed.), *Organizing For Change: Social Movement Organizations across Cultures: International Social Movement Research. A Research Annual*, Bd. 2, Greenwich, CT: JAI Press, pp. 1–17.

—— (1993) 'A Theoretical Framework for Comparisons of Social Movement Participation', *Sociological Forum*, 8(3): 383–402.

—— (1997) *The Social Psychology of Protest*, Oxford and Cambridge, MA: Blackwell.

Klandermans, Bert and Oegema, Dirk (1987) 'Potentials, Networks, Motivations and Barriers: Steps towards Participation in Social Movements', *American Sociological Review*, 52: 519–32.

Klandermans, Bert and Smith, Jackie (2002) 'Survey Research: A Case for Comparative Design', in Bert Klandermans and Suzanne Staggenborg (eds), *Methods of Social Movement Research*, Minneapolis: The University of Minnesota Press, pp. 3–31.

Klein, Angela (2005) 'Das 1. Sozialforum in Deutschland: Eine Bilanz', *Sozialistische Zeitung*, September. Online, available at: www.linksnet.de/textsicht.php?id=1903 accessed February 2007.

Kolb, Felix (2005) 'The Impact of Transnational Protest on Social Movement Organizations: Mass Media and the Making of Attac Germany', in Donatella della Porta and Sidney Tarrow (eds), *Transnational Protest and Global Activism*, Lanham, MD: Rowman and Littlefield, pp. 95–120.

Kriesi, Hanspeter (1993) *Political Mobilization and Social Change*, Aldershot: Avebury.

—— (1996) 'The Organizational Structure of New Social Movements in a Political Context', in Doug McAdam, John McCarthy, and Mayer N. Zald (eds), *Comparative Perspectives on Social Movements: Political Opportunities, Mobilizing Structures, and Cultural Framing*, Cambridge and New York: Cambridge University Press, pp. 152–84.

—— (2004) 'Political Context and Opportunity', in David A. Snow, Sarah H. Soule, and Hanspeter Kriesi (eds), *The Blackwell Companion to Social Movements*, Oxford: Blackwell, pp. 67–90.

Kriesi, Hanspeter, Koopmans, Ruud, Duyvendak, Jan-Willem, and Giugni, Marco (1995) *New Social Movements in Western Europe: A Comparative Analysis*, Minneapolis: The University of Minnesota Press/UCL Press.

Ladd, Anthony, Hood, Thomas, and Van Liere, Kent (1983) 'Ideological Themes in the Antinuclear Movement: Consensus and Diversity', *Sociological Inquiry*, 53: 252–72.

Lagroye, J. (1993) *Sociologie politique*, Paris: Presse de la Fondation Nationale de Sciences Politiques.

Lazarsfeld, Paul F., Berelson, Bernard R., and Gaudet, Hazle (1944) *The People's Choice: How the Voter Makes up His Mind in a Presidential Campaign*, New York: Columbia University Press.

Leach, Darcy K. and Haunss, Sebastian (2009) 'Scenes and Social Movements', in Hank Johnston (ed.), *The Cultural Dimension in Social Movements*, forthcoming.

League for the Fifth International (2006) 'Fourth European Social Forum a Success'. Online, available at: www.fifthinternational.org/index.php?id=14,390,0,0,1,0 accessed February 2007.

Lee, Julian (2004) *The European Social Forum at 3: Facing Old Challenges to Go Forward* (Research report), Geneva: Centre for Applied Studies in International Negotiations. Online, available at: www.casin.ch/web/pdf/europeansocialforum2004.pdf accessed 20 November 2007.

Leighley, Jan (1996) 'Group Membership and the Mobilization of Political Participation', *Journal of Politics*, 58: 447–63.

Lévêque, Sandrine (2005) 'Usages croisés d'un "événement médiatique"', in Eric Agrikoliansky and Isabelle Sommier (eds), *Radiographie du Mouvement Altermondialiste*, Paris: La Dispute, pp. 75–102.

Levi, Margaret and Murphy, Gillian H. (2006) 'Coalitions of Contention: The Case of the WTO Protests in Seattle', *Political Studies*, 54: 651–70.

Lichterman, Paul (1996) *The Search for Political Community*, New York: Cambridge University Press.

—— (1999) 'Talking Identities in the Public Sphere: Broad Visions and Small Spaces in Sexual Identity Politics', *Theory and Society*, 28: 101–41.

Lijphart, Arend (1999) *Patterns of Democracy: Government Forms and Performances in Thirty-six Countries*, New Haven, CT and London: Yale University Press.

Lowi, Theodore (1971) *The Politics of Disorder*, New York: Basic Books.

McAdam, Doug (1988) *Freedom Summer*, New York: Oxford University Press.

McAdam, Doug, Tarrow, Sidney, and Tilly, Charles (2001) *Dynamics of Contention*, Cambridge: Cambridge University Press.

McCarthy, John D. and Zald, Mayer N. (1973) *The Trend of Social Movements in America: Professionalization and Resource Mobilization*, Morristown, NJ: General Learning Corporation.

—— (1977) 'Resource Mobilization and Social Movements: A Partial Theory', *American Journal of Sociology*, 82(6): 2323–41.

—— (1987) 'Resource Mobilization and Social Movements: A Partial Theory', in Mayer N. Zald and John D. McCarthy, *Social Movements in an Organizational Society*, New Brunswick, NJ: Transaction, pp. 337–91 (originally published in *American Journal of Sociology* (1977, 82[1]: 212–41).

Maeckelbergh, Marianne (2004) 'Perhaps We Should Just Flip a Coin: Macro and Microstructures of the European Social Forum Processes', in Oscar Reyes, Hilary Wainwright, Mayo Fuster I. Morell, and Marco Berlinguer (eds), 'The European Social Forum: Debating the Challenges for its Future', *Euromovements Newsletter 1*. Online, available at: www.euromovements.info/newsletter/flipacoin.htm accessed 11 November 2007.

Mahoney, James (2000) 'Path Dependence in Historical Sociology', *Theory and Society*, 29(4): 507–48.

Majone, Giandomenico (1989) *Evidence, Argument, and Persuasion in the Policy Process*, New Haven: Yale University Press.

Manin, Bernard (1987) 'On Legitimacy and Political Deliberation', *Political Theory*, 15(3): 338–68.

Mansbach, Richard, W. and Rafferty, Kirsten L. (2008) *Introduction to Global Politics*, New York: Routledge.

Mansbridge, Jane (1996) 'Using Power/Fighting Power: The Polity', in Seyla Benhabib (ed.), *Democracy and Difference: Contesting the Boundaries of the Political*, Princeton: Princeton University Press, pp. 46–66.

—— (2003) 'Consensus in Context: A Guide for Social Movements', *Research in Social Movements, Conflicts and Change*, 24: 229–53.
March, James, and Olsen, Johan (1989) *Rediscovering Institutions: The Organizational Basis of Politics*, New York: Free Press.
Marsdal, Magnus E., Halvorsen, Kristin R., Tagesson, Helena, and Dragsted, Pelle (2004) 'European Assembly: Could We Have Better Meetings?', in Oscar Reyes, Hilary Wainwright, Mayo Fuster I. Morell, and Marco Berlinguer (eds), *Euromovements Newsletter 1 – The European Social Forum: Debating the Challenges for its Future*. Online, available at: www.euromovements.info/newsletter/better_meetings.htm accessed 11 November 2007.
Martelli, Cristina and Panzani, Lara (2002) 'Il progetto Scriba', in *Testimonianze*, 425–6: 134.
Melucci, Alberto (1989) *Nomads of the Present: Social Movements and Individual Needs in Contemporary Society*, London: Century Hutchinson Ltd.
—— (1999) *Challenging Codes, Collective Action in the Information Age*, Cambridge: Cambridge University Press.
Meyer, John and Rowan, Brian (1977) 'Institutional organizations: Formal structure as Myth and Ceremony', *American Journal of Sociology*, 80: 340–63.
Meyer, Katherine and Seidler, John (1978) 'The Structure of Gatherings', *Sociology and Social Research*, 63: 131–53.
Meyer, Katherine, Seidler, John, and MacGilivray, Lois (1977) 'Youth at a Leftist and Rightist Political Rally: Reasons for Participating', *Sociological Focus*, 10: 221–35.
Michels, Robert (1959 [1915]) *Political Parties*, Dover Publications Inc.
Milbrath, Lester (1965) *Political Participation: How and Why Do People Get Involved in Politics?* Chicago: Rand McNally.
Milbrath, Lester W. and Goel, M. Lal (1977) *Political Participation*, Chicago: Rand McNally.
Mingst, Karen (1999) *Essentials of International Relations*, London: W.W. Norton.
Mitlin, Diana, Kickey, Sam, and Bebbington, Anthony (2007) 'Reclaiming Development? NGOs and the Challenge of Alternatives', *World Development*, 35(10): 1699–720.
Munck, Ronaldo (2002) 'Globalization and Democracy: A New "Great Transformation"?' *The Annals of the AAPSS: Globalization and Democracy*, 581:10–21.
Norris, Pippa (2002) *Democratic Phoenix: Reinventing Political Activism*, Cambridge: Cambridge University Press.
Nuñes, Rodrigo (2005) 'Territory and Deterritory: Inside and Outside the ESF 2004, New Movement Subjectivities', in Oscar Reyes, Hilary Wainwright, Mayo Fuster I. Morell, and Marco Berlinguer (eds), *Euromovements Newsletter 1 – The European Social Forum: Debating the Challenges for its Future*. Online, available at: www.euromovements.info/newsletter/nunes.htm accessed 30 October 2007.
Oberschall, Anthony (1973) *Social Conflict and Social Movements*, Englewood Cliffs, NJ: Prentice Hall.
Offe, Claus (1985) 'New Social Movements: Changing Boundaries of the Political', *Social Research*, 52: 817–68.
Olson, Mancur (1963) *The Logic of Collective Action*, Cambridge: Harvard University Press.
Osterweil, Michal (2004a) 'A Cultural–Political Approach to Reinventing the Political', *International Social Science Journal*, 56(182): 495–506.
—— (2004b) 'De-centering the Forum', in Jai Sen, Anita Anand, Arturo Escobar, and Peter Waterman, *World Social Forum: Challenging Empires*, New Delhi: The Viveka Foundation, pp. 183–91.

Papadimitriou, Tasos, Saunders, Clare, and Rootes, Christopher (2007) 'Democracy and the London European Social Forum', paper prepared for the 2007 ECPR joint sessions of workshops, workshop 'Democracy in movements', Helsinki.

Peterson, Abby (2006) 'Policing Contentious Politics at Transnational Summits: Darth Vader or the Keystone Cops', in Donatella della Porta, Abby Peterson, and Herbert Reiter (eds), *Policing Transnational Protest*, Aldershot: Ashgate, pp. 43–74.

Petras, James (1999) 'NGOs in the Service of Imperialism', *Journal of Contemporary Asia*, 29(4): 429–40.

PGA (2007) 'Media Lab at ESF in Paris'. Online, available at: www.nadir.org/nadir/initiativ/agp/free/wsf/paris2003/medialab.htm accessed 28 August 2007.

Pierson, Paul (2000) 'Increasing Returns, Path Dependence, and the Study of Politics', *American Political Science Review*, 94(2): 251–67.

Piven, Frances F. and Cloward, Richard (1977) *Poor People's Movements*, New York: Pantheon.

Pizzorno, Alessandro (1966) 'Introduzione allo studio della partecipazione politica', in *Quaderni di sociologia*, no. 3–4 (now in A. Pizzorno, *Le radici della politica assoluta*, Milan: Feltrinelli, pp. 85–128).

—— (1978) 'Political Exchange and Collective Identity in Industrial Conflict', in Colin Crouch and Alessandro Pizzorno (eds), *The Resurgence of Class Conflict in Western Europe*, New York: Holmes & Meier, pp. 277–98.

—— (1996) 'Mutamenti nelle istituzioni rappresentative sviluppo dei partiti politici', in Paul Bairoch and Eric J. Hobsbawm (eds), *La storia dell'Europa Contemporanea*, Torino: Einaudi, pp. 961–1031.

—— (2001) 'Natura della disuguaglianza, potere politico e potere privato nella società in via di globalizzazione', *Stato e Mercato*, 2: 201–36.

Pleyers, Geoffrey (2005) 'The Social Forums as an Ideal Model of Convergence', *International Journal of the Social Sciences*, 182: 507–19.

—— (2007) *Forums Sociaux Mondiaux et defies de l'altermondialisme*, Louvain-La-Neuve: Bruylant-Academia.

Plöger, Andrea (2007) 'Was wäre wenn eine andere Welt möglich wäre und niemand hätte davon gewusst? Eine Kommunikationsagenda für das Weltsozialforum', in Judith Dellheim, Simon Teune, and Andreas Trunschke (eds), *Ziehen wir an einem Strang?! Gewerkschaften, soziale Bewegungen, Nichtregierungsorganisationen, Parteien*, Schkeuditz: Schkeuditzer Buchverlag, pp. 114–28.

Pollack, Philip H (1982) 'Organizations as Agents of Mobilization: How Does Group Activity Affect Political Participation?', *American Journal of Political Science*, 26: 485–503.

Polletta, Francesca (2002) *Freedom is an Endless Meeting: Democracy in American Social Movements*, Chicago: The University of Chicago Press.

Ponniah, Thomas (2007) 'The Contribution of the U.S. Social Forum: A Reply to Whitaker and Bello's Debate on the Open Space', *Znet*, 19 July. Online, available at: www.zmag.org/content/showarticle.cfm?SectionID=1&ItemID=13330 accessed 2 April 2008.

Powell, Walter and DiMaggio, Paul (1991) *The New Institutionalism in Organizational Analysis*, Chicago: University of Chicago Press, pp. 183–203.

Putnam, Robert D. (1993) *Making Democracy Work: Civic Traditions in Modern Italy*, Princeton, NJ: Princeton University Press.

—— (2000) *Bowling Alone: The Collapse and Revival of American Community*, New York: Simon & Schuster.

Reese, Ellen, Kerkenrath, Mark, Chase-Dunn, Chris, Giem, Rebecca, Guttierrez, Erika, Kim, Linda, and Petit, Christine (2006) 'Alliances and Divisions within "the Movement of Movements"': Survey Findings from the 2005 World Social Forum', paper presented at the 2006 annual meeting of the American Sociological Association, Montreal.

Rifondazione Comunista (2002) 'Statuto del Partito della Rifondazione Comunista V Congresso Nazionale Rimini, 4–7 Aprile 2002'. Online, available at: www.rifondazione.it/v/doc/statuto_definitivo.html accessed February 2007.

—— (2003) 'Comitato Politico Nazionale 25–26 Ottobre 2003: Proposto dalla Segreteria Nazionale: Il documento approvato'. Online, available at: www.rifondazione.it/cpn/031025/doc_app.html accessed February 2007.

Rootes, Christopher (2001) 'Non-governmental Organizations (NGOs)', in B.J. Clarke and J. Foweraker (eds), *Encyclopaedia of Democratic Thought*, London and New York: Routledge, pp. 465–8.

Rootes, Christopher and Saunders, Clare (2005) 'Social Movements in Britain since the 1960s', DEMOS working paper no. 1/2005, Canterbury: Centre for the Study of Social and Political Movements, University of Kent.

—— (2007) 'The Global Justice Movement in Great Britain', in Donatella della Porta (ed.), *The Global Justice Movement: Cross National and Transnational Perspectives*, Boulder: Paradigm Press, pp. 128–56.

Rose, Richard (1974) *The Problem of Party Government*, London and Basingstoke: Macmillan Press.

Routledge, Paul (2003) 'Convergence Space: Process Geographies of Grass-Roots Globalization Networks', in *Transactions of the Institute of British Geographers*, 28(3), 333–49.

Rucht, Dieter (1993) 'Parteien, Verbände und Bewegungen als System politischer Interessenvermittlung', in Oskar Niedermayer and Richard Stöss (eds), *Stand und Perspektiven der Parteienforschung in Deutschland*, Opladen: Westdeutscher Verlag, pp. 251–75.

—— (1994) *Modernisierung und Soziale Bewegungen*, Frankfurt am Main: Campus.

—— (1996) 'The Impact of National Contexts on Social Movement Structures', in Doug McAdam, John McCarthy, and Mayer N. Zald (eds), *Comparative Perspectives on Social Movements: Political Opportunities, Mobilizing Structures, and Cultural Framing*, Cambridge and New York: Cambridge University Press, pp. 185–204.

—— (2004) 'The Quadruple "A": Media Strategies of Protest Movements Since the 1960s', in Wim Van De Donk, Brian D. Loader, Paul G. Nixon, and Dieter Rucht (eds), *Cyberprotest: New Media, Citizens and Social Movements*, London: Routledge, pp. 29–56.

—— (2005) 'Un movimento di movimenti? Unità e diversità fra le organizzazioni per una giustizia globale', *Rassegna italiana di sociologia*, 46: 275–306.

—— (2008) 'Social Forums as a Public Stage and Infrastructure of Global Justice Movements', in Seraphim Seferiades (ed.), *Collective Action and Social Movements in the 21st Century*, Athens: Themelio.

Rucht, Dieter and Teune, Simon (2007) 'Communicating the European Social Forum', paper prepared for the 2007 ECPR joint sessions of workshops, workshop 'Democracy in Movements', Helsinki. Online, available at: www.essex.ac.uk/ecpr/events/jointsessions/paperarchive/helsinki/ws4/Rucht.pdf accessed July 2008.

Rucht, Dieter, Teune, Simon, and Yang, Mundo (2007) 'The Global Justice Movements in Germany', in Donatella della Porta (ed.), *The Global Justice Movement: Cross National and Transnational Perspectives*, Boulder: Paradigm Press, pp. 157–83.

Salamon, Lester M. and Anheier, Helmut K. (1996) *Defining the Nonprofit Sector: A Cross-National Analysis*, Manchester: Manchester University Press.

Sanders, Lynn M. (1997) 'Against Deliberation', *Political Theory*, 25: 347–76.

Saunders, Clare (2007) 'Using Social Network Analysis to Explore Social Movements: A Relational Approach', *Social Movement Studies*, 6(3), 227–43.

Schoenleitner, Guenther (2003) 'World Social Forum: Making Another World Possible?', in John Clark (ed.), *Globalizing Civic Engagement*, London: Earthscan, pp. 127–49.

Schulz, Markus S. (1998) 'Collective Action across Borders: Opportunity Structures, Network Capacities, and Communicative Praxis in the Age of Advanced Globalization', *Sociological Perspectives*, 41: 587–617.

Seidler, John, Meyer, Katherine, and MacGillivray, Lois (1976) 'Collecting Data on Crowds and Rallies: A New Method of Stationary Sampling', *Social Forces*, 55: 507–18.

Seoane, José and Taddei, Emilio (2002) 'From Seattle to Porto Alegre: The Anti-neoliberal Globalization Movement', *Current Sociology*, 50(1): 99–122.

Sewell, William H. (1996) 'Three Temporalities: Toward an Eventful Sociology', in Terence J. McDonald (ed.), *The Historic Turn in the Human Sciences*, Ann Arbor: University of Michigan Press, pp. 245–80.

Shannon, Claude E. and Weaver, Warren (1949) *A Mathematical Model of Communication*, Urbana: University of Illinois Press.

Slegers, Frank (Belgium Social Forum) (2005) 'A Balance about the Euro-Demonstration Held in Brussels the 19th of March 2005 and Promoted by the CES and the European Movements and Networks Participating in the ESF, 23 March 2005'. Online, available at: www.openelibrary.info/autorsview.php?id_autore=180&PHPSESSID=e7376fa2abe 0365b50539e38132b16d4 accessed February 2007.

Smith, Jackie (2004) 'The World Social Forum and the Challenges of Global Democracy', *Global Networks*, 4(4): 413–21.

Smith, Jackie and Karides, Marina (2007) *Global Democracy and the World Social Forums*, Boulder, CO: Paradigm.

Snow, David A. and Benford, Robert D. (1988) 'Ideology, Frame Resonance, and Participant Mobilization', in Bert Klandermans, Hanspeter Kriesi, and Sidney Tarrow (eds), *From Structure to Action: Comparing Social Movements Research Across Cultures*, Greenwich, CT: JAI Press, pp. 197–217.

Socialist International (1989) 'Declaration of Principles of the Socialist International Adopted by the XVIII Congress (Stockholm, June 1989)'. Online, available at: www.socialistinternational.org/4Principles/dofpeng2.html accessed February 2007.

—— (2003) 'Governance in a Global Society – the Social Democratic Approach: Report Adopted by the XXII Congress in Sao Paolo, October 2003'. Online, available at: www.socialistinternational.org/5Congress/XXII-SAOPAULO/xxiiglobalgovernance-e.html accessed February 2007.

Solidaires (Union Syndicale Solidaires) (2004) 'Resolution 1: Contexte international et européen, mouvement altermondialiste', December Congress. Online, available at: www.solidaires.org/IMG/pdf/resolution1-2.pdf accessed February 2007.

Sommier, Isabelle (2003) *Le renouveau des mouvements contestataires à l'heure de la mondialisation*, Paris: Flammarion, collection Champs.

—— (2005) 'Produire l'événement: Logiques de cooperation et conflits feutrés', in Eric Agrikoliansky and Isabelle Sommier (eds), *Radiographie du mouvement altermondialiste*, Paris: La dispute, pp. 19–43.

—— (2008) 'Sur la généalogie de l'altermondialisme en France', in Isabelle Sommier, Olivier Fillieule and Eric Agrikoliansky (eds), *Généalogie des mouvements altermondialistes en Europe: une perspective comparée*, Paris: Karthala, pp. 87–114.

Sommier, Isabelle and Combes, Hélène (2007) 'The Global Justice Movement in France', in Donatella della Porta (ed.), *The Global Justice Movement: Cross-National and Transnational Perspectives*, Boulder and London: Paradigm, pp. 103–27.

Sotiropoulos, Dimitri A. and Karamagioli, Evika (2006) 'Greek Civil Society: The Long Road to Maturity', Civicus Civil Society Index Shortened Assessment Tool Report for the Case of Greece, Athens.

Staggenborg, Suzanne (1998) 'The Consequences of Professionalization and Formalization in the Pro-choice Movement', *American Sociological Review*, 53(4): 585–605.

Stokes, Susan C. (1998) 'Pathologies of Deliberation', in Jon Elster (ed.), *Deliberative Democracy*, Cambridge: Cambridge University Press, pp. 123–39.

Stratoulis, Dimitris (2006) 'The Trade-union Network's Report for the 4th ESF'. Online, available at: www.openelibrary.info/autorsview.php?id_autore=341&PHPSESSID=06e e3c907c4007cabb2d85796d58e0a3 accessed February 2007.

Tarrow, Sidney (1989) *Democracy and Disorder: Protest and Politics in Italy (1965–1975)*, Oxford and New York: Oxford University Press.

—— (1994) *Power in Movement: Social Movements, Collective Action and Politics*, New York and Cambridge: Cambridge University Press.

—— (2001) 'Transnational Politics: Contention and Institutions in International Politics', *Annual Review of Political Science*, 4: 1–20.

Teivainen, Teivo (2002) 'The World Social Forum and Global Democratisation: Learning from Porto Alegre', *Third World Quarterly* 23(4): 621–32.

—— (2004) 'Twenty-two Theses on the Problems of Democracy in the World Social Forum', *Transform!* 1. Online, available at: www.transform.it/newsletter/news_transform01.html accessed 19 April 2004.

Teorell, Jan (2003) 'Linking Social Capital to Political Participation: Voluntary Associations and Networks of Recruitment in Sweden', *Scandinavian Political Studies*, 26(1): 49–66.

Thompson, John B. (1995) *The Media and Modernity: A Social Theory of the Media*, Oxford: Polity Press.

Tilly, Charles (1978) *From Mobilization to Revolution*, Reading, MA: Addison-Wesley.

Topf, Richard (1995) 'Beyond Electoral Participation', in Hans-Dieter Klingemann and Dieter Fuchs (eds), *Citizens and the State*, New York: Oxford University Press, pp. 52–91.

Uadier, Florence and Bacache, Maya (2007) 'Emploi dans la fonction publique', *Revue de l'OFCE*, 103: 323–50.

Van Aelst, Peter and Walgrave, Stefaan (2001) 'Who is that (Wo)Man in the Street? From the Normalisation of Protest to the Normalisation of the Protester', *European Journal for Political Research*, 39: 461–86.

Verba, Sidney and Nie, Norman H. (1972) *Participation in America: Political Democracy and Social Equality*, New York: Harper and Row.

Verba, Sidney, Nie, Norman H., and Kim Jae-On (1978) *Participation and Political Equality: A Seven Nation Study*, Cambridge: Cambridge University Press.

Verba, Sidney, Schlozman, Kay Lehman, and Brady, Henry E. (1995) *Voice and Equality: Civic Voluntarism in American Politics*, Cambridge: Harvard University Press.

Ver.di (Vereinte Dienstleistungsgewerkschaft) (2003) 'Globalisierung nicht dem Markt überlassen – Handlungserfordernisse für eine politische, wirtschaftliche, soziale und ökologische Gestaltung', resolution passed by the Ver.di federal congress in October 2003. Online, available at: http://globalisierung.verdi.de/ accessed February 2007.

Verhulst, Joris (forthcoming) 'February 15, 2003: The World Says No to War', in Stefaan Walgrave and Dieter Rucht, *Protest Politics: Anti-War Mobilization in Western Democracies,* Minneapolis: The University of Minnesota Press.

Waddington, David, Jones, Karen, and Critcher, Chas (1988) *Flashpoints: Studies of Public Disorder,* London: Methuen.

Walgrave, Stefaan and Rucht, Dieter (eds) (forthcoming) *Protest Politics. Antiwar Mobilization in Advanced Industrial Democracies,* Minneapolis: The University of Minnesota Press.

Walgrave, Stefaan and Verhulst, Joris (2004) 'Worldwide Anti-war-in-Iraq Protest: A Preliminary Test of the Transnational Movement Thesis', paper presented at the second ECPR General Conference, Marburg, September.

Walzer, Michael (1983) *Spheres of Justice: A Defense of Pluralism and Equality,* New York: Basic.

Waterman, Peter (2005) 'The Old and the New Within the Global Justice and Solidarity Movement', *The Voice of the Turtle.* Online, available at: www.voiceoftheturtle.org/show_article.php?aid=425 accessed 6 April 2008.

Wellman, Barry (1988) 'Thinking Structurally', in Barry Wellman and S.D. Berkowitz (eds), *Social Structures: A Network Approach,* Cambridge: Cambridge University Press.

Whitaker, Chico (2004) 'The WSF as Open Space', in Jai Sen, Anita Anand, Arturo Escobar, and Peter Waterman (eds), *World Social Forum: Challenging Empires,* New Delhi: Viveka, pp. 111–21.

—— (2007) 'Crossroads Do Not Always Close Roads'. Online, available at: www.wsflibrary.org/index.php/Crossroads_do_not_always_close_roads accessed 2 April 2008.

Wikipedia (2008) 'Fourth International', in *Wikipedia, The Free Encyclopedia.* Online, available at: http://en.wikipedia.org/w/index.php?title=Fourth_International&oldid=188631205 accessed 4 February 2008.

World Bank (2001) 'Categorising NGOs'. Online, available at: http://docs.lib.duke.edu/igo/guides/ngo/define.htm accessed 13 February 2007.

World Social Movements (2001) *Porto Alegre 2001: Call for Mobilisation,* January. Online, available at: http://france.attac.org/a2978.

—— (2002) *Porto Alegre 2002: Call of Social Movements: Resistance to Neoliberalism, War and Militarism: For Peace and Social Justice.* August. Online, available at: www.forumsocialmundial.org.br/dinamic/eng_portoalegrefinal.asp.

WSF (World Social Forum) (2002) 'Charter of Principles'. Online, available at: www.forumsocialmundial.org.br/main.php?id_menu=4&cd_language=2 accessed July 2008.

Ylä-Anttila, Tuomas (2005) 'The World Social Forum and the Globalization of Social Movements and Public Spheres', *Ephemera* 5(2): 423–42. Online, available at: www.ephemeraweb.org/journal/5-2/5-2yla-anttila.pdf accessed 5 November 2007.

Young, Iris Marion (2003) 'Activist Challenges to Deliberative Democracy', in James S. Fishkin and Peter Laslett (eds), *Debating Deliberative Democracy,* Malden, MA: Blackwell, pp. 102–20.

Zald, Mayer and Ash, Roberta (1966) 'Social Movement Organizations: Growth, Decay and Change', *Social Forces,* 44: 327–40.

Index

activism: professional 116, 118–21; sustained 113, 116–18, 121–3, 125, 144, 162; transnational 6, 117, 121, 170, 193, 229
addressee 47–9
addresser 47–9
Agnoletto, Vittorio 14
Agrikoliansky, Eric 14–15
Aguiton, Christophe 34
alternative media 48, 60–1
Arci 42–3
argument, quality of 78, 81
Ash, Roberta 134
assembleary model 71–3, 75, 79–81, 194, 196, 198
assembly of social movements 32, 42, 57, 207, 208
Assembly of the Unemployed and Precarious Workers in Struggle 93–4
associational model 71–3, 75, 79–81, 194, 196, 198
Attac 31, 37, 59, 67–8, 140, 148n10, 158, 166, 186, 203n27
Attac France 40, 54, 208
Attac Germany 40, 179
autonomist groups 158, 175, 181, 188
autonomous spaces 35, 37, 42, 44, 52, 63n3, 65, 67, 170, 209–10, 234

Babels 39, 44n5, 53
Bello, Walden 150, 163
Benhabib, Sheyla 79
Bernocchi, Piero 43
Blanchard, Philippe 20, 22
Bohn, Lars 67
Bonacich, Phillip 153
Bourdieu, Pierre 112
Burt, Ronald S. 159

Callinicos, Alex 69, 84n5
Cardon, Dominique 14–15, 34
Central and Eastern Europe 27, 35, 42, 45n22, 61
civil disobedience 101–6
civil society 26, 31–2, 225, 234
Clemens, Elisabeth 8
Cobas 42–3, 66–7, 181, 184, 185, 188
Cohen, Joshua 79
Coleman, James 112
collective action 117
collective identity 57; identification 117
communication, 27, 70, 47, 228; direct, face-to-face 48, 50, 61; external 46–8, 54–60
complex representation 40–2
Confédération Générale du Travail (CGT) 175, 184, 187
Confederazione Generale Italiana del Lavoro (CGIL) 175, 179, 184, 185, 187
conflict 26, 29, 30, 32, 34, 41, 51, 56, 58, 63n3
consensus 5, 7, 27, 29–31, 41–2, 44n7, 65, 71–3, 75–6, 78, 139, 140, 142, 166, 230, 232
context 27, 30–1, 42; contextual characteristics 49, 60–1
Cornwell, Benjamin 151
cosmopolitan activists 75, 228, 230
Countersummits 12, 19, 49, 51, 55, 57, 174; see also Genoa Social Forum
Coy, Patrick 76
Critical Europeanists 94, 235–7
cross-fertilization in action (contamination) 9, 182, 194, 199
cultural capital 112

De Tocqueville, Alexis 8
delegation 27, 139, 166, 194, 197, 198

deliberation (deliberative democracy) 39, 71–3, 75, 81, 83, 140, 141, 150, 167, 195, 196; index of 80, 84n8, 140
deliberative democracy 5–7, 42, 79, 113, 123, 126, 226
deliberative participative model 71–3, 75, 79–81, 194, 196, 198
deliberative representative model 71–3, 75, 79–81, 197
Della Porta, Donatella 43, 150
democracy 5, 62, 114; transnational 26
democracy, models 70, 113, 114, 123, 140, 194; and action repertoires 215–17, 220, 221, 222
Democratici di Sinistra (DS) 175, 178, 183, 184, 201n2, 201n3
demonstration 48, 55–7
Deutscher Gewerkschaftsbund (DGB) 175, 179
Di Maggio, Paul 148n13
diachronic perspective 26–7
diffusion 142
direct democracy 5, 9, 113, 139, 194, 196, 198
Downton, James 116

electoral participation 101–6, 187
electoral preferences 187
embeddedness 151, 153–5
emotions 80, 237–8
equality 35, 37, 40, 45n20, 78, 81–2
European Community Organisation of Socialist Youth (ECOSY) – Young European Socialists 175, 178, 202n21
European constitutional treaty 90–1, 93, 181
European Left (EL) 32, 179–80
European Preparatory Assembly (EPA) 17, 26–9, 30, 32–5, 38–41, 44–5, 47, 50, 60–1, 63n2, 64n13, 68, 77, 186, 199, 202n26, 207, 210, 228, 230, 232–3, 236; minutes of 27–8, 30, 43
European Programme Group (EPG) *see* Working group (WG) on programme
European Social Consulta 90, 95
European Social Forum (ESF): activists 47–8, 51–4; communication with local citizens 48, 54–7, 61; finance 27, 29–30, 32–5, 43–4; Local organizing committee 47, 50–1, 55; logo 63n10; logistics of 27, 47, 50, 52, 58; memory 31, 34, 53–4, 61–2; national and local organisers 29–34, 38–9, 45n16, 47–51, 57, 62; national organizing committee 57–8, 63n9, 64n13; Nordic Organising Committee 33, 38; participants 47–8; participation 69; plenary sessions 39; programme 27–8, 37–9, 175, 184–6, 199; protest space 205–8, 221–2; thematic axes of 27, 36–8, 40; website 50, 59–60, 62, 64n13; Working groups (WGs) 27, 29, 33; Working group on enlargement 27–8, 35–8; Working group on organization 27–8, 33; Working group on programme 27, 38–40
European Social Forum, Athens 3, 14, 16, 28, 30, 32, 33, 41, 43–4, 60–1, 9, 52–5, 57, 60–1, 68–9, 86, 88, 95–6, 182, 184, 185, 188, 209, 211, 223n1, 236
European Social Forum, Florence 3–4, 13, 28–9, 33, 42–4, 49, 51–2, 55–7, 59–62, 65, 90, 92, 94–6, 182, 183, 184, 205, 209
European Social Forum, London 4, 14, 16, 28, 30, 34–5, 44n9, 49, 52, 54, 56, 59–61, 64n13, 65–9, 84n5, 86, 90, 182, 210
European Social Forum, Paris 13–14, 16, 28–9, 34, 44n8, 49–50, 52–3, 56, 58–9, 61, 65, 69, 88, 90, 93, 95, 184, 209
European Trade Union Confederation (ETUC) 178, 184, 185, 208, 223n5
European Union 3, 16, 86–9, 91–4, 104, 32, 132, 235
eventful protest 236–7
eventful temporality 9
expertise 40–1, 49

Favre, Pierre 20
Federazione Impiegati Operai Metallurgici (FIOM) 175, 179, 184
Ferree, Myra 225
Fillieule, Olivier 20, 22
Fisher, Dana 131, 147n7
Fisher, William 147n3
Fourth International 32, 45n10, 182
frames 236
free spaces 99–100, 106
friendship 31, 41, 44n7, 51

G10 Solidaires 93
general public 48, 57–60
Genoa Social Forum 58, 207, 209
George, Susan 66
Giovani Comunisti (GC) 180–1
global day of action (15 February 2003) 207
global democracy 234, 237

Global Justice Movement (GJM) definition 6
Global Progressive Forum 185, 202n24
Globalise Resistance 136, 184, 185, 202n25
Granovetter, Mark 159
Grant, Wyn 138
grassroots trade unions 181–2, 185, 199, 201n11
Greater London Authority (GLA) 34, 59, 67, 184
Gutmann, Amy 79

Harrison, Jill Ann 151
horizontal (versus verticals) 35, 49, 56, 59–61, 66, 83, 98, 210, 229, 234, 238
horizontality (as value) 150, 230–1

identification (with the Global Justice Movement) 16–17, 75–7, 82–3, 101–6, 192, 222
identification, with Europe 94
identities 9–10, 99, 238; tolerant 6, 149, 191, 227
IG Metall 175, 179
inclusiveness 30, 41, 46, 49–50, 228
incongruence between group practices and democratic ideals 80–3, 197–8, 200
Independent Media Centre (IMC) *see* indymedia
indymedia 52, 63n5, 140; Italy 51
Influential Transnational Organizations (ITOs) 132–4, 135
information 98–9
institutions 38; local 26, 34, 61, 63n4; public 27, 33–4, 49–63
interest groups 131, 147n4
International Governmental Organizations (IGOs) 3, 87, 226, 229, 235–6
International Monetary Fund (IMF) 131, 132
Internationalist Socialist Tendency (IST) 31–2, 182
Internet 51, 229
interviews in research on activism 17–22
Iron law of oligarchy *see* Michels, Robert

Jones, Dave 52
Jordan, Grant 133, 146
journalists 52, 57–61, 63n7
Juris, Jeffrey 211

Kavada, Anastasia 50, 60
Khalfa, Pierre 93
Klandermans, Bert 147n7

labour movement 4, 230; *see also* traditional left
Le Monde Diplomatique 59
League for the Fifth International 136, 182, 202n17
left-right scale 102–6, 224n14
Lévêque, Sandrine 45n15, 58–9
Ligue Communiste Révolutionnaire (LCR) 158, 182
local social forums 42, 44n5, 53, 55, 57–8, 62, 65, 140, 166, 191; European network of 64n10, 67
Lowi, Thodore 131

Maloney, William 133, 146
Manin, Bernard 79
Mansbach, Richard W. 130
Mansbridge, Jane 78
Marcos, subcomandante 230
mass media (mainstream media) 48–9, 51, 54, 56–7; coverage 38, 46, 55, 56, 58, 63n7; criticism 59; resonance 57; visibility 58
Mayer, Nonna 20
Media Center (MC) 48, 51–2
Metallos Medialab 52, 59
Michels, Robert 133, 136, 146
minimalistic conception of democracy 225
Minkoff, Debra 8
movement constituencies 46–8, 60–1
multi-organizational analysis 153
multilevel governance 87
multiple membership 11, 151, 191, 228–9

national delegations 29–31, 33, 40
national environments *see* context
neoinstitutionalism 142, 194
neoliberalism, critique of 3, 87, 89, 96, 107
network analysis 149–55; latent 149–52 organizational 50, 54, 56, 60–1; personal 31–2, 35, 47–8, 50–1, 62; social 153; thematic 29, 39
networks 11, 68, 77, 227–9, 234, 236
new left 99; *see also* radical left
new social movements 4, 9, 188, 230
newest social movement organizations 188
no vox 65–8
nomad 53–4
Non Governmental Organizations (NGOs) 71, 129–31, 188, 234
non-violence 204, 206, 207, 208, 211, 222

open space 14–16, 26–7, 32, 34, 38, 42, 228, 230, 237; openness 150

Index   269

organizational cultures 23, 40, 42, 195, 197; *see also* horizontal (versus verticals)

participatory budgeting 99–100
participatory democracy 7, 26, 31, 44n7, 67, 70–3, 76, 78, 83, 87, 195, 231
Party of European Socialists 175, 201n2
party/parties (political) 26, 29, 32–3, 42, 58, 63n8, 65, 69, 71, 132, 135, 232; activism in 97, 191, 211; communist 179–81, 199; foundations 184, 185; mistrust in 89, 98; social democratic and socialist 177–8, 199; relations with 235; youth organizations 185
Petras, James 130
Pizzorno, Alessandro 10
pluralist (values) 5–7, 228, 230–2
political opportunities 8
political participation, definition 10; research on 9–11, 101
political process approach 7–9, 87, 106
politics, conceptions of 69, 96–9
Polletta, Francesca 5, 26, 31, 40, 44n7, 45n20, 225
Porto Alegre *see* World Social Forum (WSF)
post-materialism 113
Powell, Walter 148n13
power 69, 96, 98–100
power centrality 153
prefigurative 226, 234
preparatory process *see* European Preparatory Assembly (EPA)
press office 48–9, 55, 57–60, 62, 64n12
professional activists 233
professionalisation *see* activism
protest business 133, 134, 137, 146
public relations (PR), 58–61, 63n10; professionalization of 58–61
Putnam, Robert 159

radical left 174, 199; and the social forum process 181–3, 184, 199; national differences 175
radical left activists 188; democratic ideals of 195–7, 200; incongruence between group practices and democratic ideals of 197–8, 200; participation in GJM of 193, 200; perceived democratic practices 194–5, 200; repertoire of action 191–2, 200; social characteristics of 189, 200
Rafferty, Kirsten L. 130
rational arguments 140
Reese, Ellen 131

repertoire of action 70, 97–8, 191–2, 206, 222, 227, 234; and democratic models 215–17, 220, 221, 222; and movement area 213–14, 220, 221; and political attitudes 215–19, 221, 222; and structural characteristics 215, 220, 221, 222; divergencies about 208–11; overlapping of 211, 213–14, 220, 221, 222
representative institutions 6, 69, 70, 74, 87, 106–8, 226
Réseau Intergalactique 65
resource mobilization approach 8
resources 27, 35, 46, 52; resource mobilization 134
Rifondazione comunista (RC) 180, 201n2
Rootes, Christopher 128, 130
Rose, Richard 132
Rucht, Dieter 13

satisfaction with democracy 77, 79, 81
Saunders, Clare 128
Sin-Cobas 66
Sinistra giovanile 184, 185
Snow, David A. 54
social capital 112, 113, 159, 162
social characteristics (effects on political participation) 9–10
social closure 31, 41
Social Movement Organizations (SMOs) 4–5, 8–9, 131, 132
social movement studies 225–6
Socialist Action 66, 67, 184, 210
Socialist International 177
Socialist Workers' Party (SWP) 31, 41, 44n9, 69, 136, 147n6, 182, 184, 210
solidarity (group) 10, 76
solidarity fund 27, 35
Sozialdemokratische Partei Deutschlands (SPD) 175, 201n3
Staggenborg, Suzanne 133
surveys at demonstration *see* interviews in research on activism

Teivanen, Teivo 231
Teorell, Jan 159, 160
Thatcherite legacy 138
theory of social centrality 112
Thompson, John B. 47
Tilly, Charles 8
trade unions 31, 34–5, 37, 40, 44n5, 56, 65–6, 71, 132–47, 235; national differences 175–6; *see also* grassroots trade unions; traditional trade unions

traditional left 174, 232; national differences 174–5; and the social forum process 176–81, 183–4, 199
traditional left activists 187; democratic ideals of 195–7, 200; incongruence between group practices and democratic ideals of 197–8, 200; participation in GJM 193, 200; perceived democratic practices 194–5, 200; repertoire of action 191–2, 200; social characteristics of 189, 200
traditional trade unions 178–9, 185, 199, 201n11
translation 27, 39, 45n13, 53–4, 63n6
transnational activism 6, 193, 229
transnational public sphere 46
transparency 38, 46, 61–2, 64n12
Trotskyites 158, 174, 175, 182–3, 187, 188
trust in institutions 88–92, 101–7, 192, 220

unconventional participation 10
Union Syndicale Solidaires 181
United for Peace 207
United Nations (UN) 88, 93, 104, 131, 132

Ver.di 175, 184, 187
Verba, Sidney 112
Verhulst, Joris 207
violence 56–7, 61, 103, 106, 192, 209, 211, 224n11

Walzer, Michael 40
Wehr, Paul 116
Whitacker, Chico 150, 207
World Bank 130, 131
World Economic Forum (WEF) 46
World Social Forum (WSF) 12–14, 26, 28–9, 31–2, 38, 43, 45n17, 46, 49, 55, 62, 66, 100, 111, 139, 150, 205, 207, 209, 227–34, 236–7; Charter of Principles 26, 32–3, 38, 40, 42, 43, 44n2, 201n4, 206, 208; International Council 32, 45n19
World Trade Organization (WTO) 51, 132

Zald, Mayer 134
Zapatistas 234

eBooks – at www.eBookstore.tandf.co.uk

A library at your fingertips!

eBooks are electronic versions of printed books. You can store them on your PC/laptop or browse them online.

They have advantages for anyone needing rapid access to a wide variety of published, copyright information.

eBooks can help your research by enabling you to bookmark chapters, annotate text and use instant searches to find specific words or phrases. Several eBook files would fit on even a small laptop or PDA.

NEW: Save money by eSubscribing: cheap, online access to any eBook for as long as you need it.

Annual subscription packages

We now offer special low-cost bulk subscriptions to packages of eBooks in certain subject areas. These are available to libraries or to individuals.

For more information please contact webmaster.ebooks@tandf.co.uk

We're continually developing the eBook concept, so keep up to date by visiting the website.

www.eBookstore.tandf.co.uk